Towards Unity

Ecumenical Dialogue
500 Years after
the Reformation

Towards Unity

Ecumenical Dialogue 500 Years after the Reformation

Essays in honour of Monsignor John A. Radano

EDITED BY

Donald Bolen, Nicholas Jesson & Donna Geernaert, SC

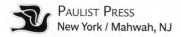
PAULIST PRESS
New York / Mahwah, NJ

© 2017 Novalis Publishing Inc.

Cover design: Martin Gould
Layout: Audrey Wells

This edition published by arrangement with
Novalis
10 Lower Spadina Avenue, Suite 400
Toronto, Ontario, Canada
M5V 2Z2

www.novalis.ca

Library of Congress Control Number: 2017931701

ISBN 978-0-8091-5349-7 (paperback)

Published in the United States by
Paulist Press
997 Macarthur Boulevard
Mahwah, NJ 07430

www.paulistpress.com

Printed in Canada.

5 4 3 2 1   21   20   19   18   17

Contents

Acknowledgements

The idea of producing a *Festschrift* in honour of the lifetime contribution of Msgr. John A. Radano was greeted with great enthusiasm by all those who had the opportunity to work alongside him in ecumenical dialogues. Profound thanks to the authors of this collection of essays for their own contribution to the ecumenical movement, and for their part in this volume.

We remember with fondness two of our friends and colleagues who submitted essays for this volume and have died in the intervening years: Dr. Margaret O'Gara and Bro. Jeffrey Gros, FSC.

The initial solicitation of essays was assisted by the staff of the Pontifical Council for Promoting Christian Unity. Particular appreciation is owed to Silvana Salvati of the PCPCU who read all the initial submissions and provided numerous suggestions. Thanks are also owed to Sr. Donna Geernaert, who joined our editing team just when we were ready to give up. Thank you also to Joseph Sinasac and Novalis, in conjunction with Paulist Press, for your enthusiasm and willingness to publish this work.

Finally and foremost, heartfelt thanks to Jack Radano for his unfailing commitment to ecumenical relations and dialogue at the service of the Gospel, and for his patience and perseverance amidst challenges.

Archbishop Donald Bolen
Nicholas Jesson
Sr. Donna Geernaert, SC

Biographical Note

Monsignor John A. Radano

Monsignor John A. Radano was born in Jersey City, New Jersey, on March 25, 1938. Ordained a priest of the Archdiocese of Newark (1965), he was appointed to the faculty of Seton Hall University, serving in the Department of Religious Studies (1965-1984), and also as its chairman (1977-1984), specialising in ecumenical studies.

During these years on the faculty at Seton Hall, his many ecumenical activities included participation in the North American Academy of Ecumenists, with three years (1981-1983) as membership secretary/treasurer, and co-director of an Ecumenical Studies Institute co-sponsored by Seton Hall University and Uppsala College, which organized ecumenical lecture programs at both institutions (1973-1975). In addition, he participated in two international assemblies of the World Conference on Religion and Peace (Princeton, New Jersey, 1979, and Nairobi, Kenya, 1984), with the responsibility for organising the assembly prayer sessions. He also served as a member of the Pax Romana (a Catholic NGO) delegation at the United Nations (1975-1979), and as head of the delegation (1977-1979).

From 1984 to 2008, he served on the staff of the Pontifical Council for Promoting Christian Unity (PCPCU), Vatican City, and in 1985 Pope John Paul II appointed him head of the PCPCU's Western Section. He participated in a number of the Catholic Church's international bilateral dialogues, including those with the Lutheran World Federation (third and fourth phases, 1986-1993 and 1995-2006, serving as co-secretary of the dialogue 1986-1990 and 1997-1999); the World Alliance of Reformed Churches (co-secretary for the second and third phases, 1985-1990 and 1998-2007); the Baptist World Alliance (co-secretary for the first phase, 1984-1988, and the first two sessions of the second phase, 2006-2007); the Mennonite World Conference (co-secretary for the first phase, 1998-2003); Classical Pentecostals (co-secretary for the third phase, 1985-1990, participant in the fourth, 1991-1997, and co-chairman of the fifth phase, 1998-2007); and the World Evangelical Alliance (member of the first phase, 1993-2002). He also participated in informal bilateral consultations with Seventh-day Adventists (2000, 2001, and 2003) and with the Salvation Army (2007), and was involved in the PCPCU's relations with the Anglican Communion and the World Methodist Council. One could legitimately ask whether anyone has ever participated in more international bilateral conversations.

In 1985, the PCPCU named him liaison with the Commission on Faith and Order of the World Council of Churches and, in 1988, a member of the Joint Working Group between the Catholic Church and the World Council of Churches (JWG). He attended four World Council of Churches (WCC) General Assemblies: at Vancouver, Canada (1983), Canberra, Australia (1991), Harare, Zimbabwe (1998), and Porto Alegre, Brazil (2006). He represented the PCPCU (1999-2008) on the Continuation Committee of the Global Christian Forum, which organized meetings between Pentecostals/Evangelicals and historical mainline churches, first on a regional basis in the USA, Asia (Hong Kong), Africa (Zambia), Europe (Germany), and Latin America (Chile), and then in 2007, an international assembly in Limuru (Nairobi), Kenya. In 1986, Pope John Paul II appointed him Papal Chaplain and in 1993 Prelate of Honour. In 2008, Pope Benedict XVI appointed him Protonotary Apostolic Supernumerary.

Since completing service to the Holy See in 2008, he has been an Adjunct Professor in the School of Theology at Seton Hall University. He has also taught, as Professore Invitato, at the Pontifical University of St Thomas Aquinas (the Angelicum), Rome (March 8-15, 2010); was Scholar-in-Residence at St. Paul Seminary School of Divinity of the University of St. Thomas, St. Paul, Minnesota (Spring Semester, 2010); and Adjunct Professor at St. Joseph's Seminary, Dunwoodie, Yonkers, New York (Fall semesters, 2009, 2010, and 2011). He has lectured at the University of Notre Dame, South Bend, Indiana, at the invitation of the Department of Theology (March 27-28, 2009). In 2012, he was appointed to the Eighth Round of the USA Reformed-Catholic Dialogue.

He is the author of *Lutheran and Catholic Reconciliation on Justification* (Eerdmans, 2009), editor of *Celebrating a Century of Ecumenism:*

Exploring the Achievements of International Dialogue (Eerdmans, 2012), and co-editor with Günther Gassmann of *The Unity of the Church as Koinonia: Ecumenical Perspectives on the 1991 Canberra Statement on Unity*, Faith and Order Paper no. 163 (Geneva: WCC, 1993). He was editor of the PCPCU's *Information Service* (1985-2008), and has published articles in the *New Catholic Encyclopedia*, the *Dictionary of the Ecumenical Movement*, and in many journals, including *Midstream*, *Ecumenical Trends*, *The Journal of Ecumenical Studies*, *One in Christ*, *Religious Studies Review*, *Angelicum*, *Marian Studies*, *Catholica*, *Centro Pro Unione Bulletin*, *Priests and People*, *Messagero Cappucino*, and *U.S. Catholic Historian*. He has published numerous articles in *L'Osservatore Romano* and in several WCC publications, as well as contributing to books edited by others. He has frequently been invited to give public lectures on topics of ecumenical interest to mark significant anniversaries and events in both university and dialogue contexts.

Abbreviations

ARCIC   Anglican-Roman Catholic International Commission. See iarccum.org

IARCCUM   International Anglican-Roman Catholic Commission for Unity and Mission. See iarccum.org

JWG   Joint Working Group between the Roman Catholic Church and the World Council of Churches

LWF   Lutheran World Federation. See lutheranworld.org

MWC   Mennonite World Conference. See mwc-cmm.org

PCPCU   Pontifical Council for Promoting Christian Unity, Vatican. See vatican.va

WARC   World Alliance of Reformed Churches, merged in 2010 with the Reformed Ecumenical Council to form the WCRC

WCC   World Council of Churches. See oikoumene.org

WCRC   World Communion of Reformed Churches. See wcrc.ch

WEA   World Evangelical Alliance. See worldea.org

Document collections

BU   *Building Unity: Ecumenical Dialogues with Roman Catholic Participation in the United States.* Edited by Jeffrey Gros and Joseph A. Burgess. New York: Paulist Press, 1989.

DC   *Deepening Communion.* Edited by William G. Rusch and Jeffrey Gros. Washington: US Catholic Conference, 1998.

DH 1   *A Documentary History of the Faith and Order Movement, 1927-1963.* Edited by Lukas Vischer. St. Louis: Bethany Press, 1963.

DH 2   *Documentary History of Faith and Order, 1963-1993,* Faith and Order paper 159. Edited by Günther Gassmann. Geneva: WCC, 1993.

DS · Denzinger, Heinrich. *Enchiridion symbolorum definitionum et declarationum de rebus fidei et morum.* Latin-English. Edited by Peter Hünermann. 43rd edition. San Francisco: Ignatius Press, 2012.

GA I · *Growth in Agreement: Reports and Agreed Statements of Ecumenical Conversations on a World Level.* Faith and Order paper 108. Edited by Harding Meyer and Lukas Vischer. New York: Paulist Press; Geneva: WCC, 1984.

GA II · *Growth in Agreement II: Reports and Agreed Statements of Ecumenical Conversations on a World Level, 1982-1998.* Faith and Order paper 187. Edited by Jeffrey Gros, Harding Meyer, and William G. Rusch. Geneva: WCC; Grand Rapids: Eerdmans, 2000.

GA III · *Growth in Agreement III: International Dialogue Texts and Agreed Statements, 1998-2005. Faith and Order paper 204.* Edited by Jeffrey Gros, Thomas F. Best, and Lorelei F. Fuchs. Geneva: WCC; Grand Rapids: Eerdmans, 2007.

GA IV · *Growth in Agreement IV: International Dialogue Texts and Agreed Statements 2005-2013.* 2 volumes. Edited by Thomas F. Best, Lorelei F. Fuchs, John Gibaut, Jeffrey Gros, FSC, and Despina Prassas. Geneva: WCC, forthcoming.

GC I · *Growing Consensus: Church Dialogues in the United States, 1962-1991.* Edited by Joseph A. Burgess and Jeffrey Gros. New York: Paulist Press, 1995.

GC II · *Growing Consensus II: Church Dialogues in the United States, 1992-2004.* Edited by Lydia Veliko and Jeffrey Gros. Washington: US Conference of Catholic Bishops, 2005.

MD · *Mennonites in Dialogue: Official Reports from International and National Ecumenical Encounters, 1975-2012.* Edited by Fernando Enns and Jonathan Seiling. Eugene, Oregon: Pickwick, 2015.

Online collections

Anglican-Roman Catholic Dialogue: Online resource centre for Anglican-Roman Catholic relations, iarccum.org

Centro Pro Unione, *Interconfessional Dialogues,* prounione.urbe.it

List of Contributors

Bert B. Beach was born in Switzerland to Seventh-day Adventist (SDA) parents serving as missionaries in Western Europe. He studied in France, Switzerland, and the United States, earning his BA at Pacific Union College, doing graduate work at Stanford, and completing a doctorate in history at the University of Paris in 1958. He has held several positions in Adventist education and in general church administration in Italy, England, and the U.S. He was an SDA observer/journalist at all four sessions of Vatican II and served for some twenty years at the World Headquarters of the SDA Church, responsible for dealing with public affairs, religious liberty, and interchurch relations. He speaks four languages fluently and is the author of seven books and many articles.

Thomas F. Best, a pastor of the Christian Church (Disciples of Christ), is retired director of the WCC Commission on Faith and Order. He is former editor and book review editor of *The Ecumenical Review*, the recent *Baptism Today* (WCC/Liturgical Press), and an editor of the forthcoming *Growth in Agreement IV*. He currently serves as a member of the International Disciples-Roman Catholic Dialogue, and as President 2016-2017 of the North American Academy of Ecumenists.

Henri Blocher has taught Systematic Theology at the Faculté Libre de Théologie Evangélique (Vaux-sur-Seine, near Paris) since it was founded in 1965, and held the Gunther Knoedler chair of Systematic Theology at Wheaton College from 2003 to 2008. He served for eight years as a vice-president of the United Bible Societies. He was part of the Task Force or delegation of the World Evangelical Fellowship/Alliance through the first round of dialogue with the delegation of the PCPCU (1993-2002). He participated for twelve years in the French Baptist-Catholic dialogue. In France, his privileged "dialogue partner" was the Jesuit theologian Bernard Sesboüé.

Donald Bolen is archbishop of Regina (Canada), and was the bishop of Saskatoon from 2010 to 2016. Originally from Gravelbourg, Saskatchewan, he studied at Campion College at the University of Regina, at Saint Paul University in Ottawa, and at Oxford. He served the Pontifical Council for Promoting Christian Unity from 2001 to 2008 as staff person for relations with the Anglican Communion and the World Methodist Council. He is currently co-chair of the international Methodist-Catholic dialogue, of the Canadian Anglican-Roman Catholic dialogue, and of the International Anglican-Roman Catholic Commission for Unity and Mission, as well as a member of the international Evangelical-Catholic consultations.

Cardinal Edward Idris Cassidy served as president of the Pontifical Council for Promoting Christian Unity and of the Commission for Religious Relations with the Jews from 1991 to 2001. He served 33 years in the Diplomatic Service of the Holy See before his appointment to the PCPCU. He is the author of *Ecumenism and Interreligious Dialogue* (2005) in the Paulist Press series *Rediscovering Vatican II*.

For the 32 years prior to his recent retirement as auxiliary bishop of Down and Connor, **Anthony J. Farquhar** was chairman of the Ecumenical Commission of the Irish Bishops' Conference. Much of this time was spent against the background of the Troubles and violence in Northern Ireland. He was Catholic co-chair for the Pontifical Council's dialogue with the World Alliance of Reformed Churches when Monsignor Radano served as secretary. In 2001, he was appointed as a member of the International Anglican-Roman Catholic Commission for Unity and Mission.

Günther Gassmann is a Lutheran theologian and ecumenist. He received his doctor's degrees at the University of Heidelberg, Germany, where he also served as assistant professor. After teaching positions in Germany, Switzerland, and the USA he became director of the Commission on Faith and Order of the WCC in Geneva, from which he retired after eleven years. He was a member of the Joint Working Group between the WCC and the Roman Catholic Church, and among his publications are *Documentary History of Faith and Order, 1963-1993* (1993) and *Historical Dictionary of Lutheranism* (2011).

Donna Geernaert, SC is a member of the Sisters of Charity-Halifax, serving as congregational leader from 2002 to 2014. As director for Ecumenical and Interfaith Relations at the Canadian Conference of Catholic Bishops from 1984 to 2002, she was involved in several national inter-church and interfaith dialogues as well as on various committees of the Canadian Council of Churches. She was one of the Vatican representatives on the WCC Commission on Faith and Order, participating in its fifth world conference in Santiago de Compostela, and in plenary assemblies at Moshi and Kuala Lumpur. She was a consultant on the third phase of the International Reformed-Roman Catholic Dialogue and a member of the International Anglican-Roman Catholic Commission for Unity and Mission.

Jeffrey Gros, FSC was a member of the De La Salle Christian Brothers and an internationally known ecumenist and theologian. Prior to his death in August 2013, he had served as a high school teacher, a university professor, an associate director of the United States Conference of Catholic Bishops' Secretariat of Ecumenical and Inter-religious Affairs, director of Faith and Order for the National Council of Churches and, president of the Society for Pentecostal Studies. The author or editor of 20 books, as well as numerous articles and book reviews, he was deeply committed to the reception of ecumenical dialogues into religious education and pastoral practice.

Helmut Harder is professor emeritus of Theology at Canadian Mennonite University, Winnipeg. Among his various ecumenical distinctions was his role as Mennonite co-chair of the international Catholic-Mennonite dialogue which concluded in 2003.

William Henn, OFM Cap. is professor of ecclesiology at the Gregorian University in Rome, and has represented the Catholic Church in bilateral dialogues with Pentecostals, the World Alliance of Reformed Churches, the Baptist World Alliance, the Lutheran World Federation, and the Mennonite World Conference. He is vice-moderator of the WCC Commission on Faith and Order and is a consultant to the PCPCU.

Nicholas Jesson is ecumenical officer for the Roman Catholic Diocese of Saskatoon. His academic work and ecumenical ministry have focused on dialogue between Evangelicals and Roman Catholics. He was director of the Prairie Centre for Ecumenism from 1994 to 1999 and has been editor of the website *Ecumenism in Canada* (ecumenism.net) from 1995 to the present. He has developed the new digital archive *Anglican-Roman Catholic Dialogue* (iarccum.org) on behalf of IARCCUM. He is a member of the national dialogue between the United Church of Canada and the Roman Catholic Church.

Cardinal Walter Kasper served as president of the Pontifical Council for Promoting Christian Unity and of the Commission for Religious Relations with the Jews from 2001 to 2010. He is the author of numerous theological texts, many of which have been translated into English. His ecumenical texts include *Harvesting the Fruits: Basic Aspects of Christian Faith in Ecumenical Dialogue* (2009), *Sacrament of Unity: The Eucharist and the Church* (2004), and *A Handbook of Spiritual Ecumenism* (2006).

Denton Lotz served as general secretary of the Baptist World Alliance from 1988 to 2007. He studied at the University of North Carolina and Harvard Divinity School before completing his Dr.Theol. in Missiology from Hamburg Universitaet in Germany. He was formerly professor of Missions at the Baptist Theological Seminary in Ruschlilkon, Switzerland, and represented the American Baptist International Ministries in Eastern Europe. Presently he serves as senior pastor of Tremont Temple Baptist Church in Boston, Massachusetts.

Odair Pedroso Mateus has been director of the Commission on Faith and Order of the World Council of Churches since 2015. A pastor of the Independent Presbyterian Church of Brazil, Mateus did his doctoral studies on the theology of the Uruguayan Jesuit Juan Luis Segundo. He then moved to Geneva, Switzerland, where he worked for the World Alliance of Reformed Churches, directing its bilateral ecumenical dialogues and editing its quarterly journal. In 2007, he joined the World Council of Churches as staff for the Faith and Order secretariat and as instructor at the Ecumenical Institute in Bossey.

Larry Miller has been secretary of the Global Christian Forum since 2012. He was formerly the General Secretary of the Mennonite World Conference for 22 years. Together with Monsignor John Radano, he served as co-secretary of the international Catholic-Mennonite dialogue. He has served also as co-secretary of other international bilateral dialogues – Baptist-Mennonite, Reformed-Mennonite, and Lutheran-Mennonite – as well as of the trilateral Catholic-Lutheran-Mennonite dialogue on baptism and of the multilateral conversations known as the "Prague Consultations."

Margaret O'Gara was a member of the Faculty of Theology at the University of St. Michael's College, Toronto, from 1976 until her death in 2012. The focus of her teaching, writing, and public lecturing was ecumenical theology. She was active in many academic and ecclesial organizations, especially those with an ecumenical dimension. She also served as a Roman Catholic member of five national or international ecumenical dialogues.

James F. Puglisi, SA served as Minister General of the Friars of the Atonement (Graymoor Fathers) from 2004 to 2014 and is currently director of the Centro Pro Unione in Rome. He is also a professor of ecumenical theology at the Pontifical Atheneum of St. Anselm (Rome), the Pontifical University of St. Thomas Aquinas ("Angelicum"), and the Institute of Ecumenical Studies (Venice), and has taught at the Pontifical University Antonianum (Rome). He is a former member of the Lutheran-Roman Catholic Dialogue in the USA. He has published articles in the *Journal of Ecumenical Studies, La Maison Dieu, Ecumenical Trends, Studi Ecumenici, Journal of the American Academy of Religion*, and *Eccesiology*. He is author of *Liturgical Renewal as a Way to Christian Unity* (2005), and editor of *How Can the Petrine Ministry Be a Service to the Unity of the Universal Church?* (2010) and *Petrine Ministry and the Unity of the Church* (1999).

Cecil M. Robeck, Jr. is professor of Church History and Ecumenics and director of the David du Plessis Center for Christian Spirituality at Fuller Theological Seminary in Pasadena, CA. Dr. Robeck is an ordained Assemblies of God minister and has been appointed "General Liaison to Christian Communities in the United States" by its Executive Presbytery. Robeck has served on the International Catholic-Pentecostal Dialogue since 1985 and as co-chair since 1992. From time to time he offers lectures to Diocesan Ecumenical Officers in the US and he co-chairs a monthly dialogue between Evangelicals and the Archdiocese of Los Angeles.

William G. Rusch is adjunct professor of Lutheran Studies at Yale Divinity School, and former director of the Commission on Faith and Order at the National Council of the Churches of Christ (USA). He is the author of numerous books, including *Ecumenical Reception: Its Challenge and Opportunity* (2007), *The Pontificate of Benedict XVI: Its Premises and Promises* (2009), and *The Witness of Bartholomew I, Ecumenical Patriarch* (2013).

Mary Tanner taught Old Testament and Hebrew at Hull University and Westcott House, Cambridge, before serving as the general secretary of the Church of England's Council for Christian Unity. She was a member of the WCC Commission on Faith and Order from 1973 and its Moderator from 1991 to 1998. She has also been a member of the Anglican-Roman Catholic International Commission and the International Anglican-Roman Catholic Commission for Unity and Mission. From 2007 to 2013, she served as president for Europe of the WCC.

Huibert van Beek served on the staff of the WCC from 1978 to 2004. One of his assignments as executive secretary of the WCC Office of Church and Ecumenical Relations in the 1990s was to initiate and develop relationships with churches not in membership with the WCC, belonging to the Evangelical and Pentecostal movements. In this capacity, he was directly involved with the Global Christian Forum (GCF) from its inception in 1998. From 2004 to 2011 he served as the first secretary of the GCF. Prior to his involvement with the WCC and GCF, he worked as a missionary in Madagascar in different capacities, sent out by the former Paris Missionary Society.

Geoffrey Wainwright is an ordained minister of the British Methodist Church. Born in Yorkshire, he spent much of his career in the United States, teaching primarily at Duke Divinity School until his retirement in 2012. From 1976 to 1991, he was a member of the WCC Commission on Faith and Order, where he chaired the final redaction of the 1982 Lima text on *Baptism, Eucharist and Ministry*. From 1986 to 2011, he was co-chair of the Joint Commission between the World Methodist Council and the Roman Catholic Church. His publications reflect his strong interest in the relationship between liturgy and ecumenism.

Foreword

by Archbishop Donald Bolen

Those who work in the field of Christian unity for any length of time are quick to point out that ecumenism is the work of the Holy Spirit. We say that not to sound pious but because we know firsthand two things: from our failed efforts, that we cannot bring about unity by ourselves no matter how hard we try; and from our successes, that something else is operative in this work of dialogue and reconciliation. God's grace shapes our efforts in countless ways, experienced in a deep yearning for unity, in the insights which come forth from dialogue, in the moments of breakthrough when new understandings are reached, in the relationships and bonds of communion that are formed when we work with other Christians at the service of unity.

Ecumenism is a work of the Holy Spirit in the churches as they put themselves at the service of Jesus' desire that his disciples be reconciled, and it is a work of the Spirit in people's lives. This volume, which reflects on ecumenical achievements and hopes as we mark the 500th anniversary of the Reformation, is a celebration of the work of the Holy Spirit in the churches and ecclesial communities of the West as they have sought to address conflicts and heal divisions. It is also a celebration of the work of the Holy Spirit in the ecumenical ministry of Monsignor John Radano, and in a secondary but very real way, of each of the contributors to this volume. John Radano, generally known by his dialogue partners and colleagues as Jack, served as head of the Pontifical Council for Promoting Christian Unity's (PCPCU) Western section for nearly a quarter century, from 1984 to 2008. In this capacity, he participated in dialogues with Lutheran, Reformed, Baptist, Mennonite, Classical Pentecostal, and Evangelical traditions, and served as liaison with the World Council of Churches' Commission on Faith and Order. Jack was also involved in relations with the Anglican Communion, the World Methodist Council, and the Global Christian

Forum, so had a truly comprehensive involvement in relations with the Catholic Church's dialogue and consultation partners in the West.

As Cardinal Kasper's introduction notes, Jack has an encyclopedic knowledge of the ecumenical movement and ecumenical texts, not least because during his years at the PCPCU, he served as the editor of *Information Service*, the Pontifical Council's journal documenting the Catholic Church's involvement in the ecumenical movement on an international level. Coupled with that deep knowledge base and widespread engagement in ecumenical relations, Jack's work was characterized by a deep confidence in the process of dialogue. While dialogue needs to be accompanied by prayer for unity, relationship building, and efforts at common witness and mission, it is the work of dialogue that is at the heart of the Pontifical Council's efforts at reconciliation among Christians. Ecumenical dialogue is dependent on men and women who have profound confidence in and knowledge of their church and its teachings, and who have an ability to bring that knowledge and commitment into dialogue with others in a way that is intelligent, respectful, open-minded and discerning. It also benefits greatly from those who are engaged in dialogue over the long haul, thus building honest and genuine relationships with the dialogue partner and an in-depth understanding of the other's tradition and history as well as one's own. Jack was eminently suited to this work and gave himself over to it with tremendous generosity. He is a living example of the Second Vatican Council's understanding that to be deeply committed to one's Catholic faith and to be seriously committed to Christian unity are profoundly compatible.

I had the privilege of serving at the PCPCU from 2001 to 2008, as the staff person for relations with the Anglican Communion and the World Methodist Council. Jack was a generous and patient *cap'ufficio* (head of department) for those of us working in the Western section, always ready to take the time to answer our questions, give feedback to our ideas, and brainstorm about how to respond to the challenging situations that were a daily occurrence at the office. Above all, I witnessed in him (and learned from him) a deep commitment to the process of dialogue and a recognition of the rich value and potential of the bilateral and multilateral texts that the dialogues produced. Jack referred to these as texts of reconciliation, and when they did not seem to have a significant impact on participating churches upon their release, he spoke of them as being "in the bank," treasures waiting to release their reconciling potential when the time was right.

In bilateral dialogues, which formed the biggest part of Jack's work at the PCPCU, commission members generally live, pray, eat, plan, discuss, and draft together during the course of their annual meetings. Motivated by the common aim of seeking reconciliation as they approach the Scriptures, tradition, and their separate histories on the theological subject under investigation, dialogue participants often come to see the integrity of the dialogue partner as one who desires to love God, to be a faithful disciple of Christ, to be obedient to the Holy Spirit. The dialogue process helps to create a context that is highly conducive to recognising the other's faith, and to finding a faithful way forward when addressing long-standing divisions. The great Catholic ecumenist Jean Tillard offered a keen insight into the working of an effective dialogue commission when speaking of his work on the Anglican-Roman Catholic International Commission: "as a Commission we found ourselves living and experiencing the tragic drama of our two churches": the unity being sought was one that "together we were already experiencing."[1] Working on a dialogue commission, the real but imperfect communion between churches can be experienced with immediacy and forcefulness.

This book witnesses to what has been achieved through the work of dialogue over the past fifty years, and to the work of the Holy Spirit in evidence through the dialogue process. It also witnesses to the importance of ecumenical friendship in advancing the cause of unity. When approaching colleagues and former colleagues of Monsignor Radano to ask if they would be willing to prepare a paper as part of a *Festschrift* honouring Jack, there was a nearly unanimous "'yes" to this invitation, even though these scholars and church leaders are all incredibly busy people. The friendship that emerges over the course of years of dialogue does not always transfer to spending a lot of time together outside of the dialogue. Rather, it is a friendship grounded in the experience of working closely together, empowered by the Holy Spirit, at a cause much bigger than ourselves, the work of God reconciling the world to himself in Christ. Such friendship is a chosen instrument in the toolbox of the Holy Spirit, and its capacity to assist in the work of reconciliation is the cement that holds the papers of this volume together and made it possible.

The text begins with an Introduction and initial chapter which offer reflections from two former Presidents of the PCPCU. Both testify to Monsignor Radano's commitment, competence, and wide knowledge of the dialogues in which he was involved over many years.

The next several chapters focus on gleanings from the bilateral dialogues. Brother Jeffrey Gros, FSC, addresses an internal audience, calling on Roman Catholics to integrate dialogue results into catechetical materials. He invites churches to rewrite history together and to promote the healing of memories. Articles by Drs. Mary Tanner and James Puglisi, SA, highlight insights from Anglican-Roman Catholic dialogue, especially in ecclesiology. Dialogues with the Methodists, Lutherans, and Disciples of Christ are featured in the texts of Drs. Geoffrey Wainwright, William Rusch, and Margaret O'Gara. Developments in Reformed ecclesiology and ecumenicity are discussed in the essays by Drs. Donna Geernaert, SC, and Odair Mateus. Growth in understanding through the dialogue process with Mennonites, Pentecostals, and Seventh-day Adventists is explored in the chapters by Drs. Helmut Harder and Larry Miller, Mel Robeck, and Bert Beach. The article by Dr. Henri Blocher offers an Evangelical reading of *Ut Unum Sint* that illustrates some of the challenges faced by dialogue partners as they seek to receive documents produced in another tradition.

The next three chapters invite reflection on the ecumenical movement as a whole. While the text by Dr. William Henn, OFM Cap., explores some specific strengths and weaknesses of the current search for Christian unity, that of Dr. Günther Gassmann chronicles the development of concepts of unity in the WCC Commission on Faith and Order. In the article by Dr. Thomas Best, mutual accountability is identified as a decisive dimension of the church and churches' relationships with one another.

The final two chapters of this volume focus on specific ecumenical organisations which give form to multilateral relationships. Dr. Denton Lotz reflects on some of the concerns raised by Baptists and Evangelicals who affirm the search for Christian unity but are not members of the World Council of Churches. Dr. Huibert van Beek describes the emergence of the Global Christian Forum and the new possibilities it offers for promoting Christian unity among churches which do not usually cultivate a strong sense of belonging to Reformation history. In his Postscript, Bishop Anthony Farquhar offers a personal portrayal of Monsignor Jack Radano, theologian, scholar, and consummate ecumenist.

---

1   Cited in "J.M.R. Tillard", in *Encounters for Unity: Sharing Faith, Prayer and Life*, ed. Gillian R. Evans, Lorelei F. Fuchs, and Diane C. Kessler (Norwich: Canterbury Press, 1995), pp. 199-200.

Introduction

by Cardinal Walter Kasper

T he twentieth century, which started with a strong impulse of faith in human progress, which is rather difficult to imagine today, became one of the darkest and bloodiest centuries in the history of humankind. No other century has known as many violent deaths. There was, at least, one glimmer of light in this dark period: the birth of the modern ecumenical movement. The divisions of the sixteenth century in the West, which continued into further divisions down to our present day, had slowly awakened in the consciousness of Christians that such divisions were a scandal. While the impetus for this reflection may have been initially focused on the pragmatic problem of the scandal of exporting divisions into mission territories, the consciousness of the scandal of division in and of itself has continued to germinate in the souls of the faithful. After centuries of growing fragmentation of the *una sancta ecclesia* – the one, holy Church that we profess in our common apostolic creed – into many divided churches, a new movement developed in the opposite direction.

In Jesus' prayer before his passion, he prayed for his disciples: "I pray not only for them, but also for those who will believe in me through their word, that they may all be one, as you, Father, are in me and I in you, that they also may be in us, that the world may believe that you sent me." (John 17:20-21) In deep sorrow and repentance, the churches realized that their situation of division, contrary to the will of Christ, was sinful and shameful. It is significant that this new ecumenical awareness developed in the context of the missionary movement. The division of the Church was recognized as a major obstacle to world mission. The foundation of the World Council of Churches in Amsterdam in 1948 represented an important milestone on this ecumenical journey.

The birth of the twentieth-century ecumenical movement more or less coincides with the World Missionary Conference held in Edinburgh in 1910, already a century in the past. Edinburgh was very important for several reasons. It was the source of two great currents which then flowed into the World Council of Churches: "Life and Work" and "Faith and Order." Edinburgh's essential contribution was to connect explicitly the Church's ecumenical and missionary commitments. Ecumenism and mission are "twins," so to speak.

The Church's ecumenical challenge is to become ever more aware of the scandal of division, which the existence of divided churches and ecclesial communities particularly highlights, in order to achieve reconciliation. In her mission, the Church must open herself to the world of nations and cultures desirous of receiving the Gospel proclamation. Ecumenism and mission, therefore, also have an eschatological dimension; they strive for the eschatological *shalom*, the universal eschatological peace proclaimed by the Old Testament prophets. It is by no means accidental that the President and Secretary of the Edinburgh Conference, the American Methodist layman John Mott and the Anglican theologian Joseph H. Oldam, were also protagonists of the peace movement initiated after the tragedy and devastation of the First World War.

However important the Edinburgh Conference may be, we must not forget that it is neither the only nor the oldest root of twentieth-century ecumenism. Two years earlier the then (still) Episcopalian minister Paul Wattson (1863-1940), co-founder of the Community of Brothers and Sisters of the Atonement at Graymoor (Garrison, New York), introduced an Octave of Prayer for Christian Unity that was celebrated for the first time from January 18 to 25, 1908. This is the origin of the Week of Prayer for Christian Unity still celebrated during that octave. The Week of Prayer can be traced to various initiatives even further back in time, and to movements of spiritual renewal in the second half of the nineteenth century: for example, the Oxford Movement, the World Evangelical Alliance, and the "World Day of Prayer" of women which, despite strong male opposition, was introduced by Presbyterian, Methodist, Baptist, and Anglican women in the 1880s, first in the United States and Canada, then worldwide.

The Catholic Church abstained from this path of ecumenism at the beginning. The encyclical letters *Satis cognitum* of Leo XIII (1896) and *Mortalium animos* of Pius XI (1928) even condemned the ecumenical movement which seemed to relativize the claim of the Catholic Church to be the true Church of Jesus Christ. Pope Pius XII paved the way to a more open attitude, albeit with caution, in an Instruction of the Holy Office of 1949. However, only the initiative of Pope John XXIII (+1963) and the Second Vatican Council (1962-65) brought a shift. The conciliar Decree on Ecumenism *Unitatis Redintegratio* stated that the ecumenical movement was a sign of the work of the Holy Spirit in our time,[1] opening the way for Catholic participation in the ecumenical movement and highlighting the importance of dialogue with other Christians and with their churches and communities.[2]

Pope Paul VI made the idea of dialogue central in his inaugural encyclical *Ecclesiam suam* (1963). This line was taken up in a document of the then Secretariat for Promoting Christian Unity entitled *Reflections and Suggestions Concerning Ecumenical Dialogue* (1970), later in the *Ecumenical Directory* (1993), and finally in the great, important, and even prophetic ecumenical encyclical of John Paul II, *Ut unum sint* (1995).

Nevertheless, the new beginning was not easy. From the outset, the first General Secretary of the World Council of Churches, Dr. Willem Visser't Hooft, raised the question as to whether the Catholic Church and the World Council of Churches understood ecumenism in the same way. This question was also related to the meaning of ecumenical dialogue, which the conciliar Decree on Ecumenism had proposed as a way of contributing towards unity.

The Catholic Church's entry into the modern ecumenical movement with Vatican II helped shift the methodology of ecumenical dialogue from multilateral dialogues, favoured by the World Council of Churches, to the both/and approach of bilateral and multilateral dialogues. The Catholic Church became a member of the multilateral Faith and Order Commission of the World Council of Churches in 1968. She also began a series of bilateral dialogues and conversations with individual Christian churches and ecclesial communions to work more concretely on specific issues between the various churches and communions.

The approach of the 500th anniversary of the Reformation in 2017 offers an opportunity to take account of the ecumenical progress that has been made, especially in the last century. The ecumenical movement in the twentieth century brought a profound recognition of the scandal of divisions, and significant efforts to address through dialogue the doctrinal conflicts that led to – and/or resulted from – those divisions. As Pope John Paul II noted in 1983 on the fifth centenary of the birth of Martin Luther: "Time, by separating us from the historical events, often permits them to be understood and represented better."

Key questions arise in this new ecumenical context. To what extent have the ecumenical dialogues, bilateral and multilateral, enabled us to address and resolve or make progress in resolving the doctrinal conflicts over which Christians divided in the sixteenth century? To what extent have they helped to identify steps towards reconstituting the unity of Christians, even if complete unity has not been reached?

This volume has a two-fold thrust: towards what has already been achieved ecumenically in recent decades; and towards the future, envisioning further steps that can be taken in our common search for the unity of all Christians. The contributors include representatives from the Christian World Communions of the West that have been engaged in dialogue with the Catholic Church since the Second Vatican Council, representatives from the World Council of Churches, as well as Catholic theologians who have been engaged in these ecumenical dialogues. The contributors look at what has been achieved – either by a particular bilateral or multilateral dialogue involving the Catholic Church or from the wider search for Christian unity. They examine the extent to which doctrinal differences have been successfully addressed, the steps that have been taken to give tangible ecclesial expression to that which we can claim as our common faith, and the conditions which have dynamized these steps towards reconciliation. Looking to the future, it is hoped that this study will encourage creative reflection in exploring where ecumenical advances could be made or steps could be taken, identifying the ecumenical challenges that we currently face or are likely to face in the future, and envisioning with greater clarity the unity we seek.

Looking to the future, the pontificate of Pope Francis fills us with new courage and hope. Pope Francis has started a new phase in the ongoing process of the reception of Vatican II, placing particular emphasis on its ecumenical orientation. Significant aspects of Francis' pontificate have already emerged: his pastoral motto "walking together" (*camminare insieme*); his insistence on the conversion of the Church, including the papacy; his idea of a Church oriented towards the peripheries (*chiesa in uscita*); the prominence that he brings to the synodical structure of the Church; his insistence on the *sensus fidelium*; his vision of unity as reconciled diversity; his personal contacts with the ancient Eastern churches and with the mainline Reformation churches; and his outreach to the Evangelical and Pentecostal churches. All of these will have an enormous impact on the future of the ecumenical movement and after an ecumenical winter can fill us with new ecumenical enthusiasm.

Monsignor John A. Radano (Jack) has spent his entire priesthood in the service of Christian unity. Ordained in 1965 for the Archdiocese of Newark (New Jersey, USA), shortly after Vatican II's Decree on Ecumenism, *Unitatis Redintegratio,* was promulgated, young Father Radano was assigned to teach in the Religious Studies department of Newark's Seton Hall University. He began a quest for Christian unity that was the subject of teaching and research until he was called to Rome in 1984 to work in the then Secretariat for Promoting Christian Unity. In his years of service to the Holy See in ecumenism, there is little in the Western Section that did not become a part of the work of Monsignor Radano. Eventually becoming the head of the Western Section, Jack served the Pontifical Council for Promoting Christian Unity until 2008. During this time, he became the living memory of Catholic involvement in ecumenism.

Never one to look for recognition or self-promotion, Jack is a tireless worker, a trusted partner for theologians working in ecumenism. Those familiar with him know that he has a clarity of logic and thought that quickly cuts to the central issues being discussed. A true and patient listener, Jack not only hears the words of dialogue partners but also listens intently. He seeks points of convergence and consensus in dialogue. An academic, he has an encyclopedic memory of the ecumenical movement. Ask him about an important moment in ecumenism, and 1) he was there; 2) he can detail who was present, what were the concerns, and what was settled upon; and 3) he can most likely tell you the weather, where people sat, and what they wore.

His concern is always to lift up the consensus achieved; highlighting what can be said together. He is interested in Christian unity, not his instrumental role in that unity.

This volume not only recounts the varied areas of western ecumenism but highlights many trusted ecumenical partner churches and persons who worked closely with Jack during these past decades. The theologians who write here describe their community's involvement in ecumenism. They could as easily have written about their relationship with Monsignor Radano. Those who know Jack know that there is little that can raise an emotional response from him. He has been described by some ecumenical partners as a consummate bridge-builder for his even-handed diplomacy; or as a tireless, determined priest who consistently goes out of his way to build those relationships that are at the heart of trust and reconciliation. To get an emotional response out of Jack, take him to a Yankees baseball game. There, a metamorphosis takes place. The consummate diplomat becomes an ardent fan. The relationship builder becomes an unapologetic backer of his team. For most of us who do not appreciate American baseball, both baseball and the transformation of Jack watching the Yankees are both mysteries deeper than any ecumenical divide. It is with great appreciation for his ministry of service to Christian unity that this volume has been prepared. Thank you, Monsignor John A. Radano, for all you have achieved in service of the unity for which Christ prays for his church.

---

1   Second Vatican Council, *Unitatis Redintegratio* (Decree on ecumenism, November 21, 1964), no. 1.

2   *Unitatis Redintegratio*, nos. 4, 9, 11, 14, 18, 19, 21-23.

✝ CHAPTER I

Reflections on the Pursuit of Christian Unity during My Years at the Pontifical Council

by Cardinal Edward Idris Cassidy

When I was appointed to the office of President of the Pontifical Council for Promoting Christian Unity (PCPCU), Pope John Paul II calmed my concern of not having sufficient experience for such an important and delicate task by assuring me that I would find at the Pontifical Council dedicated people with ample knowledge and experience in the field. That proved to be the case and I shall always be grateful for the support and collaboration that I received from Bishop Pierre Duprey and Monsignor Eleutherio Fortino, together with the priests and lay staff I found there.

Monsignor John Radano had already been at the Pontifical Council for some four years when I arrived, and I soon came to recognize in him a valuable colleague with special experience in relations with the World Council of Churches, the Lutheran World Federation and the World Alliance of Reformed Churches. It is my intention in this tribute to him to reflect on the years 1988 to 2001, which that I spent at the Pontifical Council, indicating the main achievements of those years and referring briefly to some of the problems we met on the way. In so doing, I wish to acknowledge with deep gratitude the important role that Monsignor Radano had in the work of the PCPCU during that period. The Church and the ecumenical movement owe him a great deal!

During my years at the Pontifical Council, I often found consolation and new energy by reflecting on the fact that in just forty years a great change for the better had taken place in relations between the Catholic Church and other Christian Churches. Pope John Paul II, in his encyclical letter *Ut Unum Sint* (UUS), described this achievement with a single, but deeply meaningful phrase, "brotherhood rediscovered."[1]

Looking back, it may seem that we have lost some of the enthusiasm and hope of the early years after the Second Vatican Council. We tend to forget that the challenge in those first years was more a matter of attitude and understanding than seeking to confront and reconcile the differences at the heart of our divisions. Old prejudices had to be put aside, new trust established. The emphasis was on highlighting what Christians had in common, rather than on what still kept us apart. With goodwill and by getting to know each other, we were able to make substantial progress, a progress that is clearly visible as we examine the various relationships enjoyed by the Catholic Church today. I am convinced that the communion we have achieved is destined to be long-lasting and fruitful.

I have often likened the ecumenical journey to attempts at conquering high mountains. Both in Kashmir and Nepal, I experienced the exhilaration of reaching a certain height on the majestic Himalayan Mountains. Together with a local guide, our group was able to reach the lower levels. The going at first was mainly rocky and the path up the mountain to our destination already challenging but within our possibilities. What we experienced even at those heights was truly beautiful and well worth the effort. I would have loved to have gone higher, but that needed skill and training that I did not possess.

In the first forty years of our ecumenical climb, we have covered a lot of 'rocky' ground and climbed to new heights of understanding, trust, cooperation and fraternal communion. We have been able to enjoy new visions of unity and we now desire fervently to go further towards the mountain summit, where we would be able to share the eucharistic bread and wine that Our Lord left his disciples as his parting gift. To reach the summit of full communion, however, will need continued efforts along the same lines, accompanied by the dedication and skill of the theologian and historian working together in a dialogue inspired and aided by the Holy Spirit. What has been achieved is already well worthwhile and truly beautiful, and surely is enough to encourage the Christian Communities to continue the climb until the Lord's prayer is finally answered: "that they may be one" (John 17: 21).

In *Ut Unum Sint*, Pope John Paul II sees the ecumenical edifice being raised on three pillars: prayer, cooperation and dialogue. Prayer has pride of place. His Holiness writes about the 'primacy of prayer' and begins with this statement: "Change of heart and holiness of life along with public and private prayer for the unity of Christians, should be regarded as the soul of the whole ecumenical movement, and can rightly be called 'spiritual ecumenism.'"[2]

It is very important to keep in mind that Christian unity is not something we can hope to achieve by our own efforts alone. It is true that our divisions are the result of human weakness and sin. It is also true that God will not bring about our unity without our efforts. Those efforts are inspired by the prayer of Our Lord Jesus Christ on the night before he suffered, when, regarding those who would believe in him, he prayed to the Father: "I ask not only on behalf of these, but also on behalf of those who will believe in me through their word, that they may all be one. As you, Father, are in me and I am in you, may they also be in us, so that the world may believe that you have sent me" (John 17: 20-21).

There is a delicate balance between prayer and action in promoting the ecumenical cause. Nothing will be achieved without our cooperation, but alone our efforts will fail to procure the result we seek. In a meeting with clergy from the region in the Italian mountains where he was spending some weeks of summer holiday in July 2007, Pope Benedict XVI spoke of the quest for Christian unity. He reminded those present: "If we listen carefully to the Gospel we will realize that our task is to 'let out the nets.' We are not responsible for the fish being there or for the catch! That is the Lord's work, while ours is to give of our best and *prayerfully* entrust the results to Our Lord Jesus Christ."[3]

These comments from Pope Benedict XVI reminded me of an experience of mine that occurred in the early years of my time as President of the PCPCU. I had returned to my apartment in the Vatican one Saturday afternoon after lunch with Pope John Paul II. It was a time when relations with the Russian Orthodox Church were particularly strained and an attempt at healing them had only made things worse. I was feeling quite frustrated and despondent. Fortunately, I had to prepare a short homily for the following day and took up the Gospel reading for that Sunday. It was the same incident as that to which Pope Benedict refers.

In the Gospel of Luke, chapter 5, we read how Jesus gave the disciples he had just called to his service an important lesson for their future mission. After addressing the crowd from Simon Peter's boat, he asked him "to put out into the deep water and let down your nets for a catch." Now Simon and his companions had fished all that night without any success and were washing their nets. Simon reminded Jesus of that fact: "Master, we have worked all night long and have caught nothing." Perhaps he was thinking that he knew the lake better than this teacher who was no fisherman, but he continued: "Yet if you say so, I will let down the nets." They did so and caught so many fish that their nets were beginning to break and they had to call their friends in another boat to come and help them.

Reading this, I suddenly realized that what the Lord was asking of me was to 'let down the nets'. Maybe the result would be like that experienced by Simon Peter and his companions; maybe not. That was not my responsibility. I was to let out the nets, do my part and prayerfully call on the Lord to bring those efforts to a fruitful conclusion. From then on, I was able to carry out the task entrusted to me, without being overly concerned about the results. Of course, I was anxious to have a great 'catch', and at times disappointed with the outcome, but that 'good catch' would come in the Lord's own time, if all those involved in our efforts did their part.

Reflections on Progress – 1990-2001: Two Very Special Documents

When I began my service as President of the PCPCU, I was quickly made aware of the vital role of the Council in fostering local ecumenism in the dioceses and other ecclesial institutions throughout the world. Even as papal representative in El Salvador, the Republic of China, Bangladesh, Southern Africa and the Netherlands, I had been active in encouraging those local Catholic communities to study the Second Vatican Council's Decree on Ecumenism, *Unitatis Redintegratio*. I realized already just how essential it is that the work done at the international level be known and supported by the local churches. I especially sought to encourage the priests of those countries to become involved. It was obvious that even the local bishops' best efforts would not bear the desired fruit unless they had the support and cooperation of their clergy.

If I may take an example once again from nature, I would refer to an Australian experience. My country is one in which serious droughts occur from time to time. On those occasions, farmers become excited and hopeful when they see clouds forming in the skies. Too often those clouds just roll on, and the land remains barren. Unless the rain falls and enters the soil, nothing will grow. Similarly, efforts and successes at the international level in the ecumenical field will remain fruitless unless the results enter into the life of the local churches. Only then can they produce a really lasting result.

Consequently, the Pontifical Council dedicates time and effort to assisting local churches in this task. On my arrival at the Council, a revised edition of the *Ecumenical Directory* that had been published in two parts, in 1967 and 1970, was being prepared. The *Ecumenical Directory* had been offered in response to requests made by a number of bishops during the Second Vatican Council, who had asked for detailed directives and guidelines for pastoral initiatives.

The *Directory* and other documents published by the Secretariat for Promoting Christian Unity – as the Pontifical Council was then called – had proved helpful. It seemed, however, that a more complete *Directory* was required. After consultation with Bishops' Conferences and discussion within the Roman Curia, which as a new man I found at times difficult, in 1993 we were able to publish a comprehensive *Directory for the Application of Principles and Norms on Ecumenism*, approved and confirmed by the authority of Pope John Paul II.[4]

This was followed in 1995 by a second document, which owed its inspiration and much of its content to Pope John Paul II himself. The remarkable encyclical letter already referred to, *Ut Unum Sint*, was at the same time a most valuable contribution to Catholic ecumenism and to the ecumenical movement in general. Reflecting on the Conciliar decree *Unitatis Redintegratio* and on the experience of thirty years of Catholic involvement in the search for Christian unity, the Holy Father offers a number of encouraging conclusions and new insights.

In a short space of thirty years, the Catholic Church had moved from a position of indifference to the ecumenical movement to being at the forefront of the search for greater unity among Christians. Here was an official papal document, approved word for word by the bishop of Rome, that left no room for doubt about the commitment of the Catholic Church to the ecumenical task.

Major Dialogue Achievements

By 1990, the Catholic Church had already been involved in a number of theological dialogues that had produced valuable agreed statements. At the close of a particular phase of dialogue, the final document in each case was published in the *Information Service* of the Pontifical Council, together with a critical commentary by a Catholic scholar with special competence in the particular area of doctrine that had been discussed by the relevant dialogue commission. By 1990, only one of these agreed statements had been submitted for official approval by the churches involved, namely the *Final Report* of the Anglican-Roman Catholic International Commission (ARCIC I).[5]

Some very valuable Christological agreements had, however, been achieved between the Catholic Church and the Ancient Oriental Churches. Pope John Paul II describes these as "signs of progress" in dialogue in *Ut Unum Sint,* and mentions each of them individually.[6] He concludes:

> Ecumenical contacts have thus made possible essential clarifications with regard to the traditional controversies concerning Christology, so much so that we have been able to profess together the faith which we have in common. Once again it must be said that this important achievement is truly a fruit of theological investigation and fraternal dialogue.[7]

During the period under consideration, all the theological dialogues – with the exception of the Joint International Commission for the Theological Dialogue between the Catholic Church and the Orthodox Church – reported significant progress. As already mentioned, the *Final Report* of ARCIC I had been submitted to the Holy See for formal approval. The 1988 Lambeth Conference had found the statements on Eucharist and Ministry "consonant with Anglican

Tradition"; while the third question dealt with in the Report – Author-ity – was accepted as a good foundation for further discussion. A first Vatican response was not so positive, and soon after my arrival at the Council, I was involved in intense discussions, which fortunately led to clarifications. These were eventually accepted by ARCIC and they allowed me to affirm officially that no further work needed to be done with respect to the section of the *Final Report* on the Eucharist. I was also able to state that there was agreement on the nature of Ministry in the Church, although the question of the minister able to celebrate the eucharist remained unsolved. Like the Anglican partner, we could state that the section dealing with authority in the Church was most promising, but requiring further study.

In the meantime, ARCIC II had begun its work and in the following years published a number of valuable agreed statements: *The Church as Communion* (1990);[8] the first theological dialogue document on morals and ethics, *Life in Christ: Morals, Communion and the Church* (1993);[9] a superb contribution to ecumenical dialogue entitled *The Gift of Authority* (1999);[10] and a joint study on *Mary, Grace and Hope in Christ* (2004).[11]

After some time at the Pontifical Council, I became concerned that the excellent work being done by ARCIC was not finding its proper place in the life of the local Anglican and Catholic churches. The Commission members could not be blamed for this, since they had worked hard and produced documents worthy of study and dis-cussion wherever good numbers of Catholics and Anglicans resided. ARCIC, in any case, was a theological commission, whereas the task of fostering reception in Anglican and Catholic churches is mainly the responsibility of the two hierarchies.

The celebration in Malines, in 1996, of the seventy-fifth anniversary of the informal Malines conversations between representatives of the Catholic Church and the Church of England offered me the oppor-tunity of discussing this problem with Dr. George Carey, Archbishop of Canterbury. He agreed at once that some more authoritative body was required to take the work of ARCIC forwards, and subsequent discussions led to a meeting in Mississauga, Ontario, Canada, in May 2000. Pairs of senior bishops from thirteen regions of the world as well as the ARCIC co-chairs met under the chairmanship of Dr. Carey and me. For one week we lived together in a retreat house, in prayer and deep fellowship, and were able to produce a draft plan of action as announced in the joint statement approved by the gathering.

Subsequently, a new working group, consisting of sixteen members (of whom ten would be bishops) was established, known as the International Anglican-Roman Catholic Commission for Unity and Mission (IARCCUM). This Commission began to work in 2002 on a document which aimed to prepare a "common declaration which would formally express the degree of agreement in faith existing between Anglican and Catholics, consolidate the results of more than thirty years of dialogue and commit the dialogue partners to a deeper sharing in common life and worship."[12]

Unfortunately, the work had to be suspended after the 2003 meeting, due to internal difficulties within the Anglican Communion, but resumed in 2005 and in October 2006 the Commission was able to publish an Agreed Statement entitled *Growing Together in Unity and Mission: Building on 40 Years of Anglican-Roman Catholic Dialogue*.[13]

These reflections would remain very incomplete if reference were not made to one of the most significant and personally satisfying experiences of my years as President of the PCPCU. This was the signing in Augsburg, on October 31, 1999, of the *Joint Declaration on the Doctrine of Justification* (JDDJ),[14] which was an outcome of the excellent work of the International Dialogue Commission between the Lutheran World Federation (LWF) and the PCPCU. It had begun its work soon after the conclusion of the Second Vatican Council and had completed three phases: the first (1967-1971) focused on the Gospel and the Church; the second (1973-1984) on the Eucharist and Ecclesial Ministry; the third (1986-1993) on Church and Justification.

It was during this third phase that the International Lutheran-Roman Catholic Commission for Unity (as it is now called) had come to the conviction that the two seemingly opposing understandings of Lutherans and Catholics on the doctrine of justification could be reconciled. A joint declaration was drawn up and officially submitted by the Commission to the two churches for approval.

The process of approval was itself interesting from an ecumenical point of view since this was probably the first attempt at achieving formal acceptance of a dialogue agreement between the Roman Catholic Church and a church of the Reformation. But of course it is the document itself and the method followed which offer encouragement, and I believe throw light on the whole movement towards the unity of Christians. Neither side was asked to abandon traditional teaching or change their fundamental approach to such a basic Christian belief as justification.

The aim was to see if traditional expressions of faith were, in fact, contradictory – as was claimed and seemed true for several centuries – or could rather be considered complementary and even as enriching one another. Both Lutherans and Catholics are usually particularly bound to their own expressions of faith, and hence this was no easy task. Yet in the end, both the Catholic Church and the Lutheran World Federation were able officially to sign the JDDJ, and so open the way for further progress in dialogue.

The Anglican Communion gave an early informal positive response to the JDDJ, while the World Methodist Council, after first issuing a statement of congratulations and appreciation, took the initiative to propose a meeting with the LWF and the Catholic Church in order to discuss how the JDDJ might have favourable consequences for other than the two partners to the declaration. The idea developed into a consultation, hosted by the PCPCU and the LWF, and attended by representatives of the World Methodist Council and the World Alliance of Reformed Churches. This was held in Columbus, Ohio, from November 27-30, 2001, and focused on theological and procedural issues involved in a possible formal adherence of the Methodist and Reformed ecclesial families to the agreements reached in the JDDJ.

Following on this meeting, the World Methodist Council prepared a statement on the Methodist understanding of justification and its relationship to the agreements reached in the JDDJ. This text was submitted to the PCPCU and the LWF and suggested changes incorporated into the document that was then submitted to the World Methodist Council meeting in Seoul in 2007. The document indicates an acceptance by Methodists of the basic consensus stated in the common confessions of the *Joint Declaration*. Similarly, it declares that the explanations that Lutherans and Catholics give in the JDDJ concerning their respective positions on key aspects of the doctrine of justification are not considered sufficient cause for division between Methodists and either of these two churches. The text concludes with a formal statement by the World Methodist Council and its member churches of fundamental doctrinal agreement with the teaching expressed in the JDDJ, on terms that the text makes clear.

This process has significant implications not only for Methodist-Catholic relations but also on possible future initiatives by a third partner to become part of an agreement established by two others. It signals a new genre of ecumenical text and a new means of advancing the search for unity.

On the fifth anniversary of the signing of the *Joint Declaration*, Rev. Dr. Ishmael Noko, Secretary General of the LWF, and Cardinal Walter Kasper, President of the PCPCU, wrote a joint letter calling for celebrations by Lutheran and Catholic communities on October 31, 2004. They referred to work being done to follow up on the JDDJ, mentioning, in particular, a study program on the contemporary meaning of justification, "Justification in the World's Context," and a biblical symposium being organized to broaden the biblical section of the Declaration.[15]

The International Lutheran-Roman Catholic Commission for Unity has since turned its attention to *The Apostolicity of the Church, Ministry and Church Teaching*. The discussions cover such subjects as New Testament foundations, the Apostolic Gospel and the Apostolicity of the Church, the Ordained Ministry from the Lutheran perspective, Scripture and Church teaching in a Reformation perspective, the concept and understanding of the magisterium in Catholic theology from the Council of Trent to the Second Vatican Council, and the ministry of apostolic teaching.[16]

Relations between Catholics and Lutherans have continued to develop. Leaders of the LWF and the PCPCU meet at least twice a year for discussions, alternately in Geneva and Rome. They deal with present-day issues, the planning of the international Lutheran-Catholic dialogue and ecumenical relations in general.

As already mentioned, the Pontifical Council joins in dialogue with other international ecclesial organisations, and considers each of these to be important. It is remarkable how much progress has been made, even in dialogue with Pentecostals and Evangelicals.

I must include here, however, a word on the relations between the Catholic Church and the World Council of Churches (WCC). I knew, of course, before going to the Pontifical Council that the Catholic Church was not a member of the WCC. But I had no idea of the very special relations that actually exist between the PCPCU and the WCC. We are really able to be part of the WCC without being a member, something that would create difficulties for both the Catholic Church and the WCC.

The primary form of this collaboration takes place within the framework of the Joint Working Group (JWG). Established in 1965 for the general purpose of exploring possibilities of dialogue and co-operation, the JWG is given a mandate by its parent bodies to study themes of mutual interest that help to deepen *koinonia* between the Catholic Church and the member churches of the WCC. It seeks to encourage and evaluate bilateral relations between the two partners. The JWG consists of 17 members on each side, appointed by the WCC and PCPCU for a period of seven years, and chosen from different parts of the world. In addition, the PCPCU has two Catholics attached full-time to the staff of the WCC and three representatives on the WCC Commission on World Mission and Evangelism. Some nine Catholic experts are invited regularly by the WCC to participate in various programs.

On a less formal basis, regular contact occurs between the WCC and the Catholic Church at various levels. The principal opportunity for establishing valuable friendships in a wide context is offered by the WCC Assemblies, which take place every seven years. I found the Canberra Assembly in 1991 a wonderful opportunity for meeting delegates from all over the world, representing the various Christian communities. Unfortunately, a change in the dates for the Harare meeting in 1998 did not allow me to follow up on that earlier experience. Besides the official Catholic observer delegation of some 20 or more members, about 100 other Catholics can be found at these Assemblies, under various categories of participation. During his 26 years as bishop of Rome, Pope John Paul II sent a message to each WCC Assembly held during that period, and this action was generally much appreciated.[17] At the Harare Assembly of the WCC in 1998, the Moderator of the Central Committee of the WCC, His Holiness Aram I (Catholicos of the Armenian Catholicosate of Cilicia) made special reference to Pope John Paul II's encyclical *Ut Unum Sint* and other Catholic documents on ecumenism. He stated: "although these documents addressed the internal ecumenical life of the Roman Catholic Church, their potential transcends the Roman Catholic Church."[18]

Other valuable forms of regular contact between the Roman Catholic Church and the WCC are:

- An invitation of the PCPCU to send observers to the 158-member WCC Central Committee meetings every 18 months has become a normal practice.[19]

- The WCC was invited to send a representative as a fraternal delegate to the Vatican Central Committee preparing the Jubilee Year 2000.

- WCC delegates took part in the ecumenical gatherings connected with the celebration in Rome of the Jubilee, at St. Paul's Outside the Walls on January 18, 2000, and January 25, 2001, as well as the Commemoration of Witnesses to the Faith in the Twentieth Century, at the Colosseum on May 7, 2000.

There are also frequent visits and contacts between Rome and Geneva on a more informal basis by members of the staff on both sides. These help greatly in establishing personal trust and understanding between those seeking to promote the official relationship while providing the occasion for an exchange of information and views on how best to proceed to this end.

It is obvious from what has been stated above that the relationship between the WCC and the Catholic Church is quite positive. The contribution of the Catholic Church to the work of the World Council is greatly appreciated by the authorities in Geneva since it certainly provides valuable assistance to the WCC in certain fields of its activities.

The relationship of the Catholic Church to one of the important organs of the WCC, the Commission on Faith and Order, is more official. Within the context of the multilateral theological dialogue, the WCC Commission on Faith and Order has a special role in promoting the search for greater doctrinal unity among the churches.

Since the Uppsala Assembly of the WCC in 1968, twelve of the 120 members of the Commission have been Catholic theologians, appointed by Faith and Order in collaboration with the PCPCU. They serve as full voting participants. The Commission meets every three or four years and aims, according to its by-laws, "to proclaim the oneness of the Church of Jesus Christ and to call the churches to the goal of visible unity in one faith and one Eucharistic fellowship, expressed in worship and in common life in Christ, in order that the world may believe."[20] A Standing Commission of thirty members, of whom three are Catholic, meets annually.[21] From time to time, Faith and Order calls a world conference. I was privileged to attend the Santiago de Compostela conference in 1993. The value and importance of a world conference are that it reaches out to involve more people in Faith and Order issues than those who would normally work with the Commission. In this way, it can enable Faith and Order efforts to achieve visible unity to have a greater impact on the various churches and ecclesial communities. The Commission on Faith and Order is also responsible, together with the PCPCU, for the preparation and distribution of material for use each year during the Week of Prayer for Christian Unity by Christian communities throughout the world.

One Shadow over a Promising Picture

My first experience with the Orthodox-Catholic theological dialogue was not a happy one. The Joint International Commission for the Theological Dialogue between the Catholic Church and the Orthodox Church had, during its eleven years of existence, approved three documents. The Munich meeting in 1990, which I co-chaired for the first time, was unable to proceed with discussion of a follow-up fourth document on the "Ecclesiological and Canonical Consequences of the Sacramental Nature of the Church" prepared for this meeting. Instead, we were left with no option by the Orthodox delegation but to discuss the question of so-called 'Uniatism,' that is the existence within the traditional borders of the Orthodox Churches, of churches having the same rite and customs, but in union with the bishop of Rome and not with the local patriarch. After the end of the communist regimes in some countries of Eastern Europe, the Greek Catholic Churches had regained their legal status and were seeking the return of property that had been confiscated by the communists and was in the hands of the Orthodox.

A meeting of the Joint International Commission for the Theological Dialogue between the Catholic Church and the Orthodox Church was held at Balamand, Lebanon, in 1993. Again it was not an easy meeting, and not all of the Orthodox Churches were in fact represented. Nevertheless, the meeting approved an agreed statement,[22] which sought to bring back a climate of peace in the troubled areas of Central and Eastern Europe. Uniatism was, therefore, the topic discussed and certain principles were agreed, including one that stated: "Uniatism is not the present method in the search for full unity" (4). The meeting accepted "the inviolable freedom of persons and their obligation to follow the requirements of their conscience" (15) and "the right of the Oriental Catholic Churches to exist and act in answer to the spiritual needs of their faithful" (3). Unfortunately, the document encountered opposition, especially among the Churches that had not been represented at Balamand, and the Commission remained suspended until a meeting at Baltimore in 2000, which, however, failed to get the dialogue back on track. It was obvious to me already at Balamand that we had gone as far as we could go with this question, which is after all essentially linked to the primacy of the bishop of Rome. This primacy would, therefore, have to be taken up by the Commission before a question so intimately linked to it could be fruitfully discussed.

After Baltimore, the Commission remained suspended. In the meantime, I had retired and the Orthodox co-chairman, Archbishop Stylianos of the Greek Orthodox Church in Australia, had resigned from the Commission. Cardinal Walter Kasper took over as head of the Catholic delegation, and the well-known Orthodox theologian Metropolitan Prof. Dr. John of Pergamon became head of the Orthodox delegation. Persistent and patient work by my successor, Cardinal Kasper, involving the Orthodox Churches individually, and a more positive approach by Metropolitan John of Pergamon resulted finally in the decision to have the Joint International Commission meet again in 2006 in Belgrade. This was followed by a meeting in Ravenna in 2007. The document that had been prepared for Munich in 1990 was finally discussed and agreement reached on a revised version. This document was made public on November 15, 2007, with the title *Ecclesiological and Canonical Consequences of the Sacramental Nature of the Church: Ecclesial Communion, Conciliarity and Authority.*[23] In this document, for the first time, the Orthodox Churches recognize the existence of the universal level of the Church, and at that level conciliarity, synodality, and authority. The consequence is that there is a primate at that level and according to the practice of the ancient Church, that primate is the bishop of Rome.

Moreover, the dialogue will continue and the theme chosen for the next meeting will be "The Role of the Bishop of Rome in the Communion of the Church in the First Millennium." This is, of course, wonderful news and offers new hope for the future. It was exactly what I unsuccessfully sought to achieve in the years following Balamand. There will be no easy return to full communion between the Orthodox and Catholic Churches, but there is reason now for new hope.

At the same time, relations with the singular Orthodox Churches continue to improve. This is true in particular with regard to the Patriarchate of Moscow and the Church of Greece.

The relations with Russia went from being very cordial in the 1980s to rather icy after the return to legal life of the Ukrainian Greek Catholic Church in 1989-1990, followed by the elevation of the Roman Catholic vicariates apostolic in Russia to dioceses and the setting up of a Bishops' Conference there. Pope John Paul II was not able to fulfil his ardent desire of making a visit to Russia to meet with Patriarch Alexis. The Holy Father had hoped to hand over personally the ancient Icon of Kazan that had been stolen from Russia during the Communist regime and had finished up at Fatima. The owners very generously placed this historic icon at the disposal of the Holy Father, to be returned by him to Russia.

In August 2004, only a few months before he died, Pope John Paul II entrusted the icon to Cardinal Kasper and a high-level Catholic delegation to be returned to Russia. It was taken solemnly from a special ceremony in St. Peter's Basilica to Moscow and received there with great joy by Patriarch Alexis. This has certainly helped the ice to melt! A further positive development has been the recognition on the part of the Russian Orthodox Church of the urgent need for Catholics and Orthodox to be able to speak together in the defence of Christian values in Europe and throughout a world that tends more and more to marginalize such voices. At a meeting in Naples in November 2007, Metropolitan Kirill of Smolensk, the Head of the Russian Orthodox Department for Ecumenical Church Relations, even spoke of the possibility of "an alliance between the two Churches," both of which, he said, "understand more clearly today than they have ever done before the importance of their joint testimony to the secular world about Christian values, which this world is trying to marginalize."[24]

The relations with the Church of Greece were never really cordial, as the memories of the past, especially of the Crusades, seemed to remain fresh in the minds of the Greek community. This has gradually changed since Pope John Paul II's visit to Athens in May 2001, as was clear from subsequent exchanges of visit between Rome and Athens, and the presence of the Archbishop of Athens at the funeral of Pope John Paul II. The road ahead may still prove difficult, but the on-going efforts of the PCPCU to foster greater spiritual ecumenism and fraternal relations with the individual Orthodox Churches give renewed hope for the future.

Looking to the Future

As we look forwards to the future of the ecumenical movement, we can be sure that the Lord Jesus will support our efforts with the guidance of the Holy Spirit. It is his prayer that we may be one – *Ut Unum Sint!* But, will those responsible for our relations be ready "to let down the nets" and make what Pope John Paul II called the "sacrifice of unity"?[25] It is there that I believe lies the main challenge for the future. I have no doubt that most if not all Christian Churches, including the Catholic Church, want this unity and are committed to the cause. I am not sure from our experience so far, however, that all are ready for this sacrifice of unity. Only the future will answer that doubt. For while God's grace is always available to us, experience shows that we are not always ready to make the sacrifice that may be required. God will not force us into unity. Through our own fault, we have lost the unity that Christ's Church enjoyed. God's grace will not be lacking to those who seek to restore the lost unity, but they will have to "let down the nets."

I have before me as I write a photograph that I consider an icon of hope. It was taken at the Basilica of St. Paul's Outside the Walls in Rome on January 16, 2000, the first day of the Week of Prayer for Christian Unity in the Holy Year. It shows Pope John Paul II, with the representative of the Ecumenical Patriarch, Metropolitan Athanasios of Heliopolis and Theira, and the Anglican Archbishop of Canterbury, George Carey, on either side, opening together the Holy Door of St. Paul's Basilica, so as to lead their communities into the new millennium, together with representatives of ten other Eastern Orthodox Churches, five Oriental Orthodox Churches, the Old Catholic Church-Union of Utrecht, the Lutheran World Federation, the World Methodist Council, the Disciples of Christ, the Pentecostal churches and the World Council of Churches. Only a few years earlier, such an event could not have taken place. Moreover, to illustrate well that this was no illusion, just five years later, representatives of all these Churches and others were present in St. Peter's Square for the funeral of Pope John Paul II on April 8, 2005. The continued presence of these ecumenical representatives at major events in the life of the Catholic Church is an ongoing testimony to Monsignor Radano's commitment and fidelity during his many years at the Pontifical Council for Promoting Christian Unity. And, I am happy to acknowledge, as well, the special service he provided to the whole ecumenical movement through his faithful documentation of events and dialogues as editor of the PCPCU *Information Service.*

---

1   John Paul II, *Ut Unum Sint* (Encyclical on commitment to ecumenism, May 25, 1995), no. 41.

2   *Ut Unum Sint,* no. 21; cf. Second Vatican Council, *Unitatis Redintegratio* (Decree on Ecumenism, November 21, 1964), no. 8.

3   *L'Osservatore Romano* (English edition), 40th year, no. 32-33 (August 8-15, 2007).

4   Pontifical Council for Promoting Christian Unity, *Directory for the Application of Principles and Norms on Ecumenism* (Vatican City: Libreria Editrice Vaticana, 1993).

5   ARCIC I, *Final Report* (London: SPCK; Cincinnati: Forward Movement Publications; Washington, DC: United States Catholic Conference, 1982), in GA I, pp. 62-118.

6   *Ut Unum Sint,* no. 62.

7   *Ut Unum Sint,* no. 63.

8   ARCIC II, *The Church as Communion* (London: Church House Publishing and Catholic Truth Society, 1991); *Origins* 20 (April 11, 1991): pp. 719-27, in GA II, pp. 328-43.

9   ARCIC II, *Life in Christ: Morals, Communion and the Church* (London: Church House Publishing and Catholic Truth Society, 1994); *One in Christ* 30, no. 4 (1994): 355-87, in GA II, pp. 344-70.

10 ARCIC II, *The Gift of Authority* (Toronto: Anglican Book Centre; London: Catholic Truth Society; New York: Church Publishing, 1999); *Origins* 29, no. 17 (May 27, 1999); *One in Christ* 35, no. 3 (1999): 243-66, in GA III, pp. 60-81.

11 ARCIC II, *Mary: Grace and Hope in Christ* (London: Continuum; Harrisburg: Morehouse Publishing, 2005), in GA III, pp. 82-112.

12 IARCCUM, Communiqué (November 19-23, 2002), *Information Service* 111 (2002): 230.

13 IARCCUM, *Growing Together in Unity and Mission: Building on 40 Years of Anglican-Roman Catholic Dialogue* (London: SPCK, 2007); *Origins* 37, no. 19 (October 18, 2007): 289-307; *Information Service* 124 (2007): 44-66; https://iarccum.org/doc/?d=32.

14 Lutheran World Federation and Roman Catholic Church, *Joint Declaration on the Doctrine of Justification* (Grand Rapids: Eerdmans, 2000); *Information Service* 103 (2000): 3-35; *Origins* 28 no. 8 (July 1998): 120-127 and *Origins* 29 no. 6 (July 1999): 85-87; *One in Christ* 36, no. 1 (2000): 56-74, in GA II, pp. 566-82.

15 Walter Kasper and Ishmael Noko, "Letter on the Occasion of the Fifth Anniversary of the Ratification of the Common Declaration on the Doctrine of Justification" (February 6, 2004), http://vatican.va.

16 Editor's note: The final report of this phase of dialogue was published in 2006. Lutheran-Roman Catholic (International) Commission on Unity, *The Apostolicity of the Church: Study Document* (Minneapolis: Lutheran University Press, 2006); *Information Service* 128 (2008): 60-133; http://www.prounione.urbe.it.

17 *Information Service* 99 (1998): 192. Pope Benedict has continued the practice of greeting the WCC assembly with a letter on January 25, 2006; www.vatican.va/roman_curia/pontifical_councils/chrstuni/information_service/pdf/information_service_99_en.pdf.

18 Diane Kessler, ed., *Together on the Way: Official Report of the Eighth Assembly* (Geneva: WCC Publications, 1999), 3.2, no. 4.

19 Editor's note: At the WCC 10th General Assembly, the Central Committee was restructured to become a body of 150 members which meets every two years.

20 WCC, *By-Laws of the Commission on Faith and Order*, 3.1.

21 Editor's note: At the WCC 10th General Assembly, the Faith and Order Commission was restructured to become a single body of 40 members of whom 10% are Catholic.

22 Joint International Commission for the Theological Dialogue between the Catholic Church and the Orthodox Church, "Uniatism: Method of Union of the Past, and the Present Search for Full Communion," *Information Service* 83 (1993): 96-99; *Ecumenical Trends* 22 (December 1993): 173-77; *Sobornost* 13, no. 2 (1992): 49-54; *The Quest for Unity: Orthodox and Catholics in Dialogue*, ed. John Borelli and John H. Erickson (Crestwood, NY: St. Vladimir's Seminary Press, 1996): pp. 175-83, in GA II, pp. 680-85.

23 Joint International Commission for the Theological Dialogue between the Roman Catholic Church and the Orthodox Church, "Ecclesiological and Canonical Consequences of the Sacramental Nature of the Church: Ecclesial Communion, Conciliarity and Authority," *Greek Orthodox Theological Review* 52, no. 1-4 (2007): 215-32; *Europaica Bulletin* 130 (October 21, 2007); http://orthodoxeurope.org/page/14/130.aspx.

24 *Europaica Bulletin* 131 (November 24, 2007); http://orthodoxeurope.org/page/14/131.aspx.

25 *Ut Unum Sint*, no. 102.

✝ CHAPTER 2

Artisans of Reconciliation: Catechesis of Memory and Freedom[1]

by Jeffrey Gros, FSC

A s we approach the 500th anniversary of the beginning of the Reformation the churches, especially in Europe and North America, will need to work together most diligently to see that this commemoration lifts up agreements, provides a spirituality nurtured on the *Joint Declaration on the Doctrine of Justification*,[2] and offers resources for a historical narrative of the 2,000 years of Christianity that situates the 16th century in its appropriate and reconciling interpretative perspective. Some even speak of the Reformation as being "over."[3] Among the resources for this rereading and rewriting of history and charting a new future are the dialogues into which the Catholic Church has entered with Reformed and Evangelical partners. A new look at the hermeneutics of history and a new appropriation of religious freedom by the Catholic Church at the Second Vatican Council make for a new, creative, and challenging agenda for Catholic catechesis.

The Pontifical Council for Promoting Christian Unity (PCPCU) is among the significant contributions of the Holy See to the process of evangelization for the last fifty years and into the foreseeable future. It calls Catholics to conversion in order to become the pilgrim people of God drawn by the unity for which Christ prayed. Such a conversion entails moving to a Christ-centered spirituality from an ecclesiocentric piety; to a communion-centered understanding of the Church from an institution-oriented ecclesiology; and to a catholicity in faith, space, and time, from an ethnocentric – and even occasionally politically established – Catholicism. It calls all Christians to be renewed by the faith of the Church through the ages, by serious attention to the Great

Tradition and its primary embodiment in Scripture, and by the grace of contact with one another in dialogue.

The honouree of these essays, Monsignor John Radano, has been a gracious servant of this instrument of the Gospel for a quarter of a century during one of its most fruitful periods of ministry and service to the unity of Christians. However, neither the Pontifical Council nor Radano are the subject of this essay. Its primary focus will be the educational mandate of the Church, illustrated by two of the dialogues which Radano has served most generously: the Reformed-Catholic contribution to the catechesis of history; and the various Evangelical-Catholic dialogues with their focus on educating for freedom and about proselytism.[4] Radano has boldly called for an "ecumenical reflex" to replace our "reformation reflexes"; one might add the Catholic Counter-Reformation or "apologetic reflex." Reordering old habits and ingrained reflexes is a formidable educational task.

Educational Challenges of the Dialogues

Each of the dialogues – so expertly staffed by the Pontifical Council – have different methodologies, styles, levels of challenge, or claims to convergence or consensus. As an example, I will take two of the lesser-known Catholic dialogues, with Reformed churches and with Evangelicals; and two themes, history and freedom. Other dialogues have been more productive, claim higher levels of agreement, or exhibit more theological depth. However, these modest initiatives have a monumental potential for changing the religious landscape, moving the reconciling agenda forwards, and demonstrating how the careful and quiet work of dialogue presages a very different future for the pilgrim Church in its faithfulness to the Gospel call.

Reformed-Catholic Call for Rereading History

The over forty years of Reformed-Catholic dialogues internationally and in local contexts around the world have been particularly fruitful in witnessing to Christ's reconciling will for the churches. Radano himself has offered "a survey of Catholic contacts with Reformed churches and a prospectus of ecumenical possibilities."[5] The Reformed tradition is a complicated but welcome discussion partner.[6] In this section, I will note some contributions of the international dialogue and some examples from the United States context.

Unfortunately, the Reformed tradition is largely unknown by many Catholics. As George Tavard notes:

> By and large the works of John Calvin remain generally unread by Catholic theologians. The result is of course that questionable clichés are often adopted, notably regarding predestination, pessimism as to the human situation, extremism in addressing the consequences of original sin, harshness in judgment, a legalism that can destroy the freedom of the children of God, a reduction of spiritual life to asceticism, and suspicion of denial of mystical graces. In addition, the memory of colonial Puritanism has been detrimental to the reputation of Calvin and his disciples among Catholics in North America.[7]

For this reason, the direct dialogue between these two living traditions today is important to Catholic understanding and catechesis: to build trust, dispel this ignorance and caricature, and eventually lay the groundwork for deepening communion. Anyone who has the most superficial knowledge of the 16th century realizes that Calvin is one of the greatest systematic theologians of the era, regardless of how his individual arguments are evaluated.[8]

The International Reformed-Catholic Dialogue

The Reformed-Catholic dialogues are less well known than Catholic dialogues with the Lutherans, Anglicans, and Orthodox. Nevertheless, they provide an important component in the pilgrimage towards full communion. There have been three international dialogues sponsored by the World Alliance of Reformed Churches (WARC)[9] and the PCPCU[10]: on *The Presence of Christ in Church and World* (1968-1977),[11] *Towards a Common Understanding of the Church* (1984-1990),[12] and *The Church as Community of Common Witness to the Kingdom of God* (1998-2005).[13]

From a Catholic point of view, these dialogues help both laypeople and clergy to understand that the Reformed tradition has a sense of the biblical imperative for unity, even with its more inclusive ecclesiology and its emphasis on the invisible Church.[14] They should dispel the Catholic prejudice that the lack of bishops means the absence of the biblical *episcopé*, or any commitment to elements of Apostolic Succession even if not embodied in episcopal ordinations. And most pastorally important, it will help Catholics realize that a doctrine of the real presence of Christ in the Lord's Supper can be embodied in other formulations than those used in the polemics of the Reformation and the theories used to explicate the fourth Lateran Council (1215) and Trent. While these issues are by no means resolved in the dialogue, this set of texts provides a totally new context for interpreting one another and for teaching our respective people to appreciate the fundamental convictions we share.

The key issue in reconciling these churches is ecclesiology – what understanding, practice and witness of these churches are necessary before full communion is achieved. This dialogue has tackled core issues of the Christian faith, such as the Trinity and the Incarnation. The ecclesiological issues themselves are driven by this Christological confession of the churches. "Jesus Christ, in whose name our forbearers separated themselves from one another, is also the one who unites us in a community of forgiveness and kinship."[15] The second chapter of the 1990 report is even entitled *Our Common Confession of Faith*. While the drafters are clear on how this text differs from a confession or a magisterial text in the classical understanding, it is their reflection on the common elements of the Christian faith shared by the Catholic and Reformed churches that emboldens them to use such a formulation. Not only does this text claim agreement on the work of Christ, Justification, Grace and the Trinity, it also professes to have reconciled differences over the relationship of these to the Church:

> Together we confess the Church, for there is no justification in isolation. All justification takes place in the community of believers, or is ordered towards the gathering of such a community. Fundamental for us all is the presence of Christ in the Church, considered simultaneously as both a reality of grace and a concrete community in time and space.[16]

Because of the success of this dialogue, especially its section on Justification (nos. 77-88), and the collaboration of Reformed scholars in the German scholarship leading up to the *Joint Declaration on the*

Doctrine of Justification, Catholics have shared the disappointment of Reformed leaders who report a lack of interest in their churches in participating in the international process of affirming this agreement.[17] Diligent attention will need to be given to educating our people and their leadership to the positive results and ecclesial implications of such a development were it to become possible.[18]

An educationally important section of the 1990 report is on *Towards a Reconciliation of Memories.* It should be a guide to the reformulation of Catholic catechetical materials, and those of our ecumenical partners.

The process of reconciliation will be greatly enhanced with positive portraits of one another without the "selectivity and polemics" of the past, and with an affirmative view of the "present reality in our churches."[19] On the basis of this discussion, the dialogue leaves historical scholars and educators with a challenge:

> We need to set ourselves more diligently, however, to the task
> of reconciling these memories, by writing together the story
> of what happened in the sixteenth century, with attention
> not only to the clash of convictions over doctrine and church
> order, but with attention also as to how in the aftermath our
> two churches articulated their respective understandings into
> institutions, culture and the daily lives of believers. But, above
> all, for the ways in which our divisions have caused a scandal,
> and been an obstacle to the preaching of the Gospel, we need
> to ask forgiveness of Christ and of each other.[20]

I personally have found this text most helpful in providing a hermeneutical guide for teaching courses on the Reformation in Protestant, Catholic, and ecumenical contexts.[21] However, I have yet to find an adequate textbook to guide seminary-level students with this perspective in view. We need resources that make the conviction of this dialogue a concrete reality in the narrative we share with our ministry and people.

The late Pope John Paul II has picked up on this theme as integral to the reconciling and reforming moments in Catholic ecclesiological developments, as recognition of the shadow side of Catholic history, and taking account of the painful memories that continue to leave divisions among us.

> Christians cannot underestimate the burden of long-standing misgivings inherited from the past and of mutual misunderstandings and prejudices. Complacency, indifference and insufficient knowledge of one another often make this situation worse.[22]

His many gestures of apology and reconciliation, especially during the Jubilee Year in 2000, will be remembered by many especially in the Reformed and Orthodox worlds as hallmarks of his pontificate. Providing opportunities for Catholic formation to inculcate such a spirit of repentance, healing, and reconciliation is an important priority. Catholics, especially in their formative years, should have opportunities for rituals and gestures of repentance and reconciliation. Certainly, this spirit should infuse the preparation for and commemoration of the 2017 anniversary.

The Reformed-Catholic dialogue is not the only one to lift up this dimension of the Church's mission. In the light of the *Joint Declaration*, the Lutheran-Roman Catholic Commission on Unity proposes that differences between these churches "must be examined in common, with the aim of discovering convictions held in common and of clarifying whether differing theological explanations are open to reconciliation."[23]

Just to give two examples of revisions that are urgently necessary: first, both Protestant and Catholic history texts incorrectly identify the papal centralization of modern Catholicism with 16th-century developments, in particular, the Council of Trent. In fact, Paul III assiduously kept the ecclesiological question, other than reform of the exercise of episcopacy, off of the agenda. Had the Spanish students of Francisco de Vitoria (1483-1546) prevailed over the more ultramontane Jesuits and Italian bishops at Trent, Catholicism may have emerged as a moderate conciliarist Church. Forms of conciliarism, such as Gallicanism, were live options until the French Revolution and Vatican I. Even Bellarmine was of the opinion that conciliarism was not a heretical position, even though it was not his own.[24]

Likewise, the *Augsburg Confession*'s (1530) affirmation of the episcopacy as of divine right is also lost in both Catholic and Protestant texts.[25] The fact that the Reformers took one side of open questions, only to be resolved later by an already divided Catholicism, or that, while in full communion, Orthodoxy and Catholicism had quite different points of view on papal primacy or marriage, makes the common ecumenical rereading of history an imperative for both catechetical material and ecumenical research.[26]

A second historical revision is urgently needed. Protestant texts often treat prayers for the dead and purgatory as though they emerged in the Middle Ages on the eve of the Reformation, without rooting these practices in the theologies of the catacombs, Tertullian, or Augustine, from which they emerged.[27] Some even read as though Tetzel (1465-1519) invented indulgences! In fact, Protestant students are amazed when they are exposed to the origins and meaning of concepts like indulgences, transubstantiation, or infallibility, often noting that their Catholic classmates seem not to understand their own heritage. A common account of the history, an irenic reading of the positive content of different theological decisions, and an accessible rendering of the results of the dialogues, are essential to Catholic catechesis if the results of the dialogues are to become a "common heritage."

It is to be hoped that the theology and spiritual legacy of these traditions can be received as gifts and that we can "set ourselves more diligently ... to the task of reconciling these memories, by writing together the story of what happened in the sixteenth century, with attention not only to the clash of convictions over doctrine and church order, but with attention also to how in the aftermath our two churches articulated their respective understandings...."[28] These dialogues take up a specific set of ecclesiological issues, always in the context of the Church's mission and the world in which God works through the Church and beyond it. This context is particularly important for these two churches because they have both been very self-conscious in their heritage about the social mission of the Church and its visible, tangible relation to the world and to culture.

Both Catholic and Reformed churches have the experience of being the established church in confessional states. Therefore, as will be seen especially in the US dialogue, not only social and evangelical collaboration are important for this reconciliation, but also a common ethical and ecclesiological understanding. Indeed, many of the difficulties that inhibit collaboration are rooted in divergent ecclesiologies, unreconciled memories, and different ethical options.

Ordained ministry and the Eucharist have been particularly intractable issues between Reformed and Catholic traditions. However, with more specificity than in the World Council of Churches' *Baptism, Eucharist and Ministry* (1982), the dialogue is able to affirm: "We believe we have reached a common understanding of the meaning and purpose and basic doctrine of the Eucharist, which is in agreement with the Word of God and the universal tradition of the Church."[29] Making the link between reform of worship, theological agreement, and the consciousness of our people in developing their ecumenical identity is a vital educational challenge at this moment in the ecumenical journey.

The US Reformed-Catholic Dialogue

The US dialogue has been remarkably productive, though there was a long hiatus in the 1980s because of the energies going into the reunion of the dialogue's largest Reformed member, the Presbyterian Church, after 1983. Early statements on such issues as Scripture and Tradition,[30] ministry,[31] the roles of women,[32] stages towards unity,[33] the laity,[34] and pastoral approaches to marriage, baptism, and the Lord's Supper[35] provide important proposals for reconciliation. On the one hand, they have provided significant resources for later international and multilateral developments on these issues. On the other hand, some of the earliest dialogues moved so quickly towards agreement that they may appear näive about the openness of the Reformed and Catholic churches internationally, and even within the United States. It will be important for all future dialogues, not only in the US, to continue to draw upon this early and very promising work.

Ethical Themes

Especially important to the Catholic catechetical mission is the moral formation of our people. Ethics can be both a reconciling element of common witness and a tension-producing cause of polarisation, especially when churches come down on different sides of issues in public political debates. Two sets of US dialogues are truly pioneering in that they take up the significant ethical issues of our time: human rights, abortion, peace, and education. These discussions, with the possible exception of that on peace, have yet to bear the fruitfulness of which they are capable. This is due to the politicized character of religion in the US context and the fact that common reconciling statements do not assist those most energized by public advocacy. Catholic moral formation will need to provide not only the content of the Catholic tradition but also the results of these dialogues and strategies for both reconciliation and common witness.

The statement on abortion, for example, provides a case study of dialogue on a major church-dividing ethical issue by giving a common account of the ethical traditions underlying the positions. It also suggests some moral principles that might be helpful to the American religious community in finding a basis for a national common ground, in fidelity to common Christian values.[36] The dialogue proposes five concrete areas of common faith and four areas of continued discussion.

While the American impulse for advocacy and issue-oriented organisation runs counter to the irenic impulse of ecumenical agreements generally, the very nature of our unity in Christ makes common witness to reconciliation even more urgent. Catechetical ministry needs to give people an honest appraisal for the Christian bases on which fellow Christians differ in ethical decisions and witness in public life. Likewise, the cultural, economic and political role of the United States in the world urges ecumenical collaboration on the US churches.

In addition to the formal US dialogues, several Reformed churches have reassessed earlier evaluations of Catholic doctrine, especially on the Lord's Supper, in light of contemporary liturgical reforms, common ecumenical scholarship, and the pastoral urgency of interchurch families. Of particular theological significance is the process and conclusion of the Christian Reformed Church in North America and its understanding of the *Heidelberg Catechism* question and answer number 80, which presents the Catholic Mass in extremely unflattering terms. The CRC Synod of 2004 concluded that the Mass – when celebrated in accordance with official Roman Catholic teaching – neither denies the one sacrifice and suffering of Jesus Christ nor constitutes idolatry. In consequence, the Synod declared: "Q&A 80 can no longer be held in its current form as part of our confession."[37] This conclusion may be understood as an example of how a proper catechesis of history can lead to a new perception of the points of division among us.

Evangelical Dialogue on Freedom and Proselytism

One of the most dramatic developments at Vatican II was the Declaration on Religious Liberty.[38] It provides a basis of civil equality on which theological dialogue, mutual trust, and common witness can develop. It also opens up the possibility for dialogue for a host of churches not represented at the Council among the observers, or even open to dialogue during the 1960s. For many of these Evangelical, Holiness, Pentecostal and Peace Church Christians, old prejudices lingered and points of contact were few in the aftermath of the Council so that evaluations were individual, tentative, and varied.

While Catholics formally profess the freedom of all to share their convictions with one another, Catholics from cultures with a memory of Catholic hegemony often characterize those who share their faith as "proselytising." These dialogues have been very useful in specifying very clearly what is meant by proselytising in a pejorative sense, and what is appropriate evangelising in a free society, for which the Catholic Church advocates. Educating for this free society is a challenge, especially in southern Europe and Latin America. Catholics are often embarrassed when their leaders use the language of "sect" in a pejorative sense about other believers, without giving precise definitions of what is meant and who are being so characterized. Catholic ecumenists do not use language about the other, like "sect," except when the group in question uses that language of itself.[39]

Baptists

Baptist origins in the United States and England are intimately tied to the affirmation of religious freedom, long before it was a general American Protestant hallmark. Roger Williams (1603-1684) was exiled from Massachusetts Colony to Rhode Island for his advocacy of religious freedom and adult baptism. At the time of the newly emerging United States, the Virginia Baptists were strong advocates of separation of church and state as well as religious freedom in the new nation. Two hundred years later, the post-conciliar position of the Catholic Church on freedom was central to discussions initiated with American and Southern Baptists in the US and with the Baptist World Alliance internationally. The Vatican Council's affirmation of freedom in matters of religion does not reject those historic relations where churches were established in law, like Anglican England or Catholic Spain. The narrow, juridical understanding of the Declaration on Religious Liberty, however, did not come to the core of the issue as Baptists have traditionally confessed it. For Catholics and many other Christians, there is a tendency to see the freedom issue in terms of the relationship of the Church to secular society, and not as integral to Christology and Soteriology.

This commitment to freedom in matters of religion, however, emerged from a religious impulse very different from the European anticlerical laicist sense of "liberty" which caused persecution of the Church on the continent and in Latin America. For Baptists, it is the doctrine of grace, Baptism, and salvation which evoke the deepest commitments to human freedom. Baptists do not baptize infants since children cannot freely enter into the covenant of grace to which they are called by the Gospel. Therefore, in dialogue with Baptists, questions relating to sacramental initiation and Christian formation must be rooted in discussions of the role of human freedom in God's saving will.[40]

For Catholics, on the other hand, the question of proselytism and what is perceived as unfair evangelism has a priority in this dialogue. The dialogue with the Baptist World Alliance, in particular, spells out some of the characteristics of unworthy evangelism and, in a repentant tone for both Catholics and Baptists, renounces these violations of religious freedom in the past. An affirmation of religious liberty renounces every kind of physical violence, moral compulsion, psychological pressure; the use of situations of distress, weakness or lack of education to bring about conversion; of political, social and economic pressure as a means of obtaining conversion or hindering others, especially minorities; of casting unjust and uncharitable suspicion on other denominations; or comparing the strengths and ideals of one community with the weaknesses and practices of another community. The dialogue goes on to say that proselytism is often used inaccurately to characterize the free witnessing to the Gospel as our churches understand it, without violating the religious rights of others.[41]

Certainly the Baptist link between religious freedom and God's saving work in the human person, and between participation in the Ordinances and the freedom of the individual, will lead to a deepening of the understanding of religious freedom for Catholics. In predominantly Catholic-heritage cultures, like the Hispanophone, it will require a new understanding of Catholic identity and culture.[42] In cultures where the Church exists in a pluralist society, it will necessitate providing all Catholics with a robust and personal sense of their faith to share with others in their society through dialogue and evangelism.[43]

Evangelicals

Early Catholic contacts with Evangelicals, in the late 1960s, occurred through the bible societies in translation work together.[44] Difficulties in these early encounters enabled the Pontifical Council and national bishops' conferences to develop sensibilities and an understanding of where common ground needed to be found. As the Catholic Church moved into the 1970s and beyond, it became possible to initiate conversations with these churches, to begin the healing of memories, and to recognize the importance of speaking about religious freedom and proselytism as a prelude to common witness. The results of these dialogues are important contributions to Catholic catechesis, especially in countries where Catholics predominate.

In some places, such as Spain and Colombia, a first evaluation of the Council by the local bishops was that it would not influence their situation. Elsewhere, council fathers from other Catholic countries, such as Cardinals Rossi of Brazil and Silva of Chile, were clear on the catechetical revolution that would be necessary to hand on the Catholic faith in a context that now affirmed the liberty of all persons in matters of belief. Even these visionary leaders did not envision how necessary this catechesis of freedom and ecumenical commitment would become as Evangelical Protestantism began to mushroom in the 1970s to the present.

Within the Latin American Catholic Church, there is still no consensus on ecumenical priorities, the response to an inevitable religious pluralism, or the advocacy of the religious rights of all citizens, for example in matters of education or marriage. With popular religion as the primary bearer of Catholic identity for many in Latin America, including US Hispanic Catholics, differences over catechesis of the Council become an important challenge for Catholic ecumenical progress.

To this catechetical task, the variety of dialogues with these Evangelical churches is an irreplaceable contribution to Catholic ecumenical formation and education for pluralism and religious liberty. These relationships were not predicted in the Council, are very fragile, and are least known where they are most needed: in the Evangelical Protestant community and in Catholic contexts where Catholics are a majority and have a memory of hegemonic times where religious freedom was not at the centre of the Catholic agenda for social advocacy. In this section, we will survey some of these dialogue results as an example of the fruitful contribution these dialogues on freedom have made to mutual understanding, convergence and opening up new issues for Catholic exploration.

Among the dialogues sponsored by the Pontifical Council for Promoting Christian Unity, conversation with a group of Conservative Evangelical Christians produced *Evangelical-Roman Catholic Dialogue on Mission* in 1983.[45] It included some from churches with whom the Catholic Church has regular dialogue and others from churches or movements which are not even open to the ecumenical movement. Therefore, at that stage, the text had a very unofficial and ad hoc character.

However, since this body of Christians has an important international presence, especially in mission and evangelism, these talks were a significant early part of a long process. It is in these groups, for example, that much of the historic anti-Catholicism has still to be overcome. Likewise, it is here that the most aggressive evangelism, sometimes proselytism, is likely to take place relative to Catholics.

The text that was produced has no standing with any of the participants or with the Catholic Church, and its diffusion is purely individual though it has become an important resource, particularly in dealing with areas of tension. Indeed, the World Evangelical Fellowship (now Alliance) found it necessary to develop a relatively negative statement on Catholicism in reaction to what was perceived to be irenic compromises towards Catholics.[46] This statement provided the impulse for more formal dialogue, this time sponsored by the World Evangelical Alliance and the PCPCU. Both the earlier informal dialogue and the later formal dialogue touched on issues related to religious freedom.

Among the many topics taken up in the first dialogue, two lay the foundation for important common developments on religious liberty: the discussions of Gospel and culture, and of unworthy witness. Both Catholics and Evangelicals express past insensitivities to the freedom and autonomy of cultures into which the Gospel was introduced and different approaches they have had to one another. The 2002 text takes up the question of evangelization in the context of different understandings of the church and agreements on biblical *koinonia*. It relies heavily on texts from each tradition and takes the line on unworthy witness that we have reviewed in the section on the Baptist dialogue above.[47]

Catholics can be grateful for the patience and persistence of members of the Pontifical Council in stewarding this somewhat fragile but pioneering dialogue, and can only pray that its work may be deepened in the future. Educators are challenged to provide models for educating for firm Catholic conviction, willingness to witness openly to the content of their faith, and openness to ecumenical engagement; resisting proselytism on the one hand, and not falling prey to polemical presentations of the Catholic faith on the other.

Pentecostals

For over thirty years there has been an important dialogue between Pentecostals and the Catholic Church. The 1997 text *Evangelization, Proselytism and Common Witness* takes up this theme also in the context of common witness and outlines again some of the characteristics of un-Christian behaviour that both communities hope will be avoided.[48] This text is particularly important for the US Hispanic community and Latin America where the Pentecostal and Catholic communities are the largest and often experience tensions.[49] It was heartening to see the Council of Latin American Bishops' Conferences (CELAM) take up this dialogue as a priority.[50] Christians can only hope that this Latin American engagement with Pentecostals will be fruitful in that context and for global Catholicism.

Anabaptists

It has taken many years for a formal dialogue to develop with Mennonites, though the multilateral discussions in Faith and Order have brought Catholics and Peace Churches together over many years.[51] The Anabaptist churches, Mennonite and Brethren, confess religious freedom, separation of church and state, and the relationship of personal freedom to sacramental life as central to their understanding of the Apostolic Faith proclaimed in the Gospel.

The ecclesiological and confessional issues involved here are very complex. With many churches, Catholic among them, a case must be made that Christian pacifism is a confessional, church-dividing issue of the same stature as justification, the sacraments, ministry, and the order of the Church. However, a rather fundamental test of the reception of the vision of ecumenism and the centrality of religious freedom to Catholic identity has been the ability to carry on this dialogue, eventually, with the same vigour and integrity as those with the other Reformation churches.

The 2003 text *Called Together to be Peacemakers* is a significant marker in the reception of Catholic commitments to ecumenical engagement with religious freedom for three reasons. It begins with a healing of memories, confessing the Catholic Church's failures in the past. Secondly, it affirms together the passing of the Constantinian era, which was the position of the 16th century Mennonite Reformation. Finally, it begins to explore the Gospel imperative for peacemaking with a community that confesses the biblical imperative for the Christian to remain free of state-sponsored violence of any sort.[52] Any commemoration of the Reformation will need to take account of these changes in society, foreshadowed and prepared for by the Anabaptist pioneers, and the common future which entails all of us learning to live as believers' churches in a free society, witnessing together to peace and justice, solidarity and the Reign of God.

65

While not claiming agreement on the separation of religion from society or the Christian from violence, this text does begin a process of dialogue with the community that pioneered religious freedom in the West, even to the point of martyrdom. It is an important catechetical resource both for looking again at our painful history together, and also for looking forward to a common witness in a society where Catholicism has an important peace witness, but no longer the claim to hegemony once exercised in the West.

Conclusion

For Catholics, rewriting history together with our ecumenical colleagues and handing on our faith so that Catholics are prepared for their ecumenical vocation remain inescapable dimensions of the catechetical task. These two dialogues – Reformed-Catholic and Evangelical-Catholic – are a call for renewal, indeed reform, in each of our churches. They provide educators with both a rich array of resources and a challenge to make their results a "common heritage." Much change has occurred in the last forty years. Many have been converted to Christ's call for the unity of the Church. Many remain to respond to Christ's call.

These are the good works of the Christian leader, growing from the grace of unity with which we have been gifted in Christ. Monsignor John Radano's inescapable contribution is a testimony to both the grace of unity and the flowering of good works that flow therefrom. What is said of the ecumenical saints and pioneers is well applied to his generous ministry: In every age of history, the principal artisans of reconciliation and unity were persons of prayer and contemplation, inspiring divided Christians to recommit themselves to walk the path of unity.[53]

---

1   Editor's note: This essay was submitted by Bro. Jeffrey before his untimely death in August 2013. It collects notes and ideas from various sources, some of which he did not have an opportunity to put into print in other forms. Although he has not approved the final form of this essay, we include it in the conviction that it makes an important contribution to ecumenical reflection.

2   Lutheran World Federation and Roman Catholic Church. *Joint Declaration on the Doctrine of Justification* (Grand Rapids: Eerdmans, 2000); *Information Service* 103 (2000): 3-35; *Origins* 28 no. 8 (July 1998): 120-127 and *Origins* 29 no. 6 (July 1999): 85-87; *One in Christ* 36, no. 1 (2000): 56-74, in GA II, pp. 566-82.

3   William Rusch, "How May the Reformation Best be Continued?" *One in Christ* 30, no. 4 (1994): 301-9. Geoffrey Wainwright, *Is the Reformation Over?* Pere Marquette Theology Lecture (Milwaukee: Marquette University Press, 2000). Mark Noll and Carolyn Nystrom, *Is The Reformation Over? An Evangelical Assessment of Contemporary Roman Catholicism* (Grand Rapids: Baker Academic, 2005).

4   For his own reading of the present situation, see John Radano, "The Future of Our Journey: Issues Facing Ecumenism," Oberlin Conference on Faith and Order, July 18-23, 2007.

5   John Radano, *Catholic and Reformed*, Occasional Paper, no. 8 (Louisville: Office of Theology and Worship, Presbyterian Church in the USA, 1996); http://www.pcusa.org.

6   Martien Brinkman, "Unity: A Contribution from the Reformed Tradition," in Michael W. Goheen & Margaret O'Gara, eds., *That the World May Believe: Essays on Mission and Unity in Honour of George Vandervelde* (Lanham: University of America Press, 2006), p. 114.

7   George Tavard, "A Reflection on the Joint Declaration on Justification and the Reformed Tradition," in Goheen & O'Gara, *That the World May Believe*, p. 187.

8   Two recent contributions to this conversation: George Hunsinger, *The Eucharist and Ecumenism* (Cambridge: Cambridge University Press, 2008). Joseph Small, "The Professor, the Prefect, and the Pope: Joseph Ratzinger – A Reformed Appreciation," in William G. Rusch, ed, *The Pontificate of Benedict XVI: Its Premises and Promises* (Grand Rapids: Eerdmans, 2009), pp. 144-67.

9   WARC merged with the Reformed Ecumenical Council in 2010 to form the World Communion of Reformed Churches (WCRC).

10 An additional dialogue was held between WARC, the PCPCU and the Lutheran World Federation on *The Theology and Problem of Mixed Marriage* in 1976, in GA I, pp. 277-306.

11 Geneva: World Alliance of Reformed Churches; Rome: Secretariat for Promoting Christian Unity, 1977, in GA I, pp. 433-63; http://www.prounione.urbe.it.

12 *Towards a Common Understanding of the Church: Reformed/Roman Catholic International Dialogue: Second Phase, 1984-1990* (Geneva: WARC, 1991), in DC, pp. 179-229; *Information Service* 74 (1990): 91-118; http://www.prounione.urbe.it.

13 *Information Service* 125 (2007): 110-56; http://www.prounione.urbe.it.

14 For a discussion of Reformed exclusiveness and inclusiveness, see Richard Mouw, "True Church and True Christians: Some Reflections on Calvinist Discernment," in Goheen & O'Gara, *That the World May Believe*, pp. 103-112. See also *Mission and Unity*, Section II Discussion Paper for 22nd General Council of World Alliance of Reformed Churches, Seoul, Korea, August 15-27, 1989 (Geneva: WARC, 1989), esp. pp. 45-50.

15 *Towards a Common Understanding of the Church*, no. 65, in DC, p. 198; cf. *The Presence of Christ in Church and World*, no. 32, in GA I, p. 442.

16 *Towards a Common Understanding of the Church*, no. 80, in DC, p. 203.

17 Pontifical Council for Promoting Christian Unity and Lutheran World Federation, *Unity in Faith: The Joint Declaration on the Doctrine of Justification in a Wider Ecumenical Context*. Presentations and relevant documents from a Consultation held in Columbus, Ohio, U.S.A., November 27-30, 2001 (Geneva: LWF Office for Ecumenical Affairs, 2002). See also Tavard, in Goheen & O'Gara, *That the World May Believe*, pp. 187-202.

18 Editor's note: further progress has indeed occurred since this chapter was written. The World Communion of Reformed Churches (WCRC) has drafted a proposed statement of association to the *Joint Declaration* and sent this to its member churches for consideration. The WCRC General Council will be convened in Leipzig, Germany, from June 27-July 7, 2017.

19 *Towards a Common Understanding of the Church*, nos. 12-63, in DC, pp. 181-98.

20 *Towards a Common Understanding of the Church*, no. 63, in DC, pp. 197-98.

21 Jeffrey Gros, "Building a Common Heritage: Teaching the Reformation in an Ecumenical Perspective," *Ecumenical Trends* 35, no. 5 (May 2006): 11-15. For a more detailed and theological treatment of this historical challenge, see Jeremy Morris, "Whose History? Historical Method and Ecclesiology in Ecumenical Context," *Ecclesiology* 2, no. 1 (2005): 90-106; Jeffrey Gros, "Toward a Reconciliation of Memory: Seeking a Truly Catholic Hermeneutics of History," *Journal of Latino/ Hispanic Theology* 7, no. 1 (August 1999): 56-75.

22 John Paul II, *Ut Unum Sint* (Encyclical on Commitment to Ecumenism, May 25, 1995), no. 2.

23 Lutheran-Roman Catholic Commission on Unity, *The Apostolicity of the Church: Study Document* (Minneapolis: Lutheran University Press for the Lutheran World Federation and the Pontifical Council for Promoting Christian Unity, 2006), no. 429. Also at http://www.prounione.urbe.it.

24 See Richard Costigan, *The Consensus of the Church and Papal Infallibility: A Study in the Background of Vatican I* (Washington: Catholic University of America Press, 2005), p. 24; and Avery Dulles, *Models of the Church* (Garden City: Doubleday, 1987), p. 36.

25 See Randall Lee and Jeffrey Gros, eds., *The Church as Koinonia of Salvation: Its Structures and Ministries* (Washington: US Conference of Catholic Bishops; Chicago: Augsburg-Fortress, 2005).

26 Walter Kasper, "Introduction to the Theme and Catholic Hermeneutics of Dogmas of the First Vatican Council," in Walter Kasper, ed., *The Petrine Ministry: Catholics and Orthodox in Dialogue* (New York: Newman Press, 2006), pp. 7-23.

27 See James Goff, *The Birth of Purgatory* (Chicago: The University of Chicago Press, 1984).

28 *Towards a Common Understanding of the Church*, no. 63, in DC, p. 197-98. http://www.prounione.urbe.it.

29 *The Presence of Christ in Church and World*, no. 91, in GA I, pp. 455-56.

30 *Reconsiderations: Roman Catholic/Presbyterian and Reformed Theological Conversations, 1966-67* (New York: World Horizons, 1967).

31 "The Ministry of the Church," *Journal of Ecumenical Studies* 5, no. 2 (Spring 1968): 462-65; Kilian McDonnell, "Ways of Validating Ministry," *Journal of Ecumenical Studies* 7, no. 2 (Spring 1970): 209-65; "Ministry in the Church," *Journal of Ecumenical Studies* 7, no. 3 (Summer 1970): 686-90.

32 "Women in the Church," in BU, pp. 375-83, *Journal of Ecumenical Studies* 7, no. 3 (Summer 1970): 686-90; "Women in Church and Society," *Journal of Ecumenical Studies* 7, no. 3 (Summer 1970): 691.

33 Ernest Unterkoefler and Andrew Harsanyi, eds., *The Unity We Seek* (New York: Paulist Press, 1977), in BU, pp. 384-417.

34 The Roman Catholic-Presbyterian/Reformed Consultation, *Laity in the Church and the World: Resources for Ecumenical Dialogue* (Washington: US Catholic Conference, 1998).

35 Patrick Cooney and John Bush, eds., *Interchurch Families: Resources for Ecumenical Hope* (Louisville: Westminster John Knox Press; Washington: US Conference of Catholic Bishops, 2002).

36 *Ethics and the Search for Christian Unity* (Washington: United States Catholic Conference, 1981), in BU, pp. 418-23; http://www.usccb.org/beliefs-and-teachings/ecumenical-and-interreligious/ecumenical/reformed/index.cfm.

37 *Heidelberg Catechism*, Reformed Confessions Translation (2011), Q&A 80, note 2, https://www.crcna.org. See Lyle Bierma, "Confessions and Ecumenicity: The Christian Reformed Church and Heidelberg Catechism 80," in Goheen & O'Gara, *That the World May Believe*, pp. 145-54; Jeffrey Gros, "Mission and Mystery: Gospel Testimony in Service to the World," in Goheen & O'Gara, *That the World May Believe*, pp. 155-72.

38   See Steven Bevans, SVD and Jeffrey Gros, FSC, *Evangelization and Religious Freedom: Ad Gentes, Dignitatis Humanae* (New York: Paulist Press, 2008).

39   Cecil M. Robeck, Jr., "Evangelization or Proselytism? A Pentecostal Perspective," *Journal of Latino/ Hispanic Theology* 4, no. 4 (1997): 42-64; José Antonio Rubio, "Bearing False Witness," in Peter Casarella and Raúl Gómez, eds., *El Cuerpo de Cristo: The Hispanic Presence in the U.S. Catholic Church* (New York: Crossroads, 1998), pp. 213-27. It is interesting to see the difference between the preliminary notes for the V General Conference of CELAM and the final document, which is much more analytically sophisticated, self-critical and in line with the ecumenical initiatives of the universal Church than either the preliminary notes or the opening address of Pope Benedict (cf. CELAM, *V General Conference Aparecida*, nos. 227-34; http://www.celam.org).

40   Jeffrey Gros, "*Dignitatis Humanae* and Ecumenism: A Foundation and a Promise," in John Ford, ed., *Religious Liberty: Paul VI and Dignitatis Humanae* (Brecia: Istituto Paolo VI, 1995), pp. 124-28.

41   Baptist-Roman Catholic International Conversations, "Summons to Witness to Christ in Today's World," in GA II, pp. 373-84; *Information Service* 72 (1990): 5-14; http://www.prounione.urbe.it.

42   See CELAM, *V General Conference Aparecida*, nos. 156, 225, 297, 479.

43   See Jeffrey Gros, "The Challenge of the Lasallian Catechist in the Late Twentieth-Century United States: One Lasallian Journey," *AXIS: Journal of Lasallian Higher Education* 4, no. 3 (2013), http://axis.smumn.edu; Daniel Mulhall and Jeffrey Gros, eds., *The Ecumenical Christian Dialogues and the Catechism of the Catholic Church* (New York: Paulist Press, 2006).

44   John Radano, "International Dialogue between Catholics and Evangelicals since the Second Vatican Council," in Goheen & O'Gara, *That the World May Believe*, pp. 173-75.

45   *Evangelical-Roman Catholic Dialogue on Mission, 1977-1984*, in GA II, pp. 399-437; http://www.prounione.urbe.it.

46   World Evangelical Fellowship, "A Contemporary Evangelical Perspective on Roman Catholicism", *Evangelical Review of Theology* 10, no. 4 (October 1986): 342-64 and 11, no. 1 (January 1987): 78-94.

47   International Consultation between the Catholic Church and the World Evangelical Alliance, 1993-2002, "Church, Evangelization, and the Bonds of Koinonia," in GA III, pp. 268-94; *Evangelical Review of Theology* 29, no. 2 (April 2005): 100-30; http://www.prounione.urbe.it.

48   International Dialogue between the Roman Catholic Church and Some Classical Pentecostal Churches and Leaders, 1990-1997, *Evangelization, Proselytism and Common Witness* (1997), http://www.prounione.urbe.it.

49   See Jeffrey Gros, "Reconciliation and Hope: The Contribution of the US Hispanic Community: Recovering a Reconciling Heritage," *Ecumenical Trends* 35, no. 10 (November 2006): 1-6 and "Building a Common Future," *Ecumenical Trends* 35, no. 11 (December 2006): 1-4, 15.

50   See Francisco Sampedro Nieto, *Ecumenismo y Tercer Milenio: Nuevo Manual de Formación Ecuménica* (Bogotá: Consejo Episcopal Latinoamericano, 2003), p. 442.

51   Marlin Miller and Barbara Nelson Gingrich, eds., *The Church's Peace Witness* (Grand Rapids: Eerdmans, 1994); John Rempel and Jeffrey Gros, eds., *The Fragmentation of the Church and its Unity in Peace Making* (Grand Rapids: Eerdmans, 2001).

52   International Dialogue between the Catholic Church and Mennonite World Conference, 1998-2003, *Called Together to be Peacemakers*, Final Report (2003), in GA III, pp. 206-67; http://www.prounione.urbe.it. See also Gros in Ford, *Religious Liberty*, pp. 141-42.

53   Walter Kasper, *A Handbook of Spiritual Ecumenism* (Hyde Park: New City Press, 2007), p. 11.

† CHAPTER 3

The Church: Towards a Common Vision – Ecumenical Breakthrough and Ecumenical Hope[1]

by **Mary Tanner**

I remember first meeting Monsignor John Radano in Rome in the mid-1980s when a small group of members of the Faith and Order Commission of the World Council of Churches (WCC) met to work on the Apostolic Faith Study. In the years that followed, we worked closely together in the Faith and Order Commission, where Jack assumed a special responsibility for keeping the Commission aware of the results of the bilateral dialogues and was a strong advocate for the holding of regular meetings of the Bilateral Forum. This was an important role and explains, in part, why the fears of earlier years that there would be competition between the multilateral and bilateral conversations never became a reality. Quite the reverse, in fact, for the multilateral documents, not least of all *Baptism, Eucharist and Ministry* (BEM), came to serve as an overarching context in which to set the results of the bilateral conversations, and the results of the bilateral conversations often inspired the multilateral conversations. There was a fruitful interchange. Because of the contribution of Jack Radano to the work of Faith and Order for more than 20 years and in gratitude for his support and friendship, it seems appropriate to offer in his honour a reflection on the latest ecclesiological statement from the Faith and Order Commission.

The journey to *The Church: Towards a Common Vision* (TCTCV) can be traced back to the missionary conference in Edinburgh in 1910 when Bishop Brent, an Episcopalian from the USA, called for a world conference to explore honestly the points of agreement and of disagreement which were the original cause of separations and which continued to keep churches apart when the mission of the church demanded unity. It took another seventeen years before the First World Conference on Faith and Order gathered in Lausanne, and set the future agenda of faith, sacraments, ministry and the Church – an agenda which became foundational for the World Council of Churches when it was established in 1948 and whose first function remains:

> for churches to call one another to the goal of visible unity in one faith and one eucharistic fellowship expressed in worship and in common life in Christ.[2]

The Constitution of Faith and Order is almost identical. Its first aim and function is:

> to proclaim the oneness of the Church of Jesus Christ and to call the churches to the goal of visible unity in one faith and in one eucharistic fellowship, expressed in worship and in common life in Christ in order that the world may believe.[3]

It is not too much to claim that Faith and Order has been, since 1948, the conscience of the Council and of the ecumenical movement, keeping churches focused on the goal of visible unity. Thus, TCTCV is directly connected to the mandate of both Faith and Order and the WCC itself.

By the 1970s, the Commission had agreed that three things were needed for visible unity: the common confession of the apostolic faith; common sacraments and a single ministry; and ways of deciding and teaching together.[4] Intensive work on sacraments and ministry was well underway when the Faith and Order Commission met in Accra, Ghana, in 1973. A miraculous moment was reached when the Commission, meeting in Lima, Peru, in 1982, agreed that *Baptism, Eucharist and Ministry* was "mature enough" to be sent to the churches.[5] Almost as influential as the text were the questions put to the churches about the text and the intensive response process that followed, which produced six volumes of responses from churches, and Faith and Order's response to the responses. One of the issues raised by some churches was the ecclesiological question "Is there an integrated ecclesiology lying behind BEM, bridging the divide between catholic and reformed understandings of the Church?"

Work on confessing the one faith followed, though it never received the attention the brilliant text deserved.[6] Studies on racism, the handicapped and the community of women and men in the Church were making the ecumenical community aware that unity also entails renewal in the human community of the Church with implications for the renewal of the language used to confess our faith, the ministry we exercise, and the way we take counsel and make decisions. Unity and renewal belong together. We have to be renewed into unity if the Church is to be a convincing sign to the world of its own possibility.

By the end of the 1980s, the idea for a Fifth World Conference on Faith and Order was gaining support, to answer the frequently asked questions "Where are we, and where are we going in the ecumenical movement? What has Faith and Order to say in the light of its completed work on BEM, Apostolic Faith and Church and World?" The theme of the Conference emerged as a preliminary answer to that question—"Towards *koinonia* in faith, life and witness." This theme would provide an opportunity for Faith and Order to harvest its work since the last World Conference and give a preliminary answer to the question of the goal of visible unity. The Conference in Santiago de Compostela in 1993 opened with a magisterial biblical exposition of *koinonia* by John Reumann; Wolfhart Pannenberg presented the work on apostolic faith; Elizabeth Templeton spoke on communion in sacramental life and service; and Metropolitan Khodr, from Lebanon, on communion in witness. Perhaps the most important affirmation of the Conference came in its final message:

> There is no turning back either from the goal of visible unity
> or from the single ecumenical movement that unites concern
> for the unity of the Church and concern for the engagement
> in struggles of the world.[7]

It was out of this harvesting of Faith and Order's work at Santiago that work on ecclesiology came to be the focus of the Commission's agenda, producing first, *The Nature and Purpose of the Church,* and then, *The Nature and Mission of the Church,* both with the modest subtitle "On the Way to a Common Statement." These two proto-texts were sent to churches for a response. The comments received helped to mature the text, though the responses were not as many as in the case of responses to the BEM proto-text sent from the Accra meeting of the Plenary Commission, *One Baptism, One Eucharist and a Mutually Recognized Ministry.*[8] Did that reveal a dwindling commitment to unity, visible unity, with the growing urgent interest in issues of justice and peace taking priority?

There is much at stake in TCTCV. If the text is an answer to the questions "Where are we?" and "Where are we going?" then it means that much rests on the response the churches make to the text. Reactions will show whether churches any longer believe in unity, visible unity, and whether there is convergence in the understanding of the nature and purpose of the Church.

Like BEM, TCTCV is a convergence document. It sums up what Faith and Order believes the churches can say together about the Church and its unity. It paints in words an emerging portrait of what life together might entail and, in italicized paragraphs, remarkably few and all extremely irenically phrased, invites churches to consider whether some of the remaining differences might just be legitimate differences, not destructive of unity. The questions put to the churches encourage further dialogue: e.g., *Could this be the time for a new approach?* (no. 24). It is a document inviting churches into an ongoing conversation of discovery. Another very helpful feature of the document is the inclusion of footnotes referring to convergences or agreements in other international bilateral documents. This gives a sense of a convergence movement in the one ecumenical movement.

It is a great achievement that such a diverse ecumenical forum has produced a convergence text on ecclesiology, helping churches to face the question of what sort of Church God is calling us to be together and what is the Church's role in God's plan for the whole creation. Looking back over more than forty years, involvement in the work of Faith and Order, it seems to me that TCTCV has made significant advances in each chapter.

The document does not start with abstract, ideal statements about the Church but, rather, with God's great design for the whole creation. God's purpose is to establish communion with God and with one another, a purpose thwarted by sin but opened up as restored possibility through the life, death and resurrection of Jesus Christ. Only in the context of God's grand design in creation can we understand the Church, called to continue the life-giving mission of Jesus in prophetic and compassionate ministry, by participating in God's work of healing in a broken world.

The clue to the Church's nature is signalled in the opening paragraph:

> Communion, whose source is the very life of the Holy Trinity, is both the gift by which the Church lives and, at the same time, the gift that God calls the Church to offer to a wounded and divided humanity in hope of reconciliation and healing (no. 1).

Throughout the text, *koinonia* is the key to understanding the nature, the unity, and the mission of the Church.

It is striking that Faith and Order's compelling vision is not of a self-absorbed Church turned in on itself, interested in its own organization and structure, but, rather, a Church living in the life of God, facing outwards in service to the needs of the world, proclaiming the good news, and working for justice and peace for all.

There is an emphasis throughout on mission. Mission, we are warned, is not an easy vocation. Not in the early years of the Church's life and not today in a world of rapidly changing circumstances (no. 7). The Church's mission faces new challenges: the claims of other faiths; the communications revolution; emerging churches which propose new ways of being church; a global secular culture which questions the possibility of faith at all; the radical decline in membership and a need to re-evangelize.

The chapter's conclusion is that Christian unity is vital for mission, adding that visible unity requires that Christians are able to recognize in one another what the creed calls the One, Holy, Catholic and Apostolic Church, and warns that this may call for a change in doctrine, or practice, or forms of ministry for each church. Here is a call to renewal. There is an implied warning of the need to be alert to how what follows may challenge each of us.

The first chapter is reassuring. The Church is set within God's grand design for the whole creation. We are not offered a picture of a cosy, inward-looking Church that God is calling us to be. It has been clear that there will always be new challenges: there always have been; there always will be.

The second chapter focuses on the Church, picking up the trailed theme of the Church as *koinonia*, affirming the central place that communion ecclesiology has come to have in our understanding of the life and unity of the Church and the call to visible communion. It is reassuring that Faith and Order has not given up on an ecclesiology of communion as it seemed to be doing in earlier versions of the text. Communion, a communion of love, describes the life of the Holy Trinity and is the source and ground of the Church's life. In the Church, through the Holy Spirit, believers are united with Jesus Christ and thereby share a living relation with the Father and with one another (no. 13). We are told that *koinonia* ecclesiology is not simply the union of existing churches in their current form. Does this rule out a federal model of unity? It is rather a state of being drawn together into the life and love of God and making that visible in our life together.

Drawing on the ancient Creed of Nicaea, the text explores the Church as One, Holy, Catholic and Apostolic and helps us to understand the nature and purpose of the Church by using two familiar ecumenical insights: the Church as both sign and servant. This means that the mission of the Church is both in active service and also in being, in its life, a reflection of God's own life, pointing towards the sort of life God desires for all people. The quality of the life of Christians together really matters. It is not only unity in the service of others – the important justice and peace agenda – but the way we are together in worship, in fellowship, in service of each other, and in the enjoyment of one another, secure in our common identity: the ecology of unity. The italicized paragraph within the text addresses the question of the apparent difference between those who refer to the Church as sacrament and those who do not use this language and asks tentatively:

> *Might this, therefore, be seen as a question where legitimate differences of formulation are compatible and mutually acceptable?* (no. 27).

So far the text has offered an ideal picture of what the Church is called to be in God's plan for the world. The text turns now to two aspects of the actual, visible life of the Church. As if to reassure us that visible unity is not imposed uniformity, it deals with diversity – legitimate diversity – as a gift from God (no. 28). This is important as so often the accusation is made that Faith and Order's work has no room for diversity, offering instead a structured, monolithic view of unity. TCTCV is clear that the Gospel has to be incarnated in different languages, symbols and imagery relevant to particular times and contexts. It has to be lived out authentically in each time and place. Diversity is a gift, yes, but that does not mean that anything goes: there are limits to diversity. The Church has struggled with this from the Council of Jerusalem on. When diversity goes beyond acceptable limits it can be destructive of God's gift of unity, as we know from history and from our experience today. We can sense a problem here. The italicized paragraph nails it. Churches have no common criteria or structures to discuss the question of what is legitimate diversity. Then we are gently invited to consider: "*what positive steps can be taken to make common discernment possible?*" (no. 30). This is one of the most important questions in TCTCV. The issue has been raised but we have to wait for the next chapter for a substantive reflection and advance.

This second chapter ends with a second important advance for Faith and Order – a reflection on the local church and its relation with all the local churches. Each local church contains within itself the fullness of what it is to be the Church. "It is wholly Church but not the whole Church." The communion of local churches is *not* an optional extra. The local church cannot be isolationist. Communion ecclesiology entails belonging to the whole Church both across space and through time. Again Faith and Order poses the question as an invitation:

> *we invite the churches to seek more precise mutual understanding and agreement in this area: what is the appropriate relation between the various levels of life of a fully united Church and what specific ministries of leadership are needed to serve and foster those relations?* (no. 32).

Such reasonable and important questions.

The chapter has seen an advance in the handling of diversity in unity and the relation of the local churches across the world and through time. The portrait of visible unity is being filled out in significant ways.

The third chapter turns to what it calls "the ecclesial elements" required for full communion or full visible unity. In a nutshell:

"The ecclesial elements required for full communion within a visibly united church – the goal of the ecumenical movement – are communion in the fullness of the apostolic faith; in sacramental life; in a truly one and mutually recognized ministry; in structures of conciliar relations and decision-making; and in common witness and service in the world." These attributes serve as a necessary framework for maintaining unity in legitimate diversity.[9]

This is an important statement from Faith and Order. The insistence with which these elements are stressed as "a necessary framework" for unity is perhaps more emphatic than has been claimed in recent Faith and Order work. The full realisation of God's gift of communion requires Christians to agree about these fundamental aspects of the life of the Church (no. 37). A bold assertion which challenges each tradition to ask whether this is really what it believes? The text goes on to take the ecclesial elements one by one.

First, a communion in faith. There is substantial agreement among Christians concerning the faith grounded in Scriptures and focused in the Nicene-Constantinopolitan Creed, a faith which has to be expressed in each generation in words and lived out in life.

Secondly, a sacramental communion. The responses to BEM revealed how much the churches share in common in their understanding of the two dominical sacraments, and pointed to where old divides might yet be overcome. The italicized commentaries in TCTCV invite churches to consider whether they can reach even closer convergence: for example, on who may receive baptism, or preside at liturgical celebrations, or between those who celebrate sacraments and those who do not. There is also an important discussion to be continued with the Society of Friends who have much to teach the ecumenical community about their understanding of the sacramentality of all life.

It is no surprise that the greatest number of differences remain in the area of ministry constituting considerable obstacles on the path to unity (no. 46). Issues need facing: the understanding of priesthood; the threefold ordering of the ministry and whether such a pattern is

God's will for the Church; episcopacy and apostolic succession. Are episcopacy and apostolic succession a barrier, a blockage, or simply an excuse? Without greater convergence in the area of ministry, progress in some relationships is hardly possible. But ministry is not just a matter of the ordained. A question for all is how lay and ordained can share and work together more effectively in the future.

Perhaps the most significant advance in this ecclesiology text comes in what is said about authority in the Church and about a ministry of oversight. It was clear that the subject was coming from the hint in the opening chapter which asked: "who says what is legitimate diversity?" It is the authority of the crucified Christ that is lodged in the Church; an authority different in character and exercise from worldly power and authority. The question is again posed as an invitation:

> *May not the seeking of ecumenical convergence on the way in which authority is recognized and exercised play a creative role in this missionary endeavour of the churches?* (no. 51).

This sets the scene for all that is said about the "service" of authority, making for a more sympathetic and more attractive approach to the role of a ministry of oversight. Oversight is understood as a ministry of coordination and leading in mission. The personal ministry of oversight is never to be exercised in isolation, but collegially with all the ordained, and communally with the whole people of God. The BEM triad, "personal, collegial, and communal," was one of the important, though underdeveloped, insights of that document and it is good that it is being developed in the present ecclesiology text. No church has got the exercise of authority right. We have much to learn from one another. In conversation around this text, we may learn new things about ecclesial structures of graced belonging. The personal and relational life of the people of God requires structure to nurture, sustain, and guide its life and mission.

The text goes on to make a very bold step for Faith and Order, one which some wanted at Lima in 1982 to see put into BEM. However, the Commission took the view then that it would be unwise to add anything on the subject without first undertaking significant background work. TCTCV says that for the sake of good order there is need for someone to summon and to preside over gatherings and goes on to ask how,

> *If, according to the will of Christ, current divisions are overcome, how might a ministry that fosters and promotes the unity of the Church at the universal level be understood and exercised?* (no. 57).

By including the matter of authority and a serving ministry of oversight, and at least raising the question of whether visible unity requires the service of a personal focus of unity at the universal level, Faith and Order has provided the churches with a more complete ecclesiological portrait of visible unity and its essential characteristics to consider in the years ahead. Perhaps churches can dare to enter that discussion as they watch Francis, Bishop of Rome, in his ministry of service, turned towards the poor, leading in a serving ministry of justice and peace, and gathering leaders together to reflect on some of today's difficult issues.

The final chapter returns to where TCTCV began, with God's plan for creation and the role of the Church in God's plan. The Church is faced with new issues today, including the fact of religious diversity and the varying responses of the churches to this and to moral issues. Then comes what is perhaps a surprise for some. Communion, *koinonia*, entails not only shared faith and the celebration of common worship but also shared moral values based on the Gospel. Faith and Order has never been so clear that moral values are "an essential characteristic" of visible unity. It is, of course, common moral values – and not agreed responses to moral issues – that are being stressed. There is a caution that due to our ecumenical closeness, what one denomination does now has consequences for all of us. We need to be accountable to one another, even now, listening to one another and engaging in mutual questioning. Our responses to new moral issues challenge not only our understanding of the unity to which God calls us but also the degree of unity we already share.

The document ends by returning to the beginning, to the relation between Church and world, reminding us that the Church has a responsibility to help those without power to be heard, to respond to human suffering, HIV and AIDS, violence and the threats of war, and to promote justice, peace and the care of the environment. It is in light of these huge challenges in today's world that unity, the visible unity of the Church, is an imperative and can never be an optional extra. Paragraph 68 sums it up.

> Our brokenness and division contradict Christ's will for the unity of his disciples and hinder the mission of the Church. This is why the restoration of unity between Christians, under the guidance of the Holy Spirit, is such an urgent task. Growth in communion unfolds within that wider fellowship of believers that extends back in the past and forward into the future to include the entire communion of saints. The final destiny of the Church is to be caught up in the *koinonia*/communion of the Father, the Son and the Holy Spirit, to be part of the new creation, praising and rejoicing in God forever (cf. Rev. 21:1-4; 22:1-5).

TCTCV is an important convergence text on ecclesiology. Like BEM, it comes with an invitation to churches to consider five questions. The first may seem to some disappointing when it asks, "to what extent this text reflects the ecclesiological understanding of your church?" BEM asked whether churches could recognize in the document BEM, "the faith of the church through the ages." This was a deliberate phrasing of the question to turn churches away from themselves and their own identity and consider the continuity of the Church through the centuries and only then to consider themselves in light of faithful continuity. Further questions ask whether this text offers a basis for growth in unity; what it suggests for renewal of life; whether it offers a firm basis for forming closer partnerships with those who can also recognize a positive account of the Church in the text; and what still remains for further discussion in future.

It is now over to the churches. But there also remains an important task for Faith and Order. The Commission will need to monitor and encourage responses, to publish them and respond to issues raised in the ongoing work of the Commission. There is much at stake in the responses of the churches, or indeed, the lack of responses, for this will indicate whether some churches remain committed to the goal of visible unity and, if they are, with what issues Faith and Order now needs to help them engage. Responses might also show whether priority is now focused on concerns of justice and peace. TCTCV is clear that it is not a matter of either/or; rather, concern for justice and peace and concern for unity belong inextricably together in an ecclesiology of communion. There is much at stake in TCTCV for Faith and Order, for the WCC and for all our churches. The world needs signs of reconciled life, and of life in unity with amazing diversity. May the response process flourish!

TCTCV both represents the ecumenical achievement won over many decades and provides ecumenical hope for the future. In all of this, Monsignor John Radano played an important and patient role, not least of all in keeping the insights of the multilateral conversation and the bilateral conversations together.

---

1   This chapter is based on a paper presented to the Joint Commission on Doctrine of the Church of Scotland and the Roman Catholic Church at their Edinburgh conference in December, 2015, "Sharing Future Church." The Conference papers are published in the journal *One in Christ* 49, no. 2 (2015): 171-81. I am grateful to the Editor for allowing me to use the substance of the article for this essay.

2   WCC Constitution; see WCC website: http://oikoumene.org.

3   By-laws of Faith and Order, *Called to be the One Church*, ed. John Gibaut, Faith and Order paper 212 (Geneva: WCC, 2012), p. 236.

4   *The New Delhi Report: The Third Assembly of the World Council of Churches, 1961* (London: SCM, 1962), pp. 117-19.

5   *Baptism, Eucharist and Ministry*, Faith and Order paper 111 (Geneva: WCC, 1982).

6   *Confessing the One Faith*, Faith and Order paper 153 (Geneva: WCC, 1991).

7   "Message to the Churches", no. 3, in *On the Way to Fuller Koinonia: Official Report of the Fifth World Conference on Faith and Order*, Faith and Order paper 166 (Geneva: WCC, 1994), p. 225, in GA II, p. 939.

8   *One Baptism, One Eucharist and a Mutually Recognized Ministry*, Faith and Order paper 73 (Geneva: WCC, 1975).

9   TCTCV, no. 37, quoting Joint Working Group between the Roman Catholic Church and the World Council of Churches, *The Church: Local and Universal* (Geneva: WCC, 1990), no. 25, in GA II, pp. 862-75.

✝ CHAPTER 4

Synodality: When Is It Necessary to Decide Together?

by James F. Puglisi, SA

One of the important issues that comes to the fore as the churches deepen their discussion around the theme of ecclesiology is the question of authority. What kind of authority and how shall it be exercised and by whom? All of these questions are extremely important and will become clearer as the churches focus on the meaning of what it means to be church.

One of the collateral issues that arises when speaking of authority is the question of ministry. Who may be a minister within the churches and how can a church make a change on an important issue such as this? At the time of the Reformation and subsequently, Anglican and Reformation churches have made various decisions regarding the issue of who may minister within their respective churches. On such an important issue, which has likewise touched the churches in their various ecumenical dialogues and relationships with one another, the matter of *how* one church may arrive at a decision in regards to the ministry is key.

Monsignor John Radano has collaborated in many of these dialogues and has demonstrated an extraordinary talent in helping to craft final statements of dialogues that at times have had to struggle with these difficult issues. In this essay, I wish to consider an example of the discussions that have gone on within the Church of England as it grapples with these questions. Moreover, the issue does not concern the Church of England and the Anglican Communion alone. What needs to be considered, especially by the Catholic Church, is the very synodical structure that Vatican II was unable to integrate fully with the theology of collegiality in its documents.

Introduction

The purpose of this presentation is not to argue for or against the ordination of women to the ordained ministry. The position of the Catholic Church on this point has been presented in several documents in recent times.[1] Rather, I would like to take up one of the agreed statements from the Anglican-Roman Catholic International Commission, *The Gift of Authority*, published in 1999.

Most will be aware of the great progress that came about in the Catholic Church because of the Second Vatican Council, especially its Dogmatic Constitution on the Church, *Lumen Gentium* (LG). One of the major points that are affirmed in that document is the theology of episcopal collegiality that is linked to a communion ecclesiology (*communio ecclesiarum*), and rooted in ordination. For the ecclesiology of Vatican II, the universal church is not an immediate reality but rather a communion of local churches. Because the local church is the presence and full manifestation of the church of Christ, the entire church is realised concretely in the communion between the churches and in that which manifests their mutual reception (*Christus Dominus*, CD 11; LG 23).

Vatican II resurrected institutions that allow for the renewal of local churches as subjects of law and initiative. Some of these are: episcopal conferences (CD 36-38); regional or national conferences (CD 38, 5); presbyteral councils (*Presbyterorum Ordinis* 7); pastoral councils (CD 27); council of laity (*Apostolicam Actuositatem* 26); diocesan synods and provincial councils (CD 36); and special synods of bishops (CD 5). Hence, the position of the Council may be seen in favour of a synodical praxis. In spite of this theoretical position, the Council never fully articulated how these institutions would be actualized. This lack in the actual application and reception of the Council in the church at large may be linked to the deep-rooted clericalism of many pastors. This, coupled with the weakness of the Western canonical disposition, tended to reduce the position of the Council to a minimalist level. The *Code of Canon Law* (can. 515, 536) does not render pastoral councils obligatory just as it makes the convocation of a diocesan synod rely solely on the wish of the bishop (can. 461). The synodical structures of the church are seen as more or less optional and mainly dependent on a superior authority. For example, if a regional council is convoked its acts may not be enacted until the Holy See has approved them (can. 439-46).[2] It is well known that shortly after the Council, Paul VI instituted the Synod of Bishops. However, in current Catholic practice, synods are not *deliberative* but rather consultative.[3]

These facts concerning the relationship of collegiality and synodality are important to establish at the beginning because they illustrate how important it is to obtain an ecclesiological balance in the decision-making structures of the church. What are the limits and boundaries of the participatory structures of the church? These processes are likewise important especially when the decisions that are made will have implications for relations with other churches.

One further observation may be made. The model for a synodical form of ecclesial existence is found in the New Testament in the first "council" of the church. When a serious problem arose in the Jerusalem church over the question of admitting uncircumcised Gentiles, it is interesting to note that the manner in which the early church dealt with this issue was to listen to all concerned. A delegation was then sent to hear the opinion and to see the results of the mission in Antioch. "The apostles and the elders with the consent of the whole church" (Acts 15:22) decided to send the message of the decision of all concerning the conditions of the Gentiles' admission to the church as they concluded that "it seemed good to the Holy Spirit and to us" (Acts 15:28). This decision was extremely difficult due to the seriousness of the issues at stake. Nevertheless, the resulting decision would impinge upon the "whole church" for the future of Christianity. Yves Congar observed that the general norm in ecclesiology is derived from this New Testament incident: "*Quod omnes tangit ab omnibus tractari et approbari debet*."[4]

Ordination and Communion

The Council makes a very important statement in *Lumen Gentium* 22: "One is constituted a member of the episcopal body in virtue of sacramental consecration and hierarchical communion with the head and members of the body." Vatican II restored the relationship between orders and jurisdiction, which since the Middle Ages had been separated into two spheres of power, that of orders and that of jurisdiction.[5] This explained why even after a bishop was ordained, he had to receive a second, juridical act from the head of the college, the pope, to be able to minister and have jurisdiction within his church. *Lumen Gentium* taught that through ordination the bishop receives all that is necessary to sanctify, teach, and govern (LG 26). The Council identifies the jurisdiction of the bishop as related directly to Christ: "Bishops, as vicars and ambassadors of Christ ... are not to be regarded as vicars of the Roman Pontiffs" (LG 27).

This was a tremendous step forward in the understanding of the relationship of bishops to the pope and to one another. This new understanding encouraged reflection on new structures to express the collegiality that had been rediscovered, but something was missing. There was an insufficient articulation between the person of the bishop and the communion among churches that the bishop presided over. In *Lumen Gentium* 22, ordination is seen as the foundation of communion. Yet, because of the large number of bishops who are *sine populo*, without a people (i.e., auxiliary, titular or retired), the document relates ordination to the universal church. The weakness observed here comes from an absence of correlation between the college of bishops and the communion of local (diocesan) churches. This is due to the fact that the bishop is being situated *vis-à-vis* his church and not *in* his church.

Why is this point so important? Principally, because it omits the primary focus of the relationship that must exist between the bishop and his church and the ministry of the communion that, because of this first relationship, he articulates between the churches. He is minister of the communion of churches and, therefore, its unity.

The awareness of communion in the early church was something that is articulated clearly by Paul. Especially in the letters to the church in Corinth, he underscores the fact that "we are one body" (1 Cor. 10:17). The rationale for this is found in the eucharist where all are called to "recognise the Body of the Lord" (1 Cor. 11:29). Since in the body all are gifted with the Spirit and all have the possibility to exhibit their gifts for the sake of all (cf. 1 Cor. 12:7) then there is the obligation for the one who presides to listen to all and to discern how the Spirit is working for the good of all.[6] Likewise in other passages, we can see that the early church had an awareness of having a responsibility to listen profoundly to each other since all had the anointing of the Spirit to recognise the truth (cf. 1 John 2:20-27).

Synodality – The Missing Piece of Vatican II?

While the Council articulated a theology of collegiality, what is not clearly expressed is the ministry of communion between the churches (which was the end purpose that Vatican II attributed to Roman primacy). This cannot be defined unilaterally starting from itself. Obviously, all the bishops taken as a body are co-responsible for the communion between local churches and the entire church. This means applying the general rule announced by *Ut Unum Sint* in number 95 when John Paul II says "together..." and in 96: "I cannot carry out by myself." This "together" is the grace of the ecumenical movement that John Paul II wished the church to be submitted to "irreversibly."

In point of fact, this is an understanding of synodality that was not articulated at Vatican II but has been developing since the Council. That which is called *synod* (in Greek) or *council* (in Latin), deals with the question of assemblies that have as their specific goal going beyond the context of the local Church and uniting several communities in the same place.[7] Several conditions existed for the holding of these institutions:

- there were a number of important organised groupings of Christians;

- the material possibility of meeting;

- there was a minimum of agreement on the essentials (the rule of faith);

- there was a desire to find a solution *together* to new questions that were beginning to be resolved by different means, indeed by opposite means;

- there was a certain desire for unity and cohesion among the different groupings of Christians, at the same time that some points of disagreement presented the conflict as dangerous for the future of the Christian faith; and

- above all there was a wish to gather together to recognise each other, namely, to see in the other the faith that gives identity.

For these synods to be held there needed to be extreme cases, internal to the ecclesial group, that were threatening its identity.

It seems clear that not in every case was there a need to celebrate together, or decide together, or to teach together. However, in certain cases, the extreme cases, it was necessary to celebrate, decide, and teach together for the sake of the whole of the communion of churches.

This way of "walking together" was present in the form of life that these communities embraced because it enabled them to hold together in communion. This communion was not the communion of individuals but rather the communion of churches. The Council's dogmatic constitution on the Church is "flawed" in this respect. It seems that rights were established for individuals (especially when we consider the fact that bishops had access to the college without representing a people except one that was fictitious – titular bishops or those in curial posts or in the diplomatic service of the Holy See) – and not for the relations between churches. This means that an effective relationship of communion was missing between these communities. It is true that the bishop forms the link between churches, however, he is not to be considered as an individual, but as a collective reality in so far as he represents the faith of his church.

Bishop as Servant of Unity within the Church

The Anglican Communion and the Catholic Church speak of the role of the bishop as serving the unity that Christ gives to his Church. This is illustrated by the questions put to the elect at the time of ordination:

In the Roman Pontifical:

> Are you resolved to build up the Church as the body of Christ and to remain united to it within the order of bishops under the authority of the successor of the apostle Peter?

> Are you resolved as a good shepherd to seek out the sheep who stray and to gather them into the fold of the Lord?

In the Alternative Service Book:

> Will you promote unity, peace, and love among all Christian people, and especially among those whom you serve?

In the revised Ordinal of the Church of England:

> Will you promote peace and reconciliation in the Church and in the world; and will you strive for the visible unity of Christ's Church?

A review of texts from the international Anglican-Roman Catholic dialogue (ARCIC) highlights the very specific function of the bishop at the service of unity: "According to our two traditions the bishops are (because of their ordination in the 'apostolic succession') the link with the so-called apostolic Church, and with all the Churches in *communion* with this apostolic Church. This is a function given in their ordination. They are called to be *together* the living *memory* (in the biblical sense of ZKR) of the twelve. For it is *together* that the Apostles were the authentic witnesses of the Risen Lord."[8]

Ordination as a sign and visible means of apostolic succession must be an *insertion* into the life of the community. When this happens, the ordained bishop *both gives and receives* apostolicity from the community into which he is inserted. Apostolic continuity cannot be created *ex nihilo* through episcopal ordination unless it is somehow already there. And it cannot be taken for granted unless it is somehow affirmed, sealed, and proclaimed through episcopal ordination. There is no apostolic succession that could be limited to the episcopal college as such or to some form of apostolic collegiality. Every bishop participates in the episcopal college *via his community*, not directly. Apostolic succession is a succession of apostolic communities via their heads.[9]

The theological evolution of apostolic continuity and succession in the Latin West during the Middle Ages gave rise to the view that apostolic succession passes from an *individual* apostle to an *individual* bishop and not from the *entire* apostolic college headed by Peter as vicar of Christ. This resulted in the loss of two fundamental ideas that were present from the first centuries: (a) that each bishop is the successor of *all* the apostles and (b) that each succession involves *the community* of the church headed by Christ. Another consequence of the loss of this Christological dimension of succession was the need to look for a *vicarius Christi* outside and independently of the apostolic college.[10]

No minister of the Lord, however, is alone but is always minister in communion because the very ministry of the ordained is to be minister of the *communion of the Holy Spirit.*[11] One is, in fact, a member of a college, the whole body of bishops who are in communion *together* because of its communion with the Twelve. Jean Tillard will note that:

> The mere 'recognition' of ministers is not sufficient. *Togeth-erness* is also needed. And because the bishop has to be the one who 'watches over' the quality of *communion* in his local church, it is thanks to this *togetherness* that we may know how the *same* understanding of the Word and the *same* means of grace are, *substantially,* in all the churches.[12]

He will conclude:

> Thus, the unity we are looking for is the rich eucharistic *koinonia* of Churches demonstrating by their harmonious diversity the richness of faith, unanimous in the application of the principles governing moral life, served by ministers that the grace of their ordination unites *together* in an episcopal body grafted to the group of the Apostles.[13]

In the process of ordination of a bishop, the role of the other bishops present during the ordination is that of giving to the vacant see its head and of receiving that bishop into the *communion* of those who *together* are responsible for the promotion of unity within the local church and between the local churches, namely the unity of the Body of Christ.

Synodality in "The Gift of Authority"

This is a short section (nos. 34-40) in the agreed statement of ARCIC II "The Gift of Authority" but I think it goes to the heart of the question that is at the base of the discussion of whether a church may decide alone certain dimensions of church life and discipline. The text is punctuated with the "Amen" of the communion of faith.

In these brief paragraphs, the statement affirms the activity of the Spirit in the local church and in the life of the churches together. It recognises the jurisdiction of the bishop not as a *personal power* of an individual but rather as an *ecclesial power* ("[jurisdiction] is not arbitrary power given to one person over the freedom of others. Within the working of the *sensus fidelium* there is a complementary relationship between the bishop and the rest of the community": no. 36). It is the Eucharist in the local church that is seen as the "fundamental expression" of the synodality of the people of God.

In number 37, the text articulates the principle for what I believe will need to be the question that guides ongoing ecumenical discussion about decisions that are taken that affect the whole of the church. These sentences I feel are at the heart of the matter:

> The mutual interdependence of all the churches is integral to the reality of the Church as God wills it to be. No local church that participates in the living Tradition can regard itself as self-sufficient... The ministry of bishop is crucial, for this ministry serves communion within and among local churches. Their communion with each other is expressed through the incorporation of each bishop into a college of bishops... The maintenance of communion requires that at every level there is a capacity to take decisions appropriate to that level. When those decisions raise serious questions for the wider communion of churches, synodality *must* find a wider expression.[14]

Conclusion

In closing, I offer the following questions dealing with the difficult subject of who may or may not be ordained to the episcopate: Does the decision to ordain women to the episcopate in the Church of England belong to this synod of bishops *alone* to decide? Is it a decision that "raises serious questions for the wider communion of churches" and if so, how then is it posed to the wider communion? Is this a situation when it is necessary that all decide and all teach *together*? Does one church have the authority to make this decision alone which might endanger the unity of its own communion and certainly will endanger the communion it has with the Catholic Church and possibly other churches? What is the value of our ecumenical agreements?

The experience of ecumenical dialogue for over four decades has taught us that we each have gifts to receive and gifts to give. We Catholics have much to learn from the Anglican experience of synodical government as we seek to engage more fully all of the church membership in decisions of faith and Christian living. Hopefully, we also have something to offer in exchange.

From this punctual context, it may be seen that one question opens into another and into another. Perhaps the greatest of these questions is the one of unity. I wish to conclude then with these words of Jean-Marie Tillard:

> What is the unity ARCIC has the mandate to prepare? It is a eucharistic *communion* of Churches demonstrating by their harmonious diversity the richness of faith, unanimous in the applications of the principles governing moral life, served by ministers that the grace of ordination unites *together* in an episcopal body, grafted to the group of the Apostles, and which is at the service of the authority that Christ exercises over his Body with the Spirit of Truth, for the Salvation of the World and the glory of the Father. In one Word, it is the communion of the Body of Christ, here and now on earth.[15]

1 The Catholic Church's teaching has recently been expressed in the following documents: Congregation for the Doctrine of the Faith, *Inter Insigniores* (October 15, 1976); John Paul II, *Mulieris Dignitatem* (Apostolic Letter, August 15, 1988); John Paul II, *Ordinatio Sacredotalis* (Apostolic Letter, May 22, 1994); *Responsum Ad Dubium* (Note of the Congregation for the Doctrine of the Faith, October 28, 1995); John Paul II, *Ad Tuendam Fidem* (Apostolic Letter *Motu Proprio*, May 28, 1998). There is not absolute agreement on the dogmatic value of these texts among Catholic theologians, historians, and canonists. To enter into this debate would take us far too long to expose here. See Hervé Legrand, "*Traditio perpetuo servata*? La non-ordination des femmes: tradition ou simple fait historique?" in *Rituels - Mélanges offerts au Père Gy* (Paris: Cerf, 1990), pp. 393-416; English trans. "*Traditio perpetuo servata*? The Non-ordination of Women: Tradition or Simply an Historical Fact?" *Worship* 69 (1991): 482-508; the two volumes edited by two Catholic scholars, Bernard Cooke and Gary Macy, eds., *A History of Women and Ordination* (Lanham, MD: The Scarecrow Press, 2002); Richard R. Gaillardetz, "Infallibility and the Ordination of Women," *Louvain Studies* 21 (1996): 3-24; Sara Butler, *The Catholic Priesthood and Women: A Guide to the Teaching of the Church* (Chicago: Hillenbrand Books, 2007).

2 Severino Dianich, "Sinodalità," in *Teologia*, eds.Giuseppe Barbaglio, Giampiero Bof, and Severino Dianich (Cinisello Balsamo: Edizioni San Paolo, 2002), p. 1525.

3 See *Code of Canon Law* (1983), canons 338, 343, 344.

4 Yves Congar, "Les conciles dans la vie de l'église," in *Sainte église. Études et approches ecclésiologiques*, Unam Sanctam 41 (Paris: Cerf, 1964), p. 308. Here Congar notes how this 13th-century principle borrowed from Roman law was enlarged by its Christian interpretation of that which concerns everyone must be discussed and approved by everyone.

5 Cf. Luciana Mortari, *Consacrazione episcopale e collegialità: la testimonianza della chiesa antica*, Testi e ricerche di scienze religiose 4 (Florence: Vallecchi, 1969), who has shown that for the ancient church an ordination without election and without an office is just as impossible as jurisdiction without order.

6   See the ecumenical implications of the First Letter by Hervé Legrand, "Communion eucharistique et communion ecclésiale. Une relecture de la première lettre aux Corinthiens," *Centro Pro Unione Bulletin* 67 (2005): 21-32.

7   See the explanation and evolution of the institution of synods in the exceptional work of Alexandre Faivre, *Ordonner la fraternité. Pouvoir d'innover et retour à l'order dans l'Église ancienne* (Paris: Cerf, 1992), pp. 342-59.

8   Jean-Marie Tillard, "Our Goal: Full and Visible Communion," *One in Christ* 39, no. 1 (2004): 42. This was the last ecumenical meeting he attended before passing on to the Lord.

9   Bernard-Dominique Dupuy, "La succession apostolique dans la discussion œcuménique," *Istina* 12, no. 3-4 (1967): 398.

10 For the full documentation of the patristic sources, see John Zizioulas, "La continuité apostolique de l'église et la succession apostolique au cours des cinq premiers siècles," *SOP-Service orthodoxe de presse - mensuel supplément* 217A (1997) : 1-14.

11 See my two volumes for a commentary on the ecclesiological understanding of ordination in the Church of England: James F. Puglisi, *The Process of Admission to Ordained Ministry. A Comparative Study*, vol. 2: *The First Lutheran, Reformed, Anglican and Wesleyan Rites* (Collegeville: Liturgical Press, 1998), pp. 111-46, and vol. 3: *Contemporary Rites and General Conclusions* (Collegeville: Liturgical Press, 2001), pp. 137-52.

12 Tillard, "Our Goal", p. 42.

13 Tillard, "Our Goal", p. 42.

14 ARCIC II, *The Gift of Authority*, no. 37, in GA III, p. 71, italics added.

15 Tillard, "Our Goal", p. 43.

✝ CHAPTER 5

The Wesley Brothers in Methodist-Catholic Dialogue

by Geoffrey Wainwright

I t may seem ironic to locate the Wesley brothers in the international dialogue between the World Methodist Council and the Roman Catholic Church when both John and Charles lived and died as priests of the Church of England, from which they – and most consistently Charles – sought to avoid the separation of Methodism. Yet their historical influence, in respective ways, extended beyond its eighteenth-century Anglican origins into what became a distinct denomination and eventually a "Christian world communion," and both of them, again in different manners, have more lately gained respect among Roman Catholics. My purpose in this chapter is neither to provide a biography of the always-busy brother John (1703-1791) nor a literary account of all the sacred poetry of the prolific brother Charles (1707-1788). Nor is it my purpose here to trace every stamp left by the pair on the Methodist ecclesial family, whether by their evangelistic activity or their written works, for John Wesley's "standard sermons" in particular are recognized to have doctrinal status in most Methodist churches and the phraseology of his brother's hymns is familiar in Methodist worship and devotion – two factors which certainly help to shape Methodist contributions to ecumenical relations and are noted by our conversation partners. The presence of the brothers among us, even where they are not named, is indeed in such general ways practically ubiquitous. In order to stay within reasonable spatial bounds, however, I will limit myself to drawing attention – and then not exhaustively – to the figures that the brothers and their works cut when they are explicitly invoked or cited in the particular bilateral dialogue between the World Methodist Council and the Roman Catholic

Church and some events directly connected with that international dialogue. As to that dialogue, it must not be thought that the present chapter represents an adequate account – whether chronological or thematic – of the Joint Commission's work over the past forty-odd years, for the bilateral dialogue has of course been fed also and equally by historical developments and doctrinal insights originating from the Catholic side. The reader may nevertheless be able to gain something of the dialogue's substance and flavour.

I. An Epistolary Address

The name of John Wesley was invoked by the Joint Commission at the very beginning of its first Report, that of "Denver 1971."[1] In its narrative recital of the start of the Dialogue, the Commission reported thus on its own first meeting in the year 1967:

> All present were conscious in general of the spectacular change in atmosphere between the two Churches in the past six or seven years, but this was underlined with some hard facts. John Wesley's "Letter to a Roman Catholic" of July 18, 1749, stood out, we were reminded, as an almost isolated overture in a general picture of aloofness and suspicion which could be illustrated, e.g. from a Methodist text book as late as 1953, while changes in Roman Catholic ecumenical attitudes and policy were even more recent (Denver, no. 3).

That *Letter to a Roman Catholic*, written by John Wesley from Dublin, was aimed at easing the reception of his own evangelistic work in the face of Catholic opposition in Ireland, a country that he eventually visited twenty-two times.[2] The opening *captatio benevolentiae* was formulated graciously and theologically:

> I think you deserve the tenderest regard I can show you, were it only because the same God has raised you and me from the dust of the earth, and has made us both capable of loving and enjoying him to eternity; were it only because the Son of God has bought you and me with his own blood. How much more, if you are a person fearing God (as without question many of you are) and studying to have a conscience void of offence towards God and towards man?

The two central blocks of the Letter are then devoted by Wesley to "the faith of a true Protestant" and "the practice of a true Protestant." As to the faith, Wesley expounds the Nicene-Constantinopolitan Creed, expanding particularly the Christological confession by language from Chalcedon ("I believe that he was made man, joining the human nature with the divine in one person"); by a mention of the traditional *munus triplex* ("that he was a prophet, revealing to us the whole will of God; that he was a priest, who gave himself a sacrifice for sin, and still makes intercession for transgressors; that he is a king, who has all power in heaven and in earth, and will reign till he has subdued all things to himself"; and by affirming Christ's "absolute, supreme, universal dominion over all things", being "more peculiarly our Lord, who believe in him, both by conquest, purchase, and voluntary obligation." Christ was "conceived by the singular operation of the Holy Ghost, and was born of the blessed Virgin Mary, who, as well after as before she brought him forth, continued a pure and unspotted virgin." As to the third article of the Creed: "I believe the infinite and eternal Spirit of God, equal with the Father and the Son, to be not only perfectly holy in himself, but the immediate cause of all holiness in us..." Concerning the Church:

> I believe that Christ by his apostles gathered unto himself a Church, to which he has continually added such as shall be saved; that this catholic (that is, universal) Church, extending to all nations and all ages, is holy in all its members, who have fellowship with God the Father, Son and Holy Ghost; that they have fellowship with the holy angels, who constantly minister to these heirs of salvation; and with all the living members of Christ on earth, as well as all who are departed in his faith and fear.

The exposition ends with the forgiveness God grants to all who repent and believe the gospel, the general resurrection, and the last judgment. Wesley then turns directly again to his Catholic addressee:

> Now, is there anything wrong in this? Is there any one point which you do not believe as well as we? But you think we ought to believe more. We will not now enter into the dispute. Only let me ask, if a man sincerely believes this much, and practises

accordingly, can any one possibly persuade you that such a man shall perish everlastingly?

What next, then, about "the practice of a true Protestant"? Wesley describes it fulsomely in terms of duty to God ("he worships God in spirit and in truth") and love of neighbour ("he loves his neighbour – that is, every man, friend or enemy, good or bad – as himself, as he loves his own soul, as Christ loved us"). And again, he asks his addressee whether he finds anything to reprove on these scores either. "This, and this alone," says Wesley, "is the old religion. This is true, primitive Christianity. Oh, when shall it spread over all the earth? When shall it be found both in us and in you?"

Assuming agreement thus far, John Wesley arrives in the finale at the point of his Letter: an invitation, even a summons that both his Catholic addressee and he should behave as Christians towards one another:

> [I]f God still loveth us, we ought also to love one another. We ought, without this endless jangling about opinions, to provoke one another to love and to good works. Let the points wherein we differ stand aside: here are enough wherein we agree, enough to be the ground of every Christian temper and of every Christian action.

We shall come later to what Wesley means by "opinions." Here we simply note his prayer that the Protestants and Catholics whom they respectively represent should not harm each other in deed, word or thought; and finally, "let us ... endeavour to help each other on in whatever we are agreed leads to the Kingdom. So far as we can, let us always rejoice to strengthen each other's hands in God."

In our Catholic-Methodist dialogue, the Singapore Report, in seeking to delineate a "Pattern of Common Faith," invokes Wesley's *Letter to a Roman Catholic* to buttress on the Methodist side the common use of the Nicene-Constantinopolitan Creed in the liturgies and teaching of the respective churches (Singapore, no. 38). The Rio de Janeiro Report devotes a whole paragraph to rehearsing Wesley's Letter and endorsing his conviction that "what is believed and affirmed in common must be embodied in the life both of the believer and the community of faith" (Rio de Janeiro, no. 38). Just as characteristically, the Letter is cited for its summons to mutual help in progress towards the Kingdom (Rio de Janeiro, no. 36; Seoul, no. 137).

2. Scriptural Holiness

John Wesley's own understanding of his vocation – why he and Methodism had been raised up by God – was "to reform the nation, particularly the Church, and to spread scriptural holiness over the land" (Brighton, no. 86, quoting the "Large Minutes"; WJW Jackson ed. 8:299).[3] According to the historical recital in the Seoul Report, "Methodism was primarily a renewal movement, concerned to evangelise the people, and to foster social and personal holiness in response to the proclamation of the Gospel" – hence "scriptural holiness" (Seoul, no. 17; cf. nos. 41, 114); and historically similar efforts are recorded as having occurred on the part of individuals and new religious communities within the Catholic Church (Seoul, no. 18). Recognition is given to "the untiring efforts of John Wesley to proclaim the Gospel to all, especially the neglected and the poor, and to call them to a life of holiness and a desire for perfection" as "precious evidence of the fruitfulness of faith" (Rio de Janeiro, no. 46).

The theme of "scriptural holiness" recurs throughout the reports of the Joint Commission. Already the Denver Report, in noting "the central place held in both traditions by the ideal of personal sanctification, growth in holiness through daily life in Christ," makes a contemporary application: "If the cultivation of 'scriptural holiness' has always been seen by the Methodist as a common task, Methodists gratefully recognize the new emphasis present in *Lumen Gentium* (nos. 9-10) and its chapter V on 'The Universal Call to Holiness,' while Roman Catholics can strengthen their own new insights by study of Methodist experience" (Denver, no. 7; cf. nos. 50, 52, 68.5).

For John Wesley, the moment of justification was also the moment of regeneration, when sanctification began. The Honolulu Report spells out the harmony between Wesley's teaching and Catholic doctrine:

> The key concept is "prevenience," a concept emphasized by both the Council of Trent and John Wesley. Always it is the Spirit's special office to maintain the divine initiative that precedes all human action and reaction.... The Council of Trent

teaches that the beginning of justification in adults takes place by means of the Lord's prevenient grace which moves us to conversion, enabling us freely to choose to follow the inspiration God gives us when he touches our hearts with the light of the Holy Spirit (Honolulu, no. 14).

The Holy Spirit sanctifies the regenerate Christian. Sanctification is a process that leads to perfect love. Life in the Spirit is human life lived out in faith, hope and love, to its utmost in consonance with God's gracious purposes in and for his children. As Wesley put it, the end of human existence is the recovery and the surpassing in perfection in which that existence was first conceived and created: "Hence [in the end of creation] will arise an unmixed state of holiness and happiness far superior to that which Adam enjoyed in paradise... And to crown all, there will be a deep, an intimate, an uninterrupted union with God – a constant communion with the Father and His Son through the Holy Spirit, a continual enjoyment of the Three-One God, and of all the creatures in him" (Honolulu, no. 18, quoting from Wesley's Sermon 64, "The New Creation").

For John Wesley, "scriptural holiness" carried an inescapable social dimension. According to a frequently quoted watchword from the Preface to the "Hymns and Sacred Poems" of 1739, "there is no holiness but social holiness." For the Wesleys, "social" here assumed a wide reach: towards the brothers and sisters in the Methodist Societies; towards the immediate neighbours in need (the "works of mercy"); and even towards the wider population and what we should today call the "social structures." The dialogue notes "Catholic-Methodist cooperation" in these matters (Singapore, no. 47).[4]

3. Hierarchy of Truths

In dealing with matters of doctrine, the Methodist-Catholic dialogue has been well aware of the teaching of the Second Vatican Council concerning the existence of "an order or 'hierarchy' of truths since they vary in their relation to the foundation of the Christian faith" (*Unitatis Redintegratio*, no. 11; cited in Singapore, no. 36). For their part, the Catholic members clearly state that this distinction in proximity to the foundation differs from what might superficially appear similar to one typically drawn by Methodists between "essential doctrines" and variable "opinions":

> Methodists have learned from John Wesley to discern between, on the one hand, different "opinions" about manners of worship, about ecclesiastical polity or even about the exposition of certain scriptural truths and, on the other, the essential doctrines of the Gospel. Such essential doctrines are: the Three-One God, the divine creation of the world and the vocation of humankind to holiness and happiness; the incarnation and atoning work of God the Son; the work of the Spirit as the source of all truth, renewal and communion; the need of fallen humankind to repent and to believe the Gospel; the divine provision of grace through word and sacrament and the institution and gathering of the Church; the summons to love of God and neighbour; and the promise of a final judgment and victory, where all the redeemed will share in glorifying and enjoying God forever (Rio de Janeiro, no. 115).

From the Catholic side:

> The Roman Catholic Church is at one with the Methodists over these essential doctrines, but emphasises that the whole teaching of the Church constitutes an organic unity. Its members are therefore called upon to believe the full teaching of the Church. But within the ecumenical dialogue also "the 'hierarchy' of truths of Catholic doctrine should always be respected; these truths all demand due assent of faith, yet are not all equally central to the mystery revealed in Jesus Christ, since they vary in their connection with the foundation of the Christian faith." This may be helpful when we discuss those doctrines which are important for the teaching and spirituality of the Catholic Church, but which will not easily be accepted by Methodists, e.g. the teaching about Mary in relation to Christ and the Church (Rio de Janeiro, no. 116, quoting PCPCU, *Directory for the Application of Principles and Norms on Ecumenism*, 1993, no. 75).

When the Commission quotes the phrase "hierarchy of truths," the emphasis usually falls on the essential interconnectedness of the truths of salvation; and here comparisons are rightly and positively drawn with several phrases that John Wesley uses in that regard: "the analogy of faith" (Singapore, no. 36; Rio de Janeiro, no. 65; Brighton, nos. 23, 89), "the grand scheme of doctrine" (Brighton, no. 23), "the general tenor of Scripture" (Brighton, no. 89). At the anthropological end, the focus falls on the triplet of "repentance, justification, sanctification." All three of these human appropriations are set within the prior work of God, which extends, as Wesley declares in his Sermon 43, "The Scripture Way of Salvation," "from the first dawning of grace in the soul till it is consummated in glory" (WJW 2:156). God's salvific work both allows and requires human "co-operation," as Wesley declares in his Sermon 85, "On Working Out Our Own Salvation" (WJW 3:199-209): "God works, therefore you *can* work; God works, therefore you *must* work."

As to what may be called the "organs" of truth, the Brighton Report notes both the overlap and the differences between Catholics and Methodists, with John Wesley figuring among the latter in at least a hermeneutical role:

> Both Methodists and Catholics accept the Scriptures, the Creeds and the doctrinal decrees of the early ecumenical Councils. In the Catholic Church further development of doctrine has occurred through other conciliar decrees and constitutions, and through pronouncements made by synods of bishops and by the Bishop of Rome and the offices that assist him in his care of all the churches. In Methodism the Holy Scriptures are believed to contain all things necessary to salvation. At the same time, Methodists' reading of the Scriptures is guided by the early Creeds and Councils and certain standard texts, such as the Sermons of John Wesley, his Notes on the New Testament, and the Articles of Religion. The Methodist Conferences have the task of interpreting doctrine. Both Methodists and Catholics hold that all doctrine must remain under the Word of God, against which the value of its content should be tested (Brighton, no. 22, where appeal might have been made to Vatican II's *Dei Verbum*).

On the neuralgic point of infallibility, the Nairobi Report of 1986 made – in its final two paragraphs (Nairobi, nos. 74-75) – a tentative move in the direction of extending to the ecclesial dimension the teaching of John Wesley regarding the "assurance" given by God to believers – as their "common privilege" – that they are in a state of grace:

> An approach towards convergence in thinking about infallibility may perhaps be reached by considering the Methodist doctrine of assurance. It is the typical Methodist teaching that believers can receive from the Holy Spirit an assurance of their redemption through the atoning death of Christ and can be guided by the Spirit who enables them to cry "Abba, Father" in the way of holiness to future glory.

> Starting from Wesley's claim that the evidence for what God has done and is doing for our salvation, as described above, can be "heightened to exclude all doubt," Methodists might ask whether the Church, like individuals, might by the working of the Holy Spirit receive as a gift from God in its living, teaching, preaching and mission, an assurance concerning its grasp of the fundamental doctrines of the faith such as to exclude all doubt, and whether the teaching ministry of the Church has a special and divinely guided part to play in this. In any case Catholics and Methodists are agreed on the need for an authoritative way of being sure, beyond doubt, concerning God's action insofar as it is crucial for our salvation (Nairobi, nos. 74-75).[5]

And this perspective returns in numbers 134-135 of the Seoul Report of 2006:

> Catholics invite Methodists to ask whether their traditional reliance on the inner assurance of the Holy Spirit might not be applied to the Church as a whole. Can the Church not have a *corporate* assurance, particularly regarding the liturgical actions of its ordained ministers, and might not the ordained ministers also have a part to play in articulating the assurance of the Church?

> Moreover, Catholics would wish to suggest to Methodists that the disputed issue of "infallibility" can be approached from

within this very confidence in Christ's own action in word and sacrament. Just as Catholics believe that Christ can unfailingly wash, feed and forgive his people through the sacramental ministrations of his Church, so too they believe that he can unfailingly *teach* his people. Not only does he do so whenever the Scriptures are proclaimed (cf. Vatican II, *Sacrosanctum Concilium*, 7), for every such proclamation is in truth infallible, but he can also do so through the teaching of the Church on a matter of vital importance. Just as there are clearly specified conditions for the proper celebration of Baptism, Eucharist, and other sacramental actions, which, when fulfilled, enable the Church to trust without doubt that Christ himself is present and active, so likewise there will necessarily be specific conditions for recognising his presence and action in decisive instances of teaching... (Seoul, nos. 134-35).

At least in the matter of indefectibility, if not quite infallibility, the Brighton Report's paragraph 84 can quote a couplet of Charles Wesley's: "In our human frailty, we trust together in Christ's promise to keep the Church faithful to himself. As Charles Wesley's hymn reminds us, 'Fortified by power divine, the Church can never fail.'"

4. Ecclesiastical Order

In a letter written on June 25, 1746, to "John Smith" (WJW 26:197-207), John Wesley posed a rhetorical question and immediately provided his own substantive answer: "What is the end of all ecclesiastical order? Is it not to bring souls from the power of Satan to God, and to build them up in His fear and love? Order, then, is so far valuable as it answers these ends; and if it answers them not, it is nothing worth." Wesley was responding to charges of "breaking or setting aside order, i.e. the rules of our own Church, both by preaching in the fields, and by using extempory prayer" (206). Already in a letter of 1739, once thought to have been written to James Hervey, his former Oxford pupil, Wesley justified his itinerant preaching against accusations of "intermeddling" in "other men's parishes" with his most celebrated and often slightly misquoted remark: "I look upon all the world as my parish... I mean that in whatever part of it I am I judge it meet, right, and my bounden duty to declare unto all that are willing to hear, the glad tidings of salvation. This is the work which I know God has called me to; and sure I am that His blessing attends it" (WJW 19:66-68).[6]

In such cases, Wesley is talking about (shall we say?) merely "canonical" order. When it comes (dare we say?) to *hierarchical* order, Wesley is much more respectful, precisely insofar as it serves the transmission of the gospel. In his controversy with Richard Challoner (1691), Vicar Apostolic of the London District from 1758 – to which the Seoul Report alludes (nos. 23-24, 27) – Wesley could claim that Protestant churches had a better line of succession than the Catholic Church since their pastors and teachers conveyed the apostolic gospel more accurately.[7] Reporting from the side of "the Methodist tradition," the Singapore Report gives the following account of Wesley's understanding and practice of *episcopé*:

> Wesley accepted and believed in the reality of *episcopé* within the Church of England of which he was a minister. In relation to the Methodist societies he exercised *episcopé* over the whole; all his followers were bound to be in connexion with him. He expounded the main teachings of the Church by means of his Sermons, Notes on the New Testament and Conference Minutes, and made available to his people authorized abridgements of doctrinal and spiritual work. His appointment of Francis Asbury and Thomas Coke to the superintendency in America was rooted in his belief that the Holy Spirit wished to bestow the gift of *episcopé* at that time and place for the sake of maintaining unity of faith with the Church of all ages. It was part of a fresh and extraordinary outpouring of the gift of the Spirit who never ceases to enliven and unify the Church (Singapore, no. 93).[8]

As it was about to start expounding upon "the Petrine office," the Nairobi Report confided that "for Methodists the concept of primacy is unfamiliar, even if historically John Wesley exercised a kind of primacy in the origins of the Methodist Church" (Nairobi, no. 37). According to the Brighton Report, "John Wesley's use of the phrase 'watching over one another in love' challenges all individual ministers and collegial bodies, especially those exercising the ministry of oversight" (Brighton, no. 83, citing "The Nature, Design and General Rules of the United

Society," WJW 9:69). The "mutual care of brothers and sisters for one another and for all who are in need" has been an especially important "aspect of Christian communion for the Methodist movement since the days of John Wesley" (Rio de Janeiro, no. 122).

Besides the canonical and the hierarchical, a third sense of ecclesiastical order has been acknowledged in the dialogue, not entirely unrelated to the first two. From the early part of the twentieth century, there were historians, both Methodist and Catholic, who likened John Wesley to the founder of a religious order.[9] Having declared that "we cannot expect to find an ecclesiology shaped in a time of division to be entirely satisfactory" (Nairobi, no. 22), the Nairobi Report nevertheless suggested, with a view to "a reunited Church," four "models" for "organic unity in the *koinonia* of the one Body of Christ." The second was this:

> From one perspective the history of John Wesley has suggested an analogy between his movement and the religious orders within the one Church. Figures such as Benedict of Norcia and Francis of Assisi, whose divine calling was similarly to a spiritual reform, gave rise to religious orders, characterized by special forms of life and prayer, work, evangelization and their own internal organization. The different religious orders in the Roman Catholic Church, while fully in communion with the Pope and the bishops, relate in different ways to the authority of the Pope and bishops. Such relative autonomy has a recognized place within the unity of the Church (Nairobi, no. 24.b).

Albert Outler, an official observer at the Second Vatican Council and a Methodist member of the Joint Commission in its early rounds, had already written: "We need a catholic church within which to function as a proper evangelical order of witness and worship, discipline and nurture."[10]

5. This Mysterious Bread

Eucharistic doctrine and practice were identified as matters for dialogue from the start. The Denver Report of 1971 recorded that the Eucharist had been recognized as providing "an obvious place of common agreement and appreciation with which to begin, i.e. the emphasis on frequent Communion of the Wesleys which led to a eucharistic revival in the first part of the Methodist story, and of which the eucharistic hymns of Charles Wesley are a permanent legacy" (79). The hymns were seen "giving a basis and hope for discussion of doctrinal differences about the nature of the Real Presence and the 'sacrificial' character of the Eucharist" (Denver, no. 9). "So our first conversations included an appraisal of those hymns from a Catholic view" (Denver, no. 79). Nevertheless, "Methodists on their side were candid in considering Roman Catholic questions how far the Wesleys remain a decisive influence in contemporary Methodism" (Denver, no. 9): "It was not disguised, for example, that the eucharistic devotion of the Wesleys and the hymns of Charles Wesley are no index at all to the place of Holy Communion in the life, thought and devotion of modern Methodists" (Denver, no. 80). There was, however, a glimmer of hope: "While traditional Methodist reverence for the preaching of the Gospel finds an echo in recent Roman Catholic theological and liturgical thinking, there are signs that Methodists on their part are recapturing through the liturgical movement an appreciation of the sacraments such as is enshrined for example in Charles Wesley's eucharistic hymns" (Denver, no. 19). By the time of the Dublin Report of 1976 (which at this point avowedly owed much to the English Roman Catholic-British Methodist Commission), it could even be claimed that

> in recent years there has been a notable recovery of eucharistic faith and practice among Methodists, with a growing sense that the fullness of Christian worship includes both word and sacrament. Similarly, among Roman Catholics there has been a recovery in the theology and practice of the ministry of the word. These developments have resulted in a remarkable convergence, so that at no other time has the worshipping life of Methodists and Roman Catholics had so much in common (Dublin, no. 51).

For the purpose of our own chapter, it is time to say a little more about "the eucharistic hymns." The *Hymns on the Lord's Supper* appeared in 1745 under the joint names of John and Charles Wesley. The "Preface" (doubtless the doing of John) consisted of an abridged version of a treatise by the Anglican divine Daniel Brevint (1616-1695), a former Dean of Lincoln: *The Christian Sacrament and Sacrifice, by way of discourse, meditation, and prayer upon the nature, parts, and blessings of Holy Communion* (1672-73). Then came the 166 hymns themselves, by and large the work of Charles, although a few of them are known to have come from other sources and John frequently edited his brother's verse. The hymns are grouped under these headings, somewhat rearranged from Brevint towards the end: Hymns on the Lord's Supper, I. As it is a Memorial of the Sufferings and Death of Christ (1-27); II. As it is a Sign and a Means of Grace (28-92); III. The Sacrament a Pledge of Heaven (93-115); IV. The Holy Eucharist as it implies a Sacrifice (116-127); V. Concerning the Sacrifice of our Persons (128-157); After the Sacrament (158-166). The *Hymns on the Lord's Supper* went through nine editions during the lifetime of the Wesleys, but only seven of the eucharistic hymns were included in the 1780 *Collection of Hymns for the Use of the People Called Methodists.* Varying and wider selections were incorporated into the hymnals of both British and American Methodism in the nineteenth century. The figures were quite well maintained in Britain during the twentieth century, but they were drastically reduced in America, and this latter fact may well account for the hesitations of the Joint Commission in its early Reports about their familiarity and influence among the Methodist people at large. The "rediscovery" of the *Hymns on the Lord's Supper* which in fact took place – at least among the liturgically, ecumenically and theologically interested – in the second half of the twentieth century owed much to the British Methodist J. Ernest Rattenbury (1870-1963) and his study and reprinting of them in *The Eucharistic Hymns of John and Charles Wesley* (London: Epworth Press, 1948). By the time of their official response to the "Lima text" of the World Council of Churches' Commission on Faith and Order, *Baptism, Eucharist and Ministry* (BEM),[11] the council of bishops of the United Methodist Church could welcome "the appropriation of the scriptural and traditional understanding of the eucharist recovered by twentieth-century liturgical scholarship and focused in the Greek terms *anamnesis* (the memorial that dynamically conjoins Christ past, present, and future) and *epiclesis* (the effective invocation of the Holy Spirit to 'realize the sign')": "All this," they wrote, "we find explicitly taught by John and Charles Wesley, who knew and respected the apostolic, patristic and reformed faith of the Church"; moreover, "as Wesleyans, we are accustomed to the language of sacrifice, and we find BEM's statements to be in accord with the Church's Tradition and ours."[12]

In the work of the Methodist-Roman Catholic International Commission, the hymns actually start to be quoted when the Commission moved in the direction of a "sacramental ecclesiology." The Rio de Janeiro Report quotes the final stanza of *Hymns on the Lord's Supper*, number 81 ("Jesu, we thus obey"), to illustrate what both Methodists and Catholics can affirm concerning Christ's institution of the eucharist as "a holy meal, the memorial of his sacrifice," in which its fruits are received in faith:

He bids us eat and drink
Imperishable food.
He gives His flesh to be our meat,
And bids us drink His blood:
Whate'er the Almighty can
To pardoned sinners give,
The fulness of our God made man
We here with Christ receive.

Again, both sides can declare – in the Seoul Report (no. 56) – that "intimate union with Christ is God's gift to the Church, maintained, deepened and renewed by the proclamation of the word and the breaking of the bread"; and *Hymns on the Lord's Supper*, number 29 is quoted:

O Thou who this mysterious bread
　　Didst in Emmaus break,
Return, herewith our souls to feed,
　　And to thy followers speak.

Unseal the volume of thy grace,
　　Apply the gospel word,
Open our eyes to see thy face,
　　Our hearts to know the Lord.

In its lengthy chapter on the Eucharist (Durban, nos. 73-134), the Durban Report of 2011 turns in the Wesleyan hymns to the "Remembrancer Divine" (*Hymns on the Lord's Supper*, no. 16) for pneumatological help in the question of presence (Durban, nos. 82-85; 128-30), and to the "Grand Oblation" (*Hymns on the Lord's Supper*, no. 123) for Christ's gracious inclusion of communicant believers into his own sacrifice "as more than standers by" (Durban, nos. 97-120; cf. *Hymns on the Lord's Supper*, nos. 131, 141).

All told, it is reckoned that Charles Wesley wrote over 9,000 hymns or poems on a vast range of scriptural and doctrinal themes, only a portion of which ever entered the liturgical repertoire. Still, the Denver Report could recognise the hymns of Charles Wesley as "a rich source of Methodist spirituality" (Denver, no. 9), and according to the Seoul Report they "constitute a corpus of practical theology for the Methodist people" (Seoul, no. 120). As dialogue partners, Catholics and Methodists "are committed to pursuing together the path towards full visible unity in faith, mission and sacramental life" (Seoul, no. 62), and so they may jointly invoke a stanza from "Jesus, united by thy grace":

> Touched by the lodestone of thy love,
>> Let all our hearts agree,
> And ever t'ward each other move,
>> And ever move t'ward thee.

And "the dynamic communion, connection and continuity of the pilgrim Church today with the Church of the past and of the future" can be celebrated with a great funeral hymn of Charles Wesley's (Seoul, no. 82):

> Come, let us join our friends above
>> That have obtained the prize,
> And on the eagle wings of love
>> To joys celestial rise:
> Let all the saints terrestrial sing
>> With those to glory gone;
> For all the servants of our King,
>> In earth and heaven are one.

> One family we dwell in him,
>> One church, above, beneath,
> Though now divided by the stream,
>> The narrow stream of death:
> One army of the living God,
>> To his command we bow;
> Part of his host have crossed the flood,
>> And part are crossing now.

6. Our Friends Above

The point has come to ask more formally about the views of Catholics and the Catholic Church – past, present, and perhaps future – upon the Wesley brothers. Or perhaps we should start the other way around and ask about Wesleyan views of Catholics and the Catholic Church. Certainly, when in its eighth round the Joint Commission took courage to face head-on the issue of ecclesiology, it realized that the "mutual reassessment" made possible by the "new context" of the ecumenical movement would have to integrate the earlier history that was "coloured by the religious, social and political conflicts which have generally characterized relationships between Protestants and Catholics" and "fed by mutual ignorance, defective understandings or partial views of the other" (Seoul, no. 11).

At the start of the present chapter we highlighted John Wesley's extraordinarily irenic "Letter to a Roman Catholic." That, of course, was not the whole story. In paragraph 20, the Seoul Report lists some of the "errors" with which Wesley taxed the Catholic Church as being contrary to Scripture.[13] In paragraphs 23-24, the Report recapitulates the controversy between Wesley and Vicar Apostolic Richard Challoner, already mentioned:

In *A Caveat against the Methodists* (1760), Challoner cited numerous biblical references to show that the Church founded by Christ is universal, one, holy, and orthodox in doctrine, with an unfailing succession of pastors and teachers under the direction of the Holy Spirit. In Challoner's estimation, "The Methodists are not the People of God, they are not true Gospel Christians: nor is their new raised Society the true Church of Christ or any Part of it."

Responding to Challoner's *Caveat*, Wesley agreed that the Church is universal, one, holy and orthodox, but then found it difficult to recognise these same marks of the Church in "the Church of Rome, in its present form." For him, the catholic Church founded by Christ is "the *whole body* of men endued with faith, working by love, dispersed over the whole earth, in Europe, Asia, Africa and America." In all ages and nations the Church is the one body of Christ... Wesley judged that "not Methodists only" but "the whole body of Protestants" had better title to these marks than the Roman Catholic Church as such. He was willing to recognise individual Catholics as being included in the Church despite the shortcomings of their institution. In his 1785 sermon "Of the Church" he said of the Church of Rome: "therein neither is 'the pure Word of God' preached nor (are) the sacraments 'duly administered." Yet, he would include those congregations within the Church catholic, if they have "one Spirit, one hope, one Lord, one faith, one God and Father of all." At times, then, Wesley was dismissive of the Roman Catholic Church; nevertheless he was reluctant to unchurch Roman Catholic individuals or even entire congregations (Seoul, nos. 23-24).

Tongue in cheek, a Methodist might wonder whether Wesley looked on some individual Catholics as "separated brothers and sisters" and could even view their congregations as "ecclesial communities."

In the other direction (paragraphs 28-29), the Seoul Report offers some nuanced (or "mixed") views taken of Wesley by prominent Catholics in the following century:

In his Lenten lectures at the London Oratory in 1850, John Henry Newman could declare to his former fellow-Anglicans that "if you wish to find the shadow and the suggestion of the supernatural qualities which make up the notion of a Catholic saint, to Wesley you must go, and such as him" (though "personally I do not like him, if it were merely for deep self-reliance and self-conceit"). Likewise, he went on, Wesley and his companions, "starting amid ridicule at Oxford, with fasting and praying in the cold night air, then going about preaching, reviled by the rich and educated, and pelted and dragged to prison by the populace, and converting thousands from sin to God's service," might evoke the great Catholic missionaries of former times – "were it not for their pride and eccentricity, their fanatical doctrine and untranquil devotion".

A more tranquil approach to Methodism from this period can be found in the work of Johann Adam Möhler (1796-1838). In a study of the major symbols and confessions of faith that had been formulated since the Reformation, he classified Methodism as "one of the smaller Protestant sects", and recognised that John Wesley was distinguished "by great talents, classical acquirement and (what was better still) by a burning zeal for the kingdom of God". While he blamed Wesley for, as he saw it, assuming the office of bishop and ordaining priests, he was the first to suggest a similarity between the origin of the Methodist movement and the inspiration "which led to the origin of the monastic institutes" in the Catholic Church. In this perspective, Methodism appeared primarily as a force for spiritual renewal. This positive reassessment, however, did not bear fruit in Catholic thought until the twentieth century (Seoul, nos. 28-29).

Clearly, the "mutual reassessment" must entail what has been called in other dialogues a "reconciliation of memories." In a directly positive mode, the Seoul Report declared the time had come to "look each other in the eye, and with love and esteem to acknowledge what we see to be truly of Christ and of the Gospel, and thereby *of the Church*, in one another. Doing so will highlight the gifts we truly have to offer one another in the service of Christ in the world, and will open the way for an exchange of gifts which is what ecumenical dialogue, in some way, always is" (Seoul, no. 97, referring in that last point to Pope John Paul's 1995 encyclical *Ut Unum Sint*, 28). Among the gifts that Catholics vouched they might receive from Methodism were none other than the Wesley brothers:

The gift of John and Charles Wesley themselves, outstanding and godly men, to be shared as heroes of Christian faith, would be a cause of joy and thanksgiving. The Wesleys are alive today, so to speak, because of the Methodist Church, and thereby enabled to be gifts to the entire Church. To preach so as truly to "warm the heart," as the Wesleys did, is an important model for Catholics, too, and the Wesleys' emphasis on frequent reception of holy communion is deeply edifying to Catholics. At a Methodist celebration marking the 300th anniversary of the birth of John Wesley, the President of the Pontifical Council for Promoting Christian Unity, Cardinal Walter Kasper, said: "Just as you continue to turn to the ministry of John Wesley for inspiration and guidance, we can look to see and find in him the evangelical zeal, the pursuit of holiness, the concern for the poor, the virtues and goodness which we have come to know and respect in you. For all of this, we can all afford to be profoundly grateful" (Seoul, no. 127; cf. no. 156.6).

This time, a Methodist might wonder – with fully positive intent – whether or when the day would come when Catholics and Methodists would be able to intone together "Sancti Ioannes et Carole, orate pro nobis." We have, in fact, already arrived at two Methodist tercentenaries in which there has been Catholic participation.

7. Two Tercentenaries

June 17, 2003, marked the three-hundredth anniversary of the birth of John Wesley. On Sunday, June 22, Cardinal Walter Kasper, President of the PCPCU, preached in the Ponte Sant'Angelo Methodist Church in Rome; and we have just seen his sermon quoted from in the Seoul Report (no. 127). As a Catholic, the preacher was bound to "grapple with Wesley's ambivalent understanding of the Catholic Church"; but in today's "new context," where "a genuine friendship has emerged between us," allowing "a reassessment of John Wesley's life and ministry from a very different starting point," a "wider view" will help us "to see what dynamized Wesley's ministry, to see the evangelical passion which gave direction to his life and the movement he started." In that Sunday's Scripture reading of 2 Corinthians 6, Kasper found "a framework to reflect on the call to discipleship, the call to spread the gospel of Jesus Christ, and the call to personal holiness," wherein to "make connections with the life and ministry of John Wesley, and hear some of his words which still resonate with us today." Wesley "understood the call to holiness as being both intensely personal and strongly ecclesial." Noting the Apostle's plea to "open wide your hearts," Kasper approached his conclusion:

It is a sign of the Holy Spirit's work among us that Methodists and Catholics today can hear this call and respond to it increasingly together, mindful of our common baptism, and in the context of an ever developing relationship which invites us to share, to the extent that is presently possible, in Christ's mission to the world... May we ever hold fast to both truth and love, pursuing them in tandem, and trusting that if we do so, the Holy Spirit will draw us ever more closely together.

Knowing how the Methodist tradition of hymns "has resulted in an enriching of the Catholic Church and many other Christian traditions," the preacher ended with the last stanza of Charles Wesley's "Love Divine, All Loves Excelling":

Finish then Thy new creation,
Pure and spotless let us be;
Let us see Thy great salvation
Perfectly restored in Thee!
Changed from glory into glory,
Till in heaven we take our place,
Till we cast our crowns before Thee,
Lost in wonder, love, and praise.

Later in that year of 2003, the meeting of the Joint Commission was held in the city of York. The customary day's excursion took the form of a pilgrimage to the Lincolnshire village or town of Epworth, the birthplace and childhood home of John and Charles Wesley and their siblings, where their father Samuel was rector of the parish and their mother Susanna instructed them in matters sacred and secular. Inspection was made of the font in which the brothers were baptised, and of the tombstone of their father from which John famously preached. After the Commission's own sessions, the members travelled to London in order to meet with the British Methodist-Catholic Committee, and to visit Wesley's House and Chapel in the City Road. The tour of the House was conducted by the local Roman Catholic priest; the group squeezed into the little room in which John read and wrote and prayed when he was in the capital, and common prayers were said in the chamber where John Wesley died. In Wesley's Chapel, the members of the Commission attended the All Saints' Day celebration of the 225th anniversary of the Chapel's dedication. In a message read by Bishop Michael Putney, Catholic co-chairman of the Joint Commission, Cardinal Kasper thanked and congratulated Methodists for "the ecumenical commitment you have shown in numerous ways in recent years"; and he again referred to a process of "Catholic reassessment of John Wesley" as "rich with possibilities."

December 2007 saw the tercentenary of Charles Wesley's birth, and a musical celebration was held on the third of the month in the Basilica of St. Paul Outside the Walls, Rome, where the Methodist, Catholic, and (this time) Anglican participants were greeted by the Abbot of the Benedictine community, Dom Edmund Power. Cardinal Walter Kasper's address included these words:

> With joy we join you today in celebrating the 300th anniversary of Charles Wesley's birth. It is appropriate that we celebrate this anniversary by singing several of his hymns, for it is above all through these hymns that Roman Catholics have come to know and appreciate the younger brother of John Wesley. While Charles Wesley's hymns, numbering in the thousands, had an enormous influence on Methodist self-understanding and worship, a significant number of these hymns are also sung in Catholic churches throughout the English-speaking world, and have enhanced our praise and celebration of God's saving grace for generations. His hymns, often combining eloquent language and theological depth drawn from the Scriptures and the faith of the Church through the ages, address themes which reflect the convergence between Methodists and Catholics on foundational aspects of Christian faith: God's universal love made known in Jesus Christ, the call to scriptural holiness and renewal of life, the sacramental life of the Church, Christian hope, and the presence of the Holy Spirit...

> I trust that our dialogue will continue to deepen our understanding and appreciation of the Wesleys and the Methodist movement they initiated. As we look to the legacy of the hymns of Charles Wesley, while there are a few references which might give us grief, reflecting as they do the polemical context of the times, the overwhelming number are a gift to be received, with our eyes attentive to full communion in faith, mission and sacramental life which is the stated goal of the Methodist-Catholic dialogue.

His Grace the Archbishop of Canterbury, Dr. Rowan Williams, said this about Charles Wesley in the message he sent to the celebration:

> He was a man whose life was not without paradox. A completely committed Anglican throughout his life, he is associated with the creation of one of the most significant Protestant traditions in the English-speaking world; a man of the eighteenth century, possessed of extraordinary skill in using the metrical riches of English verse, he succeeded in recreating within that idiom the thought-world of the Greek Fathers and indeed the early mediaeval monastic theology of the West. In a century marked so deeply by rationalistic religion, he uncovered the living heart of the Christian theology of incarnation and sacrament, adoption and deification.
>
> His work has never lacked enthusiasts – not least because he made his theology so brilliantly accessible through his hymns, which taught generations of Anglicans and Methodists, and an increasingly large number of others, how to inhabit the world of Scriptural and traditional imagery with grace and fervour and intelligence. It is wonderful to know that he is being commemorated in this way in Rome. I join you in thanking God for the gift of this great baptised mind and imagination, and I wish you every joy and blessing in your reflections together.

The occasion at St. Paul Outside the Walls ended with the singing of Wesley's great Advent hymn, "Lo, he comes with clouds descending." On the following day, a joint Methodist-Anglican Eucharist was celebrated in the Catholic Church of St. Francis Xavier Caravita.

Conclusion

As the Brighton Report observed, "Catholics and Methodists have begun to enjoy a 'union in affection' on their way to that 'entire external union' for which Wesley in his time hardly dared to hope" (Brighton, no. 28, quoting John Wesley's Sermon 39, "Catholic Spirit"; WJW 2:81-95, in particular p. 82). In our new, ecumenically shaped context, we can more easily discern the divine gifts that were bestowed or maintained even in times of separation, and we are more ready to profit from them jointly. The repeatedly stated goal of the Methodist-

Roman Catholic dialogue is "full communion in faith, mission and sacramental life" (Nairobi, no. 20; Singapore, no. 94; Rio de Janeiro, Preface; Brighton, Preface; Seoul, Preface, nos. 12, 62, 98, 144, 147, 163). Our hope and prayer must be that it contributes – with other ecumenical dialogues and enterprises – to that "restoration of unity among all Christians" to which the Second Vatican Council looked (*Unitatis Redintegratio*, no. 19; cited in Seoul, no. 12).

---

1   From its start in 1966-67, the Commission has worked in "rounds" of five years in order to be able to present its reports to the quinquennial meetings of the World Methodist Council, while at the same time presenting them to the Holy See through the Secretariat (later Pontifical Council) for Promoting Christian Unity (hereafter PCPCU). The reports – written in English – are published officially in the *Information Service* of the Secretariat/Pontifical Council, and as brochures by the World Methodist Council (Lake Junaluska, North Carolina). They can be found – also in translated forms – in various journals and collections of dialogue documents (see GA I-IV). The reports have become informally and stenographically designated – even on the Catholic side – by the place and date at which they were presented to the World Methodist Council. Only with the fourth report did a formal title come into use. Thus the sequence runs as follows: Denver 1971; Dublin 1976; Honolulu 1981; Nairobi 1986, "Towards a Statement on the Church"; Singapore 1991, "The Apostolic Tradition"; Rio de Janeiro 1996, "The Word of Life: A Statement on Revelation and Faith"; Brighton 2001, "Speaking the Truth in Love: Teaching Authority among Catholics and Methodists"; Seoul 2006, "Catholics and Methodists Reflect Further on the Church"; Durban 2011, "Encountering Christ the Saviour: Church and Sacraments"; Houston 2016, "The Call to Holiness: From Glory to Glory."" In this chapter, shorthand designations will be used as far as possible, and references will be given by paragraph number.

2   An ecumenical edition of the epistolary text with a substantial prologue by Cardinal Augustin Bea is found in Michael Hurley, *John Wesley's Letter to a Roman Catholic* (London: Geoffrey Chapman; Nashville: Abingdon Press, 1968).

3   *The Works of John Wesley* (WJW) will be cited according to the Bicentennial Edition (Nashville: Abingdon Press, 1984-) unless otherwise noted, as here according to the 19th-century edition by Thomas Jackson.

4   In his Sermon 107, "On God's Vineyard" (WJW 3:502-17), John Wesley weighed the respective strengths and weaknesses of Lutheran and Catholic teaching in the matters of justification and sanctification before boldly declaring that it had "pleased God to give the Methodists a full and clear knowledge of each" (pp. 505-506). By the year 2006, it had become possible for Catholics and Lutherans to recognize a statement of Methodist teaching – drawing heavily on Wesley – as in "agreement with the consensus in basic truths of the doctrine of justification" as formulated by the two original partners in their Joint Declaration of 1999 on that doctrine. At Seoul (Korea), on July 23, 2006, an *Official Common Affirmation of the Methodist Statement of Association with the Joint Declaration on the Doctrine of Justification* was signed on behalf of the Catholic Church, the Lutheran World Federation, and the World Methodist Council and its member churches. For the text and the procedures, see Geoffrey Wainwright, "World Methodist Council and the Joint Declaration on the Doctrine of Justification" in *Pro Ecclesia* 16 (2007): 7-13.

5   See Geoffrey Wainwright, "The Assurance of Faith: A Methodist Approach to the Question Raised by the Roman Catholic Doctrine of Infallibility" in *One in Christ* 22 (1986): 187-206; reprinted in Wainwright, *Methodists in Dialogue* (Nashville: Abingdon/Kingswood, 1995), 57-71, 295-99.

6   The Seoul Report mentions, when listing some possible gifts from Methodism to Catholicism, that one of the great twentieth-century members of the Order of Preachers, Yves Congar, "was inspired by these words to entitle one of his own books on the nature and scope of salvation, *Vaste monde ma paroisse*" (124).

7   For the controversy with Challoner, see Wesley's *Journal* for February 19, 1761, in WJW 21:303-308.

8   For John Wesley's view that "bishops and presbyters are (essentially) of one order" see already his *Journal* for January 20, 1746, in WJW 20:112. And, in a letter of March 25, 1785, to Barnabas Thomas, he could write: "I know myself to be as real a Christian bishop as the Archbishop of Canterbury."

9   So already, at the beginning of the twentieth century, Herbert Workman, in *A New History of Methodism*, ed. William J. Townsend et al. (London: Hodder & Stoughton, 1909), vol. 1, pp. 1-73 ("The Place of Methodism in the Life and Thought of the Christian Church"), where the Methodist author makes an extensive comparison between Wesley and the early Methodists, on the one hand, and Francis and the Franciscans, on the other (pp. 43-49). Others have ranged more widely: thus the Franciscan Maximin Piette, in his Louvain dissertation from the 1920s, extended the comparison "à S. Benoît pour sa piété liturgique, à S. Dominique pour son zèle apostolique, à S. François d'Assise pour son amour du Christ et son détachement, à S. Ignace de Loyola pour son génie organisateur, à S. Alphonse de Liguori, son contemporain, pour son appel terrorisant aux jugements de Dieu comme point de départ de la conversion"; see Maximin Piette, *La réaction de John Wesley dans l'évolution du protestantisme*, 2e édition revue et augmentée (1927), 654; cf. Maximin Piette, *John Wesley in the Evolution of Protestantism* (London: Sheed & Ward, 1937), 480.

10 Albert C. Outler, "Do Methodists have a doctrine of the Church?" in Dow Kirkpatrick, ed., *The Doctrine of the Church* (Nashville: Abingdon, 1964), 11-28, in particular p. 27. For another article by an eventual member of the international dialogue, see the Catholic theologian Francis Frost's "Méthodisme", in G. Jacquemet et al., eds., *Catholicisme: hier, aujourd'hui et demain* (Paris: Letouzey & Ané, 1948 onwards), vol. 9 (1982), cols. 48-71. Frost (whose grandmother was a Methodist) writes of John Wesley's teaching as "un enseignement d'ordre spirituel plutôt que dogmatique," saying that "le méthodisme moderne doit en premier lieu cet héritage à John Wesley, tout comme, dans l'Église catholique romaine, un ordre religieux ou une famille spirituelle tient son esprit d'un fondateur."

11 WCC Commission on Faith and Order, *Baptism, Eucharist and Ministry*. Faith and Order paper 111 (Geneva: WCC, 1982).

12 See further my Introduction to the facsimile edition of *Hymns on the Lord's Supper* published by the Charles Wesley Society (Madison, NJ, 1995).

13 Wesley "extracted" a "Roman Catechism faithfully drawn out of the allowed writings of the Church of Rome, with a Reply thereto" that had been critically assembled under a similar title by Bishop John Williams of the Church of England in 1686 (see WJW, Jackson ed., 10:86-128). In his own "Popery Calmly Considered," the adverb is euphemistic (see WJW, Jackson ed. 10:140-158).

✝ CHAPTER 6

The History, Methodology, and Implications for Ecumenical Reception of *The Apostolicity of the Church* [1]

by William G. Rusch

Over the years of his service as a priest, professor, and ecumenist, Monsignor John A. Radano has consistently and exemplarily shown to his colleagues a deep commitment to the visible unity of Christ's Church. He has been a faithful witness to his church's stance on ecumenism, articulated at the Second Vatican Council. This opinion could be documented at considerable length. In this context it is sufficient to mention Monsignor Radano's participation in the Consultation on Church Union in the United States, various dialogues internationally, and the Central Committee and the Commission on Faith and Order of the World Council of Churches.

Since 1984, Monsignor Radano has exercised his ecumenical vocation within the framework of the Vatican's Pontifical Council for Promoting Christian Unity. Among his other responsibilities there, he served as a co-secretary for the international Lutheran-Roman Catholic dialogue, sponsored by the Lutheran World Federation and the Pontifical Council for Promoting Christian Unity. Perhaps the most outstanding contribution of that particular bilateral conversation, along with certain national dialogues and international studies, was the work that helped make possible in 1999 the *Joint Declaration on the Doctrine of Justification*.[2]

For a number of years, including the time before his service in Rome and during his Roman years, I have been privileged to regard John Radano as a close friend and ecumenical colleague. Thus, I wish to express my appreciation to the editors of this *Festschrift* for the opportunity to contribute an essay on a topic that, I believe, reflects the ecumenical commitment that both John Radano and I share.

My intention here is to offer some comments on the latest report from the international Lutheran-Roman Catholic dialogue, entitled *The Apostolicity of the Church: Study Document of the Lutheran-Roman Catholic Commission on Unity*.[3] Specifically, I propose to look at this document in terms of its history and methodology.

It seems to me that such an examination is in keeping with the overall theme of this volume: to note what has been achieved ecumenically in recent years and to explore what future steps may be taken in the light of those achievements. I believe that such a process can be especially informative in regard to the ongoing challenge and opportunity before both the Lutheran and Roman Catholic churches to engage in ecumenical reception in this second century of the modern ecumenical movement.[4]

I. The Pre-History of *The Apostolicity of the Church* in the Lutheran-Roman Catholic Dialogue

The origins of the international Lutheran-Roman Catholic dialogues lie in discussions that took place in the closing days of the Second Vatican Council in 1965.[5] The dialogue itself began in 1967 with a mandate to study the topic of "the gospel and the church." It issued its first document in 1972, *The Gospel and the Church*, commonly referred to as the Malta Report.[6] This text included a considerable number of topics: Tradition and Scripture, justification, gospel and the world, ordained ministry, and the papacy. This report noted progress in overcoming doctrinal disputes and the structural issues that divided the churches. It called for a mutual recognition of the ordained ministry and occasional intercommunion between Lutherans and Roman Catholics. The report was not unanimously approved by the dialogue participants, and none of the churches involved through the Pontifical Council on Promoting Christian Unity (then the Secretariat for Promoting Christian Unity) and the Lutheran World Federation took any official action in regards to it. Such a situation gives an indication of the limits of the Malta Report, and also of this period of ecumenical history.

Nevertheless, *The Gospel and the Church* because of both its accomplishments and limits resulted in the authorization of the second phase of international Lutheran-Roman Catholic dialogue. This phase produced two texts dealing with special anniversaries: *All Under One Christ* in 1980 on the 450th anniversary of the Lutheran confessional document, the *Augsburg Confession*, and *Martin Luther – Witness to Jesus Christ* on the 500th anniversary of Luther's birth in 1983. This phase of the dialogue also published texts dealing with doctrinal issues in dispute between Lutheran and Roman Catholics: *The Eucharist* in 1978; and *The Ministry in the Church* in 1981. The first text concluded that differences over presence and sacrifice in the Lord's Supper should no longer be regarded as church-dividing. The second document affirmed an agreement that "the existence of a special ministry is abidingly constitutive of the church,"[7] and a high degree of agreement has been reached on ministry, which raise the question of mutual recognition as part of a process in which the churches reciprocally accept each other.

The second phase concluded its work by releasing two further texts that described what a process of mutual acceptance would look like. These are *Ways to Community* in 1980 and *Facing Unity* in 1985. All these publications received no official response from the churches.

The third phase of the international dialogue issued a lengthy text on the subject *Church and Justification* in 1993.[8] This document is the result of seven years of dialogue work. *Church and Justification* sets forth certain basic convictions that Lutherans and Roman Catholics share about justification and the Church in such a way that excludes a fundamental conflict or opposition between the Church and justification. Thus the dialogue was probing the perceived consensus on justification by looking at its implications for ecclesiology. The dialogue in this report declared that it was quite compatible with the role of justification to see that all the Church's institutions contribute to the Church's abiding truth in the gospel which alone creates and sustains the Church.[9]

It is this history and collection of dialogue texts that form the context for the international dialogue's most recent publication, *Apostolicity of the Church*.

2. *The Apostolicity of the Church*: Its History and Contents

The Apostolicity of the Church represents the work of the fourth phase of Lutheran-Roman Catholic dialogue on the international level, from 1995 to 2006. As its introduction makes clear, although the mandate of the dialogue was wider, the participants in the conversations made the decision to concentrate on apostolicity in view of its complexity and importance ecumenically. This dialogue text is to be viewed as a further step along the process begun in 1972 with *The Gospel and the Church*.

Yet two particular features stand out in the introductory material to *Apostolicity of the Church*. First, it is self-described as a "study document of the Lutheran-Roman Catholic Commission on Unity." This specific term had not been used with earlier publications from this dialogue. The three preceding dialogue reports, *The Ministry in the Church*, *Facing Unity*, and *Church and Justification*, are not identified as "study documents."[10] The new nomenclature does raise the question of whether this text is to be viewed in a lower status than other reports coming from this dialogue. *Apostolicity of the Church* itself does not speak to this question. The rationale for the use of this new description should have been given, especially since it carries the implication that *Apostolicity of the Church* could be less significant than earlier texts.

This question takes on an added complexity when *Growing Together in Unity and Mission* from the International Anglican-Roman Catholic Commission for Unity and Mission is considered.[11] This text is described as "an agreed statement." Still, *Growing Together in Unity and Mission* itself makes clear that because of internal developments within the Anglican Communion, the present time is not appropriate for Anglicans and Roman Catholics to enter a new formal stage of relations.[12] The question presents itself: why is *Apostolicity of the Church* a "study document" and why is *Growing Together in Unity and Mission* an "agreed statement"? Perhaps both texts provide evidence for the need for some standardisation of ecumenical terminology about such reports.

Second, the introduction of *Apostolicity of the Church*, although signed by the two chairpersons, but presumably with the endorsement of the participants of the commission, is less urgent in its call for the churches to respond and receive this text. On one hand, the introduction speaks of reports and analyses of *Apostolicity of the Church*'s contribution towards hastening the recognition of greater communion between the Catholic and Lutheran churches of the world. On the other hand, the foreword of *Church and Justification* asks whether this text along with the other earlier documents from the dialogue does not constitute the sufficient consensus that would allow the churches to embark upon concrete steps towards visible unity.[13] The tone seems quite different between the two documents at this point.

These two factors could suggest that the ultimate goal of this dialogue as visible unity between the Roman Catholic Church and the Lutheran Communion is less urgent than it once was in some circles. If this interpretation is accurate, it is regrettable.

The members of the dialogue recognize that during the period of their work a major ecumenical achievement occurred with the production and the signing of the *Joint Declaration on the Doctrine of Justification*. It will become apparent in the course of this essay how the *Joint Declaration* and its methodology were contributing factors of major proportions in the creation of the *Apostolicity of the Church* itself.

Apostolicity of the Church exists in both English and German texts. Both stand on the same level of authority. For this essay, the English edition of *Apostolicity of the Church* has been used. The introduction makes clear that there are two critical limits in its contents: *Apostolicity of the Church* does not address the ordination of women to the pastoral office or episcopal office, nor does it in a comprehensive way offer an ecumenical examination of the papacy.

As dialogue texts go, *Apostolicity of the Church* is a long document of some 200 pages. In light of the formidability of its subject and the importance of agreement about it for ecumenical progress, a text of this size is not unexpected. *Apostolicity of the Church* is divided into four major sections after a short introduction. These divisions deal with the following aspects of the general topic of apostolicity: The Apostolicity of the Church – New Testament Foundations; The Apostolic Gospel and the Apostolicity of the Church; Apostolic Succession and Ordained Ministry; and Church Teaching that Remains in the Truth.

2.1 The Apostolicity of the Church – New Testament Foundations (nos. 1-64)

Apostolicity of the Church acknowledges the critical nature of its first section on the New Testament for all of its work. It declares that its desire is to avoid proof-texting and to allow the writings of the New Testament in all of their complexity on this subject to speak for themselves. In this portion of text, some twenty pages are devoted to an examination of the New Testament witness to the apostles and their mission on behalf of the gospel of Jesus Christ. The diversity of the books of the New Testament is acknowledged as is the difference of interpretation of these texts. Yet *Apostolicity of the Church* is clear that Lutherans and Roman Catholics share the conviction that Scripture is normative for both of them. The New Testament is fundamental as a witness to the Word of God; it is an invitation to examine critically the dogmatic tradition. Attention is given to the mission of the Twelve during Christ's earthly ministry, the commission of the risen Christ, and the promise of the Spirit. It is the Spirit who unites the Church for its mission. A long section stresses the diverse witness of the New Testament regarding the apostolicity of the Church and the apostles.

The topic of ecclesial structures and patterns of ministry is taken up. *Apostolicity of the Church* speaks of the emergence of a threefold order in the Church in the context of the early church's diversity. It sees the influential role of the Pastoral Letters in this regard. Finally, the New Testament section speaks of the living Tradition of the Church and its desire to remain faithful to the apostolic witness. It sees the eventual canon of the Bible as the normative exposition of this concern. The conclusion of this first part is: "No human authority is able to guarantee the truth of the gospel... On the other hand, however, the faithfulness of the church requires certain forms of traditioning and a particular ecclesial ministry of proclamation, reconciliation, and teaching in order to ensure the orderly transmission of the apostolic teachings."[14]

The pages of *Apostolicity of the Church* describing the New Testament witness contain no footnotes. They seek to have the New Testament speak for itself. Yet the overall view presented is one in harmony with contemporary biblical scholarship, especially in recognition of the diversity of New Testament witnesses and the unfolding of a structured life of the Church. This material is also in agreement with other ecumenical texts on ministry. This is certainly true when *Apostolicity of the Church* and *Baptism, Eucharist and Ministry* are compared.[15]

2.2 *The Apostolic Gospel and* The Apostolicity of the Church *(nos. 65-174)*

Apostolicity of the Church in its second part deals with the apostolic gospel and the apostolicity of the Church. This portion of the text addresses two questions: What makes the Church apostolic; and what are the resources of the Lutheran and Roman Catholic churches to acknowledge in dialogue their apostolic character as partner churches that are not in full communion? It builds on its work in the first section to offer material on biblical orientation to speak of the apostolic gospel and the apostolicity of the Church. Then this section offers an historical overview of how the apostles and the Church were treated in early and medieval interpretations. Here *Apostolicity of the Church* covers the special apostolicity of the Church of Rome, and how apostolicity is portrayed in the lifestyle, art, and liturgy of these historical periods. Apostolicity and the Church are reviewed in the Lutheran Reformation and in the developments within the Roman Catholic Church at Trent and later, including the twentieth century and the Second Vatican Council. A renewed understanding of Tradition in Catholic theology is pictured along with its ecumenical import and implications. A parallel sub-section offers an ecumenical Lutheran understanding of apostolicity of the Church. This understanding includes an appreciation of diversity and of a differentiated consensus.[16]

This second part of *Apostolicity of the Church* concludes by describing three areas: 1) foundational convictions about ecclesial apostolicity that Lutherans and Roman Catholics share. Here the *Joint Declaration* is a critical resource; 2) shared understandings about apostolicity and the Church, which this dialogue has discovered. These common understandings include the centrality of the gospel and an agreement on a manifold and many-faceted apostolic legacy; 3) differences that require deeper examination to achieve reconciliation or to clarify if they still have a church-dividing character.

2.3 Apostolic Succession and Ordained Ministry (nos. 165-293)

Part Three addresses such themes as the role of witness for testimony, and the place of institutions and structures. Ministry in its doctrinal and institutional aspects is seen as being of great significance for the apostolicity of the Church. Two critical questions are identified: Can the one office of ministry manifest itself in different structures? And what belongs to the substance of ministry and what belongs to structures, which within limits are variable? A sub-section takes up biblical orientation, stressing diversity, the universal priesthood, special ministry, and issues of succession. Then an historical review follows on ordained ministry in the early church and in the Middle Ages. This survey is followed by a discussion of ordained ministry in the Lutheran Reformation and at the Council of Trent. Attention is given to the problem of the episcopate and the tension of being faithful to the gospel and to transmission of the office in traditional forms. It is pointed out that Trent's concern was to preserve traditional teaching on ministry; it did not present a total and coherent ecclesiology. The historical material concludes with an examination of ordained ministry according to the Second Vatican Council and in contemporary Lutheran teaching.

This major section of *Apostolicity of the Church* ends by describing both agreements and differences between Lutherans and Roman Catholics on these two topics. It notes that there is an asymmetry in the situation. Lutherans recognize the Roman Catholic Church as apostolic; the converse is not presently true. But both Lutherans and Roman Catholics agree that the Church is apostolic. They further acknowledge together that Christ gives himself to humans in word and sacrament. They agree there is a universal priesthood of all believers and an ordained ministry, instituted by God, with specific functions. Lutherans and Roman Catholics also are of one voice in the recognition that induction into this special ministry is by ordination.

Yet Lutherans and Roman Catholics differ about a number of aspects of ordained ministry. Roman Catholics hold a view that the threefold hierarchy of ordained ministry is by divine institution; Lutherans do not. There is a difference over what makes a person a rightful holder of a regional ministry, and there are differing views about the local church and its relation to the universal Church. *Apostolicity of the Church* speaks of the Catholic view of *defectus* in Lutheran ministry.

In the light of these differences, *Apostolicity of the Church* offers an ecumenical perspective. It builds this perspective on the *Joint Declaration*. *Apostolicity of the Church* states that for apostolic succession, succession in faith is an essential aspect. It continues that the signing of the *Joint Declaration* implied the acknowledgement that ordained ministry in both churches has by the power of the Holy Spirit fulfilled its service of maintaining fidelity to the apostolic gospel. It notes that in history the relation between offices of priest and bishop has been defined in different ways, and ministries have undergone structural changes. Again basing its argument on the *Joint Declaration*, *Apostolicity of the Church* declares that there are many individuals in Christendom who exercise an office of supervision which in the Roman Catholic Church is undertaken by bishops. These persons bear special responsibility for the apostolicity in their churches, and the Roman Catholic Church recognizes this in the *Joint Declaration*.

Therefore *Apostolicity of the Church* asks the question of whether a differentiated consensus is not possible for Lutherans and Roman Catholics in the doctrine of ministry or ministries.[17] It notes that such a differentiated consensus could appeal to the various agreements on ministry in *Apostolicity of the Church*. This approach would follow the path taken by the *Joint Declaration*. It would recognize the possibility of differing structures of ministry, which would not be church-dividing because they would realize and serve the same fundamental intention of ministerial office. *Apostolicity of the Church* acknowledges such a step would be a risk taken while trusting in the support of the Holy Spirit.[18]

2.4 Church Teaching That Remains in the Truth (nos. 294-460)

The last major section of *Apostolicity of the Church* follows a pattern that has been observable in the previous three divisions of the work. In the setting of agreement on the gospel that makes the Church apostolic and the fundamental role of the ordained ministry of word and sacrament, this fourth part is centred on how the church remains in the truth revealed in the gospel of Jesus Christ. It notes that since the Reformation, and especially the First Vatican Council, there have been differences in the structure of ministries and how these ministries function in relation to Scripture between Lutherans and Roman Catholics. A sub-section deals with the New Testament orientation to the truth of doctrine, teaching ministries and the resolving of doctrinal conflicts. The conviction of *Apostolicity of the Church* is that Scripture bears witness to the truth of the gospel and also gives an account of disputes over the gospel. Such conflicts must be settled on the basis that all teaching must serve the truth of the gospel. In this regard, the canon of Scripture has a function to exercise. This fourth part discusses doctrine and truth in early and medieval developments. Here it gives attention to the function of the rule of faith and the creeds, and to the significance of the councils of the first eight centuries. It mentions the various approaches to interpreting Scripture in the early and medieval churches. Detailed attention is provided on how in accord with the Lutheran Reformation the Church was maintained in truth, including the place and function of the Lutheran Confessions in this task.

Then the fourth portion of the text turns to Catholic doctrine about the biblical canon, interpretation of Scripture, and the teaching office, including Catholic biblical interpretation from the Council of Trent to the Second Vatican Council. When the Catholic doctrine about the teaching office is presented, *Apostolicity of the Church* points out several areas of Lutheran-Roman Catholic agreement. They agree that correct doctrine is essential in shaping a right relation of faith with God and Christ's saving work. There is also agreement on the importance of a ministry of regional oversight of teaching. Lutherans and Roman Catholics are of one mind that it is the Holy Spirit who effectively maintains the Church in the truth of the gospel and in the correct celebration of the sacraments.[19]

The final pages of this section offer conclusions to be drawn from the dialogue's work. It states that the dialogue's intention is to contribute to bringing about full communion between the Catholic Church and the Lutheran churches of the world. Here *Apostolicity of the Church* presents its results in two steps. First, there are three foundational convictions that are held in common. The report declares this is an area of full communion. Second, there are three topics where a differentiated consensus has been discovered so that on these issues the remaining differences are not church-dividing. The report indicates this is an area of reconciled diversity.

In regard to the foundational convictions, they are the following. First, Lutherans and Roman Catholics fully agree that God has issued in human history a message of grace and truth, by word and deed. The *Joint Declaration* is referred to in this common affirmation. This is the gospel of God's grace in Christ. Second, Lutherans and Roman Catholics fully agree that God's revelation of himself in Jesus Christ for human salvation continues to be announced in the gospel that the first apostles preached and taught and that the church of every age stands under the imperative to preserve God's word in continuous succession. Third, Lutherans and Roman Catholics agree that the Scriptures are the source, rule, guideline, and criterion of correctness and purity of the Church's proclamation, of its doctrine, and of its sacramental and pastoral practice.

The area of reconciled diversity includes the topics of the canon of Scripture and the Church, Scripture and Tradition, and the necessity and context of the teaching office in the Church. In regard to canon and Church, *Apostolicity of the Church* states that Lutherans and Roman Catholics are in such an extensive agreement on the source of the Bible's canonical authority that their remaining differences over the extent of the canon are not of such weight to justify continued ecclesial division. Likewise, Lutherans and Catholics are in such extensive agreement regarding Scripture and tradition that their different emphases do not of themselves require maintaining the present division of the churches. Finally, concerning the necessity and context of the teaching office, Lutherans and Roman Catholics agree in spite of their different configurations of teaching ministries that the Church must designate members to serve the transmission of the gospel. Therefore, the teaching office, or ministry, is a necessary entity by which the Church is preserved in the truth of the gospel according to Lutherans and Roman Catholics.

3. *Apostolicity of the Church*: Its Methodology

There are three aspects of the methodology employed by *Apostolicity of the Church* that deserve special attention. They are the use of Scripture, of the *Joint Declaration*, and of the concept of differentiated consensus.

3.1 *The Use of Scripture in* The Apostolicity of the Church

The use of Scripture in *Apostolicity of the Church* is conspicuous. Approximately one-quarter of the entire text is devoted to New Testament foundations or biblical orientation. Scripture is prominent and a controlling element in all four major divisions of the text. The document seeks to build on a common biblical basis shared by Lutherans and Roman Catholics to find an approach to move beyond the sixteenth century and later disputes. The novelty of this method becomes apparent when other reports from this dialogue are considered. *The Gospel and the Church* contains neither a scriptural section nor scriptural references in the text. *The Eucharist* has a section on Scripture, and references to Scripture in the text and in footnotes. *Ministry in the Church* refers to Scripture in certain parts of the text. *Church and Justification* has no initial section setting forth a scriptural foundation, though references to Scripture run through the text. They tend to cluster in certain parts of the text, chapters 1 and 2, and a specific portion of chapter 5.

Similarly, the three documents, *Ways to Community, Facing Unity,* and *All Under One Christ* have relatively few scriptural references. In these three cases, the particular subject matter may well not lend itself to copious quotations from the Bible.[20] Nevertheless, the general impression gained from these dialogue reports is that Scripture is often employed in a proof-texting manner.

Admittedly the use of Scripture in ecumenical texts is a complex subject.[21] *Apostolicity of the Church* by its explicit comment in the introduction and in the body of its report is seeking a different procedure: "The investigation of the New Testament witness to the apostles and their mission on behalf of the gospel of Jesus Christ contributes extensive and important results to our document."[22] This methodology is quite similar to that utilized by the *Joint Declaration,* and may be another indication of the direct influence of that text on *Apostolicity of the Church*.[23] It is an approach that should be welcomed in future ecumenical texts.

3.2 *The Use of the Joint Declaration on the Doctrine of Justification in* The Apostolicity of the Church

The *Joint Declaration on the Doctrine of Justification* was signed during the course of the work of this fourth phase of Lutheran-Roman Catholic dialogue. The participants in the dialogue recognized the notable weight and authority possessed by the *Joint Declaration* as a result of this signing. The *Joint Declaration* is referred to and quoted on numerous occasions in *Apostolicity of the Church*.[24] The implications of the *Joint Declaration* for other areas of agreement in addition to justification are expressed.[25]

This use of the *Joint Declaration* is one example of its ecumenical reception by participants in an official dialogue. This practice should encourage official and practical reception of the *Joint Declaration* in both churches. As the churches begin to struggle with the question of an initial response to *Apostolicity of the Church,* they will have the opportunity to acknowledge their ongoing reception or non-reception of the *Joint Declaration*.[26]

The fact that *Apostolicity of the Church* draws out further implications of the *Joint Declaration* for ministry and maintaining the Church in truth will challenge both churches to reflect on the wider significance of the *Joint Declaration* for agreement in other areas. Until now this is a largely unknown topic, and immediate consensus on the larger connotations of the *Joint Declaration* should not be assumed. The acceptance and signing of the *Joint Declaration* placed both the Lutheran and Roman Catholic churches in a new situation which will require further exploration.

3.3 *The Use of "Differentiated Consensus" in the Joint Declaration on the Doctrine of Justification and in* The Apostolicity of the Church

An examination of dialogue reports on various levels has recently offered clear evidence that the dialogues have created a definite way of working, which was neither foreseen nor developed in advance. This method is now generally denoted by the term "differentiated consensus."[27] Its chief characteristic is the recognition of a double structure. This approach is viewed in terms of two levels: there is a first or fundamental level; this is a level of consensus. Here there is real and essential agreement that is neither a general, loose agreement nor a compromise. Yet in addition, there is a second level. Here there are remaining differences. These differences are also real and essential. But the critical point is that these differences do not challenge the agreement or consensus on the first level. This schema provides for unity and diversity. It does not require the churches in dialogue either to convert to one or the other or to achieve a synthesis of their differing positions.

It is precisely and explicitly this methodology of differentiated consensus that made the *Joint Declaration on the Doctrine of Justification* possible.[28] The *Joint Declaration* was not the first dialogue report to employ this method, but the signing on the highest level of appropriate authority of the *Joint Declaration* moved differentiated consensus in Lutheran-Roman Catholic relations out of the realm of theory and into the areas of practice and acceptance.

Therefore, it is extremely significant that *Apostolicity of the Church* in reaching its areas of agreement between Lutherans and Roman Catholics on apostolicity utilized differentiated consensus. *Apostolicity of the Church*'s use of differentiated consensus is extensive. It employs the concept to explicate the Roman Catholic application of "apostolic" to other churches.[29] It affirms reconciled diversity between churches that can only be recognized on the basis of differentiated consensus.[30] In several sections, when dealing with the "apostolic gospel and apostolicity of the church," *Apostolicity of the Church* names differentiated consensus and approves its use.[31] It concludes this major section by claiming that there is a fundamental agreement between Catholics and Lutherans on apostolicity and that the remaining differences do not call into question that agreement. The term "differentiated consensus" does not appear, but the idea is obviously expressed and affirmed.[32] In the section on "apostolic succession and ordained ministry," *Apostolicity of the Church* offers a list of fundamental agreements between Lutherans and Roman Catholics. Its language is similar to the *Joint Declaration*, where the expression "we confess together" is used, and in *Apostolicity of the Church* "Together, Catholics and Lutherans affirm." Then the differences are given. The conclusion is that this combination of agreements and differences can be described as differentiated consensus.[33] In the section of *Apostolicity of the Church* on "church teaching that remains in the truth," agreement on the basis of differentiated consensus is reached in regard to ministry and the teaching office, the canon of Scripture, and the relation of Scripture and tradition.[34]

This use of differentiated consensus in *Apostolicity of the Church* is a further example in Lutheran-Roman Catholic dialogue of the validity and acceptance of the methodology and concept. It offers evidence that ecumenical reception between Lutherans and Roman Catholics – the process by which a church under the guidance of God's Spirit makes the results of a bilateral or multilateral conversation a part of its faith and life, and thus moves to greater visible unity with another church – will be possible by means of differentiated consensus.[35] Thus the implications of *Apostolicity of the Church* for ecumenical reception can only be unmistakable – with one stipulation; the sponsoring churches must take seriously the document's challenge and opportunity.

If this insight is accurate, the implications for ecumenical reception are enhanced by the outstanding work accomplished by *Apostolicity of the Church*. This should be a development much in harmony with the commitments and life work of Monsignor Radano.

---

1   This essay previously appeared in *Celebrating a Century of Ecumenism: Exploring the Achievements of International Dialogue*, ed. John A. Radano (Grand Rapids: Eerdmans, 2012). Reprinted by permission of the publisher; all rights reserved.

2   Published in English as *Joint Declaration on the Doctrine of Justification* (Grand Rapids: Eerdmans, 2000); also *Information Service* 103 (2000): 3-35, in *Origins* 28 no. 8 (July, 1998): 120-127 and *Origins* 29 no. 6 (July, 1999): 85-87, *One in Christ* 36, no. 1 (2000): 56-74, and GA II, pp. 566-82. The official German text of the *Joint Declaration*, the *Official Common Statement* and the Annex can be found in *Gemeinsame Erklärung zur Rechtfertigungslehre: Gemeinsame offizielle Feststellung, Anhang (Annex) zur Gemeinsamen Feststellung* (Frankfurt am Main: Verlag Otto Lembeck; Paderborn: Bonifatius Verlag, 1999). Studies that contributed to the production of the *Joint Declaration* included among others, H. G. Anderson, T. Austin Murphy, and Joseph Burgess, eds., *Lutherans and Catholics in Dialogue VII: Justification by Faith* (Minneapolis: Augsburg, 1985); Karl Lehmann and Wolfhart Pannenberg, eds., *The Condemnations of the Reformation Era: Do They still Divide?* (Minneapolis: Fortress Press, 1990), especially pp. 1-69 [the original report appeared as *Lehrverurteilungen-kirchentrennend?* (Frieburg im Bresigau: Herder; Göttingen: Vandenhoeck & Ruprecht, 1986]); Pierre Duprey, "The Condemnations of the 16th Century on Justification: Do They Still Apply Today?" with response by Harding Meyer,

Occasional Papers Contributing to 1997 Decisions (Chicago: Department for Ecumenical Affairs, Evangelical Lutheran Church in America, 1995).

3 Lutheran-Roman Catholic Commission on Unity, *The Apostolicity of the Church: Study Document* (Paderborn: Bonifatius; Frankfurt am Main: Otto Lembeck, 2009); *Information Service* 128 (2008): 60-133; also at http://www.prounione.urbe.it.

4 On the topic on ecumenical reception see William G. Rusch, *Ecumenical Reception: Its Challenge and Opportunity* (Grand Rapids: Eerdmans, 2007).

5 For an overview of the international Lutheran-Roman Catholic dialogue, see *Dictionary of the Ecumenical Movement,* 2nd ed., s.v. "Lutheran-Roman Catholic Dialogue," by Michael Root.

6 The documents from the first and second phases of the dialogue appear in GA I, pp. 167-275 and GA II, pp. 438-84.

7 *The Ministry in the Church* (Geneva: Lutheran World Federation, 1982), n. 18, in GA I, p. 253.

8 *Church and Justification: Understanding the Church in the Light of the Doctrine of Justification* (Geneva: Lutheran World Federation, 1994), in GA II, pp. 485-565.

9 See Heinz-Albert Raem, "The Third Phase of Lutheran-Catholic Dialogue (1986-1993)," *One in Christ* 29 (1994): 310-27.

10 *The Ministry in the Church* is described as a statement, *Church and Justification* as a joint statement.

11 IARCCUM, *Growing Together in Unity and Mission: Building on 40 Years of Anglican-Roman Catholic Dialogue* (London: SPCK, 2007), in *Origins* 37, no. 19 (October 18, 2007): 289-307, *Information Service* 124 (2007): 44-66, and http://iarccum.org/doc/?d=32.

12 IARCCUM, *Growing Together in Unity and Mission,* no. 10.

13 *Church and Justification* in GA II, pp. 485-87.

14 *Apostolicity of the Church,* no. 64.

15 See for example, BEM, 'Ministry' nos. 20-32. At one point BEM states "The Church has never been without persons holding specific authority and responsibility." (Ministry, no. 21) *Apostolicity of the Church* indicates, "The church has never been without persons holding specific responsibilities and authority, and functions and tasks make sense only when persons carry them out" (no. 35).

16 On the precise meaning of this expression, see *Apostolicity of the Church,* nos. 138 and 3.3 below.

17 See 3.3 below.

18 See *Apostolicity of the Church,* especially nos. 292-93.

19 See *Apostolicity of the Church,* especially no. 412.

20 For all these dialogue reports, see the references in endnotes 6 and 8 above.

21 See for example the discussion in Matthias Haudel, *Die Bibel und die Einheit der Kirchen: Eine Untersuchung der Studien von Glauben und Kirchenverfassung* (Göttingen: Vandenhoeck & Ruprecht, 1993).

22 *Apostolicity of the Church,* "Introduction."

23 See *Joint Declaration,* "1. Biblical Message of Justification," nos. 8-12.

24 For example, see *Apostolicity of the Church,* nos. 142, 146-47, 167, 288, 293, 432.

25 For example, see *Apostolicity of the Church,* no. 288. Here it is stated "the signing of the *Joint Declaration* implies an acknowledgement that ordained ministry in *both* churches (italics mine) has by the power of the Holy Spirit fulfilled its service of maintaining fidelity to the apostolic gospel" in terms of justification. See also *Apostolicity of the Church,* no. 293, where it is argued

on the basis of the *Joint Declaration* an approach may be followed to recognize the possibility of differing structures of ministry which realize and serve the fundamental intention of the ministerial office.

26 See Rusch, *Ecumenical Reception*, pp. 77-80.

27 Fundamental for an understanding of differentiated consensus is Harding Meyer, "Die Prägung einer Formel: Ursprung und Intention" in Harold Wagner, ed., *Einheit – Aber Wie?: Zur Tragfähigkeit der ökumenischen Formel vom "differenzierten Konsens,"* Quaestiones Disputatae 184 (Freiburg: Herder Verlag, 2000), pp. 36-58. See also William G. Rusch, "Structures of Unity: The Next Ecumenical Challenge – A Possible Way Forward," *Ecclesiology* 2, no. 1 (September 2005): 107-22 and in *Ecumenical Trends* 34, no. 9 (October 2005): 2-8; Rusch, *Ecumenical Reception*, pp. 118-30.

28 See, for example, *Joint Declaration*, 17, 18, 19, 20, 22, 23, and 24. See also Rusch, *Ecumenical Reception*, pp. 123-25.

29 *Apostolicity of the Church*, no. 122.

30 *Apostolicity of the Church*, no. 135.

31 *Apostolicity of the Church*, nos. 136-38, 142; nos. 146-47, 149, 150. The last two paragraphs especially mention fundamental agreement between Lutherans and Roman Catholics.

32 *Apostolicity of the Church*, no. 160.

33 The agreements are given in *Apostolicity of the Church*, nos. 271-75; the differences at nos. 281-92; the differentiated consensus is articulated at no. 293.

34 *Apostolicity of the Church*, nos. 412-13, 441, 448.

35 See Rusch, *Ecumenical Reception*, p. 61.

✝ CHAPTER 7

Teaching Authority: Catholics, Disciples of Christ, and Lutherans[1]

by Margaret O'Gara

For over a quarter of a century, John Radano has been a faithful witness to the commitment of the Catholic Church to ecumenical dialogue. His perseverance in this work at the Pontifical Council for Promoting Christian Unity has helped the ecumenical movement take several significant steps. The involvement of the Catholic Church in the ecumenical movement since the Second Vatican Council has been an important development, and few people have been at the centre of the centre of this development for as long as John Radano. So it is a privilege to recognize his contribution by adding to this volume in his honour.

I want to focus on two international commissions for dialogue on which I have served during many of the years of John Radano's presence at the Pontifical Council: the Disciples of Christ-Roman Catholic International Commission for Dialogue and the Lutheran-Roman Catholic International Commission on Unity. His support for dialogue commissions has always been important for their welfare, and therefore the achievements made by these two can in some sense be credited to him.

Each of these dialogues did a great deal of its work on the topic of ordained ministry. Each contributes in important ways to the development in our understanding of ordination and apostolic succession, a widespread development within the ecumenical movement during the three decades since the publication of *Baptism, Eucharist and Ministry* in 1982. It would be possible to highlight this work and show its vital link to the wider discussion. However, I have chosen to highlight another theme that also threads its way through the work of these dialogues, a theme that has not yet been addressed as fully. That theme is the teaching authority that serves the Gospel and allows the church to remain in the truth.

The latter theme is a fundamental one, and each of the two dialogues makes a distinctive contribution to our current understanding of it. Moreover, studying the two contributions together reveals a shared pattern of thought that future investigations of teaching authority might fruitfully pursue. That is to say, in a small way this study both validates and participates in the much broader project of "harvesting the fruits" that Cardinal Walter Kasper has initiated and exhorted other ecumenists to extend – a thematic investigation of agreed statements made by all the ecumenical dialogues since the Second Vatican Council.[2]

I. Two Agreed Statements of the Disciples of Christ-Roman Catholic International Commission for Dialogue

1.1 From the Second Phase of the Dialogue (1983-1992)

The second phase of the Disciples of Christ-Roman Catholic International Commission for Dialogue began in 1983 and was completed in 1992 with the publication of *The Church as Communion in Christ*.[3] While the statement considered the eucharist as well as teaching authority, here I focus mainly on the latter.

As the statement notes, the dialogue between Disciples and Catholics has a specific character among dialogue commissions. Because Disciples of Christ participate in what the statement calls a "protestant ethos," they share such Protestant emphases as the proclamation of the Word, the binding of conscience by individual judgment, and personal appropriation of the Word of God (no. 6). Yet, because the Disciples movement actually emerged as a break from Protestant churches in the nineteenth century, "it had nothing to do with a deliberate break from the Roman Catholic Church and lacked the memories of sixteenth and seventeenth-century controversies" (no. 8). And Disciples broke from the Presbyterian tradition precisely over their commitment to the centrality of the eucharist in the church's life and to the unity among Christians which it symbolized and effected. Hence their distinctive history has much in common with that of the Roman Catholic Church, which also "proclaims that it has a specific mission for the unity of the world, and affirms that this unity is signified and given by the eucharistic communion," and "teaches that the restoration of unity among all Christians is linked with the salvation of the world" (no. 8). So Disciples and Roman Catholics in our dialogue set out to explore "whether all of these affirmations and convictions are not in fact the expression of a very profound communion in some of the most fundamental gifts of the grace of God" (no. 8).

On the question of teaching authority, it seemed at first that differences between the two church traditions were irreconcilable. While Roman Catholics see the church "throughout its history as continuous with the teaching of the apostles," Disciples have the conviction that "some discontinuities in the life of the Church have been necessary for the sake of the Gospel" (no. 11). In fact, the Disciples emerged from the Presbyterian Church as a reform movement that underlined the need for such discontinuity precisely for the sake of the centrality of the eucharist and the unity of the church. This also made Disciples "distrustful of many of the creeds, confessions and doctrinal teachings" of the Christian tradition, "finding in the way they have been used a threat to unity," whereas Roman Catholics find creeds and doctrinal definitions as a "sign of the assistance of the Holy Spirit to bind the Church into one and to lead it into all truth" (no. 11). Both desire to be faithful to the apostolic church of the New Testament, but this has led Disciples to be distrustful of the structure of episcopal authority, while Roman Catholics have found it "a necessary means for maintaining continuity with the apostles and with their teaching" (no. 11). In addition, Disciples found that they are "readily critical of some developments in the history of the Church," finding sin and error among these developments, while Roman Catholics approach such teachings with more appreciative eyes, slow to find sin and error there and "quick to see continuity with the apostolic teaching" (no. 15).

We summarized our findings on differences with a contrast: "Roman Catholics are convinced that, although they must decide for themselves, they cannot decide by themselves. Disciples, on the other hand, are convinced that, although they cannot decide by themselves, they must decide for themselves" (no. 16). At first, the notion that such differences between Disciples and Catholics could be overcome seemed "nearly incredible" (no. 17).

Despite these differences, we found real convergence about teaching authority in the church. With our strong conviction that the eucharist brings us into communion with God and with other members of the body of Christ and gives us a foretaste "of what will come in fullness through the Spirit at the end of time" (no. 24), we realize as well, members report, that the church must "live in the memory of its origin, remembering with thanksgiving what God has done in Christ Jesus" (no. 25). Living in this memory means, for both church traditions, being in continuity with the witness of the apostolic generation. "The New Testament speaks of those called apostles in the earliest period in a variety of ways; and they played a unique and essential role in formulating and communicating the Gospel. The Church is founded on their proclamation" (no. 26). We could affirm that we each "share an intention to live and teach in such a way that, when the Lord comes again, the Church may be found witnessing to the faith of the apostles" (no. 27). Both Disciples and Roman Catholics believe that they maintain continuity with the apostolic witness by preserving the memory of the apostolic teaching and by proclaiming and living it anew (no. 27). Such remembering, proclaiming, and witnessing is made possible by the Holy Spirit, who acts especially in the eucharist to make Christ present. So the commitment of the two traditions to live in the memory of the apostolic teaching is highlighted by their central emphasis on the frequent celebration of the eucharist, where "the essential elements of Christian faith and life are expressed" (no. 30).

Disciples and Roman Catholics both intend to remain in continuity with the apostles and they "understand what this demands in different ways" (no. 33). We explored together the ways such continuity has been maintained by each and also the possibility of receiving new enriching gifts from the other tradition. A striking agreement was noted on the Scriptures and the tradition of the church.

Both receive the Scriptures as a normative witness to the apostolic faith. Both agree as well that the history of the Church after the writing and formation of the New Testament canon belongs to the Church's continuity in Apostolic Tradition, even though they have different emphases in understanding the significance of that history. Both find within this history many developments which, because they are the work of the Holy Spirit, are normative for the Church. Both affirm that the Gospel is embodied in the Tradition of the Church (no. 34).

Members noted that the two traditions are committed "in different ways" to continuity with the church's history when evaluating earlier formulations of doctrine. But they also agreed that such statements "never exhaust the meaning of the Word of God and that they may need interpretation or completion by further formulations" (no. 35) for clarity, and that fresh doctrinal statements may actually sometimes be needed to preserve the Gospel or proclaim it in new contexts.

Although agreeing that the pilgrim church is affected by both finitude and sin in its remembering of the Gospel, the members also were able to reach significant breakthroughs about God's assistance to the church in its teaching. They write, "But both Roman Catholics and Disciples are agreed that the Holy Spirit sustains the Church in communion with the apostolic community because Christ promised that the Spirit 'will teach you everything and remind you of all that I have said to you' (John 14:26)." They agree that "[t]he Spirit guides the Church to understand its past, to recall what may have been forgotten, and to discern what renewal is needed for the Gospel to be proclaimed effectively in every age and culture" (no. 36). The Holy Spirit helps the church adopt fresh understandings or practices precisely in order to maintain continuity with the apostolic tradition and to preach the Gospel in different contexts and circumstances (no. 37), and even to be given "a foretaste of [the] transformation" it will know fully in the future (no. 38). Through all of this, "the Holy Spirit guarantees that the Church shall not in the end fail to witness faithfully to the divine plan," members agree (no. 37). This is a striking convergence.

As Disciples and Roman Catholics consider the means by which the church is enabled to maintain continuity with apostolic tradition, they agree that individual members receive the gift of faith within and for the communion of the church (no. 40), and that the Spirit gives a variety of charisms to the church that enable it to maintain continuity. In addition to the charisms enabling the everyday living of the Gospel, there are the charisms of teaching by parents and others in Christian formation, of care for the poor and needy, as well as the charisms of especially vivid witness to the Gospel. Within the many complementary charisms given to the church, members agree that there is also "a particular charism given to the ordained ministry to maintain the community in the memory of the Apostolic Tradition." Such ordained ministry "exists to actualize, transmit, and interpret with fidelity the Apostolic Tradition" originating in the first generation and continuing to spread through space and time (no. 44).

Turning to the issue of the episcopacy, the members acknowledge that Disciples come from those traditions "which at the Reformation rejected episcopacy as the Reformers knew it in the Roman Catholic Church" (no. 45). They then give the following explanation:

> Disciples have always recognized that the work of the ministry, shared in the local congregation by ordained ministers and ordained elders, is essential to the being of the Church and is a sign of continuity with the Apostolic Tradition. Roman Catholics believe that the bishop, acting in collaboration with presbyters, deacons and the whole community in the local church, and in communion with the whole college of bishops throughout the world united with the Bishop of Rome as its head, keeps alive the apostolic faith in the local church so that it may remain faithful to the Gospel (no. 45).

While showing the differences between the two church communions, this explanation also shows their similarities and underlines their common purpose: continuity with the apostolic tradition. This point is made again when the statement notes both that the whole church shares in the priesthood and ministry of Christ, that the ordained ministers "have the specific charism of re-presenting Christ to the Church," and that "their ministries are expressions of the ministry of Christ to the whole Church" (no. 45). The whole church, shaped by the Gospel, enables it to hold fast to the "faith which was once for all delivered to the saints (Jude 3)"; and the ordained ministry "is specifically given the charism for discerning, declaring and fostering what lies in the authentic memory of the Church" (no. 45). In this process, members note, "this charism of the service of memory is in communion with the instinct for faith of the whole body"; and they conclude, "Through this communion the Spirit guides the Church" (no. 45).

By focusing only on one aspect of the statement's content – its discussion of teaching authority – I have in a certain sense distorted it. In fact, the perspectives on teaching authority that I have highlighted are embedded within the larger discussion that also shows the centrality of the eucharist in both traditions, where the faithful hear the Gospel proclaimed with authority by those ordained for this ministry, receive the body and blood of Christ, enter into communion with the saints, and are sustained for continuing the mission of the church. For each tradition, the communion in Christ which is the church "is realized especially in the celebration of the Eucharist" (no. 48). Nevertheless, focusing just on the remarkable amount of agreement about teaching authority makes it easy to see why we agreed "that our diversities are real but not all of them are necessarily signs of division" (no. 46).

1.2 From the Third Phase of the Dialogue (1993-2002)

The third phase of the Disciples of Christ-Roman Catholic International Commission for Dialogue began in 1993 and was completed in 2002 with the publication of the agreed statement, *Receiving and Handing on the Faith: the Mission and Responsibility of the Church*.[4] This statement built strongly on the agreement from the second phase, but it addressed a different question: how can the two church traditions succeed in handing on the Gospel? Disciples wondered whether the "more elaborate hierarchical structure" of the Roman Catholic Church with "an apparent emphasis on uniformity" could give "sufficient freedom of conscience" to people, while Roman Catholics wondered "how Disciples, with an apparent lack of structure and creedal formulations, have handed on the Gospel" (no. 1.4). From the outset, then, this statement addressed the question of teaching authority; but, unlike the previous statement with its emphasis on the eucharist, it emphasized the relationship of teaching authority and individual conscience.

The statement begins with the agreement that "the Church is essentially a missionary community" (no. 2.1) and that the proclamation of God's Word takes place as a "living tradition of scriptural interpretation and prayer" through which each Christian is linked to other Christians and to other generations of Christians who have preceded them (no. 2.4). The members repeat their conviction that "the Holy Spirit guides the Church, which because of this guidance will not finally fail in its task of proclaiming the Gospel" (no. 2.4).

Turning again to the recognition of "the need to hold on to the memory of the apostolic community about what God has done in Christ," the members explore their recognition that the canon of the Scriptures, councils of the church, and creeds were "developed as instruments to do this, under the guidance of the Holy Spirit (John 14:26)" (no. 3.1). They also consider the process that first led the church to discern "these instruments of faithfulness" and that continues "whenever the Church seeks to confess the Gospel with courage in the face of new situations and challenges" (no. 3.1).

Considering the canon of the Scriptures, the agreed statement focuses on the procedure by which this canon was set. "The intention of the canon is to indicate where the heart of Christian faith is authentically to be found" (no. 3.5); in the books of the Scripture, "the Church recognized the authentic Word of God in its written form inspired by the Holy Spirit" (no. 3.2). Disciples and Roman Catholics understand that the setting of the canon "was at the same time an act of obedience and of authority" (no. 3.6) and they recognize the close relation between the canon and the unity of the church. "Because it is held in common by Christians, the Bible holds Christians together with one another as they read and proclaim the same Word of God received from the Church of the apostles" (no. 3.10).

Perhaps the agreements in the next section, on councils and declarations of the faith, are a more surprising section of the statement. While Roman Catholics turn more readily to the patristic period of the church's history than do Disciples, we discovered that "Disciples for their part have received the major teachings of the patristic period without necessarily always using its texts explicitly" (no. 3.11). When considering the authority of the first seven ecumenical councils, members found "more agreement" than previously recognized, since both Disciples and Roman Catholics "recognize the first seven councils as authentic gatherings of the Church able to speak in the name of the whole Church" (no. 3.13). In probing the reasons for this recognition, the statement notes that councils remained conscious that they were under the Gospel and that Christ was in their midst as they articulated and defined the mystery of the triune God revealed in Christ. Furthermore, the councils of bishops, seen as succeeding the apostolic community, wished to serve the Scriptures; their definitions "clarified and made explicit the main affirmations of the Scriptures" (no. 3.13). After the councils ended, all local churches were drawn into their decisions through reception (no. 3.13).

Roman Catholics "believe that their life continues to be shaped by the work of the seven ecumenical councils" and that later councils can define doctrine as divinely revealed (no. 14). While the situation is not the same for Disciples, still "the Disciples tradition has never held the theological positions condemned by the early ecumenical councils," which Disciples regard as part of God's providential ordering of the church on the path of the Gospel (no. 3.15). Members write, "To the extent that they have accepted the decisions of those councils, Disciples have acknowledged their authority" (no. 3.15). Certainly, early Disciples were critical of confessions of faith used as tests of fellowship at the Communion Table during the nineteen centuries. The main targets of their criticism were not the Apostles' or Nicene Creeds, but Reformation and post-Reformation confessions such as the *Westminster Confession* and the *Secession Testimony* (no. 3.16). So Disciples have preferred New Testament confessions of faith, and "they emphasize the dependence of conciliar creeds on the New Testament" (no. 3.16). But today both Disciples and Roman Catholics "draw on the central teachings of the first seven councils when judging new ideas or practices" without necessarily affirming the "world view or conceptual structure" of their formulations (no. 3.17). For clarity may require that some formulations be redone at a later time. In fact, members agree that councils "demonstrate that sometimes the Church finds such restatement necessary precisely in order to remain in continuity with the faith it has received" (no. 3.17).

This consideration brings members to reflect on the process of the discernment of the Gospel in history, a process that takes place over time (no. 3.22) and as the fruit of the presence of the *sensus fidei* [the sense of the faith] in all of the faithful (no. 3.24). A process of mutual reception takes place which is the result of all of the charisms given to the members of the church. "To be authentic, ecclesial agreement in matters of faith will include ordained ministers with responsibility for teaching in the Church, scholars working within the community of faith, and the body of the faithful who receive and celebrate this consensus in their worship and witness," the statement observes (no. 3.24). Disciples and Roman Catholics recognize that an immediate discernment of some questions is impossible because of the time needed for reception by the whole community; they "are not unanimous on the ways in which reception is achieved, but they agree on its necessity" (no. 3.26).

With this set of agreements about the process of the formation of the Scriptures, about councils and declarations of faith, and about the process of discerning the Gospel in every age, the statement now turns to the difficult question of the individual within the community of the church. With different emphases, Disciples and Roman Catholics both agree that "obedience to the Word of God has priority" (no. 4.1). Furthermore, they agree that persons must obey their conscience, understood at the first level as the voice of God present within each human being (no. 4.4); and that they must also shape their conscience, understood at the second level as a reasoned response to God's revelation (no. 4.5). "It is their responsibility to form a conscience which is open to what God is saying," members agreed. "Nothing can oblige them to act against their perception of the will of God" (no. 4.5).

While the church has a duty to teach the Gospel, sometimes Christians disagree with church teaching of their day because of obedience to the Word of God as they discern it. Given that Disciples' memory has been shaped by their origins, when "their leaders were unwilling to accept the restrictions which Presbyterians placed on access to the Lord's Table," their "attitude toward the issue of disagreement with prevailing views" has also been affected. Roman Catholics have "no similar dominant memory" and place their "strong emphasis on unity" (no. 4.6). Despite these differences of memory and emphasis, members recognize "two important agreements." They explain, "Disciples and Roman Catholics both recognize that commitment to the Gospel should be freely made. They also recognize that living the Christian life is a continuous process of receiving and living by the teaching handed on in the Church and making personal decisions which are themselves shaped by life in communion with other believers" (no. 4.8).

In the next section, the members explore the question of teaching with authority. Both agree that "discernment of the authentic meaning of the revealed Word belongs to the whole community." And both agree that ordained ministers "are called and empowered by the Spirit to teach the Word of God. These are the pastors" (no. 4.9). But Disciples and Roman Catholics "locate and describe the exercise of ministerial authority in different ways." In the Roman Catholic Church, the bishops in communion with the bishop of Rome are responsible for the ordinary teaching of the church, serving to inform the faithful and "also to form their consciences so that they may take responsible decisions" (no. 4.12). The Roman Catholic Church, through its teaching office, today articulates "an increasingly large number of positions on new challenges or questions" (no. 4.12); and the bishops "can at times make decisions binding on the conscience of Roman Catholics" (no. 4.16). For Disciples, teaching is "the function of theologically educated, ordained ministers" who teach in consultation with their colleagues nationally and internationally (no. 4.11). "Disciples are more reluctant than Roman Catholics to provide official teaching on a wide range of matters. They often do not seek to articulate an official position when a question is under debate" (no. 4.13), and the decisions of their General Assembly or regional Conference "do not bind the conscience of individual members" (no. 4.16).

The section on teaching with authority ends with a trenchant observation.

> For both Roman Catholics and Disciples the authority of the Church's teaching derives from a combination of elements: the truths of revelation, the theological arguments based upon them to guide human thought and behavior, the position and experience of those responsible for teaching, and reception by the whole Church. However, the relative weight attached to the elements differs between Roman Catholics and Disciples. Thus the claims made for the authority of the Church in matters of conscience differ in our two communities (no. 4.16).

While highlighting differences, the statement has also revealed the deep similarities behind these differences. In order to serve the same goal, each communion has developed somewhat different approaches on teaching authority and individual conscience.

The last sections of the statement discuss the ways that both Disciples and Roman Catholics equip the faithful for evangelization. While "all Christians are called to the work of evangelization" (no. 5.11), some have special roles of formation: parents, catechists, scholars, members of religious orders, ordained ministers, missionaries. Here the purpose of the statement's argument about the individual and the church's teaching authority is shown: "[e]vangelization and the unity of the Church go together" (no. 5.12). The church's mission of receiving and handing on the faith is undermined by the disunity of the church, a concern that marks both Disciples and Roman Catholics (no. 5.12). The members conclude, "In this dialogue, we have increasingly come to recognize that the structures and instruments for the visible unity of the Church of God are part of the necessary obedience to the command of Christ who said, 'Go ... and make disciples of all nations' (Matt. 28:19)" (no. 5.13).

In its views of ordained ministry and the nature of discerning the Gospel, the agreed statement culminating the dialogue's third phase builds with great consistency on the earlier statement. To that foundation it adds a detailed discussion of how teaching authority has been exercised during the church's history, and of the significance of such authority for personal reception of the faith within community. Taken together, these two statements express a notable convergence regarding teaching authority.

2. A Study Document of the Lutheran-Roman Catholic International Commission on Unity

The fourth phase of the Lutheran-Roman Catholic International Commission on Unity began in 1995 and was completed with the publication of a study document in 2006, *The Apostolicity of the Church*.[5] When compared with the two agreed statements of the Disciples of Christ-Roman Catholic International Commission for Dialogue that we have just examined, it is roughly four times as long and significantly different in form. While the Disciples of Christ-Roman Catholic statements are concise in style and largely systematic in structure, the Lutheran-Roman Catholic study document is more discursive and contains lengthy exegetical and historical sections. But, like the earlier statements examined, this document also contains significant agreements about teaching authority in the church. Hence it allows us to compare its conclusions with those of the earlier statements, and to appreciate the common pattern of agreement emergent in the work of the two international commissions.

The document focuses on the apostolicity of the church and is organized into four parts: (I) the apostolicity of the church: New Testament foundations; (II) the apostolic Gospel and the apostolicity of the church; (III) apostolic succession and ordained ministry; and (IV) church teaching that remains in the truth. One of the significant achievements of this document is its ambitious perspective that refuses to consider apostolic succession and ordained ministry in isolation from apostolic teaching that remains in the truth. Hence its structure in itself is already an important statement about the topic. For my present purpose, however, I will leave aside its first and third parts and examine only its general discussion of the apostolic Gospel and the apostolicity of the church in Part II and its consideration of teaching that remains in the truth in Part IV. These parts address teaching authority directly and also may be less well known than the more familiar discussion of biblical foundations of apostolicity and the issues of apostolic succession and ordained ministry.

After noting the witness of the Scriptures to the importance of the teaching that comes from the apostles, Part II treats the early affirmations of apostolicity. In the fourth and fifth centuries, "great preaching bishops brought the Scriptures to bear on both doctrinal questions and Christian life, so as to make the churches apostolic in an intense manner, without however linking this with the notion of apostolicity" (no. 84). The Creed of the Council of Constantinople (AD 381) confessed the church to be "apostolic" (no. 85), religious orders sought a lifestyle in conformity with the church's apostolic beginnings (no. 89), and the artwork of late antiquity and the medieval period regularly presented the foundational role of the apostles. Different claims about the special apostolicity of the seat of the bishop of Rome began in the second century, but these claims were contested at the time of the Reformation.

Luther himself rarely spoke about the apostolic church, but he emphasized continuity in proclaiming the message of the apostles and in apostolic practices: baptism, the Lord's Supper, the office of the keys, the call to ministry, public worship of praise and confession, and the bearing of the cross as Christ's disciples. For Luther, these are the marks of the church; and among these marks, "the gospel message ... is the decisive criterion of continuity in practice with the apostolic church" (no. 95). Thus, the Reformation wished to "refocus" church life on the Gospel, the document argues, by centring church life on Scripture and its exposition through these other apostolic practices. In its apologetic reaction to Luther, the Council of Trent narrowed the understanding of apostolicity. Trent did teach that Christ, as preached by the apostles, is the source and norm of all saving truth and practice. But it also focused on the authority of the institution where the truth of Christ is normatively taught, his efficacious sacraments administered, and pastoral governance legitimately exercised, "especially by reason of apostolic succession of Pope and bishops in a church assuredly still sustained by Christ's promised assistance" (no. 105).

Turning to contemporary discussions of the church's apostolicity, the document examines Vatican II's restatement of Trent's declaration "on the gospel as source of all saving truth" (no. 107). Locating the ministry of the bishop of Rome firmly within the college of bishops, the council also makes clear that "the heritage of teaching, liturgy and witness ... is thus bound to a corporate body of living teachers, whose apostolic succession makes them normative witnesses to what comes from Christ through the apostles" (no. 109). Vatican II also links the episcopal office with preaching the Gospel, a major Reformation concern; and it emphasizes the complex reality of the apostles' message: "the spoken word of their preaching, by the example they gave, by the institutions they established, [as] they themselves had received" (no. 114). By presenting apostolic tradition as dynamic and interwoven strands of teaching that foster faith and a life consonant with faith (no. 116), and by recognizing many of these "elements of sanctification and truth" in church communions beyond the visible boundaries of the Catholic Church (no. 119), Vatican II took important steps in responding to the concerns of the Reformation.

Meanwhile, contemporary Lutheran emphases also see apostolicity "as a complex reality embracing multiple elements" (no. 127). Lutherans look at the apostolicity of the church not simply as the presence of these elements within a community, but they look "much more to the pattern of their configuration and to the understanding and use of them" (no. 127). The Reformers saw that all the elements of apostolicity were present in the late medieval church; but they wanted them reconfigured around their proper centre, the Gospel of forgiveness and salvation. However, Lutherans today also recognize that the Gospel is embedded in community and is handed down in historically contingent expressions. "Around the central expression of the gospel in word and sacrament, the life of the community takes shape in offices and institutions, doctrines, liturgies and church orders, and an ethos and spirituality animated by the message of God's grace," members explain (no. 130). When Lutherans hear the Roman Catholic Church emphasizing the centrality of the apostolic gospel at Vatican II or hear the doctrine of justification rightly taught in the *Joint Declaration on the Doctrine of Justification*, they are able to re-evaluate their earlier judgment that the Roman Catholic Church's teaching and practice was discontinuous with the apostolic legacy (no. 139).

The new emphases allow the dialogue members to close this part with a set of shared foundational convictions about the apostolicity of the church, and also to record new "shared understandings discovered" (no. 149-59). Among these shared understandings is the centrality of the Gospel now taught by Roman Catholics as well as Lutherans. In addition, Vatican II's definition of tradition sees it as

> an ensemble of gospel preaching, sacraments, different types of ministry, forms of worship, and the apostles' example of selfless service of the churches founded by the gospel ... The apostolic heritage, expressed in a special manner in Scripture, "comprises everything that serves to make the People of God live their lives in holiness and increase their faith."[6]

But the document notes the "remarkable correspondence" of this definition by Vatican II with Luther's view connecting the Gospel with a set of practices through which the saving message comes to individuals and gives shape to community life ... Christ rules and works through the gospel proclaimed, but this comes to expression in baptism, the sacrament of the altar, and the ministry of the keys for the forgiveness of sins. The church is apostolic by holding to the truth of the gospel that is embodied continually in practices coming from the apostles in which the Holy Spirit continues the communication of Christ's grace (no. 158).

With this convergence in their understandings of tradition, the two church communions can also converge in their re-evaluations of one another's apostolic character (nos. 157, 159): "we therefore mutually recognize, at a fundamental level, the presence of apostolicity in our traditions" (no. 160). While important differences on apostolicity remain, the extent of convergence on the nature of apostolic tradition is striking.

In Part IV, the document considers "church teaching that remains in the truth," beginning again with biblical perspectives and then considering "doctrine and apostolic truth" in the early and medieval periods of the church. In a distinctive approach, the document sets three developments alongside each other in time: attention to the rule of faith, the emergence of creeds for professing the apostolic faith, and the formation of the canon of Scripture. The document relates these to one another. It observes, for example:

Earlier creeds and Church Fathers were decisive in councils because in doctrinal controversy both sides appealed to Scripture, as in the Arian appeal to texts subordinating the Son to the Father. Later Councils deliberated in the presence of the open gospels, but the doctrines that they taught served to renew for their time what they received from their predecessors in the conciliar tradition (no. 341).

This discussion of the three interlocking topics is followed by an extended reflection on scriptural interpretation in the early and medieval church, with its consideration of allegory, the plain sense of the text, the problem of diverse interpretations, and the relation between scriptural interpretation and creeds and conciliar definitions.

Next, there is a lengthy presentation of the centrality the Lutheran Reformation gave to "being maintained in the truth of the gospel" (no. 355). In the Reformation dispute, "both Luther and his opponents agreed that Holy Scripture is normative for church teaching," the members observe. "The dispute however was about the precise relationship between the church and Scripture" (no. 361). Another section follows which probes Catholic doctrine on the canon of Scripture, scriptural interpretation, and the teaching office. Members maintain that "Catholic doctrine ... does not hold what Reformation theology fears and wants at all costs to avoid, namely, a derivation of scriptural authority as canonical and binding from the authority of the church's hierarchy which makes known the canon" (no. 400). The document makes the obvious point that "the teaching office of the Catholic Church has taken on a structure and mode of operation notably different from Lutheran teaching ministries" (no. 413), but it argues that even obligatory magisterial teachings necessary in a given situation "are not the church's last word" since they must still be "received by the faith of the church, in order to be recognized in their lasting significance for keeping the church in the truth of the gospel" (no. 427).

In the conclusion to Part IV, members indicate areas of shared foundational convictions where "full consensus" (no. 431) is shared, and areas of reconciled diversity where the two traditions can "mutually recognize in each other the shared truth of the apostolic gospel of Jesus Christ" (no. 435) and so the diversity is "not ... church-dividing" (no. 431). With full consensus, the members affirm that God in Christ has issued a saving message to humankind (no. 432) which "continues to be announced in the gospel of Christ that the apostles first preached and taught" (no. 433). Again with full consensus, the document affirms that "for Lutherans and Catholics the source, rule, guideline, and criterion of correctness and purity of the church's proclamation, of its elaboration of doctrine, and of its sacramental and pastoral practice" are the Scriptures, which "emerged, under the Holy Spirit's inspiration, through the preaching and teaching of the apostolic gospel" (no. 434). By the biblical canon, the document explains, "the church does not constitute, but instead recognizes, the inherent authority of the prophetic and apostolic Scriptures." It concludes, "Consequently, the church's preaching and whole life must be nourished and ruled by the

Scriptures constantly heard and studied. True interpretation and application of Scripture maintains church teaching in the truth" (no. 434).

Turning to topics of reconciled diversity which are therefore not church-dividing, the document examines the history of discussions about the canon of Scripture and its relation to the church, and it concludes that remaining differences on the extent of the canon are not of sufficient weight to justify continued division (no. 441). Furthermore, Catholics and Lutherans agree as well that "Scripture is oriented toward a process of being interpreted in the context of ecclesial tradition" (no. 442).

In discussing tradition, Catholics affirm that tradition is indispensable in the interpretation of the word of God in order to connect the gospel and Scripture with faith as it is transmitted in history and maintained by the Holy Spirit (no. 443). But they have reappropriated the patristic and high-medieval conviction that Scripture contains all revealed truth, and so today they see tradition as the living process by which the entirety of the Word is transmitted (no. 444). Lutherans, on the other hand, while rejecting human traditions without grounding in Scriptures (no. 445), have used creeds and confessions to orient the church properly in its witness to the gospel and its reading of Scripture (no. 446). This section concludes with a striking convergence:

> Lutherans further insist that while Scripture and tradition are connected, Scripture should not be absorbed into the tradition-process, but should remain permanently superior as a critical norm, coming from the apostolic origins, which is superior to the traditions of the church. Catholics agree with this, because Scripture is "the highest authority in matter of faith" and Scripture continues to direct the church in the "continual reformation" of its life and teaching of which it has need.[7]

Hence different emphases on Scripture and tradition do not justify maintaining the present division of the churches, members agree (no. 448).

In its last section of reporting areas of reconciled diversity, the document focuses on the teaching office, its necessity, and its context. Lutherans locate the ministry of teaching primarily in ordained ministers in the local congregation, but "the Lutheran confessional tradition also holds that a supra-local teaching responsibility is essential in the church, for oversight of discipline and doctrine."[8] In addition, Lutherans take account of the processes of interaction among those in office, those practising the common priesthood of the baptized, and theologians. "Lutheran churches earnestly hope that through these processes the Holy Spirit is maintaining them in the truth of the gospel" (no. 451). The Roman Catholic magisterium includes the college of bishops with the pope as its head, who exercise their office within an extensive network of other ministers, including ordained pastors of parishes and theologians; but "the magisterium functions in virtue of a capacity for discerning the truth of God's word, based on a charism conferred by episcopal ordination" (no. 452). In spite of the different configurations of teaching ministries today among Lutherans and Roman Catholics, they agree "that the church must designate members to serve the transmission of the gospel, which is necessary for saving faith." Furthermore, without a teaching office functioning both locally and regionally, "the church would be defective" (no. 453).

The two communions also agree that those exercising the teaching office carry out their responsibilities within a network of other historical and contemporary witnesses to the Word of God (no. 457). Certainly "the teaching office or ministry is a necessary means by which the church is maintained in the truth of the gospel of Christ" (no. 458). The teaching office or ministry must proclaim the Gospel, interpret biblical witness, and reject doctrine contrary to the Gospel. Lutherans and Roman Catholics agree that the teaching ministry especially should give public voice to the saving acts of God in Christ. But because the church exists in history, its witness to the truth has "aspects of both finality and provisionality" (no. 460). This requires "an ongoing search for appropriate doctrinal expressions adequate to God's truth in this time before the ultimate eschatological manifestation of Christ as Lord and Savior of all" (no. 460). On this too the members are agreed.

Conclusion

When we compare the agreements about teaching authority that have been reached in these three documents, we can discern a remarkable degree of convergence. First, perhaps most notable is the virtual end of debate about the authority of the canon of the Scriptures and the authority of creeds, councils, and dogmatic formulations in church history. With careful nuances, each of the documents reports genuine convergence on these topics and hence on the relationship of Scripture and tradition.

Second, each document reports real convergence on the necessity of an ordained ministry with responsibility for oversight in teaching. But none envisions that such responsibility is exercised apart from the witness of other ordained ministers, of theologians, or indeed of all the baptized in their various roles and states – witness given in such diverse ways as through holiness of life, critical discernment of Scripture, or striving for justice.

Third, each of the documents focuses explicitly on the historical character of the church's search for doctrinal expressions that are, as the Lutheran-Roman Catholic document puts it, "adequate to God's truth in this time" (no. 460), emphasizing that the search takes time and involves the whole church. It is in this process of ecclesial searching that the documents situate the Holy Spirit's guidance of the church, assisting it to remain in the truth of the Gospel.

More broadly, reading these documents side by side clearly illustrates the significant contribution bilateral dialogues make to ecumenism. When two partner churches probe deeply into a single divisive topic for a period of years, genuine theological breakthroughs occur that would not be possible in shorter and less focused investigations. And when the fruit of many such dialogues is made available to the entire ecumenical movement, there emerges the possibility of a rich harvest. For John Radano's perseverance in support of such bilateral dialogues and his continuing conviction that they would yield a harvest, I am very grateful.

1   This paper prepared for this *Festschrift* has also appeared in a collection of Dr. O'Gara's essays published posthumously. See Margaret O'Gara, "Teaching Authority: Catholics, Disciples of Christ, and Lutherans," ch. 15 in *No Turning Back: The Future of Ecumenism*, ed. Michael Vertin (Collegeville, Minnesota: Liturgical Press, 2014).

2   Walter Kasper, *Harvesting the Fruits: Aspects of Christian Faith in Ecumenical Dialogue* (London and New York: Continuum, 2009).

3   Disciples of Christ-Roman Catholic International Commission for Dialogue, "The Church as Communion in Christ: Report of the Disciples of Christ/Roman Catholic International Commission for Dialogue," *Mid-Stream* 33 (April 1994): 219-39; reprinted as "The Church as Communion in Christ (1983-1992)," *Mid-Stream* 41 (October 2002): 96-114; *Information Service* 84 (1993): 162-69, in GA II, pp. 386-98; http://www.prounione.urbe.it.

4   Disciples of Christ-Roman Catholic International Commission for Dialogue, "Receiving and Handing on the Faith: the Mission and Responsibility of the Church (1993-2002)," *Mid-Stream* 41, no. 4 (October 2002): 51-79; *Information Service* 111 (2002): 241-51, in GA III, pp. 121-37; http://www.prounione.urbe.it.

5   Lutheran-Roman Catholic Commission on Unity, *The Apostolicity of the Church: Study Document* (Minneapolis: Lutheran University Press, 2006); *Information Service* 128 (2008): 60-133; http://www.prounione.urbe.it.

6   *Apostolicity of the Church*, no. 156, citing Second Vatican Council, *Dei Verbum*, no. 8.

7   *Apostolicity of the Church*, no. 447, citing John Paul II, *Ut Unum Sint* (Encyclical on Commitment to Ecumenism, May 25, 1995), no. 79, and Second Vatican Council, *Unitatis Redintegratio* (Decree on Ecumenism, November 24, 1964), no. 6.

8   *Apostolicity of the Church*, no. 450, citing *Augsburg Confession*, Art. 28.

✝ CHAPTER 8

Reign of God, *Koinonia*, Church: An Emerging Consensus?[1]

by Donna Geernaert, SC

"The time is fulfilled, and the kingdom of God has come near; repent and believe in the good news" (Mark 1:15). This phrase expresses the core of Jesus' message. Yet, questions about the reign of God, its nearness, and its relation to both Jesus and the church have been a topic of Christian debate for many centuries. These related realities will be explored in this paper through reflection on the concept of *koinonia*, "communion," as it has emerged in recent ecumenical dialogue. In these dialogues, the understanding of the church as *koinonia* has found increased attention and acceptance. Further, there is agreement that *koinonia* describes the right relationships which are integral to the eschatological reign of God. Thus, *koinonia* implies the indissoluble interrelation between the nature and mission of the church, called to proclaim and prefigure the reign of God. While ecumenical dialogue has produced remarkable growth in agreement about concepts of *koinonia*, participation in the dialogue process has also offered an experience of the *koinonia* that is being conceptualized. As the members of the third phase of the International Theological Dialogue between the Catholic Church and the World Alliance of Reformed Churches report: "In a fundamental sense, our dialogue itself is already an act of common witness, a reconciling experience that calls for further reconciliation of memories as obedience leads us to unity in faith and action, to a common witness in which the signs of the Kingdom are shared with the poor."[2]

Jesus Proclaims the Reign of God

The characteristics of the reign of God are expressed symbolically in Jesus' parables and actions such as exorcisms, healing miracles, and sharing of meals. In word and deed, Jesus proclaims salvation to those who have been excluded by others: the poor, the maimed, the lame, and the blind (Luke 14:13). The God of Jesus is a God of boundless grace who loves sinners (Luke 15:7, 10), who calls all (Matt. 23:37), who allows wheat and tares to grow together until harvest (Matt. 13:24-30). Jesus preached the reign of God as a decisive, future, final event, which is now at hand. It is also a powerful, sovereign act of God and a purely religious reign. Further, while he proclaimed the reign of God as a saving event for sinners, Jesus also stressed its demand that all must make a radical decision for God. Each of these characteristics will have an impact on the credibility of the church's witness to Jesus' message. For example, a focus on the purely religious character of the reign of God, while not inhibiting Christian commitment to social justice, means that no particular economic, social, political, or ideological system may receive unqualified support.

The church owes its origin not to a single isolated act but to the totality of the Christ-event starting from the election of Israel as the people of God. The blessing God promised to Abraham and Sarah has its climax in the promise of blessing for all the families of the earth. Zion as the centre of Israel is to become the centre of the messianic reign of God for the whole world of nations. The ministry of Jesus was addressed to a people so that the first persons who heard and accepted the proclamation of God's reign were already oriented to one another by their relationship within Israel. What Jesus proclaimed was the dawn of the eschatological reign of God, which was looked for by Israel, but effected in an entirely unexpected way. It is God's action alone. But all who accept it from Jesus' words and deeds will be wholly taken into its service and will subordinate everything else to it. Jesus' disciples become personal witnesses to the nearness of the reign of God. They are to leave everything and follow him wherever he goes (Luke 9:57-62).[3]

Koinonia in the Reign of God

Jesus proclaims God's reign as being like leaven which works until the whole – church, humanity, all of creation – has been leavened (Matt. 13:33). But, how is this reign of God to be defined? One description is found in the words of the apostle Paul: "For the kingdom of God is not a matter of eating or drinking, but of justice and peace and joy in the Holy Spirit" (Rom. 14:17). Contemporary exegesis highlights the social and political connotations of the justice, peace, and joy to which Paul refers. From a biblical perspective, God has always been king of Israel and of the universe, but creation, and Israel in particular, have rebelled and fallen away from God's righteous rule. When God's rightful claim and rule is again fully and openly established, justice and peace will be reflected in the harmony of right relationships portrayed in the first two chapters of the book of Genesis. Further, the God of Jesus whose reign is "at hand" is not a fearsome, remote, or all-powerful king, but a God of boundless love who delights in regaining the lost. This image of God is illustrated in Luke's three adjoining parables (Luke 15:3-32) of the shepherd, the housewife, and the father, who each seek and then celebrate with joy the return of a treasured object to its rightful place. In brief, the reign of God is a realm of right relationships, a dynamic symbol which conveys something definite about God's plan for and commitment to creation, including the everyday lives of human beings.

Within the context of Christian faith, the revelation of a *koinonia* of three Persons in one God becomes the model of right relationship. Like the followers of many other faith traditions, Christians maintain that God is ineffable, incomprehensible, beyond all human words and knowing. Yet, Christians also believe their encounter with God in the person of Christ and the activity of the Holy Spirit has given them a special revelation about who God is. This experience is expressed in a Trinitarian monotheism initially defined at the Council of Nicaea, and the subject of much ongoing theological reflection. In recent years, there has been a renewed interest in Trinitarian theology, attempting to integrate the insights of Greek and Latin traditions with the categories of modern thought. The concept of *perichōrēsis*, or "coinherence," has proved particularly helpful in this regard. According to Catherine LaCugna, *perichōrēsis* expresses "the idea that the three divine persons mutually inhere in one another, draw life from one another, 'are' what they are by relation to one another... *Perichōrēsis* provides a dynamic model of persons in communion based on mutuality and interdependence."[4] A radically personal and social understanding of right relationship in community (*koinonia*) flows from this perception of Trinitarian life. Assuming that persons are most fully themselves in interpersonal relationships,[5] it is the members' mutual self-giving, shared history and vision which sustain a vital identity of life in community.

In light of this understanding of a Triune God, current reflection on the new cosmology is evocative. For writers such as historian Thomas Berry and physicist Brian Swimme, the cosmos is a self-generating, essentially creative process that emerges through differentiation, subjectivity, and communion. Differentiation gives rise to more and more complex entities, from sub-atomic particles to advanced life forms, and leads as well to the increasing complexity of relationships between entities. Subjectivity highlights the self-organizing, systemic dynamics of these differentiated entities, their inner coherence that enables them to work according to their own internal organizing principles. Communion affirms the essential relatedness of existence, for no evolving subject can exist alone; it can only exist because it is in connection, a member of a bonded community. Every entity is different but every entity is operating with the others to make a whole. All are in relationship.[6] For Berry and Swimme, these cosmic principles offer the basis for a more comprehensive ecological and social ethics that situates the human community and the earth community in right relationship.

When the God who creates the universe chooses to intervene in human history, right relationships are specified in the making of a covenant. Grounded in God's action of liberating Israel from Egyptian slavery, the covenant narratives contain elements of treaty formulas commonly employed in the late second millennium B.C. Like the suzerainty treaties of the period, the covenant affirms Israel's acceptance of God as sovereign ruler. And, as the laws of the Decalogue make clear, Israel's recognition of God's rule has significant implications for all members of the covenant community who, taking on the obligations of vassals, are required to live in sacred truce with one another.[7] In brief, the terms of this covenant identify right relationship between neighbours as one of the ways in which the people are to express their fidelity to God. If Israel's covenant with God is lived rightly, the biblical tradition maintains, "there will be no poor among you" (Deut. 15:4). If there are poor, however, they are to be given special care: provisions for lending without interest (Exodus 22:25; Deut. 15:7-8), feeding with gleanings from the field (Ruth 2:1-3; Exodus 23:10-11), returning a poor person's cloak at night (Exodus 22:26-27; Deut. 24:10-13), tithing to provide for the poor (Deut. 14:28-29; 26:12). Why this special concern for the poor? They are the ones who cannot repay, and so, just treatment of the poor is a clear expression of obedience to the law of God.

When Jesus links love of neighbour to love of God in the great commandment (Matt. 22:36-40), his teaching is in continuity with covenant law. Yet, the closeness of the linking established by Jesus radicalizes the love commandment by affirming that God cannot be loved without love of neighbour or, more positively stated, that God is loved in loving the neighbour. In addition to making the commandment more radical, Jesus' teaching also universalizes it. Where covenant tradition had tended to limit the neighbour to members of the Jewish community, Jesus removes all limits to the neighbour's identity (Luke 10:29-27), even insisting that enemies be loved (Luke 6:27-36). Perfection is perceived in terms of loving enemies, and God's action models the kind of love that is required (Matt. 5:43-48). Further, in Matthew's description of the last judgement (25:31-46), it is Jesus who is loved and served, or conversely persecuted and neglected, in what is done or not done to a neighbor (cf., Matt. 10:40; Luke 10:16; John 13:20; Acts 9:5). Jesus' disciples are to love one another (John 13:35), and their love is to be expressed in practical ways, specific actions (James 1:22-27; 2:14-26).

In the reign of God, which Jesus says is both here and not yet, right relationships will be lived with God, within the whole human family and the entire created universe. Thus, the reign of God is not simply a matter of life after death but rather a horizon for action in the present world. The "message of the church is not a private pietism irrelevant to contemporary society."[8] Rather, Christians are called to be agents of justice and compassion, challenging and assisting society's attempts to achieve just judgement, never forgetting that in the light of God's justice all human solutions are provisional. Since the reign of God has not yet come in fullness, Christians "experience the dynamic tension between the 'now' and the 'not yet' for the fulfilment of [this reign] in the world by engaging in patient action and active patience."[9] The Holy Spirit guides the faithful to work for both personal and structural transformation of society, thus participating in the ongoing process and realization of the prayer for the coming of God's reign.[10]

The Church as *Koinonia*

Although he insisted that the reign of God is open to everyone, Jesus gathered groups of followers who accepted him and his message and awaited the coming of the reign of God. Groups were gathered in Galilee, Judea, Bethany, and Decapolis. Disciples are sent forth to proclaim the good news and heal the afflicted. Disciples, including women, accompany Jesus on his travels. Jesus constantly speaks of the people he is gathering: "little flock" (Luke 12:32), "city set on a mountain" (Matt. 5:14), "wedding guests" (Mark 2:19), members of the new covenant (Mark 14:24). In addition, Jesus appears to have anticipated an interim period between his death and the final coming of the reign of God. At the Last Supper (1 Cor. 11:23-24) and in the injunction to Peter (Luke 22:31-34), he looked towards the disciples' staying together after his death.

Without the raising of Jesus from the dead, Christian proclamation and faith is "in vain" (1 Cor. 15:3-20). In light of their experience of the resurrection, which enables them to see the crucifixion as an event of salvation, Jesus' disciples find renewed faith and come to understand themselves as the eschatological community of God, the church. While relationships between and among the churches are not yet clearly defined, all are "built upon the foundation of the apostles and prophets, with Christ Jesus himself as the cornerstone" (Eph. 2:20). All of the New Testament authors write as members of the one church of Christ; there is no individualistic Christianity. For the early church, the outpouring of the Spirit at Pentecost is an established fact which fulfills the ancient prophecies concerning the last days (Acts 2:16-17). Transformed by the presence of the Spirit, the community becomes the temple of God (1 Cor. 3:16), capable of proclaiming the gospel with convincing power (1 Thess. 1:5). The gifts of the Spirit are effective in the community in prophecy and acts of power as well as speaking in tongues or finding the right words when on trial. And, all of these gifts are oriented towards the building up of the church (1 Cor. 12–14).

Although they were dramatically changed by their experience of the resurrection, the disciples did not understand themselves to be taking the place of Jesus. They did not simply continue to proclaim the reign of God as they had during his lifetime. Instead, the post-resurrection period is marked by a clear transition from Jesus, the proclaimer of God's reign, to the disciples, the proclaimers of Christ. According to Edward Schillebeeckx, the very pattern of Jesus' calling of the disciples suggests the origins of a relationship consistent with this change. Specifically, he claims the conversion model in the call narratives is used to show "that turning to Jesus to follow him is the *metanoia* (complete about-turn) demanded by the coming kingdom of God."[11] The Christian community after Easter sees conversion to Jesus as the condition for membership in the community of salvation.[12] The church becomes the place of contact with Christ and his message, the place where authentic discipleship is possible. The preaching of the gospel is not merely an account of the historical saving act of God in Christ; Christ himself is at work in the word that is preached. Sacramental worship is a key moment in the life of the church when Christ is present according to his promise. In brief, the focus of mission and ministry in the church is to enable Christians to enter into an immediate relationship with Jesus in the Holy Spirit.

In Christ, the church is called to be a sign, instrument, and fore-taste of the reign of God. "What Christ achieved through his cross and resurrection is communicated by the Holy Spirit in the life of the church."[13] "The liberty promised to the children of God is nothing less than participation, with Christ and through the Holy Spirit, in the life of God."[14] Thus, *koinonia* refers first to fellowship with God and subsequently to sharing with one another. The Spirit of God, acting in history, is the main agent of that *koinonia* which is the church. Persons are brought into living relationship with the Father through the Son by the power of the Spirit. To speak of *koinonia* is to speak of the way human beings come to know God as God's purpose for humanity is revealed.[15]

The new creation is a foretaste of what will come in fullness through the Spirit at the end of time... Human relationships are ... set in a new context so that people may recognize one another as equally God's children and come to acknowledge the bonds that link them as a gift from God.[16]

The mystery of salvation is a mystery of *koinonia*. While this *koinonia* will be complete only in the reign of God at the end of time, it is already visibly present in the community of faith and love which is the church. Specifically, the church as the communion of the Holy Spirit proclaims and prefigures the reign of God by announcing the gospel to the world and by being built up as the body of Christ. Until God's reign is realized in fullness, however, the church is marked by human limitation and imperfection, always remembering its "provisional" nature. Yet, in spite of all its inadequacies, the church retains its character as a sign of the eschatological reign of God.[17]

The church's mission is to witness to the reign of God by its words and rites, by its structures and governance, by its being as well as its doing.[18] "The church as the body of Christ and the eschatological people of God is constituted by the Holy Spirit through a diversity of gifts and ministries. Among those gifts, a ministry of *episkopé* is necessary to express and safeguard the unity of the body."[19]

In Christ the victory of the reign of God over the powers of [sin and death] has begun. [Therefore,] the leadership ministry of Christ is not like the leadership in the world of sin and death... It has a character and quality determined by Christ's way of being in and for the world.[20]

The new humanity, which the gospel makes possible, is present in the community of those who live according to the law of the Spirit. All "members of the church share a responsibility for discerning the action of the Spirit in the contemporary world, for shaping a truly human response, and for resolving the ensuing moral perplexities with integrity and fidelity to the gospel."[21] In its life as *koinonia*, the church is a sign of God's gracious purpose for creation, a sign of the right relationships that are integral to the reign of God.

The Church Proclaims the Reign of God

"The Church as *koinonia* requires visible expression because it is intended to be the sacrament, sign and instrument, of God's saving work. The *koinonia* is a sign that God's purpose in Christ is being realized in the world by grace."[22] By proclaiming the truth of the gospel, witnessing to it by its life, and thus entering more deeply into the mystery of the reign of God, the church is also an instrument for the accomplishment of God's purpose. In this perspective, "the Church is the visible form of God's grace. It opens the way to salvation through preaching, sacraments, and other institutions derived from apostolic authority. Participation in these means of grace constitutes the deeper [*koinonia*] that unites members of the church in the Spirit."[23] Through their common life and *koinonia,* the members of the church witness to salvation as they pray and worship, forgive, love one another, and stand together in time of trial. Their *koinonia* is made possible by a deeper *koinonia* in the means of grace that comes from God who makes the people of the church a new creation in Christ.[24]

While the action of the Spirit of God is not limited to the community of Christians, "it is within the church, where the Holy Spirit gives and nurtures the new life of [God's reign], that the gospel becomes a manifest reality."[25] As the *koinonia* of believers with God and with each other, the church is the community where the redemptive work of Jesus Christ has been recognized and received and is, therefore, being made known in the world. *Koinonia* with God in Christ is constantly established and renewed through the power of the Holy Spirit. The church as *koinonia* is "called to be a living expression of the gospel, evangelized and evangelizing, reconciled and reconciling, gathered together and gathering others."[26]

By its communal life, the church bears witness to that society of love in which the reign of God will consist. This becomes evident in the Christian community's affirmation of a world reversing understanding of authority and of leadership exercised in a way that is radically different from that of "the rulers of the Gentiles" (Matt. 20:20-28). When the church, through its exercise of authority, displays the healing and reconciling power of the gospel, then the wider world is offered a vision of what God intends for all creation. The *koinonia* of the church "demonstrates that Christ has broken down the dividing wall of hostility ... to create a single new humanity reconciled to God in one body by the cross (cf. Eph. 2:14-16). Confessing that their [*koinonia*] signifies God's purpose for the whole human race, the members of the church are called to give themselves in loving witness and service to their fellow human beings."[27]

"The church participates in Christ's mission to the world through the proclamation of the gospel ... by its words and deeds." Sustained through word and sacrament, Christians are liberated from self-centeredness and empowered to live at peace with God and with one another.[28] The church is called to embody the good news that forgiveness is a gift to be received from God and shared with others (Matt. 6:14-15). "It is called to affirm the sacredness and dignity of the person, the value of natural and political communities, and the divine purpose for the human race as a whole; to witness against the structures of sin in society, addressing humanity with the gospel of repentance and forgiveness."[29] In fulfilling its vocation, the church is called to follow the way of Jesus Christ, the suffering servant. It is to serve God's reign, rather than be self-serving or an end in itself. Just as the reign of God redeems the lost, so too it imposes on those who are saved the duty of solidarity with the lost and prepares them to accept persecutions, slanders, and sufferings for the sake of the gospel. This is "a sign of God's choice of the way of the cross to save the world."[30]

The concept of *koinonia* challenges the church to live the communion it celebrates with God, with one another, and with the whole created world. Specifically, the church as *koinonia* witnesses to the world-reversing character of the reign of God. Based on a Trinitarian understanding of God, Christian *koinonia* is to be lived in a simultaneous affirmation of mutuality and difference. This concept of differentiating union endorses neither uniformity nor individualism. In the living of *koinonia*, there can be no priority of one over another but only mutual concern for the good of each. Further, it seems evident that such a way of life would reverse many contemporary categories of judgement and allow for the paradoxical forgiveness, mercy, and compassion illustrated in the parables of Jesus. In a world that is increasingly marked by individualism, isolation, and alienation, the church's witness to *koinonia* could make a significant contribution to the evangelization and transformation of current social structures.

Dialogue towards *Koinonia*

Since the end of the Second Vatican Council, there has been an "explosion" of ecumenical dialogues, eventually involving almost every worldwide Christian communion.[31] This has led to a good deal of reflection on the qualities and dynamics of authentic dialogue. In his encyclical on commitment to ecumenism, *Ut Unum Sint*, Pope John Paul II includes a lengthy section on dialogue.[32] He begins by noting that the capacity for dialogue is basic to the very nature of persons and their dignity. Rooted in today's personalist way of thinking, he asserts, dialogue is an indispensable step towards the self-realization of human individuals and communities. Dialogue is not just cognitive but involves the human subjectivity of each participant. More than just an exchange of ideas, the pope says, dialogue is an "exchange of gifts."[33]

Pope Paul VI, in his encyclical on the church, *Ecclesiam Suam*, affirms dialogue as one of the three priorities of his pontificate. Catholics are called to dialogue, he maintains, principally because of their faith. The basis for this involvement lies, first of all, in the mystery of God, Three-in-One, where Christian revelation perceives a life of communion and interchange. Secondly, this same Trinitarian God creates human persons free and able to enter into relationship with God and with one another. And, when freedom is lost through sin, God, in an age-long dialogue, continues to offer salvation to humanity. Clearly, it is God who takes the initiative in this dialogue of salvation. In fact, the very person of Jesus Christ, fully human and fully divine, gives concrete expression to this call to dialogue. Thus, those who follow Christ are called by their human and Christian vocation to live dialogue in their daily lives wherever they find themselves. Pope Paul VI then goes on to identify dialogue as a "recognized method of the apostolate" and to name its four characteristics as clarity, meekness, confidence, and prudence. Dialogue conducted in this way, he says, unites truth and charity, understanding and love.[34]

"Dialogue," Pope John Paul II states, is "a natural instrument for comparing differing points of view and, above all, for examining those differences which exist among Christians."[35] With regard to the study of areas of disagreement, he recalls, "the Council requires that the whole body of doctrine be clearly presented... Certainly, it is possible to profess one's faith and to explain its teaching in a way that is correct, fair and understandable, and which at the same time takes into account both the way of thinking and the actual historical experiences of the other party." Further, he notes, "Full communion of course will have to come about through the acceptance of the whole truth into which the Holy Spirit guides Christ's disciples. Hence all forms of reductionism or facile 'agreement' must be absolutely avoided. Serious questions must be resolved, for if not, they will reappear at another time, either in the same terms or in a different guise."[36]

In June 2000, the North American Orthodox-Catholic Theological Consultation issued a statement on the meaning of ecumenical dialogue. This text was developed both to celebrate the dialogue's thirty-fifth anniversary and to respond to members of both churches who fear that "to enter into dialogue with other Christian bodies is to run the risk of exposing the church to the possibility of compromise or syncretism, and even to the loss of the Christian faith itself."[37] Published under the title *Sharing the Ministry of Reconciliation*, in summary it states:

> [O]ur effort in dialogue is to look beyond what appear to be contradictory verbal formulas to the faith that underlies them, to determine whether or not those formulas are witnessing to the same faith in different ways... Our conviction is that dialogue is not the abandonment of the truth of the Christian faith but rather an attempt to deepen together our understanding of that truth, free from the polemics of the past, by listening to the witness of the one truth that is given by our two traditions. Far from encouraging relativism, genuine dialogue begins with an immersion in one's own tradition and a desire to share its richness with others for the sake of the salvation of the world.[38]

In May 2004, the Joint Working Group between the WCC and the Roman Catholic Church published a study paper on *The Nature and Purpose of Ecumenical Dialogue*. Presented as a follow-up to its 1967 report, *Ecumenical Dialogue*, this text intends "to encourage the churches to continue their ecumenical dialogue with commitment and perseverance." In contemporary society, fueled by fundamentalism, new experiences of vulnerability and the impact of globalization, "Dialogue has become a *sine qua non* for nations, churches and cultures ... [it] is an imperative arising from the Gospel, which thus presents a counterchallenge to those who would adopt exclusivist positions."[39] In whatever formal or informal setting dialogue takes place, it is always a demanding exercise. Even at the human level, it is hard to keep an open mind, to try to enter into another way of thinking and seeing things. The difficulties are compounded when dialogue touches on matters of faith. Painful memories of the past (wars, inquisitions, ethnic conflicts) and present experiences of stereotyping, mistrust, and everyday misunderstandings hinder dialogue. Thus, those who wish to enter into contact and establish collaboration with others first of all need to be open to conversion. Authentic dialogue "asks for what is most painful to human nature: disinterested love."[40] At its deepest level, therefore, dialogue offers an experience of *koinonia* and a witness to the right relationships characteristic of the eschatological reign of God.

As dialogue leads to growth in agreement and its participants grow in mutual understanding, there is an increasing awareness of the need for common witness and cooperative action. In particular, a dialogue which sees the reign of God not only as an eschatological hope but also as a context for Christian mission will seek ways of transforming society according to the pattern of God's reign. "The church is that part of humanity which has been led to accept, affirm and acknowledge ever more fully the liberating truth of the kingdom for all people... The church is therefore called to live as that force within humanity through which God's will for the renewal, justice, community and salvation of all people is witnessed to."[41] Commitment to action has been a major focus of two recent dialogues. In a call to action addressed to members of the episcopate around the world, the International Anglican-Roman Catholic Commission for Unity and Mission identified a number of practical examples of collaboration, particularly in the areas of social justice and joint pastoral care. The third phase of the Reformed-Roman Catholic dialogue included an intense discussion about the methodology most suited to linking the struggle to overcome Christian divisions with the struggle to overcome what divides societies, nations, cultures, and religions in today's world. As a result, the dialogue report offers three witness narratives that outline how Christians have tried to bring their convictions about the reign of God into complex contemporary situations. In light of these case studies, the report states: "Progress in dialogue must be accompanied by a deepening communion in the life of the churches... And sometimes a growing solidarity among Christians provides a vigorous spur to seek further progress in theological dialogue."[42]

Conclusion

As it was not a major source of dispute at the time of the Reformation, the reign of God has not been of particular concern in the international bilateral dialogues. Only the Anglican-Reformed dialogue on *God's Reign and Our Unity* (1984) and the Reformed-Roman Catholic dialogue on *The Church as Community of Common Witness to the Kingdom of God* (2007) have directly addressed this topic.[43] At the same time, differing understandings about the nature and mission of the church have been either an overarching or an underlying theme in most of the dialogues that have taken place over the past 50 years. In many of these dialogues, moreover, the concept of *koinonia* has emerged as central to the quest for a common understanding of the church and its visible unity. Dialogue about the reign of God has also affirmed the notion of *koinonia* as descriptive of the right relationships God wills for the whole of creation. Further, ecclesial *koinonia* is frequently identified as a witness to God's reign, integral to the church's mission. There is an emerging consensus about the relationship between the church and the reign of God in which the church, precisely as *koinonia*, is affirmed as a sign, instrument, and foretaste, as a "kind of sacrament" of that eschatological reign. Thus, by revisiting ongoing issues of ecclesiology in light of more recent reflection on the reign of God, new ecumenical insights do become possible.

---

1   Material in this paper on the concept of 'kingdom of God in ecumenical dialogue' was researched for the third phase of the Reformed-Roman Catholic Dialogue (1998-2005) and published as an appendix to its report, "The Church as Community of Common Witness to the Kingdom of God," *Information Service* 125 (2007): 151-55; http://www.prounione.urbe.it. Monsignor Jack Radano served as staff and was a major contributor to this dialogue, as well as to its second phase (1985-1990).

2 Reformed-Roman Catholic Dialogue, *The Church as Community of Common Witness to the Kingdom of God*, no. 12.

3 Lutheran-Roman Catholic Dialogue, *Church and Justification: Understanding the Church in the Light of the Doctrine of the Justification* (1993), nos. 11, 17, 20, in GA II, pp. 489-92; Methodist-Roman Catholic Dialogue, *Towards a Statement on the Church* (1986), no. 2, in GA II, p. 584.

4 Catherine Mowry LaCugna, *God for Us: The Trinity and Christian Life* (San Francisco: Harper, 1973), pp. 270-71. The concept of Trinitarian Persons distinguished from one another through mutual inter-relatedness is well expressed at the Council of Toledo, 675: "For the Father is Father not with respect to himself but to the Son, and the Son is Son not to himself but in relation to the Father; and likewise the Holy Spirit is not referred to himself but is related to the Father and the Son, inasmuch as he is called the Spirit of the Father and the Son" (DS 528). As the Council of Florence affirms, in God everything is one except for the relative opposition of the persons (DS 1330).

5 According to Jesuit paleontologist Pierre Teilhard de Chardin, humans are born as individuals but become persons in community. Persons come to know who they are when they see themselves reflected back in other persons. In a loving relationship, the identity of the other is not abolished or absorbed but is rather confirmed and fulfilled. For Teilhard, "union differentiates" at the level at which the union occurs – the more deeply a couple is in love, the more fully each is themselves.

6 Brian Swimme and Thomas Berry, *The Universe Story* (San Francisco: Harper, 1992), pp. 66-79.

7 John Bright, *A History of Israel* (Philadelphia: Westminster Press, 1959), pp. 132-42.

8 ARCIC II, *Salvation and the Church* (1986), no. 30, in GA II, p. 324.

9 Pentecostal-Reformed Dialogue, *Word and Spirit, Church and World* (2000), in GA III, p. 493.

10 See also Disciples-Roman Catholic Conversations, *Report* (1981), no. VII.b, in GA I, p. 165; ARCIC II, *Life in Christ: Morals, Communion and the Church* (1993), no. 24, in GA II, pp. 350-51; Methodist-Roman Catholic Dialogue, *The Word of Life: A Statement on Revelation and Faith* (1996) nos. 63, 79, in GA II, pp. 632, 635.

11 Edward Schillebeeckx, *Jesus: An Experiment in Christology* (New York: Seabury, 1979), pp. 224-29.

12 "What now mediates salvation is one's relation to Jesus." Schillebeeckx, *Jesus*, p. 226.

13 ARCIC II, *Salvation and the Church* (1986), no. 26, in GA II, p. 323.

14 ARCIC II, *Life in Christ: Morals, Communion and the Church* (1993) no. 19, in GA II, p. 349-50.

15 See also Baptist-Roman Catholic Dialogue, *Summons to Witness to Christ in Today's World* (1988) nos. 19-23, in GA II, pp. 377-79; Disciples-Roman Catholic Dialogue, *The Church as Communion in Christ* (1992) nos. 23-24, in GA II, p. 391.

16 Disciples-Roman Catholic Dialogue, *The Church as Communion in Christ* (1992), no. 24, in GA II, p. 391.

17 See also Anglican-Lutheran Conversation, *The Pullach Report* (1972), no. 60, in GA I, p. 21; ARCIC I, *The Final Report* (1981), no. 5, in GA I, p. 65; Baptist-Reformed Conversation, *Report* (1977), no. 30, in GA I, pp. 147-48; Anglican-Reformed Dialogue, *God's Reign and Our Unity* (1984), no. 15, in GA II, p. 119; Lutheran-Roman Catholic Dialogue, *Church and Justification* (1993), nos. 22, 73, in GA II, pp. 492, 505.

18 Anglican-Lutheran Dialogue, *Episcope* (1987), no. 24, in GA II, p. 16.

19 WCC Commission on Faith and Order, *Baptism, Eucharist and Ministry* (1982); "Ministry" no. 23, in GA I, p. 488.

20 Anglican-Lutheran Dialogue, *The Diaconate as Ecumenical Opportunity* (1995), no. 10, in GA II, pp. 41-42.

21 ARCIC II, *Life in Christ: Morals, Communion and the Church* (1993), no. 97, in GA II, p. 368.

22 ARCIC I, *The Final Report* (1981) no.7, in GA I, p. 66.

23 Disciples-Roman Catholic Dialogue, *Report* (1981), section VI, no. 4, in GA I, pp. 163-64.

24 See also Lutheran-Roman Catholic Dialogue, *Church and Justification* (1993), nos. 303, 305, in GA II, pp. 556-57; Methodist-Roman Catholic Dialogue, *Towards a Statement on the Church* (1986), no. I.8, in GA II, p. 585; Eastern Orthodox-Roman Catholic, *The Sacrament of Order in the Sacramental Structure of the Church* (1988), no. 22, in GA II, p. 674; Reformed-Roman Catholic Dialogue, *Towards a Common Understanding of the Church* (1990), no. 111, in GA II, p. 805.

25 ARCIC II, *Salvation and the Church* (1986), no. 28, in GA II, p. 324.

26 ARCIC II, *Salvation and the Church* (1986), no. 28, in GA II, p. 324; see also Lutheran-Roman Catholic Dialogue, *The Malta Report* (1972), nos. 41, 45, in GA I, pp. 177-79; Reformed-Roman Catholic Dialogue, *The Presence of Christ in Church and World* (1977), nos. 53-59, in GA I, pp. 447-48.

27 ARCIC II, *Church as Communion* (1991) no. 22, in GA II, p. 334; see also WCC Commission on Faith and Order, *Baptism, Eucharist and Ministry* (1982); "Ministry" nos. 15-16, in GA I, p. 486; Anglican-Lutheran Dialogue, *The Diaconate as Ecumenical Opportunity* (1995), nos. 10, 13-15, in GA II, pp. 41-42; ARCIC II, *The Gift of Authority* (1998), no. 50, in GA III, p. 76.

28 ARCIC II, *Salvation and the Church* (1986), no. 30, in GA II, p. 324.

29 ARCIC II, *Salvation and the Church* (1986), no. 31, in GA II. pp. 324-25.

30 ARCIC II, *Salvation and the Church* (1986), no. 26, in GA II, p. 323; Lutheran-Roman Catholic Dialogue, *Church and Justification* (1993) no. 22, in GA II, p. 492; Pentecostal-Reformed Dialogue, *Word and Spirit, Church and World* (2000) , in GA III, pp. 492-93.

31 Reflection on this phenomenon highlights the influence of the Catholic Church, which sees itself as a spiritually and structurally united worldwide communion with a strong conviction of its special identity. This created a climate for bilateral relationships which other churches and faith communities were ready to develop in dialogue with the Catholic Church and among themselves. Cf. GA I, p. 3.

32 John Paul II, *Ut Unum Sint* (Encyclical on commitment to ecumenism, May 25, 1995), nos. 28-39.

33 *Ut Unum Sint*, no. 28.

34 Paul VI, *Ecclesiam Suam* (Encyclical on the Church, August 6, 1964), Part III, especially nos. 70-85.

35 *Ut Unum Sint*, no. 36.

36 *Ut Unum Sint*, no. 36.

37 North American Orthodox-Catholic Theological Consultation, *Sharing the Ministry of Reconciliation: Statement on the Orthodox-Catholic Dialogue and the Ecumenical Movement* (2000), GC II, p. 369. Also published as "What Ecumenical Dialogue Is and Is Not," *Origins* 30 (2000): 79. http://www.usccb.org and http://www.scoba.us/resources/orthodox-catholic/31.html.

38 *Sharing the Ministry of Reconciliation*, GC II, pp. 369-70.

39 Joint Working Group between the WCC and the Roman Catholic Church, "The Nature and Purpose of Ecumenical Dialogue," no. 1, in Appendix D, *Eighth Report, 1999-2005* (Geneva: WCC, 2005); *Information Service* 117 (2004): 204; http://www.oikoumene.org.

40 William Johnston, *Letters to Contemplatives*, in Frederick M. Bliss, *Catholic and Ecumenical* (Franklin, Wisconsin: Sheed & Ward, 1999), p. 55.

41 WCC Commission on Faith and Order, *Church and World: The Unity of the Church and the Renewal of the Human Community* (Geneva: WCC Publications, 1990), p. 23. Available at: http://www.oikoumene.org.

42 Reformed-Roman Catholic Dialogue, *The Church as Community of Common Witness to the Kingdom of God*, no. 67.

43 There are significant references to the reign of God in several dialogues and major discussions in three dialogue reports: Reformed-Roman Catholic Dialogue, *The Presence of Christ in Church and World* (1977) nos. 43-66, in GA I, pp. 444-49; Lutheran-Roman Catholic Dialogue, *Church and Justification* (1993) nos. 10-33, 297-308, in GA II, pp. 489-95 and 554-57; Pentecostal-Reformed Dialogue, *Word and Spirit, Church and World* (2000), in GA III, pp. 492-95.

✝ CHAPTER 9

Beyond "Confessionalism": The Specificity and Challenge of Reformed Ecumenicity

by Odair Pedroso Mateus

If we get our hearts large enough to embrace all our Presbyterian brethren, the proofs of enlargement will go on, and we shall begin to long earnestly for wider fellowship. I, for my part, never desired that this Alliance should end, as it were, with itself: but rather that it should be a step towards an Alliance that one day would have a vastly larger constituency, and that would form a more important contribution than we can make towards the swifter fulfilment of our Saviour's prayer – "That they all may be one."[1]

This paper deals with the ecumenical engagement of a global confessional body: the World Alliance of Reformed Churches (WARC). The expression "Beyond Confessionalism" in its title points at the same time, as the subtitle suggests, first of all to the particularity of WARC's ecumenical engagement and also to the challenges of its supra-confessional self-understanding and institutional situation in an ecumenical landscape which seems to increasingly call for confessionally profiled actors. I will briefly retrace the history of the emergence of this "beyond confessionalism" self-understanding, then describe its institutional inscription in WARC's foundational texts, and finally, point to its challenges.

My concern with the dialectics of the confessional and the ecumenical has a lot to do, on the one hand, with my ecumenical ministry at WARC and, on the other hand, with the present and future of organized ecumenism in general and the World Council of Churches (WCC) and its future assemblies in particular. As negotiations begin between the WCC and the Christian world communions on the possibility of future concurrent world assemblies, for instance, it is important to reflect on what they might mean for our common commitment to grow in conciliar fellowship.

I. The Confessional Movement in the Ecumenical Age

Let me start by outlining the background. We often think of the last quarter of the 19th century and the first half of the 20th century as the modern ecumenical age, as the age in which separated Christian churches, particularly those marked by the 16th-century Reformation, progressively realize in fact "that there is such a thing as *the Church*" and that even in their existing divisions they "must seek to *be* the Church in all possible fullness."[2] The ecumenical movement, writes the Presbyterian ecumenist Lewis Mudge in the early 1960s, "does not submerge churches in the bigness of a world enterprise which claims to do everything better and more authoritatively than it can be done by them. On the contrary, correctly understood, it lifts churches up, and shows them what they are."[3] The national councils of churches, the WCC, and the regional councils or conferences of churches are, in a certain chronological order, expressions of the churches' search to be the Church.

However, if it is true that we often think of that age as the time in which walls of separation began to be broken down, it is also true – and somewhat paradoxical – that during that very same ecumenical age the same churches experienced the need to come together as confessional families, to revisit their traditional confessional identity and go as far as to provide it with international institutional expression.[4] The first Lambeth Conference of Anglican bishops from provinces in communion with the Archbishop of Canterbury met in London in 1867. The Presbyterian Alliance,[5] gathering the Reformed and the Presbyterians mainly from Anglo-Saxon countries, was organized in 1875, also in London. The Ecumenical Methodist Conference met for the first time in 1881. The Old Catholic Union of Utrecht was created in 1889. The International Congregational Council was founded in London in 1891. The Baptist World Alliance was organized in 1905. The first Lutheran World Convention was held in Eisenach, Germany, in 1923. The Disciples of Christ from different countries met for the first time as a Convention in 1930. We nowadays call these confessional bodies and other worldwide church bodies "Christian world communions."

The encounter, the interaction between the ecumenical movement and the confessional movement, between ecumenical conciliar organizations and international expressions of different church families, and more specifically between the WCC and the Christian world communions, has a long history marked by institutional tensions,[6] theological debate on the unity we seek[7] and, more recently, by the laborious search for a complementarity which remains to be spelled out in a clear and consensual way.[8]

Why is it so? Because in this encounter between the confessional and the ecumenical what has been at stake is no less than the *raison d'être*, the sense, the ultimate aim, the integrity of the ecumenical movement itself. If a divided witness in the mission lands of Asia and Africa is seen as the scandal to overcome, then the building of united churches, of Christian communities which no longer identify themselves along the lines of what has divided them elsewhere in the past, is a test-case of ecumenical integrity in the present and a foretaste of the real possibilities of the ecumenical movement in the future. The rise of confessional organizations appears, against this background, as a threat both to the ecumenical ideal and to its most important instruments, namely the International Missionary Council and the WCC.

II. Against "Confessionalism": The Emergence of WARC's Ecumenical Self-Understanding

I will now turn to more narrative and adopt the present tense in order to try to demonstrate as vividly as possible that, after the foundation of the WCC in 1948, the self-understanding of the Alliance of Reformed Churches as an ecumenical actor is shaped by these two dynamics of the ecumenical age, by what was yesterday often the tension – and is often seen today as the laborious complementarity – between the ecumenical and the confessional. My red thread will be the life of a church servant, a person who incarnated both the tensions and the laborious search for complementarity between the ecumenical and the confessional. I am speaking of John Mackay.

Born in Inverness, Scotland, in 1889, Mackay studies in Aberdeen and Princeton (USA), and is for some years a Presbyterian missionary in Peru. This leads him to study Iberian culture and philosophy and to reflect and write on gospel and culture in Latin America. We find him also in Montevideo, Uruguay, and Mexico City, Mexico, as the religious work secretary with the South American Federation of the YMCAs from 1926 to 1932.

When we meet Mackay in 1948 he is the first professor of the newly created chair of ecumenics at Princeton Theological Seminary and also president of that traditional (in more than one sense) North American Presbyterian institution. But not only this. Mackay has just been appointed the chairman of the International Missionary Council (IMC) and the head of the joint IMC-WCC Committee, which will prepare the integration of the IMC into the WCC. He is also a member of the Executive Committee of the World Presbyterian Alliance – which will become the World Alliance of Reformed Churches in 1954 – and he will be WARC's president from 1954 to 1959.

Geneva 1948: Confessionalism is Rising, but Presbyterianism is "Naturally Ecumenical"

The World Presbyterian Alliance holds its world assembly in Geneva, Switzerland, August 11 to 17, 1948, shortly before the WCC holds its first world assembly. The assembly program includes two addresses on "the present ecumenical situation." One of them is by John Mackay, who offers at the outset an overview of the existing ecumenical situation. For the first time in history, he says, the church has become "*ecumenical* in a geographical sense."[9] Within non-Roman Christianity, this "ecumenical" movement is marked by two different trends. One, centripetal, is "a trend towards greater understanding, unity and co-operation among non-Roman Catholic churches." The other is described in the following terms: "certain Protestant denominations constitute what might be termed ecumenical denominations or confessional blocks. There is thus emerging world Lutheranism, world Anglicanism, world Methodism, etc." And he asks: What then should be the Reformed attitude "on an issue of this kind"?[10]

Mackay goes on to spell out, in the second part of his address, "the actual relations of the Reformed churches to the ecumenical movement." While some of them take no part in the general ecumenical movement, Reformed churches in general "have ordinarily been very co-operative in their relations with other churches." They have played "a leading part in determining the thought and in shaping the policy of the contemporary ecumenical movement."[11]

Mackay enumerates, in the third part of his address, some elements in the Reformed tradition "which have a bearing on the attitude which the Reformed Churches should adopt towards the ecumenical movement." John Calvin was "the most ecumenical figure of his time." His doctrine of the Church and the Reformed doctrine of the communion of saints "produce naturally a spirit of friendly relationship towards all Christian churches…" When true to itself, Presbyterianism "is naturally ecumenical." Due to the developing ecumenical situation, it is imperative that Reformed churches work out a Reformed doctrine of the church as the Catholics, Orthodox, Anglicans, and Lutherans have done in recent times. Reformed churches should achieve "closer solidarity" in their relations. In a given country, they should do all in their power "to achieve unity, and if possible, organic union, between all the members of the Reformed family within that country, giving to the consummation of organic union between Reformed churches priority, other things being equal, over union with churches belonging to a different ecclesiastical tradition."[12] The contributions which the Reformed tradition has to make to the ecumenical movement include, in his view, "a vertebrate Christo-centric theology," the ethical insistence that "all truth is in order to goodness," and the affirmation that Jesus Christ is the sole Head of the Church, as an antidote "to any trend to Romanize Protestantism."[13]

But what is right now pushing Chairman Mackay to be so concerned with the rise of "confessionalism" in general and to insist in particular on the fact that Presbyterianism is "naturally ecumenical"? For the answer, we need to meet him in Cambridge in 1949.

Cambridge 1949: Against Confessional Mission in the South

The Alliance's Executive Committee meets in 1949 in Cambridge, England. The agenda includes two items on the "problems of the missionary movement and of the younger churches as related to the

Alliance." Chairman Mackay, just back from a session of the joint IMC-WCC Committee, introduces the issue. He stresses the importance for the Alliance "to keep in close touch with the Missionary movement," that means in close touch with attempts to create united churches especially in Asia and in Africa.

Mackay is "strongly of the opinion" that the Alliance "should not imitate the Lutherans and promote Missions as an Alliance," which means confessional mission.[14] If this really happens, "it will give a new character to international denominationalism," for this will perpetuate among young churches in the South past intra-Protestant divisions inherited from their mother churches in the North.

Presbyterianism should pursue "an ecumenical policy, true to the spirit of Calvin" and encourage younger churches "to take the lead in the formation of United Churches." If a certain trend in the confessional missionary movement develops, he concludes, "it will break the ecumenical movement"; it will tend "to crystallize for the future the ecclesiastical traditions of the past. That would be a tragedy."[15]

The 1949 Executive Committee restates the 1948 attitude of the Alliance to the ecumenical movement by affirming that "while we want to be true to our Reformed and Presbyterian convictions, we are glad to be in the larger body of the World Council of Churches. We want to take our full share in the building of the 'Una Sancta.'"[16] It also agrees on three points concerning "the Alliance and the other Confessional groups": we are not ready "to follow other confessional groups in what we believe to be narrow and dangerous confessionalism"; in foreign mission fields, "we work for union with other Protestant forces"; we are ready "to exchange information with other confessional groups and work together whenever possible."[17]

It is clear now that Mackay and the Reformed Alliance discern a potential conflict not only between the growth of the "confessional blocks" and the ecumenical movement but also between their action and the urgent need to search for visible Christian unity in the mission fields in the South. Mackay and the Alliance leaders are convinced that the Alliance needs to drink from its own well and justify itself in clear complementarity with the ecumenical movement. The specificity of this ecumenical self-understanding needs to be spelt out. This happens two years later.

1951: Confessionalism Betrays Jesus Christ

The agenda of the Alliance's 1951 Executive Committee meeting, held in Basel, Switzerland, includes a discussion on "the future activity of the Alliance." It takes place under the chairmanship of John Mackay. According to the minutes, the chairman pointed out that "we were living in an era of neo-confessionalism and that it was essential for us to define our attitude." After a "good exchange of views," it is felt desirable "to leave the problem of the future activity of the Alliance until after the adoption of the statement on the role of the Alliance in the present ecumenical situation."[18] The statement is adopted in the same meeting and submitted to member churches for study and comment.

The first section of the Basel Statement offers an overview of the main ecumenical trends with which we are familiar. The life of Protestant churches in the present time is marked by three main trends. The first is "a potent movement towards ecumenical understanding and unity." The second, in opposition to the WCC, is a movement towards "the world unity of sectarian groups." The third, neo-confessionalism or "ecumenical denominationalism," represents "the desire on the part of each major Protestant communion to rediscover and purify its own religious heritage and to unite the churches which belong to it in a denominational world fellowship."

In view of this church situation, says the statement in its second section, it is important that the Alliance should "define its significance and objectives in the present church situation."[19] The Reformed tradition in post-Reformation Christianity is "by nature ecumenical." It is committed "to the pursuit of Christian unity upon the basis of loyal commitment to the essential verities of the Christian faith." The Church is an instrument of God's glory. In the same way, it is the true nature of Presbyterianism "never to be merely an end in itself, but to serve the Church Universal of Jesus Christ." The highest glory of the Reformed tradition is "to maintain the vision and viewpoint of the Church Universal, seeking continually its welfare and unity."[20]

The statement goes on to affirm the need "to increase solidarity among the members of the Reformed family." It offers and thus advocates "a strengthening of the Alliance of Reformed Churches." The promotion of solidarity among Reformed churches "would help to emphasize aspects of the Reformation heritage which are of permanent significance for the Christian Church and the secular order at the present time." The younger Presbyterian churches would then be led "to understand that it is the true glory of this tradition to seek and promote Christian solidarity and also church union where the local or national situation demands it." Membership in the Alliance is important for those Reformed churches which are not part of the "ecumenical movement for Christian unity." It strengthens them "against schismatic elements in their own ranks" and prevents them "from giving their adhesion to any organisation designed to disrupt ecumenical unity and to thwart Presbyterian solidarity."[21]

The Executive Committee of the Alliance, concludes the statement, "is acutely aware" of the perils presented by "ecumenical denominationalism." The Alliance "would never desire to be a party to preventing the incorporation of one of its member churches into wider ecclesiastical relationships." Presbyterianism, on the other hand, is called to see to it "that the resurgence of denominationalism, which is manifest around the globe, shall not become sectarian, but shall remain ecumenical in character." If the great world denominations, the Reformed churches among them, "pursue denominational preeminence and make their great world bodies ends in themselves, they will betray Jesus Christ." Conversely, if they desire "to make denominational emphasis an enrichment of that common evangelical heritage, they will, by so doing fulfil the designs of the one Head of the Church and be true organs of the Holy Spirit."[22]

1954: Reformed, Therefore Ecumenical

The World Alliance holds its 1954 general council in Princeton, New Jersey, once again just a couple of weeks before the WCC meets for its second Assembly in Evanston, Illinois. The 1954 general council is very ecumenically oriented.[23] Well-known Reformed theologians and church leaders such as Joseph Hromadka and W. A. Visser't Hooft address that world gathering on the Reformed churches and the ecumenical movement. In his opening address on the main theme of the Princeton general council, John Mackay, *l'incontournable*, reflects first of all on the witness of the "Reformed heritage," then on the witness of the "Confessional Alliance."[24]

The Reformed, he writes, share with all evangelical Christians the "four great foundations" of Christian religion, namely "the supreme authority of the Bible, Jesus Christ as God and Saviour, the reality of the new man in Christ, and the Christian Church as the community of Christ." At the same time, they hold certain "specific emphases" that constitute their "particular contribution" to the Church catholic. The first one is "the sovereign rule of God in the affairs of men." The second is "the instrumental role of the Christian and the Christian Church." God was supremely manifest within history "in the form of a Servant." The Christian and the Church belong to God, are the servants of God. They can never be an end in themselves. The Church is most truly the Church "when it is God's servant, the medium whereby He expresses His redemptive love to mankind." This Reformed emphasis, he goes on to say, "needs to be blazoned forth in the present ecumenical situation." No Church "can ever be regarded as an end in itself or the master of its members."[25]

Mackay then addresses the witness of the "confessional Alliance" in the present ecumenical context. This time, he discerns just two basic trends in the ecumenical movement. One is "towards world-wide unity among the Churches" and the other is "towards confessional unity." There is no greater need than to think through "the problem of the new confessionalism in its relation to the ecumenical movement of our time."

He goes on to propose five statements. Firstly, that "we are not, and we should never become, an ecclesiastical block." Secondly, that "we are loyally committed to Christ's Church Universal." While Christians are one in Christ and are called "to give the maximum visible expression to unity," structure "is not of the essence of the Church." There are two things we Presbyterians must repudiate "with all our might": one is what has been called "ecclesiastical tribalism" and the other is "the idea of a super Church." This means that "we do not regard the Roman ideal as the ideal for the Church of Jesus Christ." We do not consider that "the ultimate historical form of Christian unity involves a 'single, unified Church structure, dominated by a centralized administrative authority.'"[26]

Thirdly, Mackay proposes that "we emphasize the place of the local in the sphere of the ecumenical." Fourthly, he wishes "to stress the importance of theology." And lastly, he proclaims that "a Church is validated as a Church of God not by its organized structure, but by its missionary action." Structure is not an end in itself, "nor can it be made the supreme criterion of a true Church." The Church becomes the Church, he concludes, "not when it extols its virtues, but when it accepts its God-given mission."[27]

The Alliance's 1954 world assembly adopts a statement on *The Reformed Churches and the Ecumenical Movement*. Here is its argument. The ecumenical movement is "a singularly significant fact about the Christian Church in our time." This "deep stirring" towards the unity of the churches "is of God, not men, a sign of the work of the Holy Spirit."[28] The Reformed churches throughout the world "have taken an active part" in the ecumenical movement. A confessional alliance such as ours "can and must provide the opportunity and the means for furthering the ecumenical reality of the Church." It has not always been clearly understood by some Reformed churches that "the Reformers never intended to create a new Church but to restore the faith and life of the Church in obedience to the word of God."[29]

The unity of the Church is a gift in Christ. Jesus Christ transforms us and makes us fully human in and through our fellowship with one another. He breaks down all barriers of separation. He reconciles and unites. Wherever and whenever his gathered believers preach and practice his gospel of reconciliation and communion and administer the sacraments according to his institution, there he is and "where Christ is, there is the Church," one and holy, catholic, and apostolic. Whenever the community of believers is divided by "the various forms of faith and life of the Church," Christ himself "calls these churches to unity and wills to accomplish it in them through his Word and Spirit." Unity is also a task: Christians are, therefore, "under a particular and pressing responsibility to give visible expression to the unity which the Lord of the Church will and works among them."[30]

The visible structure of the Church "is not identical with the unity of the Church," though "structure and unity cannot be separated." There is a living relation between Christ and the members of his body. This is continually and continuously expressed "in the living adaptation of the structures of the Church's faith and life to the sovereign and redemptive work of Christ in the Church and in the world."[31]

As Reformed and Presbyterian Churches, we thus "recognise the ministry, sacraments and membership of all churches, which, according to the Bible, confess Jesus Christ as Lord and Saviour." Their members are all invited and gladly welcome "to the table of our common Lord." The table is the Lord's, says the statement, not ours. "We believe that we dare not refuse the sacrament to any baptized person who loves and confesses Jesus Christ as Lord and Saviour." We cannot proclaim the gospel of reconciliation "without demonstrating at the Table of the Lord that we are reconciled to one another." Therefore "we would welcome face to face talks with our fellow Christians in other churches, looking towards the time when all sincere Christians will be welcome around a common Table."[32]

Calvin's doctrine of the true Church "enables the Reformed Churches to stand at the centre of the ecumenical movement." He severely condemned those "who encourage schism from motives other than those which proceed from absolute obedience to the word of God." It is therefore "urgently necessary" to resist "any increase of division in the Body of Christ and to labour to compose all differences of faith and order which are not justified by obedience to the word of God…" Especially today "there is a kind of 'ecumenical sectarianism' which gravely disturbs the peace and unity of the community of believers."[33]

Some kind of structure "is necessary to the Church." Our adherence to the Presbyterian Order "is inspired by the fact that it expresses certain fundamental aspects of the nature and life of the Church." But we do not consider it to be "the one indispensable government structure of the Church." Likewise we cannot regard any particular existing form of episcopacy as a "fundamental condition of the restoration of the unity of the Church."[34]

Finally, the statement notes that obedience to Christ involves not only unity but also mission. The oneness of believers in Christ, it says, quoting a well-known 1951 WCC statement on the meaning of ecumenical, "is inseparable from dynamic and effective outreach of the Church into every part of the world and into every phase of the world's life."[35]

What then is "the role of the Alliance in the present ecumenical situation"? A confessional alliance such as ours "can and must provide the opportunity and the means for furthering the ecumenical reality of the Church"; it can "give strength and living reality to every effort to express the mission and unity of the universal Church." The Alliance "is only an instrument in the service of more ultimate purposes" as much as it is the nature of Presbyterianism "never to be an end in itself." It desires therefore "to collaborate closely with the World Council of Churches and the International Missionary Council as the main organisational expressions of that movement." Thanks to the WCC basis, the way is open to all Alliance member churches to join the Council. Churches which are the fruit of the missionary work "should be free to enter into local or regional union with other Christian bodies if, in this way, they can bear a better witness to Christ."[36]

However, at least three reasons call "for a strong and active Presbyterian and Reformed confessional agency." The first is the need for "bearing witness to the basic doctrinal position of the Reformed Churches." In the framework of ecumenical conversations, "the task of the Alliance is steadily to exhort the Reformed Churches to have recourse to the Holy Scriptures as the only rule of faith and practice." There are aspects in which the aid of a confessional organization to the exercise by the churches of their ecumenical doctrinal responsibility "may play an important role in the contemporary ecumenical situation." The second reason is the need for emphasizing "the fundamentals of our Presbyterian polity." The Alliance can serve as an instrument "by promoting our joint study of polity, by bringing us to greater unity in our convictions regarding it, and by gaining for these convictions a hearing in ecumenical circles which no single Church could command." The third reason is the need for "rendering certain practical services to members of the Presbyterian and Reformed family," including "the initiation of studies of union or reunions (...) of the constituent churches of the Alliance with each other or with other churches."[37]

This six-year reflection on the Alliance and the modern ecumenical movement – which will inspire the creation of the Conference of
Christian world communions in 1957[38] and the merger between the
Alliance and the Congregational Council in 1970 – can be summarized in the following propositions. First, the international movement
towards greater Christian fellowship among churches is marked by at
least two major trends: one of them is the ecumenical movement, the
search for Christian unity; the other one is the confessional movement,
the search for a renewed sense of belonging to a given church family.
Confessionalism has the potential of causing great damage to the search
for Christian unity. Second, Presbyterian and Reformed churches have
been actively involved in the ecumenical movement. The Reformed
tradition offers significant impulses to ecumenical engagement. Third,
Presbyterianism is not an end in itself. As it adopts the point of view
of the church universal, it should resist confessionalism. Lastly, there
are reasons that speak in favour of a strong WARC. These reasons are
complementary to the engagement of Reformed churches in the search
for Reformed unity and united churches.

III. Towards a Supra-Confessional Fellowship of Churches

I will now demonstrate how this particular ecumenical self-
understanding, formulated in opposition to "confessionalism," progressively shapes the whole self-understanding of WARC and transforms
it into a family of church families, into a sort of supra-confessional
fellowship of Reformation churches sharing a common Reformation
and theological memory.

I will demonstrate this remarkable transformation by briefly
reviewing the references to the confessional and to the ecumenical
in the three successive versions of the foundational document of the
World Alliance: its constitution. I will consider two questions for each
of those three different versions of the Alliance's constitution: Which
churches are eligible for membership in the Alliance, and what are the
purposes of the Alliance? I will then try to discern in the language of
the answers the dynamic interaction between the confessional and
the ecumenical.

The 1875 Constitution

The first constitution of the Alliance is adopted by representatives of twenty-one churches mainly from Britain and the United States – but also from Western Europe – who gather in London, in July 1875, as a "Pan-Presbyterian Council" to manifest their "substantial unity" and promote "harmony of action" in mission.[39]

Which churches are eligible for membership in the Alliance? They are those that are "organised on Presbyterian principles," affirm the "supreme authority" of the Scriptures and whose creed is "in harmony with the consensus of the Reformed Confessions."[40] What are the purposes of the Alliance? The aims of its world assembly are to "consider questions of general interest to the Presbyterian community...; seek the welfare of the Churches, especially such as are weak or persecuted...; commend the Presbyterian system as Scriptural, and as combining simplicity, efficiency, and adaptation to all times and conditions..."; and to address topics directly connected with the work of Evangelisation, such as "the best method of opposing infidelity and Romanism."[41]

Are there "ecumenical" references in this first constitution? There are at least two. Firstly, according to the preamble, the Presbyterian Alliance is not to be seen in opposition to other forms of inter-church cooperation. The "essential oneness" of the members of the Presbyterian Alliance is not confined to their Reformed faith and Presbyterian government or polity. The churches that are forming the Presbyterian Alliance are ready to join with the other churches "in Christian fellowship, and in advancing the cause of the Redeemer." They are ready to do so on the basis of "the general principle maintained and taught in the Reformed Confessions," namely that "the Church of God on earth, though composed of many members, is one body in the communion of the Holy Ghost, of which body Christ is the supreme Head, and the Scriptures alone are the infallible law."[42] Secondly, there is a reference to the methods of opposing "Romanism." It shows the limits of the first point, by implying that the true body of Christ is to be found only in the Reformation family.

The Alliance is a fellowship of churches that affirm the supreme authority of the Scriptures, hold the Reformed faith as their confession in harmony with the consensus of Reformed confessions, and are organized on Presbyterian principles. They seek, through the Alliance, to study together issues of common Presbyterian interest, and to promote the Presbyterian system as Scriptural. The Alliance is ecumenically pan-protestant because its member churches are ready to join and cooperate with other non-Roman churches.

The 1954 Constitution

The second constitution[43] is adopted only in 1954, almost eighty years later. As we have seen above, this is a time in which, under the leadership of John Mackay, the Alliance, seeking to take distance from what it calls "confessionalism," is formulating its self-understanding as a fellowship of Reformed churches which see their future post-confessionally, within the ecumenical movement.

Which churches are eligible for membership in the Alliance? They are those that accept "Jesus Christ as Lord and Saviour," and hold the Scriptures to be "the supreme authority in matters of faith and life"; their doctrinal position "is in harmony with the consensus of the Reformed Confessions" and their polity "is in accord with the Presbyterian order." United churches with a "sufficient and substantial part of the Reformed heritage" and Reformed bodies within interconfessional associations of churches are also eligible. Membership in the Alliance "does not restrict the relationship of any Church with other churches or with other interchurch bodies."[44]

What are the purposes of the Alliance? The new constitution lists ten items, some of which include more than one purpose. They can be grouped together under the following five headings: 1) to deepen fellowship, intercourse, and solidarity among member churches; 2) to unite forces in common service, study of the faith, mission and evangelism, and information sharing; 3) to commend the Reformed faith, the preaching of the word of God, worship rightly ordered, and the Presbyterian order; 4) to study and advise on church union or reunion negotiations; and 5) to advocate religious and civil liberty.

The 1954 constitution – adopted at the moment in which the Alliance formulates its self-understanding as a fellowship of Reformed churches which see their future post-confessionally – does not innovate in its confessional references. The Alliance remains a fellowship of churches that affirm the supreme authority of the Scriptures, hold the Reformed faith as their confession in harmony with the consensus of Reformed confessions, and are organized on Presbyterian principles. They seek, through the Alliance, to promote Reformed faith and life, and the Presbyterian order.

The same lack of innovation cannot be said of its supra-confessional or ecumenical references. They are abundant and mirror both the emerging "beyond confessionalism" self-understanding of the Alliance and the new ecumenical situation. The churches eligible for membership are those that, prior to their confessional identity, affirm the basis of the newly constituted WCC, namely "Jesus Christ as Lord and Saviour." United churches with substantial Reformed heritage and Reformed bodies within interconfessional associations are also eligible. Membership in the Alliance "does not restrict the relationship of any Church with other Churches or with other interchurch bodies." The member churches seek, through the Alliance, to study, advise, and support church union or church reunion negotiations not only among the Alliance's member churches but also with other churches. They no longer seek together to design ways of opposing the Roman Catholic Church.

The 1970 Constitution

The third constitution of the World Alliance was adopted in 1970, when the Alliance took a step forwards in the implementation of its "beyond confessionalism" self-understanding and merged with another Christian world communion, the International Congregational Council (ICC), founded in London in 1891.[45] This is to date the only case – but hopefully not the last one – of a merger involving two international confessional bodies.[46]

The historical roots of Congregationalism lie in the Protestant resistance to church establishment and church uniformity in England in the 16th and 17th centuries. Congregational Christians translate their recognition of God's sovereignty in salvation and Christ's lordship in the world, through the Spirit, into a way of ordering the church which, unlike Presbyterianism, affirms first of all the autonomy of the local congregation and, secondly, the mutual recognition of these congregations and cooperation among them and with other Christian communities. The purposes of the ICC include "strengthening the Congregational contribution to the WCC and the ecumenical movement generally."[47] By the time of the merger with the Alliance, 85% of the member churches of the ICC were also members of the WCC.

Which churches are eligible for membership in the newly created World Alliance of Reformed Churches? Eligible for membership is any church that "accepts Jesus Christ as Lord and Saviour," holds the Scriptures to be "the supreme authority in matters of faith and life," acknowledges "the need for the continuing reformation of the Church catholic," whose position in faith and evangelism is "in general agreement with that of the historic Reformed confessions," and which recognizes that the Reformed tradition "is a biblical, evangelical, and doctrinal ethos" rather than "any narrow and exclusive definition of faith and order." United churches that "share this understanding of the nature and calling of the Church" are also eligible for membership. Membership in the Alliance "does not restrict the relationship of any Church with other Churches or with other inter-church bodies."

What are the purposes of the newly created WARC? They include to further "all endeavours to proclaim the Word of God faithfully" and to order the Church's life and worship accordingly; to further the work of evangelism, mission, stewardship, and the common study of the Christian faith; to encourage the diversity and fraternal character of ministries in the Church; to widen and deepen understanding and fellowship among member churches and churches eligible for membership; to further intercourse between the member churches; to unite the forces of the member churches in common service; to be in solidarity with the oppressed or persecuted churches; to promote and defend religious and civil liberties, and – the last purpose deserves to be quoted in full:

> to facilitate the contribution to the ecumenical movement of the experiences and insights which Churches within this Alliance have been given in their history, and to share with Churches of other traditions within that movement, and particularly in the World Council of Churches, in the discovery of forms of church life and practice which will enable the people of God more fully to understand and express together God's will for his people.[48]

The constitution adopted at the moment in which the Presbyterian and Reformed Alliance merged with the Congregational Council cannot but recast once again its confessional references in order to adapt them to the self-understanding of the newly created fellowship of churches. In the 1875 constitution, these references were essentially the Presbyterian system of church government, a confessional position in harmony with the consensus of the Reformed confessions, and the commitment to promote the Presbyterian system as scriptural. In 1954, these references are a church government in agreement with the Presbyterian order, a confessional position in harmony with the consensus of the Reformed confession, and the commitment to commend the Reformed and Presbyterian order "as a polity founded and agreeable with the New Testament." In the 1970 constitution, only the reference to the Reformed confessions is retained, although it is formulated differently: eligible for membership are those churches "whose position in faith and evangelism are in general agreement with that of the Reformed confessions."

While the specific confessional references disappear, a supra-confessional Reformed language seeks to provide a new sense of identity to the old Presbyterian Alliance. From 2004, the article on the name of the organization includes a specific reference to two "first Reformation" movements: Waldensians and Hussites. Membership requirements retain the reference to the WCC basis in its first version (Jesus Christ as Lord and Saviour), and to the united churches. But they now include the acknowledgement of the need for "the continuing reformation of the Church catholic" and, against confessionalism, define the Reformed tradition as "a biblical, evangelical and doctrinal ethos," rather than "any narrow and exclusive definition of faith and order."

While the constitutional purposes of the new organization no longer make any reference to the words Presbyterian, Reformed, or Congregational, their recasting is once again clearly Reformed catholic. The list of purposes, as we have just seen, starts by a reference to the proclamation of the Word of God. It then envisages in that light church life, worship, ministry, and mission, and culminates in the affirmation of the member churches' participation in the ecumenical movement in general and the WCC in particular.

Once a fellowship of Reformed churches holding the Presbyterian system and open to pan-Protestantism, the Alliance is now a supra-confessional fellowship of first and second Reformation churches which share a biblical, evangelical, doctrinal Reformed ethos and envisage their future within the wider ecumenical movement. Placed between the past isolation of its member churches and the future world fellowship of truly united churches in each place, the World Alliance of Reformed Churches will incarnate this self-understanding in an institutional life often envisaged not only as instrumental but also as provisional, because ultimately shaped by the so-called Lund principle: WARC member churches would do together through WARC only what they could not yet do together with other Christian churches in and through the World Council of Churches. Although it has considerably changed its institutional configuration in recent years, the Alliance has not undertaken a major revision of its supra-confessional self-understanding as a fellowship of churches sharing a certain biblical, evangelical, and doctrinal ethos called Reformed, which challenges them to be the Church.

IV. The Supra-Confessional in the Age of Reconciled Diversity

By the time the Alliance becomes a supra-confessional fellowship of churches which are called to envisage their future preferably as united churches, the ecumenical movement begins to undergo major changes. While the awareness of the ecumenical indicative (that the Church is one, that its oneness is God's gift in Christ, and that this gift mirrors the koinonia of the Holy Trinity) continues to inspire Christians and churches, the understanding and practice of the ecumenical imperative (that is, the task of making manifest the gift of unity) begins to be challenged, if not enlarged, by the emergence of a new critical sense of Christian discipleship which embraces justice in opposition to discrimination and structural poverty, peace in opposition to nuclearization and militarization, and the integrity of creation in opposition to anthropocentrism and environmental degradation. This critical sense of Christian discipleship, that challenges the traditional understanding and practice of the ecumenical imperative, reaches us today as we experience the need to promote inter-religious encounter and solidarity in evangelical opposition to the language of a "clash of civilizations" that masks the ambitions of Empire.

As the understanding and implementation of the ecumenical imperative gains in complexity, we realize that ours is a time of ecumenical uncertainty. And perhaps the best evidence to this affirmation is the fact that there is limited agreement among the different attempts to explain this uncertainty. Is the ecumenical movement going through a time of transition in which the classical ecumenical paradigm built around a Christocentric universalism is being integrated "into a more comprehensive perspective that meets the challenges and contradictions which have arisen"[49] and that expresses itself in the different yet mutually related meanings of the word *oikoumene*?[50] Is the present uncertainty the symptom of a crisis engendered by the ambivalence of ecumenical achievements which requires the reaffirmation of the integrity and indivisibility of the ecumenical movement?[51]

It is clear, nonetheless, that significant elements of the emerging ecumenical perspective challenge the Alliance's traditional self-understanding as a supra-confessional fellowship of Reformed churches oriented to church union as church unity. One of them, perhaps the most important, is the "rehabilitation" of denominational or confessional identities. Challenged by the Faith and Order and WCC vision of the unity we seek as a conciliar fellowship of truly united churches, the Christian world communions respond – along the lines of the 1973 Concord of Leuenberg – by formulating the notion of reconciled diversity as a concept of church unity.[52]

The ecumenical and institutional challenges are clear. How can the Alliance make relevant sense today of its "beyond confessionalism" ecumenical profile in a time in which a plurality of concepts of unity and models of union presuppose that confessional identities are "an element of future structures of church unity"?[53] How can the Alliance make relevant sense of its supra-confessional institutional self-understanding in a time in which profiled denominational or confessional identities progressively become requirements for our staying together and even for our common prayer for the manifestation of the visible unity of the church?

1   William G. Blaikie, first President of the Alliance of the Reformed Churches Presbyterian Alliance (the forerunner of the World Alliance of Reformed Churches) to the 1884 General Council. Cf. G. Mathews (ed.), *Alliance of the Reformed Churches Holding the Presbyterian System – Minutes and Proceedings of the Third General Council, Belfast 1884* (Belfast: Assembly's Office, 1884), p. 100.

2   Lewis S. Mudge, *One Church: Catholic and Reformed* (London: Lutterworth, 1963), pp. 16, 18.

3   Mudge, *One Church*, p. 19.

4   On this topic, see for instance, Ruth Rouse and Stephen Charles Neill, eds., *A History of the Ecumenical Movement, 1517-1948*, 3rd ed. (Geneva: WCC, 1986), pp. 613-20; Harold E. Fey, ed., *The Ecumenical Advance: A History of the Ecumenical Movement, v. 2, 1948-1968*, 2nd ed. (Geneva: WCC, 1986), pp. 117-42.

5   Its full name was then: The Alliance of The Reformed Churches Throughout the World Holding the Presbyterian System.

6   I am thinking, for instance, of the admonition addressed by the Asian Churches to the World Methodist Council, the Anglican Communion and the Lutheran World Federation in 1964 and its follow-up. Cf. Fey, ed., *The Ecumenical Advance*, pp. 124-28.

7   This time I am thinking of the 1974-78 debate opposing two conceptions of the one Church: conciliar fellowship and reconciled diversity. See for instance Harding Meyer, *That All May Be One: Perceptions and Models of Ecumenicity* (Grand Rapids: Eerdmans, 1999).

8   This is the case of ongoing discussions on the possibility of having Christian world communions holding their assemblies in closer cooperation with WCC assemblies. See Stephen Brown, "Towards a common global ecumenical assembly?" *Reformed World* 56, no. 2 (June 2006): 221-47.

9   John Mackay, "The Reformed Churches and the Ecumenical Situation", *Proceedings of the Sixteenth General Council of the Alliance of Reformed Churches Holding the Presbyterian System Held at Geneva, Switzerland 1948* (Edinburgh: Office of the Alliance, 1949), p. 110.

10 Mackay, "The Reformed Churches and the Ecumenical Situation", p. 110.

11 Mackay, "The Reformed Churches and the Ecumenical Situation", pp. 110-11.

12 Mackay, "The Reformed Churches and the Ecumenical Situation", pp. 111-12.

13 Mackay, "The Reformed Churches and the Ecumenical Situation", p. 112.

14 This is how Mackay interprets the Lutheran World Federation's decision to take direct responsibility for what were called after World War II the German "orphaned missions." Mackay's interpretation of this decision as a potential ecumenical risk seems to be reinforced by the decision of the Lutheran churches in India to remain outside the formation of the Church of South India and by the decision of Lutheran churches in Germany to create their own structure alongside the Evangelical Church (EKD). Mackay does not comment on several resolutions, adopted in 1947 by the first LWF Assembly, indicating that "all Lutheran churches were being urged to cooperate in mission efforts, not only among themselves but also with the International Missionary Council" and that "a serious attitude toward the latter agency was seen as an integral part of a common Lutheran ecumenical obligation." Cf. Jens Holger Schjørring, Prasanna Kumari, Norman A. Hjelm, and Viggo Mortensen, eds., *From Federation to Communion: The History of the Lutheran World Federation* (Minneapolis: Fortress Press, 1997), p. 18.

15 Alliance of Reformed Churches Throughout the World Holding the Presbyterian System, *Minutes of the Executive Committee held at Westminster College, Cambridge, England, July 4-6, 1949*, pp. 10-11.

16 *Minutes of the Executive Committee*, Cambridge, 1949, p. 10.

17 *Minutes of the Executive Committee*, Cambridge, 1949, p. 9.

18 John Mackay, "The World Presbyterian Alliance in the Present Ecumenical Situation," in *Meeting of the Executive Committee of the Alliance of Reformed Churches Throughout the World Holding the Presbyterian System – Missionshaus, Basle (Switzerland), August 13-15, 1951*, p. 5.

19 Mackay, "The World Presbyterian Alliance in the Present Ecumenical Situation," p. 25.

20 Mackay, "The World Presbyterian Alliance in the Present Ecumenical Situation," p. 26.

21 Mackay, "The World Presbyterian Alliance in the Present Ecumenical Situation," pp. 26-27.

22 Mackay, "The World Presbyterian Alliance in the Present Ecumenical Situation," p. 27.

23 My survey, *The World Alliance of Reformed Churches and the Modern Ecumenical Movement* (Geneva: WARC, 2005), includes seven documents from Princeton 1954. No further WARC general council matches such a score.

24 John Mackay, "The Witness of the Reformed Churches in the World Today," *Proceedings of the Seventeenth General Council of the Alliance of the Reformed Churches Holding the Presbyterian Order Held at Princeton, NJ, USA, 1954* (Geneva: Office of the Alliance, 1954), pp. 109-20.

25 Mackay, "The Witness of the Reformed Churches," pp. 110-14.

26 Mackay, "The Witness of the Reformed Churches," pp. 114-17.

27 Mackay, "The Witness of the Reformed Churches," pp. 117-20.

28 Alliance of the Reformed Churches Holding the Presbyterian Order, "The Reformed Churches and the Ecumenical Movement", in *Proceedings of the Seventeenth General Council*, p. 73.

29 "The Reformed Churches and the Ecumenical Movement," pp. 73-74.

30 "The Reformed Churches and the Ecumenical Movement," p. 74.

31 "The Reformed Churches and the Ecumenical Movement," p. 74.

32 "The Reformed Churches and the Ecumenical Movement," p. 75.

33 "The Reformed Churches and the Ecumenical Movement," pp. 75-76.

34 "The Reformed Churches and the Ecumenical Movement," p. 76.

35 "The Reformed Churches and the Ecumenical Movement," p. 77. Cf. "The Calling of the Church to Mission and to Unity," in *Minutes and Reports of the Fourth Meeting of the Central Committee of the World Council of Churches, Rolle, Switzerland, August 4-11, 1951* (Geneva: WCC, 1951), p. 65: the word ecumenical "covers equally the missionary movement and the movement towards unity…"

36 "The Reformed Churches and the Ecumenical Movement," p. 77.

37 "The Reformed Churches and the Ecumenical Movement," pp. 77-79.

38 Cf. Odair Pedroso Mateus, "The Alliance, the Christian World Communions and the Ecumenical Movement (1948-1957)," *Reformed World* 54, no. 2 (June 2004): 91-106.

39 William G. Blaikie, "Introductory Narrative", *Report of Proceedings of the First General Presbyterian Council Convened at Edinburgh, July 1877* (Edinburgh: Thomas and Archibald Constable, 1877), pp. 1-13.

40 Edinburgh 1877, Article II.

41 Edinburgh 1877, Article III.4.

42 Edinburgh 1877, Preamble.

43 "Constitution of the Alliance," in *Proceedings of the Seventeenth General Council*, pp. 55-58.

44 "Constitution of the Alliance - Article II – Membership," in *Proceedings of the Seventeenth General Council*, p. 55.

45 "Constitution", *Nairobi 1970 – Proceedings of the Uniting General Council* (Geneva: Offices of the Alliance, 1970), pp. 40-42. All quotations from the 2004 amended version: *Accra 2004*, Proceedings of the 24th General Council of the World Alliance of Reformed Churches (Geneva: WARC, 2005), pp. 290-96.

46 This essay was written before June 2010 when WARC and the Reformed Ecumenical Council merged into the new World Communion of Reformed Churches, WCRC.

47 Ruth Rouse, "Other Aspects of the Ecumenical Movement 1910-1948," in Rouse and Neill, eds., *A History of the Ecumenical Movement 1517-1948*, pp. 613-14.

48 *Accra 2004*, p. 292.

49 Cf. Konrad Raiser, *Ecumenism in Transition: A Paradigm Shift in the Ecumenical Movement* (Geneva: WCC, 1991), p. 122.

50 Cf. Konrad Raiser, "Ecumenism in Search of a New Vision," in Michael Kinnamon and Brian E. Cope, eds., *The Ecumenical Movement: An Anthology of Key Texts and Voices* (Geneva: WCC; Grand Rapids: Eerdmans, 1997), pp. 70-77.

51 Institute for Ecumenical Research, Strasbourg, *Crisis and Challenge of the Ecumenical Movement: Integrity and Indivisibility* (Geneva: WCC, 1994).

52 Cf. Conference of Secretaries of Christian World Communions, "The Ecumenical Role of the World Confessional Families in the One Ecumenical Movement" and Günther Gassmann and Harding Meyer "Requirements and Structure of Church Unity," in Günther Gassmann and Harding Meyer, *The Unity of the Church: Requirements and Structure*, LWF Reports, 15 (Geneva: Lutheran World Federation, 1983), pp. 27-31 and 3-10.

53 *Dictionary of the Ecumenical Movement*, 2nd ed., s.v. "Unity," by Günther Gassmann; cf. also Michael Root, "'Reconciled Diversity' and the Visible Unity of the Church", in Colin Podmore, ed., *Community – Unity – Communion: Essays in Honour of Mary Tanner* (London: Church House, 1998), pp. 237-51.

† CHAPTER 10

Mennonite Engagement in International Ecumenical Conversations: Experiences, Perspectives, and Guiding Principles[1]

by Helmut Harder and Larry Miller

At the time of the sixteenth-century Reformation, the Anabaptists, forerunners of the Mennonites, distinguished themselves as "radicals," particularly in light of their missionary zeal and the resistance they encountered for their commitment to believers baptism, economic sharing, and an ethic of nonviolence. But that legacy proved to be short-lived. Under the pressure of severe persecution the Mennonites, particularly those groups with roots in Switzerland and South Germany, became known as "the quiet in the land." Over time, they withdrew from the mainstream of society and had relatively little contact with the state churches or, in North America, with Catholics or the mainline Protestant denominations. This situation persisted to a greater or lesser degree until well into the twentieth century.

However, in recent decades much has changed. While some Mennonites still fortify their faith and life within tightly knit religious communities, many have moved into the mainstream of society and into constructive relationships with other church bodies. Over the past century, conversation and cooperation between the Mennonite family of churches and their ecclesial counterparts have improved. Though this is noticeable at both national and international levels, the present essay focuses on the latter.

The first stage of development came at about the midpoint of the twentieth century, although there had been occasional exchanges between Mennonites and other church bodies for several decades before that time.[2] The two gruesome world wars that highlighted the first half of the twentieth century provided the occasion. At the time, the churches were asking hard questions: What is the will of God with respect to war and peace? What is the role of the churches in advocating for world peace? These questions were prominently on the agenda of the newly formed World Council of Churches (WCC) in 1948. Because of their historic peace position, the Mennonite community was, for the first time, drawn into ecumenical discussion. To this day, the peace agenda remains a dominant feature of ecumenical dialogue where Mennonites are involved. Part I of what follows here provides an overview of the Mennonite engagement with the other churches in conversations on peace.

A second stage of Mennonite engagement with the other churches began about three decades later, in the late 1970s. By then, two movements were influencing the churches to pursue ecumenical discussion with a view to Christian unity, or at least to consider closer cooperation. The first was the momentum created in and around the WCC. The second movement was initiated by the Catholic Church in the early 1960s. Its Second Vatican Council called for vigorous pursuit of ecumenical conversations with Christians of all persuasions.[3] The second part of this essay provides an overview of the Mennonite engagement in interchurch dialogues, with particular attention to the Catholic-Mennonite dialogue (1998-2003). While the peace agenda played a role in these dialogues, the primary focus was on interchurch reconciliation to overcome past schisms.

In view of the increasing Mennonite engagement in ecumenical dialogue, a pressing question arises: What are the principles that should guide Mennonite churches in their pursuit of church unity?[4] And, can these principles also be of use to other Christians engaged in ecumenical conversations? With the exception of several Mennonite theologians who have occasionally addressed issues related to ecumenical participation, Mennonite churches as such have given little attention to principles of ecumenical conversation. In the third part, we offer a series of guidelines for interchurch dialogue. While these come from a Mennonite perspective, they are not meant for consideration by Mennonites alone, but by all who engage in interchurch conversations in the context of the 500th anniversaries of the Reformation (2017) and the Radical Reformation (2025). Nor are these principles set forth as exhaustive. Rather, we offer them as a complement to those recommended by other churches with experience in ecumenical dialogue.[5]

Mennonite Peace Witness in the Context of the World Council of Churches

The WCC came into being in 1948, shortly after the end of the Second World War. While only two Mennonite groups took up membership in the WCC at the time (the Dutch and the North German Mennonite churches), some representatives of the global Mennonite family participated in the WCC's discussions of the day. They did so as part of a group of three pacifist communions – the Mennonites, the Church of the Brethren, and the Friends (Quakers) – which came to be known as the historic peace churches (HPC). Joining frequently with the International Fellowship of Reconciliation (IFOR), the agenda in which the historic peace churches participated had to do primarily with ethical issues related to war and peace, and to church and state.[6] Since discussions of the day centred on these issues, it seemed reasonable for these churches to present their case for peace together; and indeed, they were invited to do so.

Over the years, the HPC group has focused on ethical issues related to peace and justice.[7] In this, they mainly responded to what was asked of them, since the peace witness seemed to be their "specialty." One of the first notable contributions by the peace churches in the early post-war ecumenical context was a document submitted on behalf of the HPC group prior to the WCC's assembly (1954) in Evanston, Illinois, under the title *Peace is the Will of God*.[8] This evoked a response from Reinhold Niebuhr in defence of the just war position.[9] The peace churches' document, entitled "God Establishes both Peace and Justice" (1958), written largely by Mennonite scholars, took Niebuhr's arguments into account in its counter-defense of the pacifist position.[10]

The historic peace churches were also among the initiators of a series of four major WCC-related "Puidoux conferences" (1955-1962).[11] These meetings engaged peace churches and state churches on the theme "The Lordship of Christ over Church and State." Another conference planned by the WCC Study Department, held at Bossey,

Switzerland (1968), brought pacifist and nonpacifist theologians together for debate on war and peace. Mennonites were involved in this dialogue.

Notable also, as a Mennonite contribution to the work of the WCC in the early years, were the frequent presentations, both as public addresses and published articles, that Mennonite theologian John Howard Yoder contributed, often unsolicited, to the WCC's ongoing agenda.[12] These presentations addressed such themes as "Peace Without Eschatology?"[13] presented at a theological study conference in the Netherlands (1954); "The Otherness of the Church,"[14] a lecture originally delivered at Drew University (1960); "Christ, the Light of the World,"[15] an essay reflecting the theme of the Third Assembly of the WCC at New Delhi in 1961; and "Christ, the Hope of the World,"[16] a series of two lectures first presented in Argentina in 1966.

Beginning in the late 1960s, the historic peace churches and the International Fellowship of Reconciliation contributed to the WCC discussions on violence and nonviolence, an issue related not only to warfare, but also to economic, political, and social structures of injustice. Events such as the assassination of Martin Luther King Jr. and the American war in Vietnam gave new impetus to the importance of the peace witness in the ecumenical context. The WCC's Fourth Assembly (Uppsala, 1968) made some effort to deal with the issue of violence. However, the results left the historic peace churches dissatisfied. At a subsequent consultation, a Mennonite, Paul Peachey, presented a paper entitled "The Problem of Violence: Let's Start All Over Again." At about the same time an ad hoc group, including two Mennonites, formed an HPC Consultative Committee devoted to bringing peace church perspectives to bear on WCC deliberations. The consultative committee continued to advocate for more courageous steps to overcome violence.[17] At the WCC's Nairobi Assembly (1975), historic peace church delegates, representing a "pacifist minority," advocated for nonviolent alternatives to military engagement. John Howard Yoder was particularly proactive in these initiatives. The HPC group came away from the Nairobi assembly convinced that their voice in support of demilitarization and nonviolence had been less effective than hoped. By the mid-1970s, the WCC began to shift its attention to issues and programs related to militarism and disarmament.[18]

In preparation for the WCC Vancouver Assembly (1983), Mennonites once again became involved, through the HPC, in developing strategies for voicing concerns at the Assembly.[19] Following the Vancouver Assembly, a new WCC program theme emerged under the title "Justice, Peace, and the Integrity of Creation." Yoder was a participant in the development of the program theme. At that time, the historic peace churches considered drafting a new document against the background of Justice, Peace, and the Integrity of Creation. A committee, with Yoder as coordinator, went to work. The result was a lengthy statement, released under the title *A Declaration on Peace: In God's People the World's Renewal Has Begun* (1990). The publication was widely promoted at WCC's Canberra Assembly (1991). There, Mennonites again collaborated with the other historic peace church groups to bring peace church concerns to the process.[20]

We conclude this brief resumé with a reference to the WCC's recent and still ongoing voice against violence. In 1994, the WCC introduced its "Program to Overcome Violence." The program was designed "with the purpose of challenging and transforming the global culture of violence in the direction of a culture of just peace."[21] The HPC Consultative Committee worked with vigour to support and extend the vision of this new program. What resulted was the WCC's "Decade to Overcome Violence (2001-2010),"[22] which concluded with the International Ecumenical Peace Convocation (2011, Jamaica). The convocation harvested the fruits of the decade and urged all Christians, especially WCC member churches, to commit themselves to nonviolence, justice, and peace. The WCC's own commitment was made clear two years later, at the council's Tenth Assembly, when it launched the "Pilgrimage of Justice and Peace," which provides the overall programmatic orientation of the WCC until the next assembly. Mennonites were integrally involved in the development of each of these initiatives, and subsequently in providing resources and leadership for them.[23]

In summary, it becomes apparent that while Mennonites did not function at the centre of the ecumenical movement, and with very few exceptions did not become members of the WCC or of national councils, Mennonite representatives were deeply involved with ecumenical initiatives that challenged and shaped a major component of the witness of the ecumenical movement. The Gospel message of peace, Mennonites would insist, represents an essential component of the Gospel as such.[24] This conviction provided an important part of the impetus and the confidence Mennonites needed to venture into the world of ecumenical discourse. Mennonite engagement in ecumenical issues of peace and justice may have prepared them for another kind of involvement with the ecumenical community, namely church-to-church dialogue.

Mennonite Engagement in Church-to-Church Dialogue

Beginning in the early 1980s, the Mennonite World Conference entered into international bilateral dialogue with five world communions: the World Alliance of Reformed Churches, the Baptist World Alliance, the Lutheran World Federation, the Seventh-day Adventist Church, and the Catholic Church.[25] Of these, the Lutheran-Mennonite and the Catholic-Mennonite dialogues – both focusing on "reconciliation" – have been the most extensive and fruitful, judging by the length of the dialogue reports and the kinds of post-dialogue initiatives that the dialogue has spawned. They have also been the most "dramatic" given the "distance" that needed to be spanned in bridging the chasm that separated Mennonites from these two communions for almost five centuries.

Following a brief review of the Mennonites' international bilateral dialogues with Reformed, Baptists, Lutherans, and Seventh-day Adventists, as well as a multilateral dialogue with a wider circle of churches, we will turn our attention to a more extensive discussion of the international Catholic-Mennonite dialogue. A question underlying our review of all these dialogues is this: Given the purpose of church-to-church dialogues, namely the quest for Christian unity, what are the principles and aims that guide our "effort to maintain the unity of the Spirit in the bond of peace" (Eph. 4:3)? In Part III of the essay we will propose for consideration a list of guiding principles for interchurch dialogue.

Bilateral Dialogue with Reformed Churches

At the invitation of the World Alliance of Reformed Churches in the early 1980s, representatives of the Mennonite World Conference entered into bilateral dialogue with representatives of Reformed Churches.[26] An initial exchange took place in Strasbourg, France, in 1984. The consultation was called "to ask if the time had come for Mennonite and Reformed Christians to look afresh at their relationship to one another."[27] Despite the fact that these two churches trace their beginnings to a time marked by schism and persecution, the Strasbourg dialogue, long overdue, was characterized by a readiness to affirm common historic roots and numerous points of foundational theological convergence, beginning with *sola scriptura, sola gratia,* and *sola fide.* At the same time, the participants identified differences, especially with regard to the theology and practice of baptism, ecclesiology, and state-church relations, including war and peace. At the end of this brief first meeting, the two groups parted, "sensing a common call to live under the Lordship of Christ in a changing, divided and threatened world."[28] The image of Reformed and Mennonites as bitter enemies was set aside.

A second round of dialogue between representatives of the Mennonite World Conference and the World Alliance of Reformed Churches took place in Calgary, Alberta, in 1989.[29] The parties intended to articulate their common Reformation heritage and to identify remaining differences between them. Papers and discussions focused on baptism, peace, and church-state relations. Discussion of these themes set the stage for the affirmation of significant commonality among Reformed and Mennonites. While outstanding issues remain, representatives of the two churches meeting in Calgary agreed that differences could be resolved if the two communions search the Scriptures together.[30]

Dialogue between Mennonites and Reformed, brief as it was, served the process of reconciliation well, particularly in light of the history of persecution at the time both groups were emerging. This in itself represented a significant step forwards in their relationship. Furthermore, theological discussions on the role of Scripture, ecclesiology, the rite of baptism, and various ethical matters have brought the two denominations closer together, at least in mutual understanding. It is encouraging to note that, except for issues related to peace and war, and the practice of infant baptism, there is little that would be considered "church dividing" between representatives of the Mennonite World Conference and of the World Alliance of Reformed Churches.

Indeed, it appears that by and large Mennonites would be welcome at the communion tables of Reformed churches, and the Reformed would be welcome to participate in the Lord's Supper in Mennonite congregations. Generally, the two communions now regard each other as brothers and sisters in Christ. Still, there are groups of Mennonites and of Reformed that would think and practice otherwise.

Bilateral Dialogue with Baptists

Between 1989 and 1992, representatives of the Baptist World Alliance and the Mennonite World Conference engaged each other in bilateral dialogue.[31] Historically, the relationship between Baptists and Mennonites was not marked by bitterness. Indeed, the sentiment is widespread, for good reason, that the two are quite compatible in many views and practices. Both belong to the "believers church" tradition. Their agreement on believer's baptism and their opposition to infant baptism provided a ready basis for fraternal relations. It was now a matter of seeking a greater degree of understanding of their similar, yet also differing, histories and theologies and setting the stage for greater collaboration. One matter of divergence concerns views of the relationship between church and state, including the question of military engagement. Unlike Mennonites, many Baptists accept some variant of the just war theory and support military engagement. Also, many Mennonites underline the centrality of discipleship in Christian life, while Baptists more typically emphasize personal evangelism. The dialogue revealed that while these differences are significant, they are not accented so stringently as to threaten respectful ecumenical relations.

Dialogue between Baptists and Mennonites has helped to reconnect two global families that have significant historical and theological overlap. However, the two still are often not closely allied, partly because of their differing stances on church-state relations relative to the question of military engagement. For many Mennonites, the issue of participation in warfare represents a church-dividing issue. Given a willingness to revisit deeply held views on this matter while searching the Scriptures together, there is good reason for continuing dialogue aimed at Christian unity.

Bilateral Dialogue with Lutherans

In 2009, the Lutheran World Federation and the Mennonite World Conference concluded a dialogue that began in 2005, publishing the final report in 2010.[32] There had been earlier dialogues with the Lutherans on the national level, in France (1981-1984), in Germany (1989-1992), and in the United States (2002-2004).[33] Dialogue with Lutherans proved to be more challenging than conversations with the Baptists or the Reformed.

One of the underlying issues is the condemnation of the Anabaptists in the *Augsburg Confession*, a foundational and normative text for Lutheran churches. Does this mean that the condemnations still hold and that they apply to Mennonites today? The report distinguished primarily between condemnations that (1) were based on erroneous judgments about what sixteenth-century Anabaptists believed and practiced and (2) those that treat doctrinal matters where Lutherans and Mennonites still differ, specifically in regard to the themes of infant baptism and the relationship between the church and civil authority.

Though the initial plan was to address these theological differences, it soon became clear that an unresolved problem of the past was intruding on the present: Mennonites remembered Lutheran persecution of their sixteenth-century ancestors, a fact that most Lutherans themselves had long since forgotten. So the dialogue changed strategy, undertaking instead an unprecedented ecumenical project – jointly telling the history of their relations in a form that both communions could fully acknowledge as accurate. Mennonites discovered that Lutherans had not executed as many of their ancestors as they had thought. Lutherans, however, concluded that executing any Anabaptists was executing too many. They had to address the justifications of this persecution by Luther and Melanchthon while being relieved to discover Lutheran reformer Johannes Brenz's outspoken opposition to it.

In response to this rewriting of history together, the Lutheran World Federation initiated an internal process to offer a public apology to, and request forgiveness from, the Mennonite community. At its 2010 Assembly in Stuttgart, the Lutheran World Federation voted unanimously to take such action. In turn, the Mennonite World Conference representatives granted Lutherans their forgiveness and the assurance of God's forgiveness. This was an unprecedented ecclesial breakthrough that has received broad ecumenical commendation and, though not widely known, served as a model for the historic Lutheran-Catholic dialogue report (2013) and resulting special commemoration event (October 31, 2016), *From Conflict to Communion: Lutheran-Catholic Common Commemoration of the Reformation in 2017.*

While the conversations between Lutherans and Mennonites have not bridged all church-dividing differences, they have moved these two communities along the path that leads from condemnation to confession, forgiveness, and renewed dialogue. As we shall see below, a further stage of conversation between the Mennonite World Conference and the Lutheran World Federation is underway. But this stage has become a trilateral dialogue, on baptism, involving not only the Mennonite World Conference and the Lutheran World Federation, but also the Catholic Church's Pontifical Council for Promoting Christian Unity.

Dialogue with Seventh-day Adventists

In 2011 and 2012, representatives of the Mennonite World Conference and of the General Conference of Seventh-day Adventists met together for official conversations under the theme "Living the Christian Life in Today's World."[34] Mennonites and Adventists have had frequent encounters during the past forty years, both in the annual meetings of the Conference of Secretaries of Christian World Communions and in service endeavours. These contacts led to the conviction that an official conversation might be instructive for both communions, especially in relation to the practical living out of the Christian life.

Participants realized that they have much in common: for example, the desire to recover the authenticity of the New Testament church, a similar understanding of Christian history, a strong commitment to Christian discipleship, and the experience of Christian life as a minority church. The representatives identified "areas of resonance": the centrality of Jesus Christ; the relation of the church to the state; peace and nonviolence; the practice of believer's baptism; a nonsacramental view of the Lord's Supper; and social service to humanity.

The delegations also addressed areas of theological difference, including the day on which the Sabbath is celebrated, eschatology, the status given to the writings of Ellen G. White by the Adventist Church, the ministry of Jesus in the heavenly sanctuary, and the state of the dead.

After articulating recommendations for the two communions, including the exploration of joint endeavors, the delegations concluded with an affirmation and a confession that may be applicable in many dialogues between separated churches: "These conversations have been a testimony to the critical role of the historical context in shaping values, beliefs, and ethics, but in each case they have been founded on the sincere desire to affirm the authority of scripture and the authority of Jesus Christ in faith and practice. They have been an opportunity to acknowledge the need for humility as we have vulnerably and transparently tested each other in the ways we perceive ourselves and in the ways that we may be perceived by others."[35]

Multilateral Dialogue on Reformation and Renewal

A further level of ecumenical involvement of Mennonites, together with the historic peace churches, deserves mention here. A series of seven multilateral interchurch conversations, known as the Prague Consultations, began in January 1986. The last of these meetings took place in Prague in late fall 2003.[36] The Prague Consultation organizers distinguished three historic segments of the Reformation: the "first" (pre-1500), the "second" (Lutheran, Reformed, Anglican), and the "radical" (historic peace church) reformations. In this framework, the gatherings initially brought together churches of the "first" and "radical" reformations: the Church of the Brethren, the Czechoslovak Hussite Church, the Evangelical Church of Czech Brethren, Hutterian Brethren, Mennonites, Moravians, the Society of Friends (Quakers), and Waldensians. Subsequent meetings included representatives of the Reformed, Lutheran, Baptist, Methodist, and Catholic churches.[37] By the fourth consultation, held in Geneva in 1994, the meetings were officially sponsored by three world communions: the Lutheran World Federation, the World Alliance of Reformed Churches, and the Mennonite World Conference.

The intent of these multilateral meetings was to learn what the histories of eschatological and prophetic impulses within these movements have in common and can teach us. The focus was consistently on Christian ethics and "lived faith." This focus meant that the deliberations took seriously the voices "from below" as the dynamic of the Reformation spirit moved eastwards to include the Slavic world. The Prague Consultations show this progression and enable an approach to the Reformation and Radical Reformation anniversaries (in 2017 and 2025) for all churches, including Mennonites, that is more comprehensive and appreciative of the multiplicity of "Reformations."

In summary, bilateral and multilateral dialogue between Mennonites and their Protestant-related neighbours has been conducted in a harmonious atmosphere, and has proven to be, above all, an invaluable "school of learning." While facing issues that divide churches, both in doctrinal and in ethical matters, participants found much more that unites than divides. The dialogues advanced ecumenical relations. While specific questions and issues arose in each of these dialogues, from a Mennonite point of view, the dialogues raise an implicit question that needs to be addressed explicitly: What are the principles according to which ecumenical dialogue should be pursued? Before we address this question, we turn to a review of the international Catholic-Mennonite dialogue, which owes so much to Monsignor Radano.

Dialogue with the Catholic Church

On October 14, 1998, fourteen persons – seven Catholic and seven Mennonite – gathered around a conference table at the offices of the Mennonite World Conference in Strasbourg, France, for an initial week of long overdue church-to-church dialogue. Not since the mid-sixteenth century had representatives of these two international church communities conversed constructively with each other on fundamental matters of faith and life. At that time, almost five centuries earlier, the exchanges were marked by conflict. This time would be different. Now the two groups anticipated an atmosphere of mutual good will. The intent was to embark together on a spiritual journey towards the healing of memories.

The groundwork for the meetings had been prepared largely through the efforts of John A. Radano of the Pontifical Council for Promoting Christian Unity and Larry Miller of the Mennonite World Conference. Since Miller's appointment as general secretary of the Mennonite World Conference in 1990, the two church leaders had met regularly in the context of the annual meetings of the Secretaries of Christian World Communions. It was during those conversations that the possibility of an international Catholic-Mennonite dialogue was broached. Both Radano and Miller were convinced that the time had come for Catholics and Mennonites to pursue a constructive relationship between the two churches.

Eventually, with the approval of the Executive Committee of the Mennonite World Conference and the blessing of Pope John Paul II, the Mennonite World Conference and the Vatican's Pontifical Council for Promoting Christian Unity appointed delegations to enter into an initial five-year dialogue. They intended "to learn to know one another better, to promote better understanding of the positions on Christian faith held by Catholics and Mennonites, and to contribute to the overcoming of prejudices that have long existed between us."[38] The five-year process, which included six annual meetings of about a week in length, extended from October 1998 to the spring of 2003. The dialogue concluded with a report issued in July 2003 under the title *Called Together to be Peacemakers*. The report was submitted to both the General Council of the Mennonite World Conference and the Pontifical Council for Promoting Christian Unity of the Catholic Church for dissemination and consideration in their respective constituencies.

Both groups were quite aware that a restoration of conversations between them would be no simple task. The schism that had torn them apart was bathed in the blood of persecution. Bitter memories and biases continued throughout the centuries. Yet among those who gathered at Strasbourg in 1998, commitment to the dialogue ran deep. While ecumenical engagement has not been high on the agenda of the Mennonite churches, there had been the growing conviction, especially during the latter half of the twentieth century, that reconciliation with other Christians belongs to the biblical mandate to "seek peace and pursue it" (1 Pet. 3:11). Surely those who espouse the gospel of peace should "make every effort to maintain the unity of the Spirit in the bond of peace" (Eph. 4:3). At the same time, there had been an increasing call among Catholics to develop the Catholic Church's understanding of peace theology and peacemaking. But of greater weight than the ecumenical imperative and the peace agenda was the desire on the part of both churches to seek a healing of memories, to rectify the "sins of the past." This seemed particularly urgent on the eve of the beginning of a new millennium. As the concluding chapter of *Called Together to be Peacemakers* states:

> Bitter memories have resulted from past conflicts and divisions between Christians and from the suffering they have produced over ensuing centuries. Mutual hostility and negative images have persisted between separated Christians of the Catholic and Reformation traditions from the time of the divisions of the sixteenth century until today. It has therefore been the intention and hope from the beginning of this dialogue between Mennonites and Catholics that our conversations would contribute to the healing of memories.[39]

The dialogue group was well aware that the goals of dialogue must remain modest. The process is about undertaking a journey, about moving in a direction, about contributing to the healing of memories. The process of healing can be painstaking, and always takes time. Repentance and forgiveness cannot be superimposed upon constituencies. There must be reception and ownership on a broad level. While much can be accomplished in a dialogue that proceeds with openness and integrity, reconciliation requires more than an annual meeting or two over a five-year period.

The Vatican document *Memory and Reconciliation*[40] identified four components that belong to the process of the reconciliation of memories: 1) purification of memories, which requires the groups in conflict to attain an historically accurate and mutually acceptable picture of their common past; 2) ascertaining shared faith, so as to test the degree to which the groups embrace or divide on basic convictions; 3) seeking forgiveness from God and from each other for hostilities directed at one another in the past; and 4) fostering new relationships, the fruit of concrete steps of reconciliation. To what extent were these modest goals advanced in the Catholic-Mennonite dialogue? And have they brought the churches closer to the realization of Christian unity?

1) *Purification of Memories*. A survey of response to the dialogue reveals widespread support among Mennonites for the effort to seek a common interpretation of history with Catholics. At the same time, the historical reconstruction reflected in *Called Together to be Peace-*

makers has evoked some criticism. Some Mennonite scholars point out that those around the dialogue table failed to bring forwards all of the information available. Some point out that Mennonites know themselves as much more strongly opposed to the "state church" than the report implies. In that respect, and in others, the discussion needs to be much more rigorous.

Some Mennonites believe that the Catholic case for infant baptism was not as rigorously critiqued by the Mennonite delegation as it should have been on the basis of "all the information available."[41] Still others asserted that the report underplays the structural effects of Christendom, particularly its contribution to the extermination of heretics. This was not simply a matter in which the "weaknesses of so many of the Catholic Church's sons and daughters" gave in to intolerance.[42] Rather, Mennonite critics contend, this was a system built upon coercion that the Christians of the early centuries had specifically repudiated, but which popes, theologians, and councils joined Aquinas in justifying. These same critics urge the Mennonite delegation not merely to "doubt" the Catholics' claim that "the doctrine of the Church that no one is to be coerced into faith has always stood firm."[43] Rather, such a claim should be severely opposed. All of this leads to the suggestion that Mennonites and Catholics have not yet completed their historical research on such matters.

2) *Ascertaining Shared Faith.* Did the dialogue reveal that Mennonites and Catholics have a significantly shared faith despite centuries of separation? As *Called Together to be Peacemakers* reports, the question was tested in three areas of theology: a) ecclesiology; b) the sacraments/ordinances of baptism and the Eucharist/Lord's Supper; and c) peace theology and practice.[44]

In the area of ecclesiology, Mennonites and Catholics readily discovered agreement on foundational matters.[45] For example, there was agreement on conceiving the church as the people of God, the body of Christ, and the temple of the Holy Spirit; and on Christ as foundation and Lord of the Church. Major differences were noted in such areas as apostolicity and authority.

With references to the sacraments/ordinances, again, there was agreement on some basic matters. For example, at its heart, baptism is understood by both communions as a sign of dying and rising with Christ. Both churches affirm that the Eucharist/Lord's Supper has its basis in God's marvelous gift of grace. The report also lists "divergences" in each of these areas.[46] Nonetheless, the report concludes that "we hold in common many basic aspects of the Christian faith and heritage [which] ... allows us ... to see one another as brothers and sisters in Christ."[47]

The section of *Called Together to be Peacemakers* entitled "Our Commitment to Peace" begins as follows:

> Through our dialogue, we have come to understand that Catholics and Mennonites share a common commitment to peacemaking. That commitment is rooted in our communion with "the God of Peace" (Rom. 15:33) and in the church's response to Jesus' proclamation of 'the gospel of peace' (Eph. 6:15). Christ has entrusted to us the ministry of reconciliation.[48]

Mennonites and Catholics were able to agree not only on a commitment to peace but also on the foundations for this commitment. Four foundations were identified as held in common: a restorative Creation; a reconciling Christology; a peace church ecclesiology; and cross-bearing discipleship.[49] As a sign of mutual commitment to peace among Mennonites and Catholics, representatives decided that the report should bear the challenging title *Called Together to be Peacemakers*.[50]

But the conversation on peace also identified disagreements between the two churches.[51] While for Mennonites peacemaking cannot include deterrent warfare, Catholics allow for the Christian's participation in the military as a contribution to the common good, and for the protection of the innocent, or as a means of restoring peace. Mennonites are critical in principle of participation in military action. Also, Mennonites hold to nonresistance in principle, while Catholics allow for exceptions. These and other divergences led the dialogue group to conclude that "many questions remain to be explored."[52]

3) *Seeking Forgiveness.* In the context of the dialogue, both groups expressed regret and repentance for sins of the past, and committed themselves to "self-examination, dialogue, and interaction that manifests Jesus Christ's reconciling love."[53] But there are Mennonite critics

who do not find the Mennonite response to the Catholics' expression of regret adequately rigorous. The admission on the part of both Catholic and Mennonite delegations that we have "mutually condemned one another" fails to differentiate between the lethal condemnations by Catholics of Anabaptists in Catholic territories and the nonlethal condemnations of Catholics in Anabaptist writings. On the Catholic side, while the papal office has issued a general statement of repentance for sins of the past millennium – a statement said to apply as well to conflicts between Catholics and Mennonites – it is not clear to what extent the Catholic delegation's statement speaks for or engages the Catholic Church.

4) *Fostering New Relationships*. Did the dialogue foster new relationships? One can claim that the dialogue was an important indicator of the willingness of the Catholic Church and the Mennonite World Conference to strive for mutual understanding and better relationships. A foundation for improved relationships has been laid, upon which a widening community can now build. Already new relationships are being formed at local and national levels. The international dialogue and its report have played a key role in fostering national Catholic and Mennonite bilateral encounters and a new sense of Christian connection between the two communions.

Certainly, for the fourteen representatives of their respective churches, the dialogue did much to contribute to better relations. The joint delegation wrote in conclusion: "After having worked with each other over these five years we want to testify together that our mutual love for Christ has united us and accompanied us in our discussions. Our dialogue has fortified the common conviction that it is possible to experience reconciliation and the healing of memories."[54]

Inspired by that common conviction and their call "to be peacemakers together," the Pontifical Council for Promoting Christian Unity and the Mennonite World Conference sponsored a Catholic-Mennonite consultation to develop suggestions for the WCC's Decade to Overcome Violence, especially the International Ecumenical Peace Convocation with which it culminated (2011). The consultation, which took place in October 2007 at the Centro Pro Unione in Rome, offered to the WCC "theological reflections which Mennonites and Catholics, committed to overcoming violence, may affirm together as a witness to peace in the ecumenical context," including the remarkable common statement that "we affirm Jesus' teaching and example on non-violence as normative for Christians."[55]

Trilateral Dialogue among Catholics, Lutherans, and Mennonites

The five-year Catholic-Mennonite dialogue concluded with the realization that there were still many themes and issues needing attention. Prominent among these was the matter of baptism. Baptism was also the most difficult unresolved issue in the Lutheran-Mennonite dialogue. The understanding and practice of baptism represents a fundamental church-dividing issue between Mennonites on the one hand and Catholics and Lutherans on the other. But the final reports of the dialogues of Mennonites with Catholics and Lutherans bear evidence that baptismal positions have developed in ways that open the possibility for fruitful conversation between all three communions on the question.

Both Catholics and Lutherans expressed their desire to continue dialogue with Mennonites and to do so on the theme of baptism. But it seemed difficult to Mennonite World Conference leadership to undertake two major international dialogues on the same question. Consequently, they proposed to the Pontifical Council for Promoting Christian Unity and the Lutheran World Federation a "trilateral" conversation. After reflection, both agreed to this unusual arrangement. Of the many church-to-church ecumenical conversations held in the last five or more decades, this would be only the second "trialogue."[56]

Currently, the three churches are in the midst of this conversation. The general theme, introduced at the first meeting in December 2012, is "Baptism and Incorporation into the Body of Christ, the Church." Specific themes have been "Baptism: God's Grace in Christ and Human Sin" (January 2014); "Baptism: Communicating Grace and Faith" (February 2015); and "Living Out Baptism" (February 2016). The fifth and final meeting of the Trilateral Commission is scheduled to take place in February 2017 when the commission is expected to finalize its report for submission to the Lutheran World Federation, the Mennonite World Conference, and the Pontifical Council for Promoting Christian Unity.

Guiding Principles for Interchurch Dialogue

In July 1998, the Executive Committee of the Mennonite World Conference issued a statement entitled *God Calls Us to Christian Unity*.[57] The statement begins by referencing the biblical basis for Christian unity. The Bible tells the story of "God working in history to create ... a people comprising members 'from every nation, from all tribes and peoples and languages. (Gen. 15:5; 17:4-7; Rev. 7:9).'" Jesus reveals the passion for unity in his prayer that all who believe in him as sent from his Father "may all be one" (Jn. 17:21). The apostle Paul worked ceaselessly for unity, often in the face of serious divisions in the church (1 Cor. 1:12, 12:12-13). On the strength of the biblical witness, and in light of twentieth-century realities, the statement draws a conclusion very different from the sometimes defensive and preservative position of centuries past: "We see Christian unity, therefore, not as an option we might choose or as an outcome we could create, but as an urgent imperative to be obeyed." Indeed, the statement recognizes that the identity and mission of the Mennonite World Conference family of churches is found in "interaction with others with whom God has placed us as fellow inhabitants of God's world in this time and place." With this comes the insight that Mennonites have not only "unique faith experiences and insights [to] contribute to other Christians," but also "much to learn from Christians of other traditions."

In view of the Mennonite churches' participation in ecumenical conversations and projects in recent years, and in light of its renewed commitment to interchurch conversation as reflected in the 1998 statement, we anticipate that the future of the Mennonite Church will continue to include ecumenical interchanges with the wider Christian family. It is timely, therefore, that Mennonites should articulate principles of interchurch dialogue in accordance with their faith and witness. With this in mind, we commend the following seven guiding principles for consideration. The list is meant as a resource not only for representatives who engage in dialogue on behalf of the Mennonite churches but also for delegates from other churches who engage in dialogue with Mennonites and with each other.

1. Interchurch Dialogue Submits to the Authority of the Lordship of Jesus Christ

The opening words of the apostle Peter's address to the household of Cornelius are applicable to interchurch dialogue: "I truly understand that God shows no partiality, but in every nation anyone who fears him and does what is right is acceptable to him. You know the message he sent to the people of Israel, preaching peace by Jesus Christ – he is Lord of all" (Acts 10:34-35). Since God shows no partiality, but made Jesus Christ "Lord of all," members of the church certainly have no right to show partiality. They recognize each other as brothers and sisters together, under the Lordship of Christ.

It follows that for interchurch dialogue to have integrity and to proceed constructively, the churches need to submit, together, to the Lordship of Christ.[58] Nothing may stand in the way of mutual submission to the authority of Jesus Christ – not ecclesial structure, nor denominational traditions, nor historic creed and confession, nor doctrinal convictions, nor sacramental preconceptions, nor a particular way of interpreting the Bible. When each of the dialoguing partners submits confessionally and functionally to Christ as Lord, resisting the temptation to look elsewhere for the primary authoritative point of reference, or to 'lord it' over the other, a community of disciples comes into existence that opens space for the Holy Spirit to nurture the divine gift of ecclesial unity.

2. Interchurch Dialogue Proceeds in a Congregational Style of Fraternal Discernment

Among Christians, there is broad agreement that koinonia is one of the primary characteristics of church. Koinonia is founded on three important biblical images: people of God, body of Christ, and community of the Holy Spirit. The three together reflect the community of the trinity. Person-to-person encounter – divine and human – is essential to the meaning of koinonia.

Koinonia has functional integrity only where there is covenant faithfulness in a community of believers. Covenant faithfulness can occur when all persons in the gathered group are invited to speak and be heard, whether by way of an 'open floor,' through representatives, or by some other means. While a congregational style of engagement is most common in the local church, koinonia can also take place in gatherings at any ecclesiological level, from the local church to the global assembly, including gatherings of delegations meeting in interchurch dialogue.[59] Interchurch dialogue, in the spirit of koinonia and in the service of oneness, would assume a mutual commitment to decision-making through fraternal discernment[60] in the "congregation," that is, in the assembled group. Dialogue that proceeds in the spirit of fraternal discernment and leads to conclusions by way of consensus is characterized in the fourth chapter of Ephesians. There, in the context of a call to oneness (Eph. 4:1-6), and with the reminder that "each of us was given grace according to the measure of Christ's gift" (Eph. 4:7), the apostle draws attention to the necessity of "speaking the truth in love" (Eph. 4:15). The purpose of addressing one another is to "grow up in every way into him who is the head, into Christ" (Eph. 4:15) so that the church might be "built together spiritually into a dwelling place for God" (Eph. 2:21f.). Interchurch dialogue as fraternal discernment, in its widest meaning, calls for the faithful to "comprehend with all the saints, what is the breadth and length and height and depth" of "the love of Christ" and "the fullness of God" (see Eph. 3:18-19).

3. Interchurch Dialogue Accepts the Scriptures as the Primary Point of Reference

The Christian churches worldwide accept the Scriptures as the primary written authority for faith, life, and witness. This agreement on a common foundation puts the churches in a good position in the search for Christian unity. As interchurch dialogue proceeds, the churches need constantly to be reminded of their mutual point of reference. Understandably, the breadth and diversity of hermeneutical approaches to the interpretation of Scripture presents a challenge to dialogue partners in their quest for unity. In the process of the search for truth, there needs to be respect for each other's interpretations as well as openness to the leading of the one Spirit. Furthermore, each church tends to carry respect for its particular tradition into the dialogue. This sometimes makes it difficult to search the Scriptures together. Nonetheless, this is the challenge that dialogical partners must take up in their common quest of faith.

The quest for Christian unity can take us some distance when we compare our contemporary views as we sort out convergences and divergences. But to search the Scriptures together, and to find our oneness in Christ there, holds the promise of a unity that is deeper and more enduring than what the accumulation of convergences can offer. The interchurch context as such creates new hermeneutical opportunities for the interpretation of Scripture. It is inevitable, given the wide variety of local contexts in which Christians find themselves around the globe, each with its particular history, tradition, language, and culture, that churches seeking unity will need to embrace a vision of "unity in reconciled diversity." Above all, we need to find our way through this maze of interpretation and accumulation of tradition by holding to the primacy of Scripture in our deliberations.

4. Interchurch Dialogue Posits Discipleship as a Primary Goal of Christian Unity

It is typical of ecumenically minded churches in our day to favour selected aspects of Christian faith and life as the goal to which we aspire in the quest for Christian unity. Prominent among these are sacramental ecumenism (for example, an open communion table and mutual recognition of baptism), doctrinal ecumenism (agreement on truth), and social ecumenism (love one another, friendship).[61] To this list of favourites, we propose the addition of ethical ecumenism, understood as discipleship (*Nachfolge Christi*). According to the Gospel of John, among the prerequisites of discipleship are believing in Jesus (Jn. 8:32), loving one another (Jn. 13:35), and following the teachings of Jesus in life (Jn. 15:10). Churches engaged in interchurch dialogue do well to consider engagement together in discipleship as an essential sign and expression of Christian unity. As an example, the Catholic-Mennonite dialogue report, *Called Together to be Peacemakers*, points in the direction of ethical ecumenism.

5. Interchurch Dialogue Seeks Unity in the Churches' Understanding of Baptism

The theme of baptism in relation to Christian unity has been of longstanding concern to the ecumenical movement, given the claim, according to Ephesians 4:4, that there is "one baptism."[62] Churches in the Mennonite tradition have also given attention to the theology and practice of baptism since their insistence on baptism upon personal confession of faith and as a commitment to discipleship played a significant role in the interchurch debates of the sixteenth century.[63] Despite the concerted attention given to the theme of baptism in recent decades, there is still much to be gained by focusing anew on scriptural texts that inform the churches on baptism, especially in its relation to discipleship, and to do so together as Christian communities. In the New Testament, there is a vital link between baptism and discipleship. To begin his earthly ministry, Jesus submitted to baptism at the River Jordan (Mk. 1:9-11). His baptism included submission to John's baptism of repentance (Mt. 3:11), the descent of the Spirit of God upon him (Mt. 3:16), and the divine affirmation of Jesus as God's beloved Son (Mt. 3:17). With this, Jesus began his ministry of preaching, teaching, and healing. At the conclusion of his ministry, he commissioned his followers to "make disciples of all nations, baptizing them in the name of the Father and of the Son and of the Holy Spirit" (Mt. 28:19). According to the disciple and apostle John (1 Jn. 5:6-8), the baptism of Jesus and, by implication, the baptism of Jesus' disciples, bears testimony to three spiritual benefits and disciplines that identify those who serve God faithfully:[64] personal cleansing from sin ("water" baptism); the power to walk in newness of life ("Spirit" baptism); and a commitment to bear witness to the truth even unto death (baptism of "blood"). Baptism supports the life of Christian discipleship.

6. Interchurch Dialogue Pursues Reconciliation, Peace, and Justice

Peace and reconciliation are central to our unity in Jesus Christ. Furthermore, justice is an indispensable companion of peace. The Letter to the Ephesians extols Christ Jesus as "our peace," and proceeds to explain that "in his flesh he has made both [Gentiles and Israelites] into one and has broken down the dividing wall, that is, the hostility between us" (Eph. 2:14). His purpose was "that he might create in himself one new humanity in place of the two, thus making peace, and might reconcile both groups to God in one body through the cross, thus putting to death that hostility through it" (Eph. 2:15b-16; see 2 Cor. 5:11–6:2). Now, "through him both have access in one Spirit to the Father" (Eph. 2:17). In a later chapter of Ephesians, the church is exhorted to "maintain the unity of the Spirit in the bond of peace" (Eph. 4:3). Reconciliation of Gentiles and Israelites for the sake of a "new humanity" is both the realization and the foretaste of the church, whose mission it is to bear united witness to God's peace and justice in a world fraught with violence.[65]

Yet, the pathway of church history is strewn with the fallout from broken relationships. The evidence is seen in the historic divide between churches of the East and West, between the "older churches" and the "younger churches," in the multiplicity of Protestant, Evangelical, and Pentecostal denominations, in the plethora of congregations, and in the history of Christian martyrdom where some Christians put to death other Christians. Where churches entering into dialogue with one another have a history of schism, the healing of memories must be an essential step in the process of interchurch dialogue. This will inevitably be a difficult step, yet absolutely necessary. Churches reconciled to one another will be in a position to bear unique witness to the Good News of reconciliation in Jesus Christ.

An *Epistle from the Historic Peace Churches*, issued in 2001, states: "Essential to the good news of the gospel is the teaching, example, and Spirit of the crucified and risen Christ, who calls us to witness to the transforming power of God's Kingdom of peace, justice and reconciliation – for this nonviolent way of life is at the very heart of the gospel."[66] Increasingly, since the Second World War, churches have recognized the need to participate with one another in the work of peace, and of its inseparable companion, justice. The outcome of the five-year Catholic-Mennonite dialogue (1998-2003), with its report, *Called Together to be Peacemakers*, highlights this impetus, as does the WCC's "Decade to Overcome Violence" and its current "Pilgrimage of Justice and Peace." Such initiatives challenge the Christian churches together to develop and promote "just peace." The historic peace churches, including the Mennonites, are not, and should not be, a monolithic bloc with a univocal position on peace. It belongs to the integrity of the churches' peace witness to search the Scriptures not only together but with all other Christians. For this, the vision of peace, justice, and reconciliation needs to be constantly and persistently on the agenda of interchurch conversation.

7. Interchurch Dialogue Leads to Radical Catholicity

One of the defining marks of the church is its catholicity, a characteristic that is commonly understood in two related senses: in terms of location, as "extending throughout the world"; and doctrinally, as "the fullness of the apostolic faith." The concept of catholicity embraces the global and the local, the universal and the particular, the one and the many. The church universal is represented in each local congregation and parish, while the local congregation contributes to the constitution of the church as a whole, and is integral to the whole.[67] It follows that every local congregation, every extended church community, and every denomination that gathers and scatters in the name of the Lord Jesus Christ, reflects, represents, and contributes to the constitution of the catholicity of the church in both senses of its meaning, geographically and doctrinally.

Interchurch dialogue as such, when pursued with integrity, is a participation in the catholicity of the church universal. Catholicity is realized in part "whenever and wherever everyone concerned converses about everything they do, and should believe and do, as they respond to the Lord who sent them to all nations with all that he had taught them."[68] As a presupposition of dialogue, no issue, no doctrine, and no practice is excluded from the process of mutual discernment in the quest for truth. No consensus reached in the context of an interchurch dialogue group, received under the Lordship of Christ and "grounded in the enablement of the Holy Spirit,"[69] is without the potential for authority as representatives carry out their delegated responsibilities on behalf of their communions.

At the same time, every conclusion reached and every recommendation made by delegations in dialogue will be offered to the church, both local and global, for further discernment and consensus. The process of widening participation and ownership involves the discernment not only of those entrusted with church leadership but of the entire "assembly" of the people of God, who, under the guidance of the Holy Spirit, bear communal responsibility before God for the faith and work of the church. As consensus in accordance with the will of God grows, both from the "top down" and from the "ground up," the church becomes more radically "catholic" and increases its influence both in geographical breadth and in the fullness of the faith.

We anticipate that the eventually envisioned realization of catholicity will come as a gift from the gracious heart of God "who by the power at work within us is able to accomplish abundantly far more than all we can ask or imagine" (Eph. 3:20).

Conclusion

These seven guiding principles are addressed as an invitation to the churches to think together about the ways in which we engage in ecumenical conversations. To meet the challenges of ecumenical dialogue on the 500th anniversaries of the Protestant and Radical Reformation, we believe that churches engaged in dialogue need to consider together not only ultimate goals, such as "visible unity," but also the framework and manner of our ecumenical pursuit. Indeed, at this point in our sojourn together it may be of more importance that we give attention to the manner of our engagement in dialogue with one another than to ponder its outcome. After all, "there is no way to locate the unity we seek before the process of seeking it together."[70] We move forwards in the conviction and on the basis of the confession that the Holy Spirit will lead us into the "promised land" where "God will be all in all."

---

1   This essay has also appeared in *The Mennonite Quarterly Review* 90 (July 2016): 277-303. The authors dedicate this essay to Monsignor John Radano as an expression of deep gratitude for the historic role he played in bringing the Catholic Church and the Mennonite World Conference community of churches into dialogue with one another.

2   This essay focuses primarily on "ecumenical" conversations and does not claim to provide a full picture of theological exchange between Mennonites and other Christian groups over the past decades. Specifically, it does not do justice to the extensive theological interaction between Mennonites and "evangelicals." For an account of some early exchanges between Mennonites and some other churches in the nineteenth century and in the early part of the twentieth century, see H. Lamar Gibble, "Ecumenical Engagement for Peace and Nonviolence," in *Ecumenical Engagement for Peace and Nonviolence: Experiences and Initiatives of the Historic Peace Churches and Fellowship of Reconciliation*, ed. Thomas D. Paxson Jr. (Elgin, Illinois: Historic Peace Churches/FOR Consultative Committee, 2006), pp. 24-78. Before the mid-twentieth century, engagement with the wider Christian community was the exception rather than the rule.

3   Especially *Unitatis Redintegratio* (Decree on Ecumenism, Nov. 21, 1964).

4   Underlying this quest for principles is the persistent question: Why pursue ecumenical dialogue at all? It is not within the scope of this essay to address the "why" question directly, although our discussion of principles does so by implication.

5   For example, Pontifical Council for Promoting Christian Unity, *Directory for the Application of Principles and Norms on Ecumenism* (Vatican City: Libreria Editrice Vaticana, 1993).

6   John Howard Yoder, *The Royal Priesthood: Essays Ecclesiological and Ecumenical*, ed. Michael G. Cartwright (Grand Rapids: Eerdmans, 1994), pp. 93-105; Gibble, *Ecumenical Engagement*, pp. 33-78; Fernando Enns, *The Peace Church and the Ecumenical Community: Ecclesiology and the Ethics of Nonviolence*, trans. Helmut Harder (Kitchener: Pandora Press; Geneva: WCC Publications, 2007), chap. IV.

7   The following publications offer background to the ecumenical involvement of Mennonites within the context of the historic peace churches: Donald F. Durnbaugh, *On Earth Peace: Discussion on War/Peace Issues Between Friends, Mennonites, Brethren and European Churches, 1935-75* (Elgin, Illinois: Brethren Press, 1978); John Howard Yoder, "40 Years of Ecumenical Theological Dialogue Efforts on Justice and Peace Issues by the Fellowship of Reconciliation and the Historic Peace Churches," in Douglas Gwyn, George Hunsinger, Eugene F. Roop, and John Howard Yoder, eds., *A Declaration on Peace: In God's People the World's Renewal Has Begun* (Scottdale, Pennsylvania: Herald Press, 1991), pp. 93-105; Gibble, *Ecumenical Engagement*, pp. 24-78.

8   For a discerning analysis of "Peace is the Will of God," and a report of its reception, see Enns, *The Peace Church and the Ecumenical Community*, pp. 148-57.

9   Reinhold Niebuhr's biweekly *Christianity and Crisis* 15, no. 10 (June 13, 1955) published a statement, "God Wills Both Justice and Peace," signed by Niebuhr and Episcopalian Bishop Angus Dun, in response to "Peace is the Will of God." John Howard Yoder, "40 Years of Ecumenical Theological Dialogue," Appendix C, in Gwyn, *A Declaration on Peace*, p. 99.

10 Cf. Enns, *The Peace Church and the Ecumenical Community*, pp. 159-62.

11 For an expanded report and analysis of the "Puidoux conferences," see Enns, *The Peace Church and the Ecumenical Community*, pp. 162-170.

12 It was in 1957 that John Howard Yoder, as a young theology student, addressed the question of how Mennonites, as part of the historic "free church" tradition, should be engaged in ecumenical dialogue. His essay, entitled "The Nature of the Unity We Seek: A Historic Free Church View," first published in *Religion in Life* (Spring 1957), served as one of the resources for a WCC Faith and Order Commission study conference held in Oberlin, Ohio, that summer. In the essay, Yoder outlined an alternative to what he saw as the typical approach to ecumenical relations. See Yoder's related essays in *The Royal Priesthood*. As Enns points out, "Yoder's several decades of continuous engagement with the worldwide ecumenical movement contributed much to the reception of the peace churches' rich fund of ideas by the wider church." Enns, *The Peace Church and the Ecumenical Community*, p. 105.

13 Yoder, *The Royal Priesthood*, pp. 144-67.

14 Yoder, *The Royal Priesthood*, pp. 54-64.

15 Yoder, *The Royal Priesthood*, pp. 181-91.

16 Yoder, *The Royal Priesthood*, pp. 194-218.

17 Cf. Gibble, *Ecumenical Engagement*, pp. 44-49. A major contribution, begun by Mennonites at this time, was the movement known as "New Call to Peacemaking." The HPC group assumed a supportive role to the New Call to Peacemaking, and its effort to appeal to a broader community of churches, including the American evangelical sector.

18 Space does not permit a full recital of the participation of HPC and IFOR in debates on behalf of peace, nonviolence, militarism, and disarmament. For a detailed account, see Gibble, *Ecumenical Engagement*, pp. 49-56.

19 Gibble, *Ecumenical Engagement*, p. 57.

20 Gibble, *Ecumenical Engagement*, p. 66.

21 Gibble, *Ecumenical Engagement*, pp. 70-71.

22 Gibble, *Ecumenical Engagement*, pp. 73-76.

23 For example, Robert Herr and Judy Zimmerman Herr edited *Transforming Violence: Linking Local and Global Peacemaking* (Scottdale, Pennsylvania: Herald Press, 1998). From 1994 to 2006, Dutch Mennonites, German Mennonites, and Mennonite Central Committee together provided a staff person to the WCC's "Program to Overcome Violence" and "Decade to Overcome Violence." Hansulrich Gerber (Swiss Mennonite) was Coordinator for the "Decade to Overcome Violence" (2002-2009). Fernando Ens (German Mennonite) was a member of the "Decade to Overcome Violence" steering committee, serving as chairperson for its culminating event, the International Ecumenical Peace Convocation. Presently he is co-chairperson of the international reference group for the "Pilgrimage of Justice and Peace" and of the Pilgrimage's "Theological Study Group."

24 For an interpretive review of the ecumenical engagement of the historic peace churches in conversations on peacemaking, see John Rempel, "The Fragmentation of the Church and Its Unity in Peacemaking," *Peace Office Newsletter* (Akron, Pennsylvania: Mennonite Central Committee) 29, no. 1 (January-March, 1999): 1-7; Marlin E. Miller, "Toward Acknowledging Together the Apostolic Character of the Church's Peace Witness," in Marlin E. Miller and Barbara Nelson Gingerich, eds., *The Church's Peace Witness* (Grand Rapids: Eerdmans, 1994), pp. 196-207.

25 All bilateral dialogues through 2012 of Mennonites with other churches, both national and international, are documented in Fernando Enns and Jonathan Seiling, eds., *Mennonites in Dialogue: Official Reports from International and National Ecumenical Encounters, 1975-2012* (Eugene, Oregon: Pickwick, 2015); abbreviated as MD.

26 The report of the Strasbourg consultation (English) with additional resources can be found in Hans Georg vom Berg, Henk Kossen, Larry Miller, and Lukas Vischer, eds., *Mennonites and Reformed in Dialogue* (Geneva: World Alliance of Reformed Churches; Lombard, Illinois: Mennonite World Conference, 1986). Also in MD, pp. 376-81.

27 vom Berg, Kossen, Miller, and Vischer, eds., *Mennonites and Reformed in Dialogue*, p. 3, and MD, p. 376.

28 vom Berg, Kossen, Miller, and Vischer, eds., *Mennonites and Reformed in Dialogue*, p. 3, and MD, p. 376.

29 The report of the consultation is "Beyond Brokenness into God's New Creation," in MD, pp. 373-88. For a compendium of essays written for the consultation, see Ross T. Bender and Alan P.F. Sell, eds., *Baptism, Peace and the State in the Reformed and Mennonite Traditions* (Waterloo: Wilfred Laurier University Press, 1991).

30 For an insightful analysis and characterization of the Mennonite-Reformed dialogues, see Enns, *The Peace Church and the Ecumenical Community*, pp. 203-12.

31 *Baptists and Mennonites in Dialogue: Report on Conversations Between the Baptist World Alliance and the Mennonite World Conference, 1989-1992* (Falls Church, Virginia: Baptist World Alliance, 2013); MD, pp. 389-422. For an analysis of the Baptist-Mennonite dialogue, see Enns, *The Peace Church and the Ecumenical Community*, pp. 195-202.

32 *Healing Memories: Reconciling in Christ. Report of the Lutheran-Mennonite Study Commission* (Geneva: Lutheran World Federation; Strasbourg: Mennonite World Conference, 2010), also in MD, pp. 187-307.

33 MD, pp. 115-86.

34 Carol E. Rasmussen, William G. Johnson, Robert John Suderman, eds., *Living the Christian Life in Today's World. A Conversation between Mennonite World Conference and the Seventh-day Adventist Church* (Silver Spring, Maryland: General Conference of Seventh-day Adventists; Bogotá, Colombia: Mennonite World Conference, 2014); MD, pp. 423-33.

35 *Living the Christian Life in Today's World*, p. 270, MD, p. 432.

36 For an overview of the Prague Consultations (1986-2003), see MD, pp. 435-70. See also Walter Sawatsky, ed., *The Prague Consultations - Prophetic and Renewal Movements: Proceedings of Prague VI and Prague VII Multilateral Ecumenical Consultations (2000 and 2003)*, Studies from the World Alliance of Reformed Churches, 47 (Geneva: World Alliance of Reformed Churches, 2009).

37 At Prague VII (2003), Monsignor John Radano was present on behalf of the Pontifical Council for Promoting Christian Unity. In keeping with the theme of the consultation, "The Significance of Reforming and Prophetic Movements for Church and Society," Radano presented an "assessment of how the Roman Catholic Church understood prophecy, as both a present and special function within the church." He pointed to the Second Vatican Council as "a prophetic event with an impact well beyond its own boundaries." Radano advocated "the methodology of a historical review [in ecumenical conversation] ... because it draws attention to what was intended as well as what emerged in the end." For a report of Prague VII, including references to Radano's presentation, see MD, pp. 467-70.

38 *Called Together to be Peacemakers, Report of the International Dialogue between the Catholic Church and the Mennonite World Conference, 1998-2003*, no. 15 in *Information Service* 113 (2003/ II-III): 111-48; MD, pp. 19-114.

39 *Called Together to be Peacemakers*, no. 190.

40 International Theological Commission, *Memory and Reconciliation: The Church and the Faults of the Past* (December 1999).

41 This is said with reference to *Called Together to be Peacemakers*, nos. 115-116, 137.

42 *Called Together to be Peacemakers*, nos. 201, 202.

43 *Called Together to be Peacemakers*, no. 61.

44 *Called Together to be Peacemakers*, nos. 69-189.

45 Cf. the sections of *Called Together to be Peacemakers* that list theological convergences: nos. 93-102, 128-134.

46 Cf. the following sections in *Called Together to be Peacemakers:* nos. 103-106, 135-39.

47 *Called Together to be Peacemakers*, nos. 207, 210.

48 *Called Together to be Peacemakers*, no. 145.

49 *Called Together to be Peacemakers*, nos. 172-85.

50 Msgr. John Radano proposed this title, which was readily accepted by both delegations.

51 *Called Together to be Peacemakers*, nos. 186-88.

52 *Called Together to be Peacemakers*, no. 189.

53 *Called Together to be Peacemakers*, no. 206.

54 *Called Together to be Peacemakers*, no. 215.

55 "A Mennonite and Catholic Contribution to the World Council of Churches' Decade to Overcome Violence," p. 8; see http://www.mwc-cmm.org.

56 Cf. Roman Catholic-Lutheran-Reformed Study Commission, *The Theology of Marriage and the Problem of Mixed Marriages* (1976), in GA I, pp. 277-306, and http://www. prounione.urbe.it.

57 "God Calls Us to Christian Unity", a statement adopted by the Mennonite World Conference Executive Committee and MC-GC [Mennonite Church-General Conference] Interchurch Relations Committee, Goshen, Indiana, July 22, 1998.

58 John Howard Yoder makes the point that if conversation is to proceed with integrity towards ecclesial unity, it is necessary for partners to agree to a supernatural authority under which they place themselves. In his words: "True conversation exists only where there is movement toward agreement, motivated by appeal to an authority recognized by both parties." Yoder, *The Royal Priesthood*, p. 223. This authority is none other than "Christ himself as he is made known through Scripture to the congregation of those who seek to know him and his will" (p. 225). Expanding on Yoder's point, Fernando Enns identifies the "Lordship of Christ" as one important "regulative principle" of ecclesiology from a peace church perspective. He cautions that "Lordship" is misapplied when it is "associated with the exercise of power, force and violence." Enns, *The Peace Church and the Ecumenical Community*, p. 143. Enns points out that in the New Testament "'Lordship' is turned upside down by the event of the cross, which demonstrates the renunciation of power, now centered in the 'rule of the Lamb,' which [provides] … the foundation for an ethic of love and the way of nonviolence." *The Peace Church and the Ecumenical Community*, p. 143.

59 "There is no place where this quality of conversation is excluded. Whenever it happens, it is in some place, i.e. local. The crucial problem is not what 'local' means but what happening we are looking for." Yoder, *The Royal Priesthood*, p. 317, fn. 27.

60 In choosing the criterion of fraternal discernment, we rely to some extent on Yoder, except that he spoke of fraternal admonition. Cf. Yoder, *The Royal Priesthood*, p. 240.

61 Conceivably, churches need not choose between these options. All may have their place in discerning the nature of the unity we seek. For a discussion that compares social ecumenism with doctrinal ecumenism, see Brad S. Gregory, "Reformation History and Ecumenism: Problems and Prospects," in Peter C. Erb, ed., *Martyrdom in an Ecumenical Perspective: A Mennonite-Catholic Conversation* (Kitchener: Pandora Press, 2007), pp. 17-37. For an argument in favour of ethical ecumenism, see Helmut Harder, "Response to Brad Gregory," pp. 52-58.

62 Cf. WCC Commission on Faith and Order, *Baptism, Eucharist and Ministry*, Faith and Order paper no. 111 (Geneva: WCC, 1982), part I: Baptism.

63 For a helpful resource on the theme of baptism from a dialogical perspective, see Gerald Schlabach, ed., *On Baptism* (Kitchener, Ont.: Pandora Press, 2004).

64 Cf. *Confession of Faith in a Mennonite Perspective* (Scottdale, Pennsylvania: Herald Press, 1995), pp. 46-49.

65 For a fresh treatment of the biblical meaning of reconciliation in view of the changing social order and its potential for the churches' mission in our war-torn world, see Robert J. Schreiter, *Reconciliation: Mission and Ministry in a Changing Social Order* (Maryknoll: Orbis; Newton: Boston Theological Institute, 1989).

66 Quoted from "Epistle from the Historic Peace Churches," Meeting at Bienenberg Theological Seminary, Switzerland, June 25-29, 2001, in *MCC Peace Office Newsletter* 31, no. 4 (October-December 2001): 7.

67 *A Dictionary of Christian Theology*, s.v. "Catholicism," by R.P.C. Hanson.

68 John Howard Yoder, *The Priestly Kingdom: Social Ethics as Gospel* (Notre Dame, IN: University of Notre Dame Press, 1984), p. 319.

69 Yoder, *The Priestly Kingdom*, p. 319.

70 Yoder, *The Priestly Kingdom*, p. 311.

† CHAPTER II

Some Pentecostal Reflections on Current Catholic-Pentecostal Relations: What Are We Learning?

by Cecil M. Robeck, Jr.

In the report of the fifth round of the international dialogue between Catholics and Pentecostals, both teams observed that the twentieth century was very significant for the Church's understanding of the person and work of the Holy Spirit. Monsignor John A. Radano, then serving as the Catholic co-chair to the dialogue, voiced on more than one occasion the fascinating parallel regarding the Holy Spirit that ran through these two seemingly disparate traditions.

Pentecostals often point to the fact that on January 1, 1901, the Holy Spirit was poured out in a fresh way in Topeka, Kansas, and over the next several years, under the ministry of Charles F. Parham, it spread to Houston, Texas.[1] On that same day and half a world away, Pope Leo XIII entrusted the twentieth century to the Holy Spirit.[2] In 1906, the movement that had begun in Topeka, Kansas, and spread to Houston, Texas, arrived in Los Angeles, where the famous Azusa Street Revival, complete with an array of the Holy Spirit's charisms, exploded under the oversight of William J. Seymour.[3] This would become one of the most significant events leading to the independent establishment of Pentecostal denominations worldwide.

Had the events of New Year's Day in 1901 been the only place where these two traditions – Catholic and Pentecostal – shared an interesting intersection, each unknown to the other, it might simply be labelled a coincidence. But that is not the case. As the century unfolded, there were other places where these two important traditions intersected. In

1958, Pope John XXIII prayed for a "new Pentecost" as he opened the windows of the Vatican to the fresh wind of the Holy Spirit.[4] The Second Vatican Council was the result, complete with its call for changes in the way that things were done in the Catholic Church, not the least of which was a new ecumenical openness.[5] The Council would run from 1962 to1965.

One of the actions that Pope John XXIII took, even before the Council was convened, was to announce the opening of a Secretariat for Promoting Christian Unity (SPCU), on June 5, 1960.[6] While the Second Vatican Council was still in session, the Pentecostal ecumenist David du Plessis visited Rome, where he was warmly received by Augustin Cardinal Bea, President of this new Secretariat. As a result of their meeting, in September 1964, Cardinal Bea wrote a letter inviting du Plessis to serve "under private title" with the same rights as any delegated observer at the third session of the Council.[7] Thus, du Plessis became the sole Pentecostal observer at the Council.

Four years later, at the Fourth Assembly of the World Council of Churches (WCC) in Uppsala, Sweden (1968), David du Plessis met Fr. Kilian McDonnell, OSB, a Benedictine monk and theologian from Collegeville, Minnesota. It was the friendship that developed between McDonnell and du Plessis that ultimately led to the establishment of an international Catholic-Pentecostal dialogue. But there is yet more to the common story of these two traditions.

The new ecumenical openness that the Second Vatican Council precipitated led to greater mutual respect and reconciliation between many Pentecostals and Catholics at the local level.[8] Some of this came in 1967, when the Catholic Church was visited by the Holy Spirit in a new way, through the emergence of the Catholic Charismatic Renewal that had been heavily influenced by Pentecostals from the beginning.[9] Through the Renewal and, shortly thereafter, through the international dialogue overseen by the Secretariat (now Pontifical Council for Promoting Christian Unity) large segments of these two traditions have remained in conversation ever since.[10]

Today, the Catholic Charismatic Renewal remains a vital movement with as many as 120 million participants or about one in ten

Catholic believers worldwide.[11] In 1998, Pope John Paul II proclaimed to some 400,000 members of this movement,

> We could say what happened in Jerusalem 2000 years ago is renewed in this square tonight. As the apostles then, so we find ourselves together in this Upper Room, full of longing and praying for the out-pouring of the Spirit.[12]

In spite of these significant intersections, Catholic-Pentecostal relationships have not always been good, nor are they always good today. There are many Pentecostals who do not yet trust that Catholics view them as brothers and sisters in Christ, especially when Catholic leaders accuse Pentecostals of being members of sects.[13] In countries where there has been a long presence of the Catholic Church, places where their hegemony has been secure, Pentecostals complain of unfair treatment and even of persecution.[14] At the same time, there are many Catholics who do not yet trust that Pentecostals view them as brothers and sisters in Christ. In these same regions, for instance, Catholics complain that they are accused of not being Christians or of being idolaters. As a result, they claim that they are subjected to various forms of Pentecostal proselytism.[15]

The third round of the international dialogue, which began in 1985, brought a change in the way the dialogue was conducted. The first two rounds of discussion were largely introductory in nature with multiple subjects being addressed, and a variable list of participants, especially on the Pentecostal team. By the third round, the steering committee was ready to explore a single theme over the five-year commitment. They chose *koinonia* as that theme. They also made changes on the teams. Members were drawn from the realm of scholarship, pastoral ministry, and denominational leadership with the understanding that as much as possible they would remain together for the duration of the five-year period. It was during that round that Monsignor Radano and I were invited to join the dialogue. We would remain there, serving together first as participants and then as co-chairs from 2001 until Monsignor Radano's retirement in 2008.[16]

The fruit of these growing points of intersection in Catholic-Pentecostal relations has been rich, especially since the beginning of the dialogue in 1972. For one thing, Catholics have reminded Pentecostals repeatedly that there is only one Church. Currently, all of us recognize that the one Church exists as a Church in division. We may not yet agree on the details surrounding what that Church looks like today, that is, whether it is a mere spiritual reality or whether it is visible, and if it is visible in what way(s) it might be visible. But one thing is clear. For Catholics, there is only one Church.[17] This is a good reminder to Pentecostals who also affirm the oneness of the Church, but who have split so frequently over the past century that not even the renowned ecclesial statistician David Barrett was able to keep track of their numbers.[18]

In Catholic thinking, the Church's institutional expressions cannot be opposed to its spiritual reality. The Church is the one, holy people of God.[19] It includes all of those who have died in the faith as well as the faithful yet to come, standing alongside all who are part of the faith today. In this sense, then, it is a spiritual reality, and as such, it is in large part also invisible. On this much, Pentecostals are in agreement with Catholics. But Catholics contend in a more substantive way than do Pentecostals, that it is always also a visible Church. The visible and spiritual dimensions of the Church "form one complex reality comprising a human and divine element" (LG 8). It takes on both a visible and an institutional character in which it is said to *subsist* (*subsistit*) in the Catholic Church.[20] Yet, in Catholic thinking, there is room for other Christians, who are recognized on the basis of Trinitarian baptism.[21] This way of thinking is difficult for many Pentecostals to understand or accept since, by this definition, those who are not in full communion with the Bishop of Rome may be Christians, but their "churches" are not viewed as being part of the Church. It does, however, explain much of the Vatican's recent rhetoric that has upset many Christians, and it does make clear Catholic belief in the One Church of our Lord Jesus Christ.[22]

This emphasis upon one Church should not come as a surprise to any Christian. The New Testament knows of only one Church. It is the Church of Jesus Christ. We can read about local congregations in various cities – Jerusalem, Antioch, Rome, and Ephesus – but they are all linked together by the Lord Jesus Christ. They might even have been identifiable as having individual and specific mailing addresses. In the end, however, they are linked together because they are indwelt by the same Holy Spirit. And if we are honest with the biblical text, these regional manifestations of the Church are also linked by human leadership, first through the apostles and their associates and the Council at Jerusalem (Acts 15), and then through the bishops, presbyters, and pastors who led them into subsequent generations.

Any faithful reading of early Christian history recognizes that there is a line extending from the New Testament through these early leaders.[23] The *unity* of the Church was critical to its survival, especially during its first few centuries. As a result, the Apostolic Fathers and apologists such as Irenaeus spoke repeatedly about the need for the church to submit to the bishop, always with one thing in mind – *preserving their unity.*[24] In the middle of the third century, the North African bishop Cyprian went further when he argued that those who broke their relationship with the bishop were no longer part of the Church, that is, there was no such possibility for an independent church.[25] There was only one Church, and it was centred on the bishop, acting on behalf of Christ. During the fourth century, the Councils of Nicaea in AD 325 and Constantinople in AD 381 – with the support of the Cappadocian Fathers, Basil the Great, Gregory of Nyssa, and Gregory of Nazianzus in the latter instance – led to the development of the Nicene-Constantinopolitan Creed, also in the interest of preserving the unity of the Church.

While the New Testament is suggestive of other ways of viewing ecclesial polity, such as congregationalism (Matt. 18:20) or a presbyterian order of governance (largely based on the definition of presbyter), the Fathers of the Church were generally committed to its episcopal character.[26] It is equally clear that Pentecostals do not grant the same level of significance to the Fathers of the Church that Catholics do. There is no question that the Fathers were often compelling witnesses to the faithfulness of God, but for Pentecostals, they are no more authoritative for the Church today than are contemporary ecclesial leaders. In fact, Pentecostals often view the Fathers of the Church as being every bit as pragmatic within their time and place, their specific contexts, as Christian leaders are in today's contexts.[27] That being said, the message of the Fathers regarding the unity of the Church and the need for ongoing fellowship with the bishop is a very important lesson that Catholics have understood, but which, since the time of the

Reformation Protestants, and now Pentecostals, have not taken very seriously.

Pentecostals need to reconsider this emphasis upon the one visible Church to which the Catholic Church continues to bear witness. I say this, in particular, because the Pentecostal tradition is universally known for its independent and entrepreneurial spirit and, in many respects, for its celebration of individualism and the establishment of independent congregations. While at one level this may be viewed as an asset for a rapidly expanding movement, all too often it has come at the expense of the unity of the one Church. In many cases, Pentecostals have launched out on their own without regard to existing churches in the same area and with little regard for maintaining or restoring relationships with others who follow Jesus Christ. This is an area where Pentecostals and Catholics need to continue to challenge one another towards a "more excellent way" of existence and witness.

A second lesson learned from recent Catholic-Pentecostal relations is that the Church of Jesus Christ must be viewed as a global reality. The idea of the Church being one demands that we think of the Church in global terms. Over the past two millennia, the Church has spread throughout the world. It would be difficult, if not impossible, to find a nation in which the Church of Jesus Christ is not represented. With the Catholic Church representing half the Christian population of the world, and the Pentecostal/Charismatic movement arguably representing as much as another 25% of the world's Christians, it is clear that together they make up a majority of the global Church. The Church's oneness in Jesus Christ is what helps us to understand the metaphor of the Body of Christ that the Apostle Paul used on several occasions (1 Cor. 12, Rom. 12, and Eph. 4). Each of us has a role to play within that Body. But if we view that Body in global terms, it may help us to take more seriously those parts that are suffering and those parts that are rejoicing.

In my local congregation, it is our habit to pray each week for Christians who are being persecuted for the sake of Jesus Christ. It does not matter what their denomination is. It does not matter whether they are Pentecostal or Catholic. If they carry the name of Jesus Christ we pray for them, often specifically by name. And we pray for them because they are part of the same Body of Christ of which we are also a part. We pray for them because we are part of the one Church of Jesus Christ. We believe that through our prayers and through our social and political actions, we enter into their sufferings. Our hope is that we provide them with encouragement, support, and ultimately with relief. This is one way that we have come to understand the global nature of the Church.[28]

It is the tendency of all Christians, however, to begin with our own experience of the Church as it is found in our local situation and to generalize from that point. As a result, our experience, sufficiently broadened, is assumed to be the global experience of the Church, the experience of all other Christians. If I tell you that my experience and relationships with the Catholic Church is a good one, and I generalize from my experience, my expectation would probably be that in every other place the relationship between Pentecostals and Catholics is an equally good experience. But we know that this is not the case.

In the same way, Pentecostals in various parts of the world such as in Latin America or in Italy claim that things are very different from my experience. If they generalize from their observation of certain acts they have witnessed in the popular religious practices that they have observed among Catholics in their context, or their experience of tension and in some cases their claims to have been subjected to outright persecution, they might conclude that Catholic-Pentecostal relations are the same around the world. Thus, there is no possibility that Catholics and Pentecostals would be able to relate to one another in such a way as to demonstrate that they actually enjoy a common bond through the blood of Jesus Christ. But the conclusion drawn from such a generalization also is not the case.

Dialogue between Pentecostals and the Catholic Church has made it clear that within the global Church, this one Church of Jesus Christ, it is critical that we take all of our experiences of one another seriously. Some of us have had extremely difficult experiences, while others have had very good experiences. If it is important for us to take seriously the accounts of tensions and negative relationships between Catholics and Pentecostals as they are found in some parts of the world, so too must we consider with equal gravity the testimonies of positive relationships between Pentecostals and Catholics in other places. In fact, it is in these positive relationships where both communities may find clues on how better to relate to one another, a "more excellent way" towards a mutually beneficial existence together.

Third, it is clear from over four decades of working together that neither the Catholic Church nor Pentecostals are homogeneous. Internal diversity is an extremely important feature of both communities. While the Catholic Church may have a common hierarchy and it may have a common faith expressed in a common creed, it is by no means the same in every place. In some countries, the Catholic Church is a dominant political, social, and ecclesial force. In others, it stands on the margins of political, social, and religious life. The different orders with their unique vocations in different parts of the world are yet another demonstration of that diversity. In some places, Catholics push the limits of the decisions taken at the Second Vatican Council in its attempt to be a "progressive" Church. In other places, they may live their faith and life together in ways that are much closer to their more conservative pre-Vatican II past. In some regions of the world, the Catholic Church is open to and engages freely in a rich ecumenical life. In others, it is less ecumenically open. It harbours deep suspicions and resentments against other Christians, and it still views Pentecostals as "sects." In some cities, the Catholic Church functions with a vitality that rivals the vitality we see within the Pentecostal movement. In other places, the Catholic Church seems to be unable to attract its own people to a living faith, to move beyond rite and ritual and in some cases beyond an unhealthy form of syncretism to a fuller encounter with God. In some places, it conducts its life in radically biblical ways, while in other areas it might rightfully be accused of submitting so fully to the claims made in some cultural and religious contexts that its gospel message is compromised.[29]

At the same time, Pentecostals around the world differ. The suffering endured by Pentecostals in Italy under the Mussolini regime with the alleged complicity of the Catholic Church[30] is far different from the North American experience of Catholics since the emergence of Pentecostalism in the twentieth century. As I have travelled around the world, I have found many other differences between Pentecostals. In a visit to a very large Pentecostal congregation in São Paulo, Brazil,

I made the mistake of taking a seat near the rear of the congregation. I quickly found myself surrounded by four men who cordially invited and then escorted me to the side where men were supposed to sit. I had not even noticed that the congregation of several thousand people was segregated by gender. Where I come from, women and men mix freely with one another.

Among Pentecostals, the role of women differs from place to place as well. Some Pentecostals grant equal rights to women in all things, including ordained ministry,[31] while others grant ministerial credentials with certain limitations for women, and still others do not recognize women for ordained ministerial status.[32] In some places, women are silent, except when prophesying, and they are expected to worship with their heads covered.

Pentecostals also differ over the number of gifts (charisms) of the Spirit that are accepted, whether all the charisms of the New Testament (e.g. apostle) have been "restored," how these gifts are to be defined, who is expected or allowed to manifest them, and under what circumstances they may be used.[33] Even the question of what evidence or whether any evidence is necessary to determine when a person has been baptized in the Holy Spirit is debated within Pentecostal circles.[34] And if we review the ways in which Pentecostals practice baptism, we would find that some baptize infants while others baptize only confessing believers, some baptize by immersion while others pour or sprinkle, some baptize by single immersion while others embrace a triple immersion, and some baptize using the Name of Jesus Christ while most invoke the Trinitarian formula. At the same time, some would require the re-baptism of all converts from the Catholic Church while others recognize their Catholic baptism as a valid Christian baptism and, as such, do not practice rebaptism.[35]

And then there is the difficult issue of the so-called prosperity teaching. All Pentecostals and Catholics value the gifts that God has bestowed upon them, and many people in both communities are pleased to give back to God something of what he has given to them. Most Pentecostals tithe regularly and many give beyond the tithe in the form of offerings, some quite sacrificially. Most recognize their giving as a response to God's provision for them. Some clearly rely upon

God's promises to provide for his people (e.g. Prov. 28:25). But some Pentecostals push the envelope on the subject of prosperity from God meeting one's needs to God granting everything that one may desire. Clearly, there are biblical promises to individuals in this regard, but some respond to such promises as though God were a kind of genie, there to meet their desires in ways that move from faith to presumption. As a result, Pentecostals may be found along a spectrum of positions on the subject of prosperity and health.[36]

The point here is that while there is only one Church of Jesus Christ, it is important to understand that there is enormous diversity among Catholics and among Pentecostals who participate in that one Church and that diversity often stems from our historical, cultural, and theological contexts. Thus, to generalize our experience within our local context as though it were the experience of the whole Church closes us off from lessons that we might learn from other parts of the Church that may actually experience something of a "more excellent way."

Fourth, Catholics and Pentecostals hold much more in common than any of them generally recognize. One of the things that my pursuit of Christian history over the years has done is to give me an appreciation for all of those who have gone before us. In the West, this includes both Catholics and since the sixteenth century, Protestants. Their faithfulness in preserving the "Apostolic Faith," of passing on the Tradition from generation to generation, of selecting and preserving the sacred texts that we recognize as Scripture, and of sharing the gospel wherever they went should be remembered and celebrated by the Church in our own generation.

In the Americas, it is possible and even rightful to criticize the presence of the conquering sword even in relation to the Franciscan Mission chain by which the Catholic Church travelled the spine of the Andes Mountain range, making its way northwards through Central America and Mexico to California. But it is equally important to note that in the other hand came the Word of God through which many indigenous people, as well as others, came to faith in Jesus Christ.[37] It is an interesting fact that Roman Catholics have been both missionary and evangelistic throughout the centuries. Sometimes it stood in stark contrast to the positions of the Protestant Reformers who seem to have contended that the world needed no evangelization beyond the immediate family. This very fact should endear the Catholic Church to the missionary and evangelistic heart of the Pentecostal movement.

The life and example of Pope Gregory I (AD 540-604) provides a rich example of this concern, though it is a concern that was reflected by others throughout the later history of the Catholic Church. The way Gregory viewed the world and the times in which he lived, and because of his concern for the souls of men and women, his testimony sounds very much like that of many Pentecostal evangelists and missionaries today. In AD 590, Gregory returned to Rome from Byzantium where he had been representing the Pope. When he returned, he clearly believed that the Lord would return during his lifetime. The signs were all around him and he read the prophets with eschatological eyes. Rome was in turmoil. The Tiber River had overrun its banks, flooding the city. The city had been hit by an outbreak of the plague, killing thousands of its residents. The Lombards, though miles away, had effectively surrounded the region. Local secular leadership was essentially nowhere to be found. Furthermore, it was the responsibility of the Church to feed the poor, and there were thousands of people who looked to the Church for a resolution to these otherwise intractable problems. Gregory's description of what he found is depressing, to say the least – "the walls going to ruin, the houses falling down, the churches destroyed... and the buildings crumbling from old age."[38] He viewed the calamities that had befallen Rome as the manifestations of the just judgment of God on sinful humanity.

With this as his backdrop, Gregory placed a high premium on the evangelization or the re-evangelization of Western Europe, a theme that John Paul II and Benedict XVI reiterated in recent years. The forces of evil would be confronted wherever they were found. People would be encouraged to review their lives and prepare their hearts for the imminent Day of the Lord. He called the clergy to greater integrity, demonstrating consistency between what they said when they occupied the pulpit and how they lived their lives. He demanded that the clergy allow the Word of God to judge their thoughts and deeds before it was used as a platform from which the clergy addressed the people.[39] Missions would be undertaken in order to convert as many as possible before that great day so that none might be lost. Thus, he commissioned missionaries to take the gospel throughout Europe and to England.[40] Protestants had to wait until the emergence of Pietism before it took its missionary mandate seriously. Evangelization and mission are commitments that are commonly shared by Pentecostals and Catholics.[41]

One of the questions that often gets raised at this point, however, is about the nature of the gospel itself. Is the gospel that is proclaimed by the Catholic Church really the gospel, or is it some kind of syncretistic message? Such a concern might be understandable given earlier animosities between these traditions, but it is equally important to recognize that in no case is the gospel ever communicated to any culture apart from some level of syncretism – good or bad.[42] Here again, the early church may be a useful partner in the discussion. The Catholic Church confesses the ancient Nicene-Constantinopolitan Creed as a legitimate representation of its faith. Even though many Pentecostals are slow to respond to or embrace creeds of any kind, it is the case that when they are walked through this same creed, they also affirm it line by line.

One question that Pentecostals need to ask themselves in light of this fact is "What is the nature of the Gospel that Pentecostals preach?" What do they say when they invite people to make a confession of faith in Jesus Christ? They do not test potential converts on the nature of the Trinity, or their understanding of Christology. They do not ask them whether they are willing to allow the Holy Spirit to grant gifts to them or whether they even believe that there are such things as gifts or charisms of the Spirit that operate today. They do not ask their views regarding Mary, or their position on praying to the saints, whether they pray the rosary, or have a specific devotion, or what their eschatological expectations are. Nor do they ask them to recite the Creed. They simply tell them that if they acknowledge that they are sinners, confess their sinfulness to God, and put their trust or faith in Jesus Christ (Acts 2:38-39), that is, if they believe with their hearts and confess with their mouths (Rom. 10:9), they will be saved! That is a declaration that Pentecostals make time and again.

While this is not the typical approach taken by many Catholics,[43] and questions have been raised by some Catholic leaders about the need for becoming more explicit in calling for personal conversion,[44] it seems apparent that when Catholics confess the Creed, maintaining it as a legitimate representation of their belief system, Pentecostals must respond to their confession by accepting them as Christians and treating them as sisters and brothers in Christ. It is that act that has the ability to change the nature of relationships between Catholics and Pentecostals. At that moment, Pentecostals can no longer look at them as simply being "unsaved." By taking that step, Pentecostals and Catholics will find that the nature of any argument between them changes. No longer can they argue with one another as though one party is Christian and the other is not. They will argue as siblings – brothers and sisters. And siblings do argue. But beneath that argument is the basic respect and love that they deserve first, as spiritual siblings. Accountability is present in a different way between siblings than it is between those who are not members of the same family. But it is equally important to realize that mutual accountability is present in such a relationship.

When it comes to many of the issues that separate Pentecostals from Catholics, Pentecostals often betray the simplicity, or one might even say the naïveté of their invitations. Why do they treat differences between Pentecostals and Catholics as though they were primary concerns? Is it to mark their territories or in some way to provide them with a reason for their separate existence? If salvation is really as easily obtained as Pentecostals claim it to be, why are the issues that currently separate them from Catholics allowed to sap them of so much spiritual vitality? These have become church-dividing issues. Some Pentecostals have built their own kingdoms around their differences from Catholics rather than submitting to the concerns of the Kingdom by struggling with the nature of the One Church.

Recently, my wife and I experienced a different but related irony. We chose to attend Our Lady of the Angels, the new cathedral in downtown Los Angeles. It was great! God was there. We worshipped among the people of God. We enjoyed the organ. We sang hymns. And we heard a fine homily. In short, it was a very refreshing worship service for the two of us.

There were probably 2,000 people present. Three couples were chosen to carry the eucharistic elements forward. We watched as a number of couples were asked to do so, and refused. The responsible staff person finally came to Patsy and me and asked us if we would do it. We didn't know him, and he obviously didn't know us.

We told him that we were merely visiting, and we were not even Catholics. He responded with "That's not a problem, will you do it?" We kind of looked at one another and Patsy tried again, "We wouldn't know what to do." He then responded with "That's OK, we'll show you." So we looked at one another again and we both said, "OK". You have to appreciate the fact that in our congregation, Patsy is an elder. On the first Sunday of each month, as this one was, the elders, under the supervision of our pastor, serve communion to the congregation. She would have been doing this in our congregation.

In the end, Patsy and I were the couple who brought up the rear of the procession with the offering, wine, and bread, as we carried the bread forward to the Monsignor, who asked us where we lived and graciously welcomed us. Then, with the rest, we stepped down the stairs, turned in front of the altar, and bowed. Then we took our seats.

Sadly, when it came time to present ourselves to receive the elements of the eucharist, Patsy and I could not and did not participate. We could attend the service. Our baptisms would be recognized as valid. We could participate in the service both in singing and in prayer. We could worship the same God. We could confess the Creed together with no reservations. We could drop our offering into the collection basket. We could even carry forward the offering of bread for the "sacrifice." But we were not welcomed to eat of it or to sip the wine, for we are viewed as being outside the Church.

Both Pentecostals and Catholics have often tried to *force* one another to see the light from their perspective, rather than loving one another into a "more excellent way" that both could share together. Both Pentecostals and Catholics have become accustomed to living as the Church in schism; as a result, they have frequently come to regard that state of schism as normal. They have made the defense of their own position the most important thing they do, instead of asking what they might learn from the other, instead of asking how they might help the other, instead of concentrating on those many, many places where they have complete or near complete agreement in doctrine and practice, or instead of demonstrating by their lives that there is a "more excellent way."

Fifth, it is clear that Catholic leadership, at least in Rome, says that it is interested in changing the current relationship between Catholic and Pentecostal Christians. The papal visit to Australia in July 2008, where over 350,000 young people from around the world gathered to sit under the ministry of Pope Benedict XVI, was exciting to watch. In particular, three things worth noting took place at that event that were symbolic of the growing relationship between Catholics and Pentecostals. First, the entire event was given a very Pentecostal theme: "You will Receive Power When the Holy Spirit Comes upon You and You Will be My Witnesses" (Acts 1:8). Pentecostals often appeal to this passage of Scripture to describe the empowerment for witness that comes with baptism in the Holy Spirit as they understand it. Second, the planning for what was billed as the most significant meeting of World Youth Day's youth festival, a concert, was turned over entirely to the Catholic Charismatic Renewal, which has been influenced by Pentecostalism since its inception in the 1960s. Third, the Catholic leaders of this event invited Hillsong United, an internationally recognized Pentecostal worship team, to set the stage for the entire event by leading 150,000 young people in songs like "Mighty to Save" and "On Eagles' Wings."

Pope Francis has continued to reach out to Pentecostals. Even while he was serving as Archbishop Bergoglio in Buenos Aires, he met regularly with Evangelical and Pentecostal leaders, sometimes sitting in the front row during their evangelistic crusades and on other occasions sitting on the platform in support of their work. He allowed them to lay hands on him and pray over him. In 2013, an independent Anglican bishop, Tony Palmer, carried a short video message from Pope Francis to a Pentecostal gathering convened by Kenneth Copeland Ministries in Dallas, Texas, in which Pope Francis spoke "heartfully" of the sin that has separated Pentecostals from Catholics and his desire for unity.[45] In July 2014, Pope Francis sought out the Pentecostal Giovanni Traettino, pastor of the Evangelical Church of Reconciliation in Caserta, Italy, where he announced publicly, "I ask for your forgiveness for those who, calling themselves Catholic, didn't understand we're brothers." Traettino embraced the request, calling it "a gesture that opened the door to reconciliation and answered to God's request of being one church."[46]

I have spent over thirty years working with the Pontifical Council for Promoting Christian Unity, and nearly as long working with the Archdiocese of Los Angeles, California. Over the years I have attended and spoken at Catholic scholarly meetings. I have worshipped and preached in Catholic churches and published articles in Catholic journals. I have benefited from stays in various monasteries and convents. I have been engaged with Catholics in significant theological dialogue at the local, national, and international levels. I have also participated in a number of papal audiences and liturgies with Popes John Paul II, Benedict XVI, and Francis.

Beginning in 2000, John Paul II invited me to participate with him in a number of services that he led. On one occasion I was invited to lead the congregation in the third article of the Creed. On another occasion, I was invited to offer prayer for the peace of the world on behalf of the entire Christian community. In 1993, during the Week of Prayer for Christian Unity, I preached in the Cathedral of St. Vibiana in Los Angeles and in 2013, I did the same at the Cathedral of the Blessed Sacrament in Sacramento. Upon the death of Pope John Paul II, in April 2005, I spoke at his memorial service in Our Lady of the Angels, the new cathedral of Los Angeles. I even attended the inaugurations of Benedict XVI and Francis, where I was given a seat of honour on the platform adjacent to the altar. And the Pontifical Council for Promoting Christian Unity asked me to help oversee a process that would provide guidelines for the bishops of the Catholic Church, enabling them to understand Pentecostals better and build new and productive relationships with Pentecostals. My experience has led me to see that the Catholic Church is very interested in changing the nature of its current relationship with Pentecostals.

My witness may be unique, and I am sure that it is different from that which most Pentecostals have had. Nevertheless, it a valid witness of what is possible if we will make the effort to seek a way forward in Catholic-Pentecostal relations. Someone has to take the first step towards greater understanding. Without that first step, we are doomed to continue on the all too common path of tension, misunderstanding, and a failure to participate with God in the quest for the unity for which Christ prayed.

Finally, I have tried to be objective and in some ways even positive to the Catholic side in this chapter, because I find that to be a necessary corrective when dealing with Pentecostal perspectives. Pentecostal pulpit rhetoric regarding the Catholic Church is largely unchastened. There is much to be gained, much that we as Pentecostals should be able to appreciate about the Catholic witness to the gospel throughout history. Even from a Pentecostal perspective, there have always been faithful Christians within the Catholic Church. Still, the question must be asked once again. Was it really essential for the Church to be reformed in the sixteenth century? Were things really as bad as the Reformers made them out to be? In order to answer this question, I turn to two Catholic scholars.

The first of them is Anthony E. Gilles, a former professor of history at Rutgers University, a Catholic layman who is used extensively in diaconal formation programs both in Scripture studies and in church history. He observed that:

> One of the stiffest challenges any of us faces is to own up to our own failures and mistakes. That's true likewise for groups of people, especially people who make up religious bodies. We find it much easier to look at the good features of our religious tradition and ignore the bad. We Catholics have been guilty of that when it comes to the Reformation. We accurately point to the harmful effects of the Reformation, such as the splintering of the Church into hundreds of sects and the proliferation of competing doctrines. But we are sometimes not so "historical" when it comes to acknowledging the Catholic sins that contributed to the Reformation. Was the Catholic Church really as corrupt as the early Protestant Reformers said it was? The short answer is, yes it was.[47]

The second statement comes from Richard P. McBrien, a professor of theology at the University of Notre Dame. He notes that:

> While it is true that the Church is "at once holy and always in need of purification" and must constantly follow "the path of penance and renewal" (Vatican II, *Dogmatic Constitution on*

the Church, n.8), the Protestant Reformation should not have been necessary. It was the product of a series of tragic and unforgivable mistakes and corrupt actions on the part of the Church's leadership, the papacy in particular. The fourteenth and fifteenth centuries were among the worst in the Western Church.[48]

Such candid admissions are few and far between when we look at older treatments of the Reformation recorded by Roman Catholic scholars.

In the years of dialogue between Pentecostals and Catholics, the question of history and our unique memories and accountings of that history have repeatedly emerged. Especially beginning with the report of the fourth round of discussions, *Evangelization, Proselytism and Common Witness*, Pentecostals have been quite candid about their failures and weaknesses.[49] For whatever reason, it has seemed to the Pentecostals that it has been much more difficult for the Catholic teams to be as vulnerable or open on certain historical questions. What the admissions of the two Catholic authors just cited reflect, however, is the fact that since the Second Vatican Council there are those scholars in the Catholic Church who have attempted to come to terms with the Catholic Church's history in a more honest and forthright manner than had been done previously.[50]

It is this very willingness to be forthright and open that led His Holiness Pope John Paul II as well as Pope Francis to ask for and offer forgiveness for past sins and indiscretions that the Catholic Church has committed against other Christians and that other Christians have committed against the Catholic Church.

"Let us forgive and ask forgiveness!" Pope John Paul II began.

While we praise God who, in his merciful love, has produced in the Church a wonderful harvest of holiness, missionary zeal, total dedication to Christ and neighbour, we cannot fail to recognize *the infidelities to the Gospel committed by some of our brethren*, especially during the second millennium. Let us ask pardon for the divisions which have occurred among Christians, for the violence some have used in the service of the truth and for the distrustful and hostile attitudes sometimes taken towards the followers of other religions.

Let us confess, even more, *our responsibilities as Christians for the evils of today.* We must ask ourselves what our responsibilities are regarding atheism, religious indifference, secularism, ethical relativism, the violations of the right to life, disregard for the poor in many countries.

We humbly ask forgiveness for the part which each of us has had in these evils by our own actions, thus helping to disfigure the face of the Church.

At the same time, as we confess our sins, *let us forgive the sins committed by others against us.* Countless times in the course of history Christians have suffered hardship, oppression and persecution because of their faith. Just as the victims of such abuses forgave them, so let us forgive as well. The Church today feels and has always felt obliged to *purify her memory* of those sad events from every feeling of rancour or revenge. In this way the Jubilee becomes for everyone a favourable opportunity for a profound conversion to the Gospel. The acceptance of God's forgiveness leads to the commitment to forgive our brothers and sisters and to be reconciled with them.[51]

In this passage, not only did John Paul II call upon all Christians to be forgiven and to forgive, he also called on all Christians to purify the memories or perspectives that all of us carry regarding our past histories.

Memory is a very difficult factor with which to work, however. Corporate memories, kept alive by constant reiteration throughout the centuries, are among the most difficult realities to confront, and their long-term effects are even more difficult to erase. Torre Pellice, Italy, has played a long-term role in the history of the Waldensians, a group of lay preachers who were heavily persecuted by Rome in the twelfth through the fifteenth centuries. Any visitor to that town will soon realize that everyone, including many young children, is able to recite that history of religious persecution that extends back over 800 years. It is *their* story even though their persecution ended centuries ago, and they still feel the effects of that story deeply.[52] It remains very much alive in the Waldensian community, just as the Passover of the Exodus remains the historic, yet contemporary story of all practising Jews today.

The meaning in such stories has transcended the lives and times of those to whom the events actually took place. Yet today, it is more than mere memory, that is, the story of a past event that took place centuries ago. It is fresh and alive as though it were relived by each generation every day. It is like the memory (*anamnesis*; 1 Cor. 11:24-25) of Christ's death in which Christians participate each time they take part in the eucharist or Lord's Supper.

There are certain challenges that face those who seek to understand such stories, such memories, and historians are relative newcomers to these challenges.[53] The narratives of events that took place in the life of Jesus may be the same or quite similar in the different accounts that bear witness to the same basic elements. One look at shared accounts found in the Gospels should be sufficient to demonstrate this fact. They bear the unique marks of the story teller, which often point to a different usage for the same account.[54] These narratives are ultimately subject to interpretation and the interpretations may differ markedly.[55] As the basic narrative of events from the time of the Reformation onwards have come down both through Catholic and more recently Pentecostal historians, it is evident that the interpretations given to certain events or certain realities on the ground are not always viewed in the same way. Such memories are difficult to integrate or change, even when facts that emerge within the other tradition are brought to bear upon them. The usefulness of looking at historical accounts[56] and the usefulness of viewing and writing about the Church as a global reality[57] may be difficult tasks to undertake, but they are not only worth the attempt because they help to build bridges between the various parties, they are now critically important to the success of the ecumenical quest.

Dialogue between Catholics and Pentecostals has provided numerous lessons that have to do with corporate memory and historical perceptions. More often than not, these memories or perceptions have been passed on from generation to generation without being carefully examined or examined together. Past and continuing estrangement between Catholics and Pentecostals has often prevented further contact, while individual stories have grown in their significance in these respective communities. Frequently, these stories, when viewed independently, turn out to be nothing more than sources of unworthy stereotypes that have been used to maintain separation.[58]

The Pentecostal movement is a relatively recent ecclesial movement, only a century or so in existence. Yet it shares the memories of the Protestant Reformation as though they had been present at that time. Its memory of the past even extends, by means of its frequent appeal to a Restorationist reading of history, back to the time of Nicaea.[59] This position needs to be tested with those whose history is viewed through the lens of continuity rather than discontinuity.

The result of doing history in isolation is that some claim to have history on their side while challenging what they label as "perceptions" of history on the other side. This has happened more than once within discussions between Catholics and Pentecostals. It is not a helpful approach to ecumenical work. In recent years, Monsignor Radano has repeatedly called for work to be undertaken on the purification of corporate memories through an ecumenical rereading of history, a call with which I heartily concur. The most significant work to follow his suggestion to date has been the 2004 report of the Mennonite-Roman Catholic dialogue, *Called Together to Be Peacemakers.*[60]

The history of relations between Catholics and Pentecostals extends back little more than a century. The first half of that history was fraught with conflict, with little to demonstrate that we had much in common. That changed with the Second Vatican Council, which made possible both more Catholic openness to Pentecostals and, through David du Plessis, more Pentecostal openness to Catholics. While tensions continue to exist between Pentecostals and Catholics in places like Latin America and Italy, the development of the international Catholic-Pentecostal dialogue, now over 40 years old, has done much to educate a generation of younger Pentecostal scholars. A brief overview has yielded a rich tapestry of common concerns. At the present time, Catholic leadership appears to be open to the possibility that Catholic-Pentecostal relations, which all too often are still subject to vitriolic rhetoric on both sides, should continue to be a matter of priority.

Pentecostals have much to learn from Catholics, and through Charismatic Renewal and ongoing dialogue, Catholics have also demonstrated that they have been willing to learn from Pentecostals. The fact that we are both global traditions suggests that there is much that we can teach one another about the nature of the oneness of the Church, the implications of being global churches, and the diversity that both demonstrate on multiple levels around the world. In spite of our diversity, Catholics and Pentecostals may hold more in common with one another than either tradition has been willing to acknowledge because of our troubled history. In fact, we may ultimately be surprised to find that Pentecostals have more in common with Catholics than they do with many of their Protestant and even Evangelical sisters and brothers. In order to move beyond the relative impasse that still separates Catholics and Pentecostals from one another, it will be necessary for the two traditions to continue their work together on a common approach to history in which differences can be addressed *together*, and the healing of disparate memories may be purified.

---

1   The best treatment of Charles F. Parham is still James R. Goff, Jr., *Fields White Unto Harvest: Charles F. Parham and the Missionary Origins of Pentecostalism* (Fayetteville: The University of Arkansas Press, 1988), 263 pp.

2   "Already, on the eve of the twentieth century, Pope Leo XIII, taking up proposals made to him, wrote an Apostolic Exhortation (1895) and an Encyclical Letter (1897) in which he called for devotion to the Holy Spirit and recommended the nine days before Pentecost as a Novena of Prayer for the Holy Spirit: 'for the renewal of the church, reunification of Christianity, renewal of society, and for a renewal of the face of the earth'. On 1 January 1901, Pope Leo XIII prayed the hymn to the Holy Spirit in the name of the whole church." International Dialogue between some Classical Pentecostal Churches and Leaders and the Catholic Church, *On Becoming a Christian: Insights from Scripture and the Patristic Writings with Some Contemporary Reflections,* Report of the Fifth Phase (1998-2006), no. 223; *Information Service* 129 (2008): 205; http://www.prounione.urbe.it.

3   On William J. Seymour and the revival he led, see Cecil M. Robeck, Jr. *The Azusa Street Mission and Revival: The Birth of the Global Pentecostal Movement* (Nashville: Thomas Nelson, 2006), 342 pp.

4   John XXIII, *Journal of a Soul*, translated by Dorothy White (New York: McGraw-Hill, 1964), p. 391.

5   Having set forth their understanding of the Church in *Lumen Gentium* (Dogmatic Constitution on the Church, November 21, 1964), the Bishops went on to declare that 'The restoration of unity among all Christians is one of the principal concerns of the Second Vatican Council...The sacred Council...now, moved by a desire for the restoration of unity among all the followers of Christ, it wishes to set before all Catholics guidelines, helps and methods, by which they too can respond to the grace of this divine call." *Unitatis Redintegratio* (Decree on Ecumenism, November 21, 1964), no. 1.

6   On the formation and role of the Secretariat for Promoting Christian Unity, now a Pontifical Council, see Stjepan Schmidt, *Augustin Bea, The Cardinal of Unity*, trans. Leslie Waerne (New Rochelle, NY: New City Press, 1992), pp. 329-675; *Dictionary of the Ecumenical Movement*, 2nd ed., s.v. "Pontifical Council for Promoting Christian Unity," by Tom Stransky.

7   David du Plessis, *Simple and Profound* (Orleans, MA: Paraclete Press, 1986), pp. 181-82.

8   This is acknowledged in *On Becoming a Christian*, nos. 260, 273-74.

9   Kevin and Dorothy Ranaghan, *Catholic Pentecostals* (Paramus, NJ: Paulist Press, 1969), pp. 9-13.

10   The reports from the first four rounds of discussion may be found in GA II, pp. 713-79. See also Cecil M. Robeck, Jr. "On Becoming a Christian: An Important Theme in the International Roman Catholic-Pentecostal Dialogue," *PentecoStudies: Online Journal for the Interdisciplinary Study of Pentecostalism and Charismatic Movements* 8, no. 2 (Fall 2008): 1-23. This paper may also be viewed at http://www.glopent.net/pentecostudies/online-back-issues/2008-vol-7/no-2-autumn/robeck-2008. "'Do Not Quench the Spirit': Charisms in the Life and Mission of the Church", the Report of the Sixth Phase of the International Catholic-Pentecostal Dialogue (2011-2015) may be found in the *Information Service* 147 (2016/I): 47-62.

11   David B. Barratt, George T. Kurian, and Todd M. Johnson, *World Christian Encyclopedia*, 2nd ed. (Oxford: Oxford University Press, 2001), 1:20, Table 1-6a. In a special report, Alessandria Nucci, "The Charismatic Renewal and the Catholic Church", *The Catholic World Report* (May 18, 2013), claimed that there were 160 million Catholic Charismatics at the time the article was written. Edward L. Cleary, *The Rise of Charismatic Catholicism in Latin America* (Gainesville: University Press of Florida, 2011), ix. I cannot account for the estimate of 200 million Catholic Charismatics worldwide that Cleary claims to exist.

12   *On Becoming a Christian*, no. 272. For other comments by recent Popes on the Renewal, see Kilian McDonnell, ed., *Open the Windows: The Popes and Charismatic Renewal* (South Bend, IN: Greenlawn Press, 1989), 67 pp.

13   Alta/Baja California Bishops, "Dimensions of a Response to Proselytism," *Origins* 19, no. 41 (March 15, 1990): 666, for instance, states that "By sects or new religious groups, we mean those religious organizations founded in the past century which have grown progressively stronger and which reject or directly oppose the historical churches. We refer especially, to the Church of Jesus Christ of Latter-day Saints (Mormons), Jehovah's Witnesses, Seventh-day Adventists, Pentecostals in a variety of forms and others."

14   Francesco Toppi, *E Mi Sarete Testimoni: Il Movimento Pentecostale e le Assemblee di Dio in Italia* (Roma: ADI-Media, 1999), pp. 61-67. In 1957, the Assemblies of God passed a resolution on the "Persecution of Protestants" in Colombia, in which it protested the "unhuman treatment of Protestants or any religious group" by Roman Catholics there and petitioning the United States Department of State to "use every possible means to stop such persecution." *Minutes of the Twenty-Seventh General Council of the Assemblies of God Convened at Cleveland, Ohio, August 28-September 3, 1957* (Springfield, MO: Office of the General Secretary, 1957), p. 52. Pentecostals do not limit their understanding of persecution solely in terms of violence, but also include the use of pejorative terms against them, such as "Sect." Cf. Benjamín Bravo, "Sectas" in Benjamín Bravo, comp., *Vocabulario de la religiosidad popular* (Mexico City: Ediciones Dabar, 1992), p. 173.

15   See for instance the Alta/Baja California Bishops, "Dimensions of a Response to Proselytism," p. 667.

16   The Pentecostal team was led by David du Plessis through 1984. His brother, Justus du Plessis, succeeded him in the Pentecostal chair through 1991. Cecil M. Robeck, Jr. became the Pentecostal co-chair in 1992 and continues in that role. The Catholic team was led by Fr. Kilian McDonnell, OSB, from the initial meeting of the dialogue through 2000, when due to age and family requests,

he retired. Monsignor John A. Radano succeeded him in 2001 and served in this capacity until his retirement in 2008.

17 *Lumen Gentium*, no. 8.

18 Barrett, Kurian, and Johnson, *World Christian Encyclopedia*, 1:19 estimates that there are "740 Pentecostal denominations, 6530 nonpentecostal mainline denominations with large organized internal Charismatic movements, and 18,810 independent Neocharismatic denominations and networks." Much, of course, depends upon how each of these categories is defined. That they are closely related is clear, but often the differences between the Pentecostal churches and those described as "neocharismatic" are minimal. It may depend upon how much one group emphasizes healing, or signs and wonders, or prosperity or some other distinctive over another group that may teach the same thing at a less intense level.

19 *Lumen Gentium*, nos. 9-17.

20 *Lumen Gentium*, no. 8 reads, "This Church, constituted and organized as a society in the present world, subsists in the Catholic Church, which is governed by the successor of Peter and by the bishops in communion with him. Nevertheless, many elements of sanctification and of truth are found outside its visible confines."

21 *Lumen Gentium*, no. 15 reads: "The Church knows that she is joined in many ways to the baptized who are honoured by the name of Christian, but who do not, however, profess the Catholic faith in its entirety or have not preserved unity or communion under the successor of Peter. For there are many who hold sacred scripture in honour as a rule of faith and life, who have a sincere religious zeal, who lovingly believe in God the Father Almighty and in Christ, the Son of God and the Saviour, who are sealed by baptism which unites them to Christ, and who indeed recognize and receive other sacraments in their own Churches and ecclesial communities. Many of them possess the episcopate, celebrate the Holy Eucharist, and cultivate devotion of Mary, the Virgin Mother of God. There is furthermore a sharing in prayer and spiritual benefits; these Christians are indeed in some real way joined to us in the Holy Spirit for, by his gifts and graces, his sanctifying power is also active in them and he has strengthened some of them even to the shedding of their blood. And so the Spirit stirs up desires and actions in all of Christ's disciples in order that all may be peaceably united as Christ ordained, in one flock under one shepherd."

22 On this, see the responses to the words of Pope John Paul II in 1992 when he addressed the bishops in Santo Domingo, Dominican Republic, using terms such as "rapacious wolves." "Opening Address to Fourth General Conference of Latin American Episcopate," *Origins* 22, no. 19 (October 22, 1992): 326, no. 12; and *Dominus Iesus* IV.16-17.

23 Cf. Ignatius, *To the Ephesians*, no. 3-6; *To the Magnesians*, no. 6-7; *To the Philadelphians*, no. 2.7; *To the Smyrnaeans*, nos. 8-9; *To Polycarp*, nos. 2-5.

24 Clement, *Epistle to the Corinthians*, nos. 12, 37-38; Irenaeus, *Against Heresies*, I.10.1-2; III.3.2-3; IV.33.8.

25 Cyprian, *Letter* 66 (68).5.1; 8.3

26 See James D. G. Dunn, *Unity and Diversity in the New Testament: An Inquiry into the Character of Earliest Christianity*, 3rd ed. (London: SCM, 2006), 520 pp.

27 The Pentecostal understanding of the role and value of the Fathers of the Church is addressed in *On Becoming a Christian*, nos. 9-13.

28 See Cecil M. Robeck, Jr., "Christians and Persecution: Making an Appropriate Response," in Harold D. Hunter and Cecil M. Robeck, Jr., eds., *The Suffering Body: Responding to the Persecution of Christians* (Bletchley, UK: Paternoster, 2006), pp. 62-81.

29 This is clearly the concern of *Dominus Iesus*, published by the Congregation for the Doctrine of the Faith in 2000.

30 A number of incidents are mentioned in David A. Womack and Francesco Toppi, *Le Radici del Movimento Pentecostale* (Rome: A.D.I.-Media, 1989), pp. 130-33, 145-48; Francesco Toppi, *E Mi Sarete Testimoni: Il Movimento Pentecostale e le Assemblee di Dio in Italia*, pp. 61-67, 87-98; Giovanni Traettino, "The Fascist Regime and the Pentecostal Church," 25th Meeting of The Society for Pentecostal Studies and The European Pentecostal and Charismatic Research Association, 10-14 July 1995 (Mattersey, England: Assemblies of God Bible College, Mattersey Hall, 1995), 26 pp.; Mark Hutchinson, *Pelegrini: An Italian Protestant Community in Sydney, 1958-1998*, APS Supplement no. 1 (Sydney, Australia: Australian Pentecostal Studies Journal, 1999), pp. 16-23. Following World War II, the Assemblies of God made repeated resolutions appealing to the President of the United States, the Secretary of State and/or the Chair of the Foreign Relations Committee of the United States Senate to intervene in Italy to prevent "religious discrimination and suppression" that came when ministers were "forcibly prevented from conducting religious services and imprisoned." This was made necessary as a result of what they called "the old Fascist-Vatican treaty known as the Concordat ... between ... Benito Mussolini and the Pope ...." *Minutes of the General Council of the Assemblies of God Convened at Springfield, Missouri September 13-18, 1945* (Springfield, MO: Office of the General Secretary, 1945), p. 39; Giorgio Rochat, *Regime Fascista E Chiese Evangeliche: dirette e articolazioni del controllo e della repressione* (Torino: Claudiana, 1990), pp. 113-26.

31 *Minutes of the 51st Session of The General Council of the Assemblies of God: Convened in Denver, Colorado, August 2-5, 2005 with revised Constitution and Bylaws* (Springfield, MO: Office of the General Secretary, 2005), p. 111. Bylaws, Article VII Ministry, Section 2 Basic Qualifications, Eligibility of Women reads as follows: "The Scriptures plainly teach that divinely called and qualified women may also serve the church in the ministry of the Word (Joel 2:29; Acts 21:9; 1 Corinthians 11:5). Women who meet the qualifications for ministerial credentials are eligible for whatever grade of credentials their qualifications warrant and have the right to administer the ordinances of the church and are eligible to serve in all levels of church ministry, and/or district and General Council leadership."

32 *Official Manual with the Doctrines and Disciplines of the Church of God in Christ 1973* (Memphis: Church of God in Christ, 1991 edition), p. 146. The Church of God in Christ recognizes the scriptural importance of women in Christian Ministry (Matt. 28:1; Mark 16:1; Luke 24:1; John 20:1), the first at the tomb on the morning of Christ's resurrection; the first to whom the Lord appeared (Matt. 28:9; Mark 16:9; John 20:14); the first to announce the fact of the resurrection to the chosen disciples (Luke 29:9; 10:22) and etc., but nowhere can we find a mandate to ordain women to be an Elder, Bishop or Pastor....

33 Cf. "Apostles and Prophets" approved as an official statement by the General Presbytery of the Assemblies of God, August 6, 2001; http://ag.org/top/beliefs/position_papers/pp_downloads/ pp_4195_apostles_prophets.pdf.

34 Cecil M. Robeck, Jr., "Making Sense of Pentecostalism in a Global Context," unpublished paper presented at the Society for Pentecostal Studies (Springfield, MO: March 13, 1999), 34 pp.

35 Cecil M. Robeck, Jr. and Jerry L. Sandidge, "The Ecclesiology of *Koinonia* and Baptism: A Pentecostal Perspective," *Journal of Ecumenical Studies* 27, no. 3 (Summer 1990): 504-34.

36 Cal. R. Bombay, *Money, Man, and God* (Kisumu, Kenya: Evangel Publishing House, 1965), 19 pp.; Arthur M. Brazier, *Tithing: Why Give?* (Chicago: Saving Grace Ministries, 1996), 23 pp.; George Brazell, *This Is Stewardship* (Springfield, MO: Gospel Publishing House, 1962), 127 pp..; Oral Roberts, *The Miracle of Seed Faith* (Tulsa: Oral Roberts, 1970), 167 pp.; Oral Roberts, *Receiving Your Miracle through Seed Faith Partnership with God* (Tulsa: Oral Roberts Evangelistic Association, 1978), 96 pp; Charles Farah, Jr., "A Critical Analysis: The 'Roots and Fruits' of Faith-Formula Theology," *Pneuma: The Journal of the Society for Pentecostal Studies* 3, no. 1 (Spring 1981): 3-21; J.N. Horn, *From Rags to Riches: An Analysis of the Faith Movement and Its Relation to the Classical Pentecostal Movement* (Pretoria, South Africa: University of South Africa, 1989), 147 pp.

37   H. McKennie Goodpasture, ed., *Cross and Sword: An Eyewitness History of Christianity in Latin America* (Maryknoll: Orbis Books, 1989); Luis N. Rivera, *A Violent Evangelism: The Political and Religious Conquest of the Americas* (Louisville: Westminster John Knox Press, 1992).

38   Gregory I, *Homily on Ezekiel* II.6.22.

39   See Gregory, *Book* III, *Epistle* 29, of the *Register of the Epistles of Saint Gregory the Great* in Philip Schaff and Henry Wace, eds. *A Select Library of Nicene and Post-Nicene Fathers of the Christian Church*, 2nd ser. (Grand Rapids: Eerdmans, reprint 1969), 12:129. So, too, Gregory, *The Book of Pastoral Rule*, 3.40.

40   See, for example, Gregory I, *Book* VI, *Epistles* 51 and 52.

41   It is actually the Pietist movement in Europe in the latter half of the seventeenth century that brought Protestants into a position in which they begin to take missionary work seriously. In 1675, Philipp Jakob Spener published *Pia Desideria*. He was concerned with four things. 1. Christians needed to be able to witness to having had an experience of personal conversion. 2. Christians needed to live a life of holiness. 3. Christians needed to seek one another out, especially in community, for purposes of Christian fellowship. 4. Christians needed to take responsibility for passing on the gospel message to others. Nearly a century later the Lutheran King, Frederick IV of Denmark, turned to the August Hermann Francke (1663-1727) for help in recruiting missionaries. Bartholomew Ziegenbalg and Henry Plütschau responded to the invitation, and in 1706 they arrived in India.

42   Walter J. Hollenweger, *Pentecostalism: Origins and Developments Worldwide* (Peabody, MA: Hendrickson, 1997), pp. 132-34, who argues that syncretism may be unavoidable, but that it needs to be undertaken in a theologically responsible way.

43   It strikes me that the Rite of Christian Initiation of Adults is the most likely place for such an approach to begin. Given the Catholic Church's commitment to a process of "lifelong conversion," through which responsible adults encounter God – Father, Son and Holy Spirit – in an ongoing quest for God within the context of the Christian community. See Leonard Foley, OFM, *Believing in Jesus: A Popular Overview of the Catholic Faith*, 5th ed. (Cincinnati: St. Anthony Messenger Press, 2005), pp. 216-21.

44   Thomas Weinandy, "Why Catholics Should Witness Verbally to the Gospel," *New Oxford Review* 60, no. 6 (July-August 1993): 16, where he notes, "Many contemporary Catholics possess no evangelistic fervor. One reason could be that they have little or no experiential knowledge of Jesus, and may even be ignorant of the basic Gospel message: that Jesus himself is the Good News. Perhaps they simply have not been fully transformed by the power and life of the Holy Spirit that comes through faith in Jesus and thus are incapable of offering this new life to others." Pope Francis has made this point repeatedly. See for example, Kathleen Naab, "Pope's Morning Homily: 'You Can't Be a True Christian If You Don't Give Witness to Christ'," ZENIT (28 January 2016).

45   A video of this message preceded by Bishop Tony Palmer's introduction may be seen at http://youtu.be/b5TwrG8B3ME.

46   "Pope in Caserta Asks Forgiveness from Pentecostals", "Pope's Address to the Pentecostal Community in Caserta," and "Evangelical Pastor Giovanni Traettino's Words to Pope Francis in Caserta", ZENIT (29 July 2014).

47   Anthony E. Gilles, *People of God: The History of Catholic Christianity* (Cincinnati: St. Anthony Messenger Press, 2000), p. 108.

48   Richard P. McBrien, *Lives of the Popes: The Pontiffs from St. Peter to John Paul II* (San Francisco: HarperSanFrancisco, 2000), p. 275.

49　See, for instance, "Evangelization, Proselytism and Common Witness, nos. 85-87, in GA II, pp. 768-69; See also *On Becoming a Christian*, no. 258.

50　The *Decree on Ecumenism*, no. 3, in its move towards greater transparency, made it clear that through the centuries, "serious dissensions appeared and large communities became separated from full communion with the Catholic Church – for which, often enough, men of both sides were to blame."

51　The complete homily preached by Pope John Paul II on March 12, 2000, for the Jubilee Year Day of Pardon may be found and read at http://www.vatican.va.

52　See for instance, Giorgio Tourn, *The Waldensians: The First 800 Years (1174-1974)*, trans. Camillo P. Merlino (Torino: Claudiano; New York: Waldensian Aid Society, 1980), 244 pp.

53　Patrick Hutton, *History as an Art of Memory* (Hanover, NH: University Press of New England, 1993), p. 1 notes, "The topic of memory today elicits widespread scholarly interest. It serves as a crossroads of learning on which cultural anthropologists, psychologists, literary theorists, and students of oral tradition have recently converged in their efforts to make sense of its puzzles.... Historians have come late to such discussions, but their participation is becoming more prominent."

54　The incorporation of the reference to Joel 2:28-29 in the corpus of Luke-Acts, especially in Acts 2, is a fine example of this. When the Jews heard Joel prophesy, they surely understood it as a promise to Israel, not to the world. When Peter stood up to proclaim, "This is that," it involved a new interpretation to the reality prophesied by Joel. When Luke chose to incorporate Peter's understanding of Joel 2 in his two-part book to Theophilos, he had yet a different intention, one in which he tied the promise to the expansion of the Church among Gentiles as well as Jews. But when the Pentecostal movement emerged in the twentieth century, it embraced a self-understanding in which this passage applied exclusively to them.

55　One of the obvious problems in understanding the Protestant Reformation is whether it must be construed largely as an evil that put the Church into schism (a frequent Catholic interpretation), or whether it should be viewed as something good that brought a much needed reform to the Christian faith (a typical Protestant interpretation). That these interpretations are merely partial when confronted by the evidence is more apparent today than it has been in previous generations.

56　The Faith and Order Working Group of the National Council of Churches in the USA took up the question of writing ecumenical history in a study undertaken between 1988 and 1991. The results were published in Timothy J. Wengert and Charles W. Brockwell, Jr., eds., *Telling the Churches' Stories: Ecumenical Perspectives on Writing Christian History* (Grand Rapids: Eerdmans, 1995), 134 pp. It continues to serve as an excellent introduction to this theme.

57　See, for instance, Wilbert R. Shenk, *Enlarging the Story: Perspectives on Writing World Christian History* (Maryknoll: Orbis Books, 2002), 142 pp.

58　Phillip Berryman, *Religion in the Megacity: Catholic and Protestant Portraits from Latin America* (Maryknoll: Orbis Books, 1996), pp. 147-50.

59　Bennett Freeman Lawrence, *The Apostolic Faith Restored* (St. Louis: Gospel Publishing House, 1916), 119 pp., is the earliest history of Pentecostalism. It clearly carried the restorationist perspective. So, too, D. Wesley Myland, *The Latter Rain Covenant and Pentecostal Power* (Chicago: Evangel Publishing House, 1910), 215 pp., is the earliest attempt to develop a theology of the "Latter Rain," the "Former Rain" being the outpouring of the Spirit in Acts 2, and *Lost and Restored and Other Sermons by Aimee Semple McPherson* (Los Angeles: Foursquare Publications, 1989), containing her famous sermon delivered annually by Aimee Semple McPherson at Angelus Temple.

60　*Called Together to be Peacemakers*, especially nos. 23-68 and 190-215, in GA III, pp. 211-24 and 253-59.

✝ CHAPTER 12

From Isolation and Contrariety to Involvement and Consideration: An "Ecumenical" Pilgrimage

An Existential Essay in Tribute to a Friend

by Bert B. Beach

I t is with pleasure that I respond to the invitation to contribute to this *Festschrift* in honour of Monsignor John Radano. I have known and worked with Jack, as his many friends call him, for some twenty years and have come to value his intellectual acumen and to respect his knowledge and high ethical standards. During these many years, I have never heard him utter a disparaging word about the church he so loyally serves and represents. Nor have I heard him make a derogatory remark regarding the non-Catholic churches and communions with which he has dealt over the years.

While tact and diplomacy are useful when engaged in dialogue, honest and forthright expression of theological convictions is a *sine qua non* if any authentic dialogue is to take place. John Radano represents the proper balance of tact and teaching.

In thinking about what dimension I might add to this volume, I have felt that a fully footnoted academic and theological paper might not represent, at this late stage in my life, the most interesting and seminal contribution. After some hesitation, I have responded to a surprising impulse (for me, at least) to write an existential essay dealing with my personal coming to grips with interchurch relations, including relations with Roman Catholicism.

Ten Generations of Splendid Isolation

During the first thirty-four years of my life, I had very little to do with churches outside my own Seventh-day Adventist Church, probably not untypical of most Adventists. Contacts with Roman Catholicism were practically nil, except for seeing and visiting some architectural masterpieces represented by Catholic churches, abbeys, and cathedrals. I do not recall ever having a conversation with a Catholic priest, although I lived in countries like Belgium, France, and Italy. During my high school years in the gymnasium – a school sponsored by the Reformed Church in Bern, Switzerland – only one Roman Catholic student was enrolled in my class. My simple mind did not try to fathom how the young man could be Catholic while living in Protestant Bern and exposed to the teachings of Huldrych Zwingli!

This religious isolation or particularism was not untypical in the Beach family history. Ten generations back, my ancestor Ye Pilgrim John Beach and his two brothers came from England and, beginning in 1639, helped found the city of New Haven, Connecticut. Some years later John went a few miles north and founded Wallingford. All my direct Beach ancestors married women with good English names. They were all Congregationalists until they became Methodists, 200 hundred years later. My grandfather and his family became Seventh-day Adventists during the waning years of the nineteenth century. He had married an Irish lady, a Protestant from Northern Ireland. There was not a "papist connection" in the New World for over three centuries!

Vatican II – A Watershed Experience

Then in 1962, a significant change began to take place – not that I was immediately aware of this rising tide. I was living in England when I received a letter asking me to go to Rome as an observer/journalist at the Second Vatican Council and report to the *Adventist Review*, the weekly general church paper of the Seventh-day Adventist Church. Innocent as I was, I accepted this assignment, little realizing that this would lead to the beginning of my move from isolation to involvement.

If I had fully realized what this assignment would involve – writing dozens of articles (many translated into other languages) and even a book, traveling five times to Rome with stays of about two weeks each time, meeting and interviewing countless church leaders and theologians (both Catholic and non-Catholic) – I would doubtless have politely declined the invitation, saying that my other responsibilities did not allow me to accept the honor. However, God works in mysterious ways His wonders to perform. As a result of observing the Council, a whole new world of religious life and theological dimensions was opened up to me. For this, I am, in all humility, eternally grateful.

Establishing the WCC Connection

Before leaving England, I decided that on my way to Rome I would stop over in Geneva and visit the World Council of Churches (WCC), which was still in its infancy, having been established only 14 years earlier, in 1948. I had never been to the WCC and knew no one there. However, I felt that it could be useful to find out what the thinking was at this international ecumenical headquarters regarding the impending Vatican Council.

After arriving in Geneva, I phoned the home of Dr. Willem Visser't Hooft, the Dutch General Secretary of the WCC. I told him who I was and why I wanted to see him, if possible the next morning. I mentioned to him that I was a close friend of John Weidner, a Dutch Seventh-day Adventist who had headed the Dutch-Paris Line in France during World War II. Weidner had maintained contacts with Visser't Hooft, while helping about 1,000 Jews and Allied airmen to escape the Nazis by assisting their passage across the border into Switzerland or Spain. Visser't Hooft graciously agreed to see me.

After we met in his office the next day, Visser't Hooft introduced me to a couple of his colleagues, including associate general secretary Paul Verghese, who later became Metropolitan Paulos Gregorios, a well-known figure in both WCC circles and the Prague Peace Conference, and whom I later met many times. Visser't Hooft told me to be sure to meet their observer in Rome, Dr. Lukas Vischer, the secretary and later director of the Commission on Faith and Order. This I did, and we developed a lasting and fruitful relationship over many decades. Vischer, in turn, introduced me to several leading Protestant observers at the Council, such as Professors Edmund Schlink of Heidelberg and

George Lindbeck of Yale. Beginning with the second Council session, I moved over to the Pensione (run by German Lutheran Deaconesses), where many of the Protestant observers were staying. Breakfasts and other meals became valuable theological seminars. At one breakfast I met the notable, but controversial, theologian Hans Küng, one of the Council *periti*, and discovered that we were both born the same year in Switzerland. For these contacts – which increased over the years like a rolling snowball – the wide-ranging knowledge received, and the growing involvement with interchurch relations, I owe a debt of gratitude, at least indirectly, to the Catholic Church and the Vatican II process.

New Friends at the Unity Secretariat

Soon after arriving in Rome in October 1962, I gathered my courage and walked a couple of short blocks from the Council Press Office on Via della Conciliazione to Via del Erba, where the recently established Vatican Secretariat (now Pontifical Council) for Promoting Christian Unity was located, and stepped inside. What would happen to me? My mind told me that this was a logical and safe thing to do, but my heart was not so sure. After all, some rather harrowing tales exist in anti-Catholic lore! I am happy to say that I was most kindly and courteously received, and Father Thomas Stransky (now Tom) took me under his expert wing, explained what was going on, and was helpful in many ways. He later arranged for access to certain Vatican II events and on occasion to the "Aula," where the meetings took place, including access to the so-called coffee bars set up in St. Peter's Basilica. These were very useful places to meet leading figures, such as cardinals and renowned theologians, ask a few questions, and make observations. Tom invited me for lunch in one of the nearby trattorie located below the ancient passageway linking Castel Sant'Angelo and the Lateran Palace. We have remained friends ever since, even after I ended up in Washington and he, after a stint as president of the Paulist Fathers, in Jerusalem. He was one of those figures who opened doors that led me out of isolation into involvement and consideration on a world religious stage.

Religious Liberty: The Litmus Test

While there are obviously beliefs that Catholics and Adventists hold in common, there are also a number of issues that separate us. One of the issues over the years has been religious liberty. While doctrines and practices such as the sacrifice of the mass, veneration of the saints, baptism, indulgences, papal primacy, apostolic succession, and day of worship and rest are significant and have led at times to friction and separation, religious liberty lies at the very heart of interchurch relations because it touches upon *the very existence of a church* and the freedom to practice one's religion. Thus Adventists tend to look at Roman Catholicism and the papacy through the prism of religious liberty.

The Highpoint of Vatican II

While there were a number of highlights at Vatican II, such as the call to the laity to open and read their Bibles and the view of the Church as "the People of God" rather than a hierarchical structure, for me the highpoint of the Second Vatican Council was the acceptance of religious liberty in 1965. The promulgation of the document *Dignitatis Humanae* was a difficult and therefore exceptionally praiseworthy achievement due to the long history of intolerance and persecution in which the Church of Rome was involved. Pope Paul VI was certainly right in calling it "one of the major texts of the Council."[1]

While error may have no rights, the human being has rights. The Vatican II declaration regarding religious liberty differentiates between the positive right to religious liberty of the Catholic Church and its believers, allowing them to practice and preach their religion, and the negative, though important, right of all people not to be coerced or hindered in practising their religion. Nevertheless, to be in a civil society which is immune from coercion regarding religion, is, in practice, to experience religious freedom.

Past Experiences

The reader may ask why Adventists seem to have a fixation regarding religious liberty. Part of this has to do with eschatology, but also with church history and experience. For decades the Seventh-day

Adventist Church and its members had serious religious liberty problems in Catholic countries such as Italy, Spain, Portugal, and Colombia. When I arrived in Italy in the 1950s and served for six years as the principal of the Adventist School and Seminary in Florence, I was not able to get the usual right of residency. The problem was my religion. As a result, my goods (furniture, etc.) stayed in customs for some six months. It was not the most pleasant experience for a newly married couple! During that time two Adventist churches in Italy – one in Monzone (northern Italy) and the other in Carlentini (Sicily) – were closed and sealed by the government authorities for several years. Later in the 1960s, when I preached in the Adventist church in Madrid, we had to worship and sing with closed windows and leave the church building one by one, medicine-dropper style, in order not to create the significant public impression that a non-Catholic religious service was taking place. The police chief asked for the church's cooperation. He said he had no objection to our meeting, but he wanted to avoid receiving a complaint from the local bishop and having to close us down!

Significant and Irreversible Change?

Then came Vatican II and its religious liberty breakthrough! The situation in Catholic countries began to change radically. I have heard some critics of the Catholic Church say that the current Catholic statements regarding religious liberty are just window dressing. Not so! The proof of the religious liberty pudding lies in the eating. For example, both Italy, where the papacy resides, and Spain now have commendable religious liberty situations. Special laws give recognition to the rights and responsibilities of non-Catholic churches, including in a specific way the Seventh-day Adventist Church and the peculiar free exercise needs of its members. Some of the language in the Intesa (agreement) between the Italian state and the Seventh-day Adventist Church voted by the Italian Parliament[2] is taken from the *Concordat* between the Republic of Italy and the Holy See. Of course, the Seventh-day Adventist Church in countries like Italy is still a small minority, but it is an involved and no longer isolated minority. This has given me much satisfaction in my pilgrimage since 1962.

How firmly anchored is religious liberty in the Church of Rome? After all, support for religious liberty is today politically correct, though many countries violate it in practice. Back in the late 1970s, I became acquainted with Archbishop (later Cardinal) Jerome Hamer. Because he had some health problems, I arranged for him to spend a couple of weeks free of cost at the well-known Adventist Skodsborg Sanitarium near Copenhagen, Denmark. He was very pleased with his stay and the treatments received there. Later I had dinner with him in Rome. At this time, he was the secretary of the Congregation for the Doctrine of the Faith. This was formerly the Holy Office and until about 1900 the Holy Inquisition. I asked him point blank whether there was any chance that the Catholic Church could go back and abandon religious liberty. His categorical answer was (in French) "the change is irreversible!" Of course, we all know that times, circumstances, and people can change, but this was his firm conviction.

The Right to a Day of Worship and Rest

In May of 1998, Pope John Paul II published his apostolic letter *Dies Domini*. The purpose of this papal letter was to encourage Catholics to be more faithful in church attendance on Sunday. In tying the day of rest to creation, the pope struck a responsive cord among those Adventists who became acquainted with this document. At one point Pope John Paul II quoted a statement from Pope Leo XIII to the effect that the right of the working man to keep Sunday should be a protected right. I realized that this assertion could raise among Adventists the spectre of Sunday laws. I wrote a letter to my good friend Bishop Pierre Duprey, at that time secretary of the Pontifical Council for Christian Unity, saying that we would agree that a believing Sunday keeper should have the religious liberty right to observe Sunday and not be forced to work on that day. However, we wanted to know whether seventh-day Sabbath keepers, such as Adventists, Jews, and others, as well as Muslims observing Friday as their day of communal worship, should also enjoy the same right.

Several months passed and were added to my "ecumenical" pilgrimage while I received no answer. Some people suggested that I would probably not receive a reply. I told them that, in my opinion, delay simply meant the Vatican was taking my letter seriously. Finally, I received the awaited answer. Bishop Duprey apologized for the delay but said that the Council needed to check with various Vatican dicasteries and the answer was *yes*. For me, this was an important moment in interchurch relations. It affirmed once again Roman Catholic support of religious liberty for non-Catholics, even for small minorities like Seventh-day Adventists.

Catholic-Seventh-day Adventist Conversations

Since 1968, the General Conference of Seventh-day Adventists has been a consistent participant in the annual Conference of Secretaries of Christian World Communions. For 36 years, one of my responsibilities was to attend this meeting, and for 32 years I served as its secretary. Bishop Duprey would occasionally say to the group that, like the French Academy, the CWC Conference has a "perpetual secretary." Without the significant and enduring contacts and friendships made both in Geneva and Rome, this part of my pilgrimage could not have taken place. I discovered, somewhat surprisingly, that regarding several issues, particularly those dealing with morality, marriage, and socio-political activity, Adventists were closer to Roman Catholic representatives than to liberal Protestant participants. The same could be said regarding Orthodox representatives from the Phanar and the Moscow Patriarchate. This was an eye opener for me.

While in the setting of the annual meeting of CWC secretaries, Bishop (now Cardinal) Walter Kasper and I agreed that it could prove helpful to hold, in connection with the CWC Secretaries' meeting, separate theological conversations between Catholic and Adventist theologians. Such conversations took place over several years. Topics were considered and papers presented regarding Seventh-day Adventist Fundamental Beliefs, the approach to Scripture (including the role of the church and tradition), and Sabbath versus Sunday as a day of rest and worship. While these discussions revealed many commonalities, they also, as expected, disclosed significant disagreements.

Now that I have retired, as has John Radano, others will need to carry on the responsibilities of any dialogue contacts. I hope conversations and explanations of biblical truth and understanding will continue at various levels. We should explore our theological thinking, always ready to give a reason for our faith, while maintaining the three Petrine conditions of humility, respect, and honesty (I Peter 3:15, 16).

Interesting conversations could deal with the nature of man in this life and beyond. While eschatology needs eventually to be explored, it is a difficult sort of topic, dealing in part with the unknown future. Such a discussion is prone, if lacking in prudence and Christian love, to result in unpleasant and even hurtful considerations and views. While Catholic theologians have for several centuries tended to adopt either the preterist or futurist approach in dealing with eschatology, Adventist theologians have used a historicist methodology which aims at covering the whole Christian era with all its past vicissitudes and anticipated final conflict. This complicates matters.

Future Catholic-Adventist Relations

What is the future of Adventist-Catholic relations? I am not a prophet, but I do believe in biblical prophecy, some of which is conditional. At Vatican II, the Catholic Church accepted religious liberty and rejected any coercion in religious beliefs and observance. Pope John Paul II, in several of his pronouncements, particularly in his New Year's World Day of Peace messages, appears to have gone even beyond the language of Vatican II in his support of religious liberty for all, including minorities. As long as the Catholic Church continues resolutely, and without deviation, on this religious liberty *high*way, future relations should be increasingly benign.

In 1926, the Seventh-day Adventist Church adopted a statement, now included with minor revisions (in which I was involved about 25 years ago), in her *Working Policy* as O 110. It is entitled "Relationships with Other Christian Churches." Here it is stated that the Seventh-day Adventist Church recognizes "those agencies that lift up Christ before men as part of the divine plan for the evangelization of the world, and we hold in high esteem Christian men and women in other communions who are engaged in winning souls to Christ." It should not be overlooked that this statement dates from before the time when ecumenism was in vogue.

In April of 1997, the General Conference Administrative Committee (ADCOM) accepted a statement on "How Seventh-day Adventists View Roman Catholicism." Being one of the drafters of this statement was part of my pilgrimage referred to in this essay. No such statement could, in all likelihood, have been recorded even a decade or two earlier. While not ignoring the past record of Catholic intolerance and abuse of religious liberty, the statement goes on to say that "to blame past violations of Christian principles on one specific denomination is not an accurate representation of either history or the concerns of Bible prophecy... If, in expounding on what the Bible teaches, Seventh-day Adventists fail to express love to those addressed, we do not exhibit authentic Christianity." I am especially pleased by the concluding words: "We recognize some positive changes in recent Catholicism, and stress the conviction that many Roman Catholics are brothers and sisters in Christ."[3]

New Brothers and Sisters in Christ

To find along the way new brothers and sisters in Christ is a rewarding realization. We were always there, but we had to break out of our isolation and find each other. This is a precious gift that more than compensates for any criticism, hostility, and stress encountered in discovering and traveling on the new and unexplored, but living way of interchurch relations.

---

1   Quoted in John Courtney Murray, "Religious Freedom," in *The Documents of Vatican II*, ed. Walter M. Abbott (New York: Association Press, 1966), p. 674.

2   Law N 516 (November 22, 1988).

3   Seventh-day Adventist Church, *Statements Guidelines & Other Documents*, 5th expanded ed. (Silver Spring, Maryland: Communication Department of the General Conference, 2010), pp, 95-96.

✝ CHAPTER 13

An Evangelical Reading of *Ut Unum Sint*

by Henri A. G. Blocher

The very text of *Ut Unum Sint* (UUS), Pope John Paul II's encyclical letter on commitment to ecumenism, invites all the faithful *to receive* the contributions of dialogues (no. 80).[1] The encyclical itself, such a landmark in the ecumenical movement, should be among the first to enjoy the pleasures, or to suffer the pains, of reception; and since the pope's embrace generously reached his "separated brothers," I, as one of these, may be emboldened to say how I "receive," that is how I read, and respond to, this magisterial document.

Some may think that I come quite late on the task. UUS was written in view of the approaching end of the second millennium (nos. 1, 100, 102), and we have entered well beyond the porch into the third one... Yet, even apart from the benefits of prolonged reflection and hindsight, several considerations suggest that my attempt is still relevant. Ecumenical time flows rather slowly. UUS itself includes abundant quotations from *Unitatis Redintegratio* and from the teachings of Paul VI, and it maintains the same doctrinal line: "Through long stretches," Robert W. Jenson writes, "*Ut Unum Sint* is simply a careful and it seems to me faithful re-affirmation of the ecclesiology and ecumenical positions of Vatican II."[2] No observer, since, has spotted any major shift in the orientation of the Roman Catholic Church regarding ecumenism. UUS was issued near the beginning of the "round" of official conversations between representatives of the World Evangelical Fellowship/Alliance (more precisely of its Theological Commission) and of the Pontifical Council for Promoting Christian Unity which granted me the privilege of getting to know Monsignor John Radano and developing with him precious exchanges in the spirit of UUS. It is fitting, therefore, that I offer him, as a token of gratitude and friendship in the service of Jesus Christ, this attempt at reception, reading, and response.

I do so as a Protestant Evangelical, for whom the word "evangelical" does not bear the same meaning as it does in UUS,[3] though the two meanings are still vitally related. "Evangelical" as a label denotes that "Third Arm" or third main type of Christianity that distinguishes itself by characteristic enough family traits, and some institutions, from the Catholic (Roman and other) type and the more or less modernistic Protestant one, despite, it must be granted, considerable overlap.[4] Evangelicals see themselves as the only legitimate heirs of the sixteenth-century Reformers: they maintain the literal sense of the main tenets of the reformational message (that includes the "high articles of divine majesty," as Luther had it in the Smalkald articles, Christological and Trinitarian orthodoxy). Two other historical "layers" shaped their identity: the stronger emphasis on personal experience of Pietism and Puritanism, with their progeny of Revivals, and the consequent erosion of the sense of institutional prerogatives that was vigorous among the magisterial Reformers; resistance to the "liberal" or "modernistic" wave that swept most "mainline" denominations through the nineteenth century (and beyond), a resistance implying in many respects (not all) a counter-cultural stance. Evangelicals differ widely among themselves, the main two polarities being (a) that between State or *national* churches (at least in some important countries) and *Free* churches, since the sixteenth century and increasingly so through the generations, and (b) that between "*classical*" (for want of a better word) and *Pentecostal* churches or trends since the beginning of the twentieth century. Through all divergences, the four marks David W. Bebbington selected,[5] and many have adopted, may be recognized among all: *biblicism*, a practical as well as theoretical concentration on Scriptural guidance, as the only sovereign authority and fully reliable expression of God's Word[6]; *conversionism*, with a stress on personal commitment and "experience" (though not necessarily through a punctual and dramatic crisis time); *crucicentrism*: an emphasis on the Cross as the once for all, "finished," work of atonement through vicarious punishment, which the depth of human corruption and guilt rendered necessary; *activism*: with little interest in contemplative spirituality, a constant exhortation to work in the world (in the wake of Luther's rehabilitation of worldly *Beruf*) and, especially, to lead others to faith ("to win souls"). Although I am aware of reductions and distortions that easily associate with these marks, I acknowledge the four traits as contours of *my* Evangelical identity: they come into play when I try to "receive" UUS.

Among my fellow Evangelicals, I have not been able to find a crowd of predecessors, who have responded to UUS. Cecil M. Robeck refers to the encyclical three times in his chapter "Evangelicals and Catholics Together,"[7] and Timothy George once in the same symposium.[8] Richard J. Mouw includes it among the texts to which he thoughtfully responds.[9] There is also a chapter on UUS by William Abraham in a collection of essays offering an Evangelical assessment of John Paul II.[10] If one cares to include them among "Evangelicals," one can mention Reinhard Hütter (Duke Divinity School)[11] and Shafique Keshavjee (who held for a time a chair in the Faculté autonome de théologie protestante of the University of Geneva).[12] This paucity of references may be due to the limitations of my search (only checking through the resources of two libraries), but it may have something to do with the experience Richard Mouw candidly expresses, as an Evangelical: "As I read UUS, I looked without success for some overt signals that Pope John Paul II meant to find a place for us in his quest for Christian unity."[13] The contrast is striking indeed: while relationships with the "sister" Eastern Orthodox churches come up again and again, in the language of ardent courtship, Evangelicals should presumably consider themselves included in the "ecclesial communities" more briefly and coolly dealt with. The encyclical repeats the phrase "churches and ecclesial communities" but never tells who is entitled to the name "church" and who is not.[14] More generally, most Evangelicals still harbour some reservations regarding the mainline ecumenical enterprises. UUS no. 66 recalls what the Council had observed: "the ecumenical movement and the desire for peace (*concordiae*) with the Catholic Church have not yet taken root (*inveteravisse*) everywhere." Despite spectacular changes in fifty years, this is still true today.[15] Such a state of affairs participates in paradox, since the first use of "ecumenical" in the modern sense (promoting closer union among Christians of different labels) – on record at least – is credited to the founding assembly of the Evangelical Alliance (1846)[16]; the same Alliance launched the first inter-church

Week of Prayer (1847 in England, 1860 worldwide), long before the better-known "ecumenical" one (UUS, no. 24), also in January. Data of such diverse categories, at any rate, show my attempt at reading UUS to be relevant.

Since the encyclical so richly touches on many issues and does not shun repetition (compare, for instance, nos. 4 and 91, 10-12 and 48-49), commenting on the whole text as it unfolds would be neither possible nor desirable within the bounds of the present essay. My reading must be thematic and selective: and the selection itself will reflect an Evangelical theologian's interests.

Spiritual Necessity

The most striking feature of UUS is the massive emphasis put on the spiritual character and theological necessity of the commitment to ecumenism it exhibits and recommends. Christian unity, which finds its source and model in the Trinitarian life of God (nos. 8, 26) and flows from the Cross (no. 1), is no peripheral option, it "is not something added on, but stands at the very heart of Christ's mission (eius operis est cardo)" and "belongs to the very essence (naturam)" of the disciples' community (no. 9). The search for unity is an indispensable "dimension of [her] renewal" (no. 15), which John XXIII rightly refused to separate from ecumenical openness (no. 17). "Renewal," here, translates accommodationem ad praesentia, and clearly refers to the aggiornamento called for by Pope John, as the Italian version of UUS renders it. It requires "a change of heart" (no. 15, no ecumenism worthy of the name sine interiore conversione), which implies repenting "of certain exclusions which seriously harm fraternal charity, of certain refusals to forgive, of a certain pride, of an un-evangelical insistence on condemning the 'other side,' of a disdain born of an unhealthy presumption" (no. 15; cf. no. 29). Together with prayer, public and private, this conversion "should be regarded as the soul of the whole ecumenical movement" (no. 21). "Along the ecumenical path to unity, pride of place certainly belongs to common prayer" (no. 22).[17] The spiritual character of the enterprise is even deepened by the original appeal to the martyrs found in all Christian confessions, many indeed in the last century, whose perfect communion now in heaven should give us the assurance that Christian unity is possible down below (nos. 1, 12, 48, 83-84).[18]

The moving energy of the tone rules out all suspicion, as may linger in some Evangelicals' minds, that the spiritual stress may be a tactical choice. John Paul II pays a not insignificant price as a model in repentance and humility: he confesses that responsibility for unwarranted division lies on both sides (no. 11), that the members of the Catholic Church committed sins that were "betrayals" of the Savior's plan (no. 3), and these members include "pastors" and even "structures" (no. 34, *peccati "structurae,"* unfortunately unidentified). He himself, the *Summus Pontifex*,[19] asks that all pray for his own conversion (no. 4, cf. no. 91). How far from *Mortalium animos*. How far from the cast of mind, so repellent to Evangelicals, sometimes shown by ecumenical "diplomats" – ready to "trade off" beliefs.[20]

Evangelicals may, *and should*, receive the spiritual exhortation. As one of them, I must confess that the challenge hits home, the challenge to repent. Responsibility for unworthy divisions lies on all sides: also on our side. Because we have been found ourselves in small minority situations, most of the time, we have lacked the opportunity to use carnal means (political power, etc.) to push our own interests,[21] but we have been guilty of aggressive dispositions, too quick and proud a spirit of judgment, sometimes manipulative sheep-stealing, and especially guilty of *misrepresentation* of the others' reality (starting with negligence in gathering information). I confess the sin of a relative indifference (UUS, no. 79) and only lukewarm prayer for the cause of Christian reunion when I realize the place it has in the Scriptures and in the Lord's design: union already with other Evangelicals (*Quanta est nobis, evangelicis, via?*), and also with "non-Evangelical" brothers and sisters. Reminding us of the supreme message of our martyrs is also welcome: their company includes many Evangelicals (missionaries, converts in Muslim and Hindu countries), and the number of new martyrs each year, Christians who have given their lives in order to remain faithful to Christ their Lord, has not decreased since 1995.

Transparency demands, however, that I add a few comments. My reception and appropriation of the spiritual language of UUS cannot hide the fact that the union or unity we are to seek and strive for is somewhat (understatement) different from the unity John Paul had in mind – as will inevitably become clearer below. The main issue is not visibility, though Evangelicals are not prepared to say that the Church is as visible as the Republic of Venice could be: but what kind of visibility? An even thornier question relates to the identification of the "Christians" who should be one, remembering that God alone searches hearts and minds and that profession is to be examined with charity. What about apparently "sociological" Christians who do not seem to profess faith at all?

I hope I am not drifting into that "defeatism which tends to see everything in negative terms," which is rightly stigmatized by UUS no. 79, yet, I am not persuaded that the kind of visible unity that is envisioned – of all who bear the name "Christian" professing the same faith and sharing in the same eucharist – may be achieved in history; that, for Christian communities, it is not "beyond their reach."[22] Though the field is the world, not the church (Matt. 13:38), the tares sown by the enemy look too much like the wheat, before harvest time, for a true visible unity to obtain. In less parabolic language, the warnings about end-time apostasy (2 Thess. 2:3,10), about false teachers who will maintain the *form* of godliness (2 Tim. 3:5), and heresies inevitable (1 Cor. 11:19, *dei*), suggest that the Devil will always be able to raise samples of counterfeit Christianity from whom faithful disciples must separate (Rom. 16:17; 2 John 10-11, etc.): there will be people parading the name "Christians" with whom union would amount to betraying the Gospel. In this connection, I fear that I could not paint with hues as rosy as UUS[23] the situation that prevailed during the first millennium. Louis Duchesne reckoned that between the years AD 323 to 787 there were five ruptures of communion between Constantinople and Rome, totalling 203 years.[24] Though I believe God did write straight truth on crooked human lines and the ancient Ecumenical Councils rightly served the substance of revealed teaching, I shudder at the thought of the role political pressures and coercion played in obtaining visible unity.[25]

Concern for Truth

Some of the most vigorous statements in UUS reaffirm the rule of Truth, doctrinal, objective truth. They condemn everything that would amount to "altering the deposit of faith, changing the meaning of dogmas, eliminating essential words from them, accommodating truth to the preferences of a particular age, or suppressing certain articles of the *Creed* under the false pretext that they are no longer understood today. The unity willed by God can be attained only by the adherence of all to the content of revealed faith in its entirety. In matters of faith, compromise is in contradiction with God who is Truth" (no. 18). The "mutual help in the search for truth is a sublime (*suprema*) form of evangelical charity" (no. 78). "The obligation to respect the truth (*usque ad estrema*) is absolute. Is this not the law of the Gospel?" (no. 79). "Unity" and "truth" are so tightly bound to each other that one could almost stand for the other.[26]

Nowhere, maybe, does UUS meet the concerns of Evangelicals more exactly. Among them, the strongest objection against mainline ecumenism has been its implicit doctrinal laxity. Those who are prevented by their consciences from joining the World Council of Churches usually point to the absence of doctrinal discipline within that body.[27] Evangelicals gladly "receive" John Paul II's very firm stand in this regard.

The encyclical is careful to distinguish immutable doctrinal truth from the way it should be "translated" in various cultural contexts, for "the element which determines communion in truth is *the meaning of truth*. The expression of truth can take different forms" (no. 19). It quotes approvingly the 1973 Declaration *Mysterium Ecclesiae* that acknowledges that the truth enunciated by the Magisterium may "bear traces" of "the changeable conceptions of a given epoch and can be expressed without them" (no. 38).[28] Evangelicals have been wrestling with the same tension between the concern for Truth (against relativism) and the need for both hermeneutical sensitivity and flexible contextualization. In most cases, they have struck approximately the same balance as UUS offers. Though deeper-digging theological work should be done to ground the formula (no merely comfortable *via media*), I appreciate that pitfalls on the right and on the left have been avoided.[29]

Pope John Paul II also confirms the principle of the "order or 'hierarchy' of truths" (no. 37), which seems to be the basis for the frequent affirmation of a real and true *communion* between the Roman Catholic Church and other "Churches and ecclesial communities," real yet partial or *imperfect* (nos. 11, 23, 77-79, 84, *passim*). Again, I can express an exact agreement (though Evangelicals tend to speak of a communion between persons rather than church bodies). The distinction between articles of faith, already suggested by Luther's categories in the Smalkald articles, was clearly defined by John Calvin.[30] In my contribution to the Lausanne Congress on World Evangelization (1974), I developed biblical arguments in its favour, and a criteriology.[31] What I would add is a *rule of proportion*: the extent and degree of cooperation and expressed communion depends, quantitatively and qualitatively, on the extent and degree of agreement *in the Truth*.[32] The logic of UUS seems to follow similar lines, especially no. 75: "The doctrinal disagreements which remain exercise a negative influence and even place limits on cooperation."[33]

Divergences Acknowledged

Disagreements do remain – even if we agree on their practical import, even if we agree on their precise nature and location. For this is the next step in my reading of UUS. I am grateful for the lucid and forthright recognition of the main issues that still imply separation between Roman Catholics and Evangelicals: "very weighty differences ... especially in the interpretation of revealed truth" (no. 64), summarized as the relationship of Scripture and Tradition; the Eucharist and Real Presence; ordination to the threefold office; the Magisterium as entrusted to the pope and the bishops in communion with him; and the Virgin Mary, her spiritual Motherhood and intercession (no. 79). The Magisterium issue surfaces earlier several times. Limitations of space preclude any adequate treatment here of subjects that caused rivers of ink (sometimes of blood) to flow for centuries. Have UUS and ecumenical dialogues, particularly involving Evangelicals, improved the situation and brought us nearer? Undoubtedly. They have not only purified the climate and removed misunderstandings; I consider that highly significant changes have affected the language and claims of the partners I have met (such as no Evangelical would have expected fifty years ago), and these, for the better. Yet, on the vexed divisive issues, a chasm still remains between us, another *garstige breite Graben*. I will concentrate my comments around two *foci*: the place of sacraments, which is important for the eucharistic and ministry debates, and the pope's "supreme magisterium," which alone determines the Tradition issue since only the Magisterium defines what *counts* as the Tradition of the church. These two are not unrelated, since the teaching office and authority is sacramentally conferred.

The encyclical transparently presupposes a *causative* (instrumental) function of the sacraments: they confer the grace they signify (what I call "sacramentalism"). I am not surprised, but I am disappointed that nowhere UUS seeks to meet the concern of those who reject such an interpretation, historically the great majority of Evangelicals; UUS does not show any awareness that this concern exists. Calvin could lay down, as a foundational proposition:

> The Sacraments ... on God's behalf, do the same service as messengers of good news among men: i.e. *not to confer* the good to us, but *only to announce and demonstrate* the things that are given us by God's generosity, or to be a pledge *to confirm* them to us.[34]

Not to confer. In the Free church tradition, sacramentalism has been even less welcome; and even most Anglican Evangelicals and Lutheran Pietists, in modern times, have distanced themselves from the causative view.

The encyclical stresses "the ecclesiological implication of sharing in the sacraments" (no. 58) and roots the acknowledgment of "brotherhood" in the "recognition of the oneness of baptism" (no. 42), considered to be the means of our incorporation into Christ (nos. 6, 13); it rejoices over that common possession as a beginning "oriented towards a complete profession of faith" (no. 66). I must recall that Calvin, again, denied that grace be conferred "by virtue of baptism"[35] and declares that the little children baptized are "received in the Church *as being already of her body,*"[36] not, therefore, as the instrumental cause of their incorporation. More radically, those who espouse baptistic convictions (among them practically all Pentecostals) cannot, in conscience, identify the "baptism" of infants, in Catholic and other churches, with the rite our Lord commanded his disciples to administer.[37] Speaking, therefore, of the "unity among all the baptized" raises a major difficulty. One cannot expect the situation to be much easier with the other sacraments... Though some contemporary Catholic theologians so reinterpret transubstantiation, using existential categories, that it comes very near (in my opinion) to trans-signification which I could endorse, UUS (no. 67) maintains that the *substance* of the eucharistic mystery is lacking in our Evangelical celebrations: it thus upholds the older dogmatic thesis foreign to Evangelical faith. Quoting a document from the Congregation for the Doctrine of the Faith, the encyclical (5) seems to adopt the popular theme of "(re-)actualisation"[38] which I would subject to criticism. On the ministry, the somewhat ambiguous convergence expressed in the Lima Document (cf. UUS nos. 69, 78-79) carries little authority with Evangelicals: there are few of them, if any, on the Faith and Order Commission. *Quanta est via?*

The part of UUS that aroused most ecumenical discussion has been the part devoted to the papal office and prerogatives. Paul VI, in a 1967 address, designated the topic as "the biggest obstacle on the road to ecumenism."[39] Indeed, some ecumenical reactions have been unusually "frank," as diplomats say. Milan Opocensky, General Secretary of the World Alliance of Reformed Churches, declared it "unthinkable to accept the papacy as a symbol of unity among Christians"[40]; Konrad Raiser spoke of a "foremost obstacle" since the pope is not "ready to consider the necessary self-relativization of his primacy."[41] This Evangelical reader is impressed not only by the personal humility of the pope (his asking to be forgiven, no. 88), the *servus servorum Dei* title (no. 88), but also by some theological features of his plea: it is not incidental if he confesses that "the firm and enduring rock (*petra*, the New Testament word, left in the Latin text) upon which she (the Church) is founded is Jesus Christ, her Lord" (no. 4); if he underlines the collegial character of his ministry, calls all the other bishops "vicars of Christ" (no. 95) – though previously he has used the title, it seems, in a more distinctive way just for himself (no. 24)[42] – and says he speaks in their name (no. 94); if he insists that he depends entirely on the divine mercy and can only exercise mercy (nos. 92-93; cf. no. 4). He weaves into his presentation of the papal office the "weakness" traits that critics of the Roman primacy used to highlight. Moving words. But do they essentially alter the doctrinal problem? Out of conviction, the pope will not relinquish anything that belongs to his office as he received it (no. 95, "in no way renouncing what is essential to his mission"). He rightly perceives that the role he is to play would be made void (*vacuefit*) without "the power and the authority" he still claims (no. 94), and the final decision belongs to him (no. 81). *Servus servorum* expresses a magnificent ideal, but there is some force in Stephen W. Sykes' observation on ARCIC that applies to UUS: had the encyclical "faced the issue of power straightforwardly, it would have had to confront the notion explored in modern Anglo-American sociology that those attempting to defend and to advance their own power often emphasize its service component."[43] The stress on collegiality is rendered somewhat ambiguous by the prior, determinative condition of communion with the bishop of Rome; one wishes the relationship had been clarified between the pope speaking "in the name" of all the bishops (no. 94) and the *ex sese, non autem ex consensu Ecclesiae* clause of the Vatican I Decree on the pope's infallibility.[44] The crowning affirmation, maybe, in such an "ecumenical" encyclical, is that of the bishop of Rome as the "perpetual and visible principle and foundation of unity" (no. 88, from *Lumen Gentium*, no. 23).

Nobody should be surprised if I fail to be convinced. The arguments offered (I appreciate the effort) do not carry the weight that would be required. Over-interpretation (I feel) weakens the recourse to New Testament passages: they do not necessarily imply a "primacy" that gave Peter a fullness of power above the other apostles and the status of a *vicarius Christi* (not to mention the *petros/petra* difference in Matt. 16). Even more decisively: they assign a specific *historical* role to Peter and there is no hint that he should have a successor or "heir" (UUS, no. 92) with similar prerogatives. The way Brian Daley honestly summarizes the evolution on this point does not lend great persuasive power to the claim:

> This leads us to the second new emphasis in the papacy's self-understanding during the fourth and fifth centuries: a striking tendency of most of the popes from Damasus on to identify themselves personally, almost mystically, with Peter himself. The practice was not simply a rhetorical convention; it seems to have been suggested, in part at least, by the traditional Roman understanding of inheritance, in which those who succeeded to property or to the headship of an extended family

were actually understood as representing, even impersonating, their ancestors.[45]

And why the bishop of *Rome*? The fact that Peter and Paul were martyred in that city (I appreciate that UUS does not try to assign an *episcopal* ministry to Peter in Rome, twenty-five years or not) is offered as the reason: "In this way the Church of Rome became the Church of Peter and Paul" (no. 90); to an Evangelical, the appropriately Latin phrase is: *non sequitur.*

Underlying the differences on the sacraments and on the magisterium supremely entrusted to the bishop of Rome, one easily discovers divergent views of the church. They could be expressed with the contrast of two metaphors once pointed to, I have read, by John Milton: for Catholics, the Church is the majestic Mother *(Mater et magistra),* who dispenses the goods of salvation and orders the behavior of her obedient children, wielding the authority of her divine Husband; in the New Testament – as Evangelicals read it, though I do not claim Milton as an Evangelical – she is rather the young fiancée who prepares in view of the wedding, and must eliminate infelicitous features and unfitting manners in compliance with the Bridegroom's directions. UUS emphatically confesses the sins of the members, and even the pastors, of the Catholic Church, but it avoids ascribing sin to the Church (it comes nearest to doing so, it seems to me, when it says of the Catholic Church "she does not cease to do penance" (no. 3). To Evangelicals, this suggests an artificial separation of the "Church" as an entity, as another Subject, and the people or community of the faithful.[46] In a fascinating essay, the still young theologian Joseph Ratzinger was ready to speak of "the sin of the Church," albeit in a dialectical way and with the observation that "the New Testament never talks of the sinful Church."[47] Going farther, Evangelicals would claim: the promise of indefectibility (Matt. 16:18), richer indeed than the promise to the Remnant in Israel (Amos 9:8; Isa. 10:20-21, etc.) though continuous with it, does not amount to the ascription of sinlessness.

The encyclical makes room for the "constant reform of the Church" (no. 82: the Latin uses *reformatio,* which rules out a distinction here between reform and reformation), but it adds: "insofar as she is also a human and earthly institution." The clause involves a troublesome ambiguity. I can say that the church is a "divine" institution in the sense that God instituted it; I confess that he is active in her midst, adds new members through his work of regeneration or "baptism in the Spirit" (I Cor. 12:13), dwells in the church as in his living Temple; but not that one *part* of the church, one aspect or dimension of her *being*, is divine, not human. The clause calls back to mind the famous statements of Johann-Adam Möhler in his *Symbolik* affirming two natures in the Church, by virtue of the Incarnation continued. Though the Council exercised cautious restraint, it did not reform this basically "continuist" conception (*Lumen Gentium*, nos. 8, 14, 48, 52). What is at stake is the distinction, the vis-à-vis relational structure, between the church and her head, and her Lord, with whom she is united in one *pneuma*, not one *sôma* (1 Cor. 6:17).[48] A sober exegesis of the passage that looks most favourable to a pure identification of Christ and church (*totus Christus*), 1 Corinthians 12:12, does not yield that result, as Lucien Cerfaux has shown.[49] Essentially, the church is the Body as the Bride, maintaining the vis-à-vis, the distinction of subjects, and the non-symmetry.[50] The qualifications Yves Congar was compelled to bring to current statements about the divinity of the church and "Incarnation continued" flash as a warning signal that this is not the theological road to travel.[51]

The deep ecclesiological divide we cannot hide does not lead to denying also convergences and the fruitfulness of interchange, as my quoting noted Roman Catholic scholars illustrates. Lately, vigorous Catholic critics of the scheme of Incarnation continued have been heard, though I do not see them making a radical break.[52] The encyclical highlights, with the heirs of the Reformation, "mutual interaction (*insertiones*, a strong word) and complementarity" (no. 65). One interesting field for research, I suggest, would be the parallel occurrence, with or without direct influence, of renewal trends or enterprises on the Evangelical and on the Catholic sides. In our epoch, the "Charismatic" waves are a rather obvious instance. The rise of Pietism and Puritanism in the seventeenth century is not without analogy with the flourishing of spirituality among Catholics, especially in the French school. One can spot similarities in the foreign missionary movements. After the French revolution, the thought of the Restoration thinkers (Joseph de Maistre, Louis de Bonald) and the Tübingen school on the Catholic side match the Geneva revival, the birth of neo-Calvinist thought (Guillaume Groen van Prinsterer, forerunner of Abraham Kuyper) and also that of Dispensationalism (John Nelson Darby), among Evangelicals. We may be nearer to one another when we think the distance is greater.

Conclusion

Many other areas would be worth investigating. Conspicuously absent from UUS is the search for roots, for deeper *motives*: this is what the able Evangelical theologian De Chirico has undertaken, with the tools of Kuyperian neo-Calvinism. Though in my eyes, he overestimates the degree of systematic coherence of contemporary Roman Catholicism,[53] his endeavour should be pursued. He shows how the Nature-Grace motive, born of the synthesis of the Gospel message with Greek philosophy, replaces the Creation-Fall-Redemption motive that shapes biblical perspectives. I suggest that the conception of *time* (and eternity) plays an important role: it influences the way continuity is viewed, the *ephapax* of the Cross, the idea of "actualization." The Nature-Grace scheme answers to de-temporalized "metaphysical" concerns – how to bring together spirit and flesh, deity and humanity – whereas Creation-Fall-Redemption is dramatically historical.

UUS extols the possibilities and fruits of concrete *cooperation*. On this also much could be said, positively. It is increasingly the case that Evangelicals and Catholics find themselves fighting together against the "culture of death." The dialogue recommended by UUS (no. 68) is well under way between Catholics and Evangelicals.[54] Evangelicals and Catholics have already been working together to translate and spread the Bible, as highlighted by UUS (no. 44). I can testify to the value of this specific and vital cooperation, and the joy that springs from its depths.[55]

There are thus encouragements on the way, a long way though it may look. Maybe the key question is not "How far?" *Quanta via?* but: "Is the way open?" And the answer: It is.

---

1 I indicate in the text, in brackets, the paragraph number as given in the official editions of *Ut Unum Sint*, henceforth abbreviated UUS. I refer to the Latin redaction as the original one, as available from the Vatican website, but, since this paper is written in English, I usually quote from the English version, unless I specify otherwise; I have often compared the wording with that of other modern language versions from the same site.

2 "A Symposium on *Ut Unum Sint*," *Pro Ecclesia* 4, no. 4 (1995): 389.

3 No. 78, "evangelical charity," for *evangelicae caritatis*; no. 87, "Gospel law of sharing," for *evangelicae consortionis legis*; and already, in negative form, no. 15, "unevangelical insistence," for *non evangelici se claudendi*.

4 Many recent books draw a synthetic picture of Evangelicalism, e.g., Derek J. Tidball, *Who Are the Evangelicals? Tracing the roots of Today's Movement* (London: Marshall Pickering, 1994). In a brief compass, I recommend *The Dictionary of Historical Theology*, s.v. "Evangelical Theology," by Harriet A. Harris (she authored *Fundamentalism and Evangelicals*, Oxford, 1998, rather acidly critical at times, although much better informed than James Barr). A jewel in its simplicity, *Evangelical Truth: A Personal Plea for Unity, Integrity & Faithfulness* (Downers Grove, IL: InterVarsity Press, 1999), by John R. W. Stott, who could be called the world's "Mr. Evangelical" in his generation.

5 David Bebbington, *Evangelicalism in Modern Britain: A History from the 1730s to the 1980s* (Boston: Unwin Hyman, 1989), pp. 3-19 (not in the same order).

6 Against modernism, the affirmation of the total trustworthiness of the Bible does not go beyond traditional tenets; if one thinks it is too nervous, hard and stiff, one should compare with, e.g., *Providentissimus Deus*.

7 In Thomas P. Rausch, ed., *Catholics and Evangelicals: Do They Share a Common Future?* (Downers Grove, IL: InterVarsity Press, 2000), pp. 14, 27, 33.

8 "Towards an Evangelical Ecclesiology," in Rausch, ed., *Catholics and Evangelicals*, p. 143.

9 "The Problem of Authority in Evangelical Christianity," in Carl E. Braaten and Robert W. Jenson, eds., *Church Unity and the Papal Office: An Ecumenical Dialogue on John Paul II's Encyclical* Ut Unum Sint (Grand Rapids: Eerdmans, 2001), pp. 124-41.

10 William J Abraham, "Ut Unum Sint and Papal Infallibility: A Response" in Tim Perry, ed. *The Legacy of John Paul II: An Evangelical Assessment* (Downers Grove, IL: IVP Academic, 2007).

11 Reinhard Hütter, *Bound to Be Free: Evangelical Catholic Engagements in Ecclesiology, Ethics, and Ecumenism* (Grand Rapids: Eerdmans, 2004), especially chapter 10 on UUS. He can write, p. 190: "Considered strictly on the basis of the encyclical's ecclesiological core thesis – that the primacy of the bishop of Rome in its present form represents the condition for the possibility of Christian unity – visible Christian unity can only mean one thing: 'redintegratio,' that is, reunification with the Roman Catholic Church understood in terms of absorption" (this, I think, is hardly accurate: the meaning of the Latin word *redintegratio* is rather "restoration" and the Council fathers would have emphatically denied "absorption"). Yet, appealing to Melanchthon and Luther, he goes farther than most Evangelicals could accept and appears to recommend "an ecumenical primacy of the bishop of Rome ... *iure humano*..." (p. 192).

12 Shafique Keshavjee, *Vers une symphonie des Eglises. Un appel à la communion* (Saint-Maurice/ Le Mont-sur-Lausanne: Saint-Augustin/Ouverture, 1998), pp. 52-55.

13 Mouw, "The Problem of Authority," p. 124.

14 Mouw, "The Problem of Authority," pp. 124-25, raises the vexed question of the use of the pejorative "sects"; he mentions the book by Cardinal Ernesto Corripio Ahumada; Evangelicals have complained about the pope's own use during his visit to Latin America.

15 I must warn that the book by Mark A. Noll and Carolyn Nystrom, *Is the Reformation Over? An Evangelical Assessment of Contemporary Catholicism* (Grand Rapids: Baker Book House, 2005), may induce some unfounded optimism. Independently from theological appreciations, the information it provides is narrowly, "provincially," focused on North America (probably not the whole of it): the only talks between representative Evangelical and Catholic institutions at world level, the WEF(A)-PCPCU ones (with Monsignor Radano), are not even mentioned (my then colleague and esteemed friend Mark Noll gently regretted this omission in a personal

conversation); the only information about the situation in France concerns one American missionary who, at the time considered, had practically no contact with French Evangelical pastors.

16 So spoke the French Evangelical pastor Adolphe Monod, when thanking the British hosts. In Ruth Rouse and Stephen Charles Neill, eds., *A History of the Ecumenical Movement, vol. I: 1517-1948*, 3rd ed. (Geneva: WCC, 1986), p. 738.

17 In the same paragraph (no. 22), I wonder if the Latin intends a play on words which is lost in the English translation: through prayer, Christians will realize how *angustum* is what divides them and will find themselves to be together in the community the Holy Spirit is shaping despite human *angustiae* (the French version uses the same word, "limites").

18 Susan K. Wood has noticed the striking emphasis on martyrs, "A Symposium on *Ut Unum Sint*," *Pro Ecclesia* 4, no. 4 (1995): 393.

19 The title is found in the Latin original (nos. 4 and 81 for John XXIII), but replaced in the versions by "Pope"; *Pontifex Romanus* is found later (no. 97), rendered "Bishop of Rome."

20 "In a letter to the *Church Times* 28 November 1986, Bishop Moorman, who served on ARCIC I, stated that the purpose of the ARCIC discussions was to 'trade off' certain 'non-essentials' on both sides against the acceptance of other 'essentials' by the parties involved. The example he gave was the Anglicans accepting the 'essential' of the papacy in exchange for the Church of Rome giving up some of its eucharistic beliefs": quoting David Samuel, "Ecumenism: A Dilemma for Evangelicals," *Churchman* 101, no. 3 (1987): 207.

21 I read once that the great Baptist preacher Charles H. Spurgeon, addressing a large Baptist gathering, started: "We, Baptists, form the only denomination which never persecuted other Christians..." Thundering applause. And then he finished his sentence: "Because we never had the opportunity!"

22 no. 83, *haud extra suas facultates*; cf. UUS, nos. 84, 102, this is possible, yes.

23 Especially in no. 61 and already no. 55. In no. 55, the Latin "Ecclesiae igitur structurae in Oriente et in Occidente *formabantur secundum* illud apostolicum patrimonium" is weakly translated *evolved in reference*. Other modern versions are stronger, especially the French.

24 I owe this information to Yves Congar, *Diversités et communion. Dossier historique et conclusion théologique*, Cogitatio fidei 112 (Paris: Cerf, 1982), p. 34. He recalls how, down to modern times the recognition of baptism itself has been a fluctuating matter (pp. 85-87).

25 Similar considerations might be adduced concerning the medieval West. Cf. the remark by Stephen Charles Neill in Rouse and Neill, *History*, p. 20: "Those who speak warmly of the unity of Western Christendom before the Reformation sometimes forget that the price for this coercive unity was paid in a gigantic movement of dissidence from the formally established Church." And, of course, in the fires of the stakes that *martyrs* endured.

26 I am alluding to an intriguing textual detail. The last sentence in Latin no. 29 reads: "Hoc solum modo dialogus adiuvabit ad divisionem superandam et poterit ad *veritatem* admovere", "only in this way will dialogue help to overcome division and will be able to bring closer to *truth*"; but the Vatican's English translation reads "lead us closer to *unity*." Since the other versions do as the English one does, the change looks like a deliberate correction of the original.

27 One remembers Rudolf Bultmann's 1951 explanation on the Christological Confession of the World Council of Churches (the Church of which he was a pastor was affiliated to WCC), in *Glauben und Verstehen* II, pp. 246-61, translated in *Essays Philosophical and Theological* (London: SCM, 1955), pp. 273-90.

28 Adding, concerning the formulation: "while remaining forever suitable for communicating this truth to those who interpret them correctly"; surprisingly, there is no word in the Latin original

which corresponds to the "correctly" found in the modern language versions – presumably, it was considered implicit.

29 This was applied to the relations with non-Chalcedonian churches (UUS, no. 62). Considering the role of political factors in their rejection of Chalcedon, I can follow, though I still hesitate: may we imagine that the champions of orthodoxy in the 5th and 6th centuries would have similarly weighed contextual conditions?

30 John Calvin, *Institutes of the Christian Religion* 4.1.12, "All the articles of the doctrine of God are not of the same kind. There are some whose knowledge is so necessary that no one may doubt them, as no one may doubt decrees or principles of Christianity. For instance, that there is one God; that Jesus Christ is God and Son of God; that our salvation is of his sole mercy; and the like. There are others that are disputed among churches, and yet do not break the bond of unity between these. To give one example: if it so happened that one church should hold that souls, upon separation from the body, are immediately translated to heaven, while another should only affirm that they live in God, without presuming to determine the place, that such a divergence be without quarrel and obstinacy, why should they divide from each other?" and he quotes from Phil. 3:15. (My translation from Calvin's French; the passage is already found in the 1539 edition.)

31 "The Nature of Biblical Unity," in J. D. Douglas, ed., *Let the Earth Hear His Voice: International Congress on World Evangelization* (Minneapolis: World Wide Publications, 1975), pp. 380-99.

32 I have argued the case at some length, in view of Protestant interrelations, in my "Quel devoir d'unité entre protestants ?" in *Hokhma* 54 (1993): 43-57.

33 Application may well differ: the deep divide in faith, as to the truth, with representatives of other religions, makes me uneasy with the 1986 Assisi prayer invitation; the qualification *distincte sed similiter* (UUS, no. 76) is not enough to remove a dangerous ambiguity.

34 Calvin, *Institutes* 4.14.17 (my translation, italics mine). In recent decades, Calvin's views have been misrepresented by many scholars: partly because of the praiseworthy desire to narrow the ecumenical gap (with Lutherans and Catholics); partly because Calvin's own language *sounds* causative at times (not seldom). A more rigorous inquiry discovers that the instrumental causality he affirms is either (a) that of sealing, confirming and strengthening the faith of the recipient, not of conferring saving grace (sacraments are specifically seals), or (b) that of offering, as visible words, the grace that God infallibly gives to faith thus awakened (as signs, their efficacy is the same as that of the preached Word).

35 Calvin, *Institutes* 4.15.14. In the next paragraph (15), he answers the "sacramentalist's" objection he anticipates, drawn from Acts 22:16, and explains that Paul is made *more certain* by his baptism (sealing function).

36 Calvin, *Institutes* 4.15.22 (my translation and italics). In 4.16.4, baptism, just like circumcision, is the "first *external* entry into the Church of God."

37 There has been, for two or three decades, a sacramentalist trend among Baptists and other Evangelicals, but the fact does not cancel my main proposition: (a) the trend is too new for anyone to be sure that this departure from tradition is more than ephemeral fashion; (b) it is by no means universal, being essentially an English-speaking phenomenon, affecting "intellectuals"; (c) it usually goes hand in hand with a relaxation of Evangelical distinctives (on Scripture, on the Atonement) and/or attempts to woo what they call the "postmodern mind": will they retain the Evangelical identity?

38 The English version has "make present" for the Latin *actuale reddendum*; the French, Italian, Spanish and German versions have the equivalent of "actualise."

39 Quoted by Hütter, *Bound to Be Free*, p. 190.

40 Quoted by Cardinal Edward Idris Cassidy, "*Ut Unum Sint* in Ecumenical Perspective," in Carl E. Braaten and Robert Jenson, eds., *Church Unity and the Papal Office* (Grand Rapids: Eerdmans, 2001), p. 24.

41 UUS, no. 17.

42 All the modern language translations use "Pope" but the Latin original has "Christ's Vicar" in the sentence: "Concilium Vaticanum II suasit – huius rei bene conscii sumus – *Christi Vicario* ut in se susciperet hoc ministerii sui apostolici peculiare exercitium."

43 Stephen W. Sykes, "The Papacy and Power: An Anglican Perspective," in Braaten and Jenson, eds., *Church Unity and the Papal Office*, p. 69.

44 *Constitutio de Ecclesia Christi*, cap. 4 (July 18, 1870): the statement is made of the *ex cathedra* pronouncements, irreformable "of themselves, not (drawing their final authority) from the consensus of the Church"; on this addition, I owe most of what I know to Gustave Thils, *L'Infaillibilité pontificale, source-conditions-limites*, Recherches et synthèses, section de dogme (Gembloux: J. Duculot, 1969), pp. 118-21, 167-75, and already pp. 66-76 on the substance of the issue. In UUS no. 94, it is possible that the "also" (*etiam*) in the sentence that follows the affirmation of the pope speaking "in the name" of all: "He can also ... declare *ex cathedra*" is meant to separate this case and mark the pope's *independence* from the consensus of bishops. Regarding collegiality, one can also mention the difficulty of the statement of the Council of Florence, taken up by Vatican I in *Pastor Aeternus*: "Pontificem Romanum verum Christi vicarium totiusque Ecclesiae caput et omnium Christianorum patrem ac doctorem existere" without mention of the college of bishops; see also *Lumen Gentium*, no. 22.

45 Brian Daley, "The Ministry of Primacy and the Communion of Churches," in Braaten and Jenson, eds., *Church Unity and the Papal Office*, pp. 43-44.

46 Yves Congar, "Comment l'Eglise sainte doit se renouveler sans cesse" (1961), in *Sainte Eglise. Etudes et approches ecclésiologiques*, Unam sanctam 41 (Paris: Cerf, 1963), pp. 131-54, especially pp. 142-47, admirably explores the issue but does not convince me that in order to avoid nominalism (p. 144) one has to accept the church as "a person supra-individual and transcendent" (p. 141), and that "historical lapses (*fautes*)" may be imputed to the church, but not sins (p. 146). Incidentally, the forerunners of the Reformation, who were quite critical of the Roman institution, Wyclif and Jan Hus, were anti-nominalists (Augustinian realists).

47 "Theologischen Aufgaben und Fragen bei der Begegnung lutherischer und katholischer Theologie nach dem Konzil" (1966), in F.W. Kantzenbach and V. Vajta, eds., *Œcumenica: Annales de Recherche Œcuménique 1969* (Paris: Cerf, 1969), p. 262 ("sündige Kirche" with vielleicht), p. 264 (inmitten der Sünde der Kirche), p. 268 (Sünderkirche full of stains and wrinkles). Concerning the statement on New Testament usage, p. 262, I would offer a few antithetical comments. The main consideration is the one introduced above. As to specific biblical evidence, Eph. 5:27, which, precisely Ratzinger exploits, does imply stains at the present stage. He brushes off (p. 262) a reference to the seven churches of Revelation, since *the* Church is not accused but only *Gemeinden* that are threatened with being cast out of the Church; but, I object, the separation between churches and Church is artificial, and the removal of the lampstand is not explained in terms of expulsion from the Church. I would add the severe warning to the church *as the New Eve* in 2 Cor. 11:2-3 and to the branches of the Olive-Tree, the church and the Israel of God in Rom. 11:20-21, suggesting that there is more continuity than he allows between the old and the new dispensations of the Covenant-Partner of God, the Lord's Bride.

48 The issue was well perceived by Joseph Ratzinger, "Theologischen Aufgaben," p. 255-56, and I differ from his comment on 1 Cor. 6, p. 263.

49 *La Théologie de l'Église suivant saint Paul*, Unam sanctam 10 (Paris: Cerf, 1942), pp. 217-18 (with note); the parallel with Rom. 12:4-5 is important.

50 I am particularly grateful to Dom Paul Andriessen, "La nouvelle Eve, corps du nouvel Adam," in *Aux origines de l'Église: Recherches bibliques VII* (Paris: Desclée De Brouwer, 1965), pp. 87-109.

51 "Dogme christologique et ecclésiologie: vérité et limites d'un parallèle," in *Sainte Eglise*, pp. 69-104, above all pp. 96-101. "There is in the ordinary teaching given to the faithful on the Church a real danger of monophysitism" (p. 79 n.2); "In all rigour, there is no divine nature in the Church" (p. 84) though he has affirmed two natures earlier (p. 80); the mystical identification theologians are in danger of crossing the boundaries of a sound theology (p. 97, with n.1 giving instances); "In all rigour, the Incarnation does not continue" (p. 101); "To be exact, there are not, in the Church a divine and a human nature" (p. 103); "rigorously, there is no divine personality in the Church" (p. 104).

52 So Leonardo De Chirico argues, *Evangelical Theological Perspectives on Post-Vatican II Roman Catholicism*, Religions and Discourse 19 (Bern: Peter Lang, 2003), pp. 254-70.

53 In De Chirico, *Evangelical Theological Perspectives*, pp. 187-91, he refers to five thinkers only as witnesses of the systematic consciousness of Catholicism. These are: John Henry Newman, Romano Guardini, Hans Urs von Balthasar, Avery Dulles, and Richard McBrien – all of them moderately conservative.

54 The Latin quotation from *Unitatis Redintegratio*, no. 23, includes *in re morali*, dropped in the versions.

55 As I was for eight years vice-president of United Bible Societies, and the other vice-president for the region Europe and Middle-East was Alberto Ablondi, the late bishop of Livorno.

✝ CHAPTER 14

Strengths and Weaknesses of the Ecumenical Movement[1]

by William Henn, OFM Cap.

At the end of the classic *A History of the Ecumenical Movement: 1517-1948*, produced by a team of scholars who had extensive knowledge of that history, Bishop Stephen Charles Neill wrote:

> Since this History is concerned with a movement which lives and daily grows, it is impossible to end this volume with a neat classification of lessons to be learned, or of causes of success and failure drawn up in trim categories. Such a conclusion would be false, since, however accurate in detail, the static impression it would leave would not correspond to the realities and the complexities of a living object.[2]

That observation remains true today, more than fifty years later. Nevertheless, it is useful to take stock from time to time, and the following essay is premised by the conviction that it is possible to delineate a number of important strengths and weaknesses which can give both encouragement and insight for moving ahead towards the unity that Christ wills for the Church.

From the outset, it must be frankly admitted that many have voiced a certain note of disillusionment when assessing ecumenism in recent years. This was apparent in the three major presentations at an ecumenical conference held in St. Albans Cathedral in England in 2003. Archbishop Rowan Williams hinted at this malaise when he commented: "we need to balance the anxieties and challenges and struggles around unity with some sense that there is also an agenda for joy in this."[3] Commenting on the fact that Jesus prayed for unity in

John 17, Reverend Elizabeth Welch noted: "It was as if he could already see how difficult it might be for his followers to be one and he knew that he needed to entrust the work of unity to his Father."[4] Perhaps the most dour assessment came from Cardinal Walter Kasper, who stated:

> After the first wave of enthusiasm, there is now much disenchantment at unfulfilled expectations. We still cannot gather together at the table of the Lord. Ecumenical progress became slow, with churches often seeming to withdraw into old self-sufficient confessionalism. [...] Ecumenism seems to be in crisis.[5]

Cardinal Kasper did not thereby mean to offer merely a gloomy assessment of the present situation, for he immediately added that a "crisis" may be taken also in a positive sense, as an opportunity for real progress. Already twenty years earlier Joseph Ratzinger had ventured an explanation of the disappointment which some felt even then, pointing out that the rapid steps towards changed relations between churches which took place from the mid-1960s to the mid-1980s had been prepared for by a long process during the first half of the twentieth century. It was inevitable that, after some exciting changes in relations, a kind of standstill would set in, giving way to a slower phase in which divided churches would have to grow in mutual appreciation at a more profound level so as to arrive at real unity, not just what he called the "ecumenism of negotiation." While such "negotiation" can be very useful and even necessary, ultimately it is not able to produce that maturation into the reality of full communion which can never be accomplished simply by a document.[6]

An interesting interpretation of the last century of ecumenical activity was offered by veteran ecumenists Jeffrey Gros, Eamon McManus and Ann Riggs. In their *Introduction to Ecumenism*,[7] they invited readers to consider the following overview of the past hundred years. During a first stage, comprised of the first two-thirds of the twentieth century, the conviction became deeply rooted in the hearts of many Christians that they had a duty to seek full unity, and structures for fulfilling this duty – in the areas of mission, education, social action and theological dialogue – were gradually put into place. A second stage, comprising the last third of the century, saw intense dialogue and the realization of much collaboration in the aforementioned areas.

Now, a third stage of "reception" is beginning during which the seeds produced during the previous phases will hopefully sink into good soil in the lives of the churches which, for their part, will gradually take appropriate steps towards increasing their visible unity. In the more than one hundred years since the World Missionary Conference in Edinburgh (1910) and the nearly five hundred years since the beginning of the Reformation (1517), is the ecumenical movement entering into a new phase? At least, Gros, McManus and Riggs think that it is.

Keeping in mind these preliminary observations, what might be listed as some of the strengths and weaknesses of the ecumenical movement so far? "Strengths" and "weaknesses" are not so much events as qualities. In what follows, I will try both to describe particular qualities of the ecumenical movement and to suggest how strengths may be enhanced and weaknesses may be overcome.

Strengths

I believe that the first and one of the greatest strengths of the ecumenical movement is the fact that it began and continues to rest on the firm foundation of wanting to discern and carry out God's will for the Church. This is one of the greatest values of ecumenism, because, as such, it expresses discipleship in Jesus. Jesus himself sought to do the will of the Father. Disciples learn from him, as they learned to pray as he taught them "Thy will be done," a prayer echoed later in his acceptance of the Father's will in the garden of Gethsemane. As Christians commenting on the Lord's Prayer over the centuries have from time to time pointed out, the will of God inevitably shall be accomplished. Among many passages, 1 Corinthians 15:20-28 is a particularly good example of unshakable Christian hope that, in the end, Christ shall triumphantly hand over the kingdom to the Father and God will be all in all. To the extent that the ecumenical movement seeks to serve the will of the Father, it serves a cause that ultimately cannot fail. The will of God shall be done; this is the best reason for resisting discouragement in the face of the fact that we are still divided in many ways even after so much effort. It is the best reason for continuing to strive for the unity for which Christ prayed, even if we are sometimes weary. This centring of the ecumenical movement upon the will of God was put in a slightly different way, emphasizing the virtue of obedience, by the 1982 *Final Report* of the Anglican-Roman Catholic International Commission:

> Christ's will and prayer are that his disciples should be one. Those who have received the same word of God and have been baptized in the same Spirit cannot, without disobedience, acquiesce in a state of separation. Unity is of the essence of the Church, and since the Church is visible its unity must also be visible.[8]

If this is so, then we can adopt an attitude of confidence and steadfastness in continuing our efforts, no matter what obstacles seem to arise or how long the road ahead still seems.

A second strength lies in the vast extent of the spread of the ecumenical spirit among so many people within so many different Christian communities. Bishop Stephen Neill, writing a half century after the World Missionary Conference of Edinburgh began the modern ecumenical movement with the clear and determined statement "we will stay together," wrote:

> what has happened in these fifty years must needs seem astonishing. [...] Things which are taken for granted today were certainly not taken for granted a generation ago. [...] ... things which today seem incredible or impossible will seem plain and obvious to our children.[9]

Ecumenism has become deeply ingrained in the life of the churches. An assessment was offered in the second chapter of *Ut Unum Sint*, Pope John Paul II's encyclical letter on ecumenism, recalling some of the positive steps taken towards greater unity in recent decades:

> It is the first time in history that efforts on behalf of Christian unity have taken on such great proportions and have become so extensive. This is truly an immense gift of God, one which deserves all our gratitude. From the fullness of Christ we receive 'grace upon grace' (Jn 1:16). An appreciation of how much God has already given is the condition which disposes us to receive those gifts still indispensable for bringing to completion the ecumenical work of unity. An overall view of the last thirty years enables us better to appreciate many of the fruits of this

common conversion to the Gospel which the Spirit of God has brought about by means of the ecumenical movement.[10]

That this movement, under the inspiration of the Holy Spirit, has touched the hearts of so many individuals and communities is one of its great strengths.

A third strength is what I would call the multi-dimensionality of the ecumenical movement, allowing it to penetrate many important aspects of the life of the Church. This is best illustrated by looking at the unfolding history of the efforts towards greater unity in the twentieth century. Many Christians who know something of that story, when they hear the name Edinburgh coupled with the year 1910, think immediately of the relation of ecumenism to mission and evangelization. The same can be said for the great conference of Stockholm in 1925, which emphasized the importance of ecumenism for the promotion of justice and peace, and for that of Lausanne in 1927, which underlined the significance of faith and Church order for unity. Mention of other cities and years, along with the names of many outstanding Christians who were protagonists of the movement towards unity, would demonstrate how many facets of ecclesial life ecumenism has touched:

- the prayer life and spirituality of so many individuals and communities;

- the work of translating together the Scriptures into many different languages so as to make God's word available to people in their native tongues;

- the various ways of cooperation in fostering of health and education by Christian individuals and organizations;

- the establishment of structures within our respective communities and of councils of churches so as to *institutionalize* ecumenism, giving it a staying power and initiative;

- the entrance of ecumenical topics and motivation in our programs of Christian formation and catechesis, helping all Christians to see one another not as enemies but as brothers and sisters on the basis of our common baptism; and

- the training and education of ministers, theologians and Church leaders so that those playing important roles of service within our communities will be concerned to seek the unity for which Christ prayed.

A great strength of the ecumenical movement lies in the fact that it does not concern one isolated aspect of ecclesial life, of interest only to a small group of specialists.

A fourth strength pertains especially to that aspect of the ecumenical movement seeking to address the issues that caused our divisions in the first place, especially questions of doctrinal and structural reconciliation. The ability to place some of the oppositions of the past into a broader context makes it possible to see them now as *false* oppositions. One illustrative example is that tension between, on the one hand, the Orthodox and Catholics who have an aversion against speaking of the "sinfulness of the Church" because the Church is Christ's bride and is professed to be holy in the creed and, on the other, many Protestants who are very aware of the shortcomings of the Church and its leaders and who emphasize that the Church must always be reformed. The new ecclesiology study that has been developed by the Faith and Order Commission has the potential to help Christians see this as a false opposition.[11] Its first two chapters describe the Church respectively in terms of its relation to the salvific work of God and the many points commonly held by many Christian communities largely on the basis of what the New Testament teaches about the Church. This is followed by a chapter highlighting areas of continued division, partly due to the Church's vulnerability during its pilgrimage through history due to the weaknesses caused by sin, and how various bilateral conversations have made some progress, even if limited, towards overcoming some of these divisions. The final chapter describes agreement about the service that the Church is obliged to offer in the world by assisting the suffering, working for justice, peace and the protection of the environment and proclaiming the good news of Jesus Christ. Taken together, the convergence text allows the reader to see that, when some Christians are reluctant to call the Church sinful, they do not thereby deny the need for continual reform. Similarly, those who prophetically denounce sin within our communities in no way intend to deny what

Paul's Letter to the Ephesians teaches about Christ's spotless bride or what the creed professes about the real holiness of the Church.

Another classic tension was described in the Reformed-Roman Catholic agreed text entitled *Towards a Common Understanding of the Church*, which explained how Reformed Christians tend to see the Church as centred upon the word, while Catholics tend to see the Church as centred upon the sacraments.[12] In fact, both word and sacrament depend on one another. Different churches may give different emphases to one or the other, but it would not make sense to oppose them as if one had to choose and settle for one without the other. This was explicitly acknowledged in the most recent fruit of this bilateral dialogue:

> We can now affirm, in light of our investigation both of the kingdom and of the patristic literature, not only that these visions are mutually informative and complementary but also that neither is fully adequate without the other. A "sacramental" church that does not give proper place to the Word of God would be essentially incomplete; a church that is truly a creation of the Word will celebrate that Word liturgically and sacramentally.[13]

Similarly, the development of scientific biblical exegesis has shown that Scripture cannot simply be opposed to Tradition, a point forcefully brought home in the famous statement about tradition by the Faith and Order Commission at Montreal in 1963.[14] To the extent that Tradition can be understood as the Gospel which is handed on from generation to generation, the Commission affirmed that we would not be Christians at all were it not for the tradition. Montreal's statement has been further developed in the 1998 Faith and Order paper on ecumenical hermeneutics; *A Treasure in Earthen Vessels*, which especially tries to explore how various cultures and ecclesial histories affect interpretation. The text also explores issues surrounding the process of discerning the adequacy or inadequacy of any interpretation, a process engaging the whole community – scholars, authoritative ministers and the whole people of God.[15] The point is that Scripture and Tradition go together. While Christians still disagree about how they are related, it would be a caricature to oppose communities on the basis of an exaggerated opposition between them.

Finally, the 1999 Lutheran-Catholic *Joint Declaration on the Doctrine of Justification* illustrates well the principle of looking at past contradictory formulations of faith within a new and broader context. The declaration states: "Together we confess: By grace alone, in faith in Christ's saving work and not because of any merit on our part, we are accepted by God and receive the Holy Spirit, who renews our hearts while equipping and calling us to good works."[16] On the basis of this and several other fundamental shared affirmations, the two communities go on to show how they explain this central gospel truth about justification from different mindsets and using different terminologies, each of which are compatible with the fundamental agreement. A great strength of the ecumenical movement is this development towards what has been called "differentiated consensus," that is, the ability to formulate a common understanding of the gospel which allows for diversity in explanation.[17]

Thus at least four of the strengths of the ecumenical movement are its searching to carry out the will of God, its extensive reception into the convictions, attitudes and actions of Christians, its pervasiveness in touching many varied aspects of church life, and its ability to overcome false oppositions by placing former conflicts within a broader context and re-evaluating them in light of a common return to the sources of faith.

Weaknesses

A first weakness may be gleaned from the fact that after so many years we still are not united. In my preliminary remarks, I noted the sense of malaise that many have expressed. In a way, this reflects the greatest weakness which we suffer in the pilgrimage towards the unity for which Jesus prayed, that is, that it is impossible for us to achieve on our own. We simply cannot do it. At the same time, if it is true that we are saved by grace, that our salvation is not a human achievement, why should we think that the re-establishment of full unity in the Church is something "in our hands," so to speak?

The most difficult problem for Church unity seems to be unity in faith. Many documents have been produced; many agreements recorded, along with areas in which disagreement still exists. In the

Proceedings of the Conference held in St. Albans Cathedral on 17 May 2003, there was a striking comment by Cardinal Kasper which could easily bring a smile to one's face were it not about a subject of such importance. In addition to the danger of making ecumenism a "mere academic affair," he added:

> There is another danger too: to embark upon a mere ecumenical activism involving an endless series of conferences, symposiums, commissions, meetings, sessions, projects and spectacular events with the perpetual repetition of the same arguments, concerns, problems and lamentations. It may be useful to bear in mind that the ecumenical documents of only the last decades at the international level, leaving aside the many regional and local documents, now comprise two thick volumes. Who can read all this stuff, and, indeed, who wants to?[18]

In a ceremony at St. George's Cathedral in the Phanar marking the return to the Ecumenical Patriarch of Constantinople of the relics of two great bishops of that same patriarchal diocese – Gregory Nazianzen and John Chrysostom – Patriarch Bartholomew commented on Gregory's role in bringing about doctrinal agreement at the time of the second ecumenical council in 381. He then added:

> But ecclesiastical unity must be considered and experienced more profoundly than the said agreement, i.e., ontologically, as unity of persons, personal feelings, personal wills, personal goals and objectives and not as a mere organizational or administrative union, or as a coincidence of opinions and convictions or as a simple agreement on the formulation and intellectual conceptualization of truths or of truth as a whole. A doctrinal and intellectual agreement certainly helps, and can smooth the path and lead toward unity, but it is not in itself the end, it is not unity. The "unity of the acknowledgment of the Son of God" spoken about by the Apostle is the communion of an ontological nature with the Christ in Whom alone may unity be achieved.[19]

The point is that agreements are not enough. We should not expect the unity of the Church to be the result of a series of negotiations, something like the drafting of a new constitution for a country. Archbishop Rowan Williams has written:

> In those farewell discourses in St. John's gospel, unity appears as a function of the fact that believers are drawn into Jesus' own relation with God the Father, and Jesus' own movement, his eternal movement into the depths of God the Father. Unity is what we call that harmonious movement into the Father which is the life of Jesus in eternity and in time. [...] Unity is therefore never simply the appearance of unanimity, it is never simply a matter of human agreement.[20]

As such, the ecumenical movement is too weak to produce unity; it cannot do so by texts or by joint witness for justice, peace and the protection of the environment, nor by collaboration in works of charity, as much as all of those activities may contribute and hasten the day on which this unity in grace is more deeply found. But this great weakness could be considered a strength if we take into account Paul's conviction – "when I am weak, then I am strong" (2 Cor. 12:10). This first great "weakness" suggests not abandoning the various dimensions of promoting unity, but rather reinforcing them as much as possible with what might be called an "ecumenical spirituality," emphasizing especially the need for and value of prayer.

A second weakness is a separation and even competition between the various kinds of activity promoting Christian unity. Nils Ehrenström closed his account of the Life and Work movement, that is, the movement which sought to promote unity by common witness for justice and peace, with the following words, which I find to be especially helpful:

> It has been perhaps inevitable, but none the less a grave disadvantage to the ecumenical movement, that the various aspects of ecumenical concern – the unity and renewal of the Church, the evangelistic task among peoples who have never known Christ or have rejected him in the dim and distorted form in which he has been presented by the Churches, the social and political witness of the Churches – have been developed in separation from one another. Progress toward integration has been made, but the process is as yet very far from complete.[21]

In recent years, such projects as the series of ecclesiology and ethics studies initiated with *Costly Unity*[22] (1993) within the World Council of Churches (WCC) or the more recent *Princeton Proposal* (2003)[23] continue to show this weakness and even tension between various streams of the ecumenical movement. Given the limited resources available to the ecumenical movement and to the churches in general, some ask: "What is the best way of using our limited funds?" Surely the mission of the Church in the world must impel Christians to reach out together to those suffering. Often in ecumenical dialogue about theological issues, participants, especially from countries that are economically poorer or suffering from catastrophic scourges like the AIDS pandemic, wonder why attention is given to solving those problems that first divided the churches many centuries ago. The urgency of people suffering suggests setting aside theological questions, which seem so resistant to resolution in any case. On the other hand, as the *Princeton Proposal* argues, cogently in my view, no progress towards full unity can be expected by ignoring or simply by-passing the contradictions which logically led our forebears to discern that they had to part ways in the first place.

Perhaps the third phase of Reformed-Catholic international dialogue offers a way forwards. As the discussions unfolded, it became clear that there was a tension between those who wanted to focus on *contextual* issues, that is, the social situations which Reformed and Roman Catholics face in their different contexts throughout the world, on the one hand, and those who did not want to abandon the *classical issues* which divided our communities from the time of the sixteenth century, on the other. After a period of somewhat tense disagreement, an effort was made to blend the two concerns, looking at stories of common witness within the contexts of South Africa, Northern Ireland and Canada, not only to learn about how our fellow Reformed and Catholic brothers and sisters had or had not collaborated in those contexts, and what could be learned from this experience, but also to explore ecclesiological issues pertinent to these experiences, especially looking to Scripture and Tradition to reflect upon what the doctrine about the Church's relation to the Kingdom of God mandates concerning social action by Christians.[24] The subject of Church ministry and authority also entered into this discussion of questions stemming from the contextual experience of our brothers and sisters. One need not and should not opt for one or the other kind of ecumenical engagement, but rather maintain an integrated understanding of the many dimensions of ecumenical activity.

I have illustrated this weakness with examples which highlight a certain competition between common efforts promoting justice, peace and the integrity of creation, on the one hand, and theological ecumenism, which seeks to overcome past contradictory positions concerning faith and order, on the other. But fitting under this particular weakness should also be listed new challenges for the ecumenical movement which could emerge in light of the massive growth of secularism in some parts of the world, as well as the increased awareness of religious pluralism. Today there is a temptation to question the continuing relevance of seeking Christian unity when the tasks of presenting the Gospel in a credible way before our secular societies or of engaging in meaningful inter-religious dialogue with representatives of world religions seem so pressing. These real challenges stemming from the contemporary situation must not be placed in competition with that work needed to pursue the unity Christ wills.

The third and perhaps most decisive weakness of the ecumenical movement derives from our lack of agreement about the nature and mission of the Church. There is even disagreement about whether or how much we need to agree about the nature and mission of the Church. Cardinal Kasper's description of this problem is very helpful:

> We are dealing with diverse ecclesiologies that lead to different conceptions of the same ecumenical goal to which we strive. In turn, these conceptions raise different expectations that, by their very nature, lead to disappointment on the part of one or the other of the partners due to the very fact that one is not responding to the other's expectations, or cannot respond due to a different concept of the ecumenical goal. Such a situation has led in part to a sort of stalemate that makes substantial progress impossible, at least until the questions relating to ecclesiology have been fundamentally resolved.[25]

A "stalemate that makes substantial progress impossible"? Such words are less discouraging, if what was noted earlier about the overall impossibility of achieving unity on our own is true. But, in addition, several important openings that promise fuller agreement about the nature and mission of the Church appear on the horizon. I already mentioned briefly the new work by the Faith and Order Commission on this theme. At the heart of its convergence text on ecclesiology, which was presented to the Tenth General Assembly of the WCC in Busan, Korea, in 2013, is the biblical and patristic notion of communion, a way of thinking about the Church which was also prized by both the Eastern churches and by many of the leaders of the Reformation.[26] The ecclesiology of communion has deeply characterized many bilateral dialogues during the past fifteen years and, as such, is becoming more widely embraced by Christians from many different communities. One may hope that the four chapters of *The Church: Towards a Common Vision*, whose titles are "God's Mission and the Unity of the Church," "The Church of the Triune God," "The Church: Growing in Communion," and "The Church: In and for the World," may provide a clear and convincing instrument for achieving greater convergence and consensus.

Furthermore, it seems to me that more and more the Church is being seen as comprised of people engaged in three fundamental activities: believing in Christ, celebrating the new life they have received in Christ, especially through the sacraments, and serving one another and all of their fellow human beings after the example of Christ.[27] There have been significant convergences between divided Christians in each of these three areas. I have already mentioned important advances concerning Scripture and Tradition and justification by faith, which I believe provide a firm foundation for unity in the first of these three activities: believing. Regarding the celebration of the new life in Christ, the question of the sacraments emerges as a natural theme for dialogue. There has been significant convergence in this area, as two new studies on baptism – one by Faith and Order and the other by the Joint Working Group of the Roman Catholic Church and the WCC – show.[28] Both texts try to broaden the context around the traditional opposition expressed by the fact that some Christians call baptism a *sacrament* while others call it an *ordinance*. Even more, two earlier studies – the Lutheran-Catholic *Facing Unity* (1984) and the Methodist-Catholic *The Word of Life* (1996) – looked at the question of the nature and number of sacraments, agreeing that they are means used by God for the sanctification of God's people.[29] These dialogues also point out that, while Lutherans and Methodists designate only two rites with the precise word "sacrament," nevertheless, those other liturgical actions which Orthodox and Catholics call sacraments are also celebrated in many Lutheran or Methodist communities: confirmation, reconciliation, marriage, ordination, and anointing of the sick. Perhaps more churches would be able to say the same.

Regarding the third area of my triad – that of serving one another and one's fellow human beings – there have been important steps forwards, such as recognizing that all members of the Church, laity and clergy, are called to a life of service, that ordained ministry must be seen primarily in terms of service and that the life of most Christian communities gives evidence of the need for and exercise of a ministry or service of oversight, which has been referred to in any number of dialogues with the Greek word *episkopé*.[30] Under the heading of service can come also the extensive agreement and cooperation between Christians of different communities in matters of proclaiming the Gospel and of promoting justice, peace and the integrity of creation.

Conflicting views of the Church still constitute a weakness for the ecumenical movement. But, as I have tried to argue, this topic has been fruitfully explored and there are reasons to hope that the miracle of sharing a common mind is more plausible than we may once have imagined. At least three other weaknesses should be listed, even though briefly.

A fourth weakness concerns the lack of participation within the ecumenical movement as a whole of many of the largest and seemingly most quickly growing churches. Many of these are in the Pentecostal family of churches, which celebrated a major anniversary in 2006 – the hundredth anniversary of the outpouring of the Holy Spirit at the Azusa Street mission in Los Angeles, to which many of these communities look as a significant moment in their own origin.[31] Another large block of churches are those called Evangelical. Interestingly, in both cases, there have been contacts and developments, some more recent, but some stemming back already for more than thirty years, such as the Pentecostal-Roman Catholic international dialogue. Since the year

2000, several meetings of leaders from Evangelical and Pentecostal churches have taken place with representatives of those churches who have been more engaged in the Global Christian Forum.[32]

Fifth, there is the problem of reception. How have the results of the ecumenical movement been received into the lives of the various churches? Much has been published on the question of ecumenical reception.[33] One of the wisest observations, in my view, is that the aim of dialogue and collaboration is not the reception of texts but the reception by the churches of one another. Texts are important, even essential, as steps along the way to this more profound existential reception. Many have pointed out that the process of discovering, discerning and acknowledging the various kinds of unity that already exist and that are considerable is one that takes a long time. If the aim is a deep rather than superficial growth in communion, then it would be best to emphasize ecumenical formation. Commenting on Oscar Cullman's book *Unity through Diversity*, Joseph Ratzinger wrote in 1986:

> What I find very helpful for this question is the slogan that Oscar Cullmann recently injected into the debate: unity through diversity. True, schism belongs to what is evil, especially when it leads to hostility and to the impoverishment of the Christian witness. But when the poison of hostility is slowly extracted from the schism and when as a result of mutual acceptance what emerges from the difference is no longer just impoverishment but a new wealth of listening and understanding, then it can be in transition towards being seen as a *felix culpa* even before it is completely healed. [...] But this means that, even if schisms are to begin with the failure of men and women and their fault, nevertheless there is in them a dimension that corresponds to God's disposing. Hence it is only to a certain point that we can repair them through repentance and conversion; but it is only the God who judges and forgives who decides entirely on his own when the point is reached that we no longer need this split.[34]

This, he claims, is not a concept of stagnation and resignation to divisions. Rather, "it is quite simply the attempt to leave to God what is his business alone and to discover what then in all seriousness are our tasks."[35] The weakness of insufficient reception can be countered by renewed efforts to provide believers in our various churches with an ecumenical formation and spirituality which hopefully will bear fruit in more profound appreciation of and communion with one another across confessional lines.

A sixth weakness of the ecumenical movement is the ever-present danger of the emergence of new sources of division, which arise from ways in which the changes of contemporary society have an impact on our discernment about areas such as Church order (here, for example, one might mention the disagreement about the ordination of women) or ethics (examples include the moral evaluation of abortion, homosexuality, the regulation of birth, genetic engineering and so forth). These, of course, are issues which were not the original causes of Christian divisions. Nor do disagreements about them only cause tension between churches – the internal unity of communities is at times threatened by these new questions. While these specific issues cannot be taken up here, they point nevertheless to the inevitability of seeing the Church as a community of believers on the move in a pilgrimage through history.[36] New questions concerning faith and morals will always have to be addressed and the Church will forever need to remain a community of dialogue, even after, God willing, some or all of the current divisions are healed.

Thus one can list at least six weaknesses of the ecumenical movement: the impossibility of arriving at unity from human effort alone, the competition between the various streams of ecumenical activity, the lack of common vision about the Church and its mission, the absence of some of the larger and faster growing communities from the ecumenical movement, the lack of reception into the lives of the churches of ecumenical achievements, and the emergence of new church-dividing issues. At the same time, the foregoing pages suggest ways for seeing some of these weaknesses in a new light or of overcoming them.

Conclusion

Looking at these weaknesses together with the four strengths earlier mentioned – search for the will of God, the wide diffusion of ecumenism, its presence in so many aspects of ecclesial life and the growing ability to overcome false oppositions – we may be led to ask at the conclusion: What is needed in the present situation? Where can we go from here?

It seems obvious to say that we are in an intermediate stage on the road from hostility to full communion. We need to give shape to this intermediate stage by exploring ways to increase our knowledge of one another and our collaboration together in carrying out the mission Christ has entrusted to us. In November 2004, the Vatican's Pontifical Council for Promoting Christian Unity held a symposium outside of Rome inviting the ecumenical officers of all the episcopal conferences of the Catholic Church to celebrate the fortieth anniversary of the *Decree on Ecumenism*, published by the Second Vatican Council in 1964. In addition to various talks from ecumenical leaders from various churches, the symposium discussed and refined the first draft of what was entitled a *Vademecum œcumenicum*, which has since been published.[37] Its three sections – "Deepening Christian Faith," "Prayer and Worship" and "Diakonia and Witness" – strikingly parallel the three fundamental ecclesial activities of faith, celebration and service which I have listed earlier in this paper and about which I have claimed some progress towards further convergence. The handbook offers many suggestions for shared activities that could lead to deepening the reality of communion in faith, worship and service among currently divided Christians.

The point of this ecumenical handbook is to encourage the development of a spirituality of communion which may foster a strengthening of the desire for unity among Christians. This ecumenical spirituality can build upon what has already been developing for decades, deepening it and extending it to a greater number of people. This is not to replace the continuing commitment to theological dialogue and to common witness to the gospel and common advocacy of justice, peace and a healthy environment. But perhaps it can gradually create a new climate in which what Patriarch Bartholomew called the ontological reality of communion grows among us. The ecumenical movement need not worry so much about the setting of artificial deadlines. Rather it is a question of patient, persistent and prayerful seeking of that unity which God wills, in the way and at the time that God wills it. By continuing to deepen our friendship, collaboration and common witness, we may hope that miraculous breakthroughs may yet occur through the surprising grace of the Holy Spirit.

At a celebration in Chicago to mark the fifth anniversary of the signing of the Lutheran-Roman Catholic *Joint Declaration on the Doctrine of Justification,* Cardinal Kasper ended his talk with a note of hopeful optimism.[38] Who could have imagined, he asked, walking by the Berlin Wall on the morning of November 9, 1989, that that very evening the wall would begin to be torn down? Doing our best to respond to the grace already at work within us, why could we not hope that God's power might break down, in ways that now are quite beyond our imagination, those walls that now at times seem so insurmountable?

---

1   The following essay owes its origin to Monsignor John Radano, who recommended me as a Catholic presenter for a week at Iona Abbey to encourage and support a new generation of Church leaders in their ecumenical commitment. Sponsored by the Iona Community and the Society of Ecumenical Studies in Great Britain, the theme was "Breaking Down Dividing Walls in the 21st Century." Given such an origin, it seemed to me a fitting contribution to this work in honour of a great ecumenist and friend.

2   Stephen Charles Neill, "Epilogue," in Ruth Rouse and Stephen Charles Neill, ed., *A History of the Ecumenical Movement 1517-1948* (Philadelphia: Westminster Press, 1954), p. 726.

3   Rowan Williams, conference paper given at St. Alban's Cathedral, Hertfordshire, England, May 17, 2003, and published simply under his name in the booklet *May they all be one ... but how? A vision of Christian unity for the next generation,* p. 5.

4   Elizabeth Welch, conference paper in *May they all be one,* p. 14.

5   Walter Kasper, conference paper in *May they all be one,* p. 21.

6   These ideas were expressed by Joseph Ratzinger, the present Pope Emeritus Benedict XVI, in his essay "The Progress of Ecumenism," reprinted in his *Church, Ecumenism & Politics* (New York: Crossroad, 1988), pp. 135-42.

7   Jeffrey Gros, Eamon McManus, and Ann Riggs, *Introduction to Ecumenism* (Mahwah, N.J.: Paulist Press, 1998).

8   From paragraph 9 of the "Introduction" to the *Final Report,* in GA I, pp. 66-67.

9   Neill, "Epilogue," in *A History of the Ecumenical Movement 1517-1948,* pp. 730-31.

10 John Paul II, *Ut Unum Sint* (Encyclical letter on commitment to ecumenism, May 25, 1995), no. 41.

11 The ecclesiology study had earlier produced two draft texts: *The Nature and Purpose of the Church,* Faith and Order paper 181 (Geneva: WCC, 1998), and *The Nature and Mission of the Church: A Stage on the Way to a Common Statement,* Faith and Order paper 198 (Geneva: WCC, 2005). The culmination of this study process is the new convergence text *The Church: Towards a Common Vision,* Faith and Order paper 214 (Geneva: WCC, 2013). Each of these is available at http://oikoumene.org.

12   See nos. 94-113, entitled "'Two conceptions of the Church," in *Towards a Common Understanding of the Church*, in GA II, pp. 801-5.

13   Reformed-Roman Catholic International Dialogue, *The Church as Community of Common Witness to the Kingdom of God: Report of the Third Phase of the International Theological Dialogue between the Catholic Church and the World Alliance of Reformed Churches (1998-2005)*, no. 193, in *Reformed World* 57, no. 2-3 (June-September, 2007): 105-207.

14   P.C. Rodger and L. Vischer, ed., *The Fourth World Conference on Faith and Order, Montreal 1963*, Faith and Order paper 42 (London: SCM, 1964), pp. 50-61. Some of the more salient passages of Montreal's report on "Scripture, Tradition and traditions" are reprinted in *Documentary History of Faith and Order, 1963-1993*, Faith and Order paper 159, ed. Günther Gassmann (Geneva: WCC, 1993), pp. 10-18.

15   *A Treasure in Earthen Vessels: An Instrument for an Ecumenical Reflection on Hermeneutics*, Faith and Order paper 182 (Geneva: WCC, 1998); http://www.oikoumene.org; Peter Bouteneff and Dagmar Heller, ed., *Interpreting Together: Essays in Hermeneutics*, Faith and Order paper 189 (Geneva: WCC, 2001), pp. 134-60. The Reformed-Catholic text *The Church as Community of Common Witness to the Kingdom of God* also contains a third chapter entitled "Discerning God's Will in the Service of the Kingdom," which concerns the ecclesial process of discernment; see nos. 124-58.

16   Lutheran World Federation and Roman Catholic Church, *Joint Declaration on the Doctrine of Justification*, no. 15 (Grand Rapids: Eerdmans, 2000); *Information Service* 103 (2000): 3-35; *One in Christ* 36, no. 1 (2000): 56-74, in GA II, pp. 566-82.

17   A fine description of such consensus is sketched out by Harding Meyer in his "Die Prägung einer Formel: Ursprung und Intention," in Harald Wagner, ed., *Einheit – aber wie? Zur Tragfähigkeit der ökumenischen Formel vom "differenzierten Konsens,"* Quaestiones disputatae 184 (Freiburg im Breisgau: Herder, 2000), pp. 36-58. See also Meyer's "Consensus in the Doctrine of Justification," *Ecumenical Trends* 26, no. 12 (December 1997): 165-68.

18   Kasper, conference paper in *May they all be one*, p. 22.

19   Bartholomew I, "Address", Visit of the Delegation of the Holy See to Constantinople, November 27-December 1, 2004, *Information Service* 117 (2004): 151.

20   Williams, conference paper in *May they all be one*, p. 5.

21   "Movements for International Friendship and Life and Work 1925-1948," in *A History of the Ecumenical Movement 1517-1948*, p. 596.

22   *Costly Unity: A World Council of Churches Consultation on Koinonia and Justice, Peace and the Integrity of Creation* (Geneva: WCC, 1993); http://www.oikoumene.org; also in Thomas F. Best and Martin Robra, eds., *Ecclesiology and Ethics: Ecumenical Ethical Engagement, Moral Formation and the Nature of the Church* (Geneva: WCC, 1997).

23   Carl E. Braaten and Robert W. Jenson, eds., *In One Body through the Cross: The Princeton Proposal for Christian Unity* (Grand Rapids: Eerdmans, 2003).

24   See *The Church as a Community of Common Witness to the Kingdom of God*, nos. 7-13. As co-secretary of this dialogue, Monsignor John Radano played a key role in its discussions and the eventual drafting of this text, which is available at http://www.prounione.urbe.it.

25   Walter Kasper, "Introductory Report of the President," Plenary of the Pontifical Council for Promoting Christian Unity, *Information Service* 115 (2004): 28.

26   See *The Church: Towards a Common Vision*, nos. 13-16 and 28-32. The theme of communion is also dominant in recent Catholic ecclesiology and official teaching.

27 This way of thinking about the life of the Christian community is developed in William Henn, *Church: The People of God* (New York: Burns & Oates, 2004).

28 The first of these was published as *One Baptism: Towards Mutual Recognition. A Study Text*, Faith and Order Paper no. 210 (Geneva: WCC, 2011). The Joint Working Group's "Ecclesiological and Ecumenical Implications of a Common Baptism" is published in *Information Service* 117 (2004): 188-204.

29 See "Increasing agreement in understanding and celebration of the sacraments," nos. 75-82 of *Facing Unity*, in GA II, pp. 461-63, and "The sacraments and other means of grace," nos. 100-107 of *The Word of Life*, in GA II, pp. 639-41.

30 See the valuable contributions to the symposium of December 1-3, 2005 entitled "The Relation Between the Bishop and the Local Church: Old and New Questions in Ecumenical Perspective," and published as the first issue of *The Jurist* 66, no. 1 (2006): 1-338. Lutheran professor André Birmelé's "*Episcopos, Episcopé*, Catholicity and the Constitution of the Church: Important Challenges for the Reformation Churches," pp. 264-84, is especially helpful in showing that there may be more room for convergence on this question than one might have thought.

31 For a truly impressive and stimulating account of this event by a well-qualified scholar, see Cecil M. Robeck, Jr., *The Azusa Street Mission and Revival: The Birth of the Global Pentecostal Movement* (Nashville: Thomas Nelson, 2006).

32 Further information about the Global Christian Forum can be found in chapter 18 of this volume, entitled "Breaking New Ground: The Global Christian Forum," by Huibert van Beek. A brief account of the Global Christian Forum can also be found in "The Eighth Report of the Joint Working Group between the Roman Catholic Church and the World Council of Churches: 1999-2005," in *Information Service* 117 (2004): 171-72 or at http://www.oikoumene.org and http://www.globalchristianforum.org.

33 For an overview of this literature, see William Henn, "The Reception of Ecumenical Documents," pp. 362-95, with a response by Mary Tanner on pp. 396-404 in Hervé Legrand, Julio Manzanares Marijuán and Antonio García y García, eds., *Reception and Communion Among Churches*, a special issue of *The Jurist* 57, no. 1 (1997). See also the interventions by André Birmelé, William Henn, and Donna Geernaert on the theme of "Reception" in Alan Falconer, ed., *Faith and Order in Moshi: The 1996 Commission Meeting*, Faith and Order paper 177 (Geneva: WCC, 1998), pp. 58-95.

34 Ratzinger, *Church, Ecumenism & Politics*, pp. 138-39; the "need" is a reference to St. Paul's statement in 1 Cor. 11:19 that "there must be factions."

35 Ratzinger, *Church, Ecumenism & Politics*, p. 142.

36 I have attempted to expound a dynamic vision of unity in faith in *One Faith: Biblical and Patristic Contributions Toward Understanding Unity in Faith* (Mahwah, NJ: Paulist Press, 1995).

37 Walter Kasper, *A Handbook of Spiritual Ecumenism* (Hyde Park, NY: New City Press, 2007).

38 Walter Kasper, "Joint Declaration on the Doctrine of Justification," Address given in Chicago, Illinois for the 5th Anniversary of the JDDJ, in *Information Service* 117 (2004): 160.

✝ CHAPTER 15

The Unity We Seek: The Development of Concepts of Christian Unity in Faith and Order

by Günther Gassmann

Personal Prologue

In 1984, at the same time that John Radano joined what was then known as the Secretariat for Promoting Christian Unity in Rome, I joined the World Council of Churches (WCC) in Geneva as director of its Commission on Faith and Order, of which the Roman Catholic Church is a full member. This coincidence marks the beginning of a close, fruitful, and happy cooperation between the two of us. Though coming from two ecclesial traditions that represented the deep and painful division between Catholics and Lutherans since the time of the Reformation, both of us were conscious of the continuing common fundamental convictions of faith shared by our two communions. That constituted a solid basis for our cooperation. Moreover, we were both convinced that the way forwards towards visible Christian unity had to address, in an intense theological dialogue, the doctrinal differences that still divide our churches. This common approach and realism made our cooperation and contacts between 1984 and 1995 an easy and happy relationship. Our closest cooperation happened, in a way, within the Joint Working Group between the Roman Catholic Church and the World Council of Churches where Monsignor Radano and I helped to draft several of its texts. After my retirement, I observed with great satisfaction how Radano, in more difficult Faith and Order situations, continued to act as an untiring and faithful advocate of Faith and Order by highlighting its irreplaceable role and place in the WCC and the ecumenical movement. For this, we remain deeply grateful.

I. Development of First Concepts of Christian Unity between 1910 and 1937

A movement in history that is without direction, without orientation towards something to be realized, becomes aimless and loses its
dynamics and coherence. This was also recognized in the emerging
ecumenical movement with its initial organizational forms that were
developed after 1910, the year of the World Missionary Conference at
Edinburgh that is generally considered the beginning of the modern
ecumenical movement. The reflection and clarification of forms of
Christian and church unity – "the unity we seek" – naturally became
part of the agenda of the Faith and Order movement whose mandate
was to identify doctrinal differences and agreements between the
churches and to prepare ways to promote closer Christian fellowship.

The first encounters, conversations, and texts in the movement on
Faith and Order after 1910 were marked by a diversity of ideas and
concepts concerning the form of Christian unity, the goal of the new
movement.[1]

(1) On the margin of the broad spectrum of such ideas was the
idea of an *invisible, spiritual unity* of all who believe in Jesus Christ
as Lord and Savior. This basically involved a reinterpretation of the
status quo of divided Christianity as a legitimate diversity of different
theological convictions and institutional forms in the framework of an
already existing unity. Pietistic-evangelical as well as liberal-Protestant
theologians saw here no necessity for overcoming divisive doctrinal
positions in favour of sufficient agreements and institutional convergences. This was, in fact, the picture of an undynamic, unhistorical,
and "painless" ecumenism. Today this view is put forwards in modified formulations by certain voices of ecumenical postmodernism that
advocate the accommodation of Christian division as an expression
of enriching Christian diversity.

(2) More seriously conceived was the idea of a *federation of churches*
that was among concepts of unity developed after 1910. Quite a number
of voices considered such federative organizations for practical cooperation to be a sufficient embodiment of Christian unity that could
also include intercommunion. The goal was a practical and spiritual

303

fellowship of Christians and churches. For their common mission with the Gospel among non-Christians and for their Christian witness and service in response to worldwide social and political problems after World War I, a federation was considered an adequate instrument of cooperation. Other voices considered a federation an expression of an already existing spiritual unity, but only as one provisional step on the way to visible unity.

(3) Forms of *intercommunion* or *eucharistic hospitality* or *eucharistic sharing* have also been explored as possible goals of, or steps towards, Christian unity. According to one position, the open or limited intercommunion or occasional one-sided or mutual sacramental fellowship on certain occasions or in certain situations were regarded as a sufficient expression of already existing spiritual communion. According to another position, sacramental fellowship was envisaged in a more comprehensive ecclesiological framework and regarded as a spiritual strengthening on the way towards forms of visible unity. Others, finally, viewed intercommunion only as an expression of achieved and lived unity.

(4) Anglican representatives in Faith and Order who exercised a major influence during the first decades after 1910 insisted on the concept of an *organic* or *corporate unity* or *union* of the churches. They did this on the basis of the four points of the "Chicago/Lambeth Quadrilaterals" of 1886 (Chicago) and 1888 (Lambeth). This concept was grounded on an understanding of the Church (influenced by late Romantic thinking) as a living, structured organism whose external institutional structures are an integral element of its inner nature. A reunion of the churches, therefore, could only be achieved on the basis of a common affirmation and acceptance of the fundamental elements of the faith and order or structure of the Church. Such a reunion had to include the organic and organizational merger of hitherto independent churches and the bringing together of their confessional and ecclesial identities in a new and common identity.

The conclusion of this first round of discussions and clarifications in Faith and Order was marked by the Second World Conference on Faith and Order 1937 at Edinburgh.[2] Here for the first time, a large ecumenical conference formulated concepts of unity in a formal way. Three "Conceptions of Church Unity" were described:

1. Co-operative Action

This rather general title referred to concepts of an alliance or con-federation of churches. Some participants considered "federal unions for co-operative actions" already as the final goal of the efforts for Christian unity or at least as "the most we should desire." The report, however, preferred to consider a federation in a wider perspective as a preparatory, provisional step on the way to intercommunion or corporate union. "Co-operative action in itself fails to manifest to the world the true character of the Church as one community of faith and worship, as well as of service."[3] This understanding of a federation that serves cooperation or enables further steps towards Christian unity had already been implemented before Edinburgh, for example by the Federal Council of the Churches of Christ in America in 1908, and since then in numerous local, national, and continental councils of churches or Christian councils, as well as in the WCC and as the organizational structure of the Christian World Communions

2. Intercommunion

Intercommunion, at that time the general term for different forms of eucharistic sharing, is presented in the Edinburgh report as the second concept.[4] It is initially described as "the fullest expression of a mutual recognition between two or more Churches." But the report also mentions intermediate steps of an occasional and open (one-sided or mutual) communion or the exceptional practice of intercommunion at special ecumenical occasions (as happened at Edinburgh). However, by referring to "sacramental intercommunion as a necessary part of any satisfactory Church unity," intercommunion was not regarded as a concept of unity on its own but as an element of the other two concepts (federation or organic unity). The difference in connecting intercom-munion with these concepts is that for organic unity, full sacramental fellowship was considered foundational, while for a federation it was seen as desirable but not as a condition.

3. Organic Unity or Corporate Union

Corporate union or organic unity is presented as a "third form in which the final goal of our movement may be expressed" and which would include "some measure of organizational union" of churches in the same territory.[5] Thus, the Anglican Quadrilateral had achieved a limited ecumenical acceptance and reception. According to this concept, church unity is only possible on the basis of a common affirmation and acceptance of all fundamental structural elements of the Church, namely on the basis of the normative authority of Holy Scripture, the essential role of the confessions of the Early Church, the inner spiritual life of the Church based on the sacraments instituted by Christ, and the historic episcopate in apostolic succession that serves this ecclesial structure. The presentation of this concept in the Edinburgh report indicates that this is no longer a purely formal listing of the four constitutive elements of the Quadrilateral of 1888. This concept was now rooted in history by relating it to the experience of an already given unity, to the reflection on the methods of ecumenical theological efforts, to the connection between unity and diversity, and to the mission of Christianity in the world. Thus, a Christian communion had entered the ecumenical movement with its own concept of church unity and has advocated it until today. This was one of the reasons why Faith and Order was strongly influenced by the Anglican concept of organic unity in the years between 1910 and 1937, and, as we shall see, this concept has continued to influence the ongoing ecumenical reflection on concepts of church unity.

2. Broad Acceptance of Concepts of Unity in Faith and Order between 1948 and 1978

Following the creation of the WCC at Amsterdam in 1948, the task and role of the new Commission on Faith and Order within the WCC was to conduct theological ecumenical studies under its own authority and to assist the WCC in dealing theologically with important themes and events. A significant step was undertaken by the Third World Conference on Faith and Order at Lund in 1952,[6] which initiated a change of ecumenical theological methodology. The conference declared that

we have seen clearly that we can make no real advance toward unity if we only compare our several conceptions of the nature of the Church and the traditions in which they are embodied. But once again it has been proved true that as we seek to draw closer to Christ we come closer to one another. We need,

> therefore, penetrate behind our divisions to a deeper and wider understanding of the mystery of the God-given union of Christ with His Church.[7]

The task, in other words, is to manifest the oneness that is already given in Jesus Christ. Accordingly, in the further work of Faith and Order, the phrase "gift and task" is often used as a basic orientation.

This methodological Christological approach of Lund is further developed in the Lund report by proceeding from the apostolic witness regarding Jesus Christ, the Lord of the Church:

> and in obedience to Him we seek to penetrate behind the divisions of the Church on earth to our common faith in the one Lord. From the unity of Christ we seek to understand the unity of the Church on earth.[8]

The tension is outlined that exists between the unity already given by God in Christ and the recognition that "we differ in our understanding of the character of the unity of the Church on earth for which we hope."[9] The underlying unity of life already given by God in Christ makes it possible to face the divisions penitently and to live courageously in a visible way in confronting together the needs of the world and thereby move to even deeper unity.[10]

Lund achieved a highly important theological step forwards in the history of Faith and Order by introducing a new methodology that helped to identify common biblical and Christological foundations and perspectives. This led to a close interrelation between ecclesiology and Christology and the affirmation of an already given unity in Christ that implies the mandate of its visible historical manifestation.

After Lund, Faith and Order's task to assist the WCC theologically was implemented in an exemplary way by the pre-formulation of the statement on the unity of the Church by the Third Assembly of the WCC at New Delhi in 1961.[11] The Assembly accepted such a statement for the first time by including in the section report on the unity of the Church a paragraph formulated at the meeting of the Commission on Faith and Order at St. Andrews in 1960.[12] It became the much-quoted New Delhi statement:

We believe that the unity of the Church which is both God's will and his gift to his Church is being made visible as all in each place who are baptized into Jesus Christ and confess him as Lord and Savior are brought by the Holy Spirit into one fully committed fellowship, holding the one apostolic faith, preaching the one Gospel, breaking the one bread, joining in common prayer, and having a corporate life reaching out in witness and service to all and who at the same time are united with the whole Christian fellowship in all places and all ages in such wise that ministry and members are accepted by all, and that all can act and speak together as occasion requires.[13]

This dense formulation, consisting of only one sentence, together with its often-ignored "Commentary upon This Picture of Unity," clearly expresses the binding theological standards of Faith and Order in contrast to all activist or naïve-optimistic invocations of unity at that time – and throughout the history of the ecumenical movement. The goal is not to recreate or create Christian unity. Rather, unity as God's gift and task is to be made visible, and this not simply in a general way but including all Christians in all places and in a recognizably structured form that requires renewal and change. Into this unity are brought those who have been called by the Holy Spirit and baptized in Jesus Christ and confess him as Lord and Savior. Baptism and confession of Christ are presuppositions of such unity. Christians are led not on their own initiative, we might conclude, but by the Holy Spirit into a "fully committed fellowship." They do not become members of a colourful and joyful community of good will but of a community (here the term "koinonia" is already used) that is engaged in a faithful, spiritually and morally inspired life.[14]

The foundation and connecting bonds of such a community of Christians and churches, grounded in Holy Scripture and the Tradition of the faith of the Church, is the confession of the one apostolic faith, the proclamation of the one Gospel, the communion in the eucharist, in prayer, and a common life that is open to other people and the world in witnessing to the faith and in loving service.[15] In order that such a united community becomes possible, theological dialogue efforts to overcome doctrinal differences, agreement (consensus), and steps of the churches towards such unity are necessary. As a further basic element of church unity, the mutual recognition of ministries and members and the joint action and speaking in response to God's calling are again emphasized.[16]

New Delhi's statement on unity has as its perspective still the concept of an organic unity and unification in each place. "Place" is understood as a local congregation, but mainly as a diocese and national church.[17] New Delhi laid the basis and provided the direction for further considerations and statements on the unity of the Church by defining the constitutive elements and their implications for visible unity: agreement on and acceptance of the one apostolic faith, communion in baptism and the eucharist, mutual recognition of members and ministries, fellowship in proclamation, worship, and service in the world. Such organic unity is not sought for its own sake but extends in witness and service to all people. Thus, an important stimulating guidance for further work was formulated at New Delhi.

The understanding of the theological foundations that were binding for the thinking in Faith and Order were deepened and further developed after Lund and New Delhi by another world conference, the Fourth World Conferences on Faith and Order at Montreal in 1963.[18] The unity of the Church was not included as a separate item on the agenda and proceedings of this conference. Rather, the conference considered the presuppositions and criteria – the binding theological standards – for ecumenical reflection. A well-known outcome of this effort is formulated in the report of Section II on "Scripture, Tradition and Traditions."[19] Based on its hermeneutical approach to the criteria and fundamentals of Christian faith and teaching, the report proposes a distinction between *Tradition* (capital T), which is the Gospel itself; *tradition*, which is the traditionary process or the handing on of Tradition; and *traditions*, which are the different forms of Christian expression or the various confessional or ecclesial traditions.[20] This differentiation helps to affirm the close interrelation between Scripture and Tradition and to overcome their frequent opposition.

Thus we can say that we exist as Christians by the Tradition of the Gospel (the *paradosis* of the *kerygma*), testified in Scripture, transmitted in and by the Church through the power of the Holy Spirit. Tradition taken in this sense is actualized in the preaching of the Word, in the administration of the Sacraments and worship, in Christian teaching and theology, and in mission and witness to Christ by the lives of the members of the Church.[21]

Tradition in its written form as Holy Scripture must be constantly interpreted by the Church in confessions of faith, liturgical forms of the sacraments, the proclamation of the Word, and theological expositions of the doctrine of the Church.[22]

Since the declarations on the unity of the Church affirm the agreement in the apostolic faith as an essential condition, Montreal contains important perspectives of how this is to be understood. The differentiating consideration on the relation of Scripture, Tradition and traditions is one major example of the multifaceted theological work in Montreal. This is relevant for the elaboration of common foundations for the dialogue on the visible unity of the Church as well as for the realization of already possible and necessary forms of common Christian witness and service.

The concept of unity formulated at New Delhi in 1961 was broadened by the Fourth Assembly of the WCC at Uppsala in 1968 that integrated insights of Montreal.[23] The Assembly again called upon the churches to continue to seek the unity of all Christians in a common profession of the faith, in the observance of baptism and the eucharist, and in recognition of a ministry of the whole Church."[24] This perspective was more explicitly connected than at New Delhi with an emphasis on the universal dimension of Christian unity: "In a time when human interrelatedness is so evident, it is the more imperative to make visible the bonds which unite Christians in universal fellowship."[25] Taking up studies by Faith and Order since 1964 on councils and conciliarity,[26] as well as influenced by the vision of universal history so typical of Uppsala, the Assembly looked forwards to "eventually actualizing a truly universal, ecumenical, conciliar form of common life and witness." The WCC member churches are called "to work for the time when a genuinely universal council may once more speak for all Christians and lead the way into the future."[27] Uppsala combined its universally oriented concept of unity, based on Scripture and Tradition, with the perspective that was born out of the spirit of the 1960s of intertwining the unity of the Church and the unity of humankind. Accordingly, it stated slightly optimistically, "The Church is bold in speaking of itself as the sign of the coming unity of mankind."[28]

As a consequence of this new perspective, a Faith and Order study from 1969 to 1974 on the unity of the Church and the unity of humankind struggled with the lack of clarity that is inherent in this topic. This made it impossible to arrive at concluding results. However, the theme of the relationship between the efforts towards the unity of the Church and the engagement of the churches in society was again taken up from 1982 onwards in the form of a Faith and Order study project with the more narrow and precise theme "The Unity of the Church and the Renewal of Human Community."[29] In this study, the position of Faith and Order that the efforts for the visible unity of the Church have necessarily to be interrelated with the common Christian witness in proclamation and practical action within the wider human community was developed in a much more extensively argued way than before. The work for the renewal of human community, we may interpret the thesis of the text, is not just an appendix or implication of the work for church unity but an integral part of it. Accordingly, "In the unity which is God's gift and in their struggle to manifest that unity (oneness), the churches within the ecumenical movement are called to contribute to the efforts towards unity and reconciliation within the human community."[30]

It is important to note that the reflection on the unity of the Church was undertaken in Faith and Order since Uppsala with the official participation of Roman Catholic theologians. Thus, the spectrum of insights was considerably enlarged and the theological investigation on unity has become much more representative of world Christianity.

Results and impulses of this work as well as the studies on councils and conciliarity from 1964 to 1974 – in which for the first time we find an intensive consideration of *reception* in the context of conciliarity – are included in the work of a consultation of Faith and Order in 1973 at Salamanca on "Concepts of Unity and Models of Union."[31] One year later, the report of the Faith and Order Commission meeting at Accra in 1974[32] carries on the concept of organic union by combining it with the new perspective of conciliarity: "The concept of conciliarity is thus not an alternative to that of organic union but rather a way of describing one aspect of a truly organic union at every level from the local to the universal."[33] One section on "The Unity of the Church – Next Steps" of the report of the 1973 Salamanca consultation became two years later the central part of the section report of the WCC Assembly at Nairobi in 1976[34] on "What Unity Requires." In this text, New Delhi's more locally oriented concept of organic unity together with its constitutive elements is connected with Uppsala's accentuated universal view of unity as well as with the new considerations on conciliarity as a structural element of the church and its unity. The report states: "The one Church is to be envisioned as a conciliar fellowship of local churches which are themselves truly united."[35] Then, proceeding from the mutual recognition of the churches as "belonging to the same Church of Christ" within the conciliar fellowship, the basic elements of unity are again enumerated ending with the universal perspective in which sister churches express their relationship "in conciliar gatherings whenever required for the fulfilment of their common calling."[36] Here, too, it is clear that the idea of an organic unity continues to be the presupposition and goal: The term conciliar fellowship "does not look towards a conception of unity different from that full organic unity sketched in the New Delhi statement, but is rather a further elaboration of it."[37] This emphasis was already signalled in the Salamanca report of 1973:

> The unity described in the preceding section requires union of the churches which are still separated today. There is no contradiction between the vision of a conciliar fellowship of local churches and the goal of organic union ... The conciliar fellowship requires organic union. [A union will gather up] into one body the various confessional traditions of the past.[38]

However, the firm insistence on organic union still expressed at Nairobi was changed at the next Faith and Order Commission meeting at Bangalore in 1978.[39] Here, suddenly, a broader perspective was opened up when the report of the meeting stated for the first time:

> Many say that true unity requires the gathering of all in each place into one eucharistic community; there would be no room for a continuing life of the confessional traditions. Others say that unity according to Christ's will does not necessarily require

the disappearance but rather the transformation of confessional identities to such a degree that unity in full sacramental fellowship, common witness and service, together with some common structural/institutional expression becomes possible. While the first view is rather connected with the concept of 'organic unity', the second is held by those proposing the concept 'unity in reconciled diversity'. The two concepts are not to be seen as alternatives. They may be two different ways of reacting to the ecumenical necessities and possibilities of different situations and of different church traditions.[40]

Here the concern of the new and strong ecumenical voice represented by the Christian World Communions was acknowledged.

Between 1937 and 1978, Faith and Order maintained its commitment to serious theological reflection in the midst of multiple theological, ecclesiastical, and ecumenical considerations and fashions. In this way, it gained respect in the ecumenical and theological community. After 1978, Faith and Order concentrated on the preparation of the convergence texts on *Baptism, Eucharist and Ministry* (Lima, 1982),[41] the studies on "Towards the Common Expression of the Apostolic Faith Today" (1978-1991),[42] and on the relation between the unity of the Church and the renewal of human community (see above). In these studies, the theme of the unity of the Church is also present as the broader framework and perspective, but it was only in 1990 that the unity of the Church appeared again as a specific topic on the agenda of Faith and Order and the WCC.

3. A New Step: The Unity of the Church as Koinonia

Even before Nairobi in 1975, a new phase in the overall ecumenical reflection on the unity of the Church was initiated by the growing number of bilateral theological dialogues between Christian World Communions, including the Roman Catholic Church. The broad participation of the Catholic and Orthodox churches in these dialogues and the re-emerged appreciation of continuing confessional identities have led to new ecclesiological emphases and concepts of the unity of the Church such as unity in reconciled diversity, church fellowship, koinonia/communion, communion of communions, and communion of sister churches. These concepts usually integrate the already traditional and constitutive elements of "organic unity" and "conciliar fellowship" but do not maintain that the implementation of visible unity should also include an organizational merger of churches. On this background and as a result of the ongoing reflection in Faith and Order, two consultations in 1990 at Etchmiadzin, Armenia, and Dunblane, Scotland, developed a new draft text on the unity of the Church. The text was discussed, modified, and adopted by the Seventh Assembly of the WCC at Canberra in 1991.[43]

The Canberra statement on "The Unity of the Church as Koinonia – Gift and Calling" stands in obvious continuity with earlier statements, especially concerning the list of the essential elements of visible unity. But it integrates its formulations into a broader theological and historical framework and contributes new perspectives. In leading up to the central affirmations of the "unity formula" of Canberra, the report, first, commences with a much more comprehensive approach and framework than earlier statements. It proceeds from the vision of the saving action of the Triune God in relation to humanity and creation with the goal to bring "all into communion with God" (Eph. 1). The calling of the Church is described more explicitly than before, for example, the "church is the foretaste of this communion with God and with one another." It is called to make visible the communion of the people in Christ and in the Holy Spirit, to be an instrument of reconciliation and healing, to overcome division and "to live as sign of the reign of God and servant of the reconciliation with God, promised and provided for the whole creation" (no. 1.1).

Second, the Church's mission and service in the world are much more clearly integrated into this salvation-historical ecclesiological approach. But it is also admitted that the sinful divisions of the churches damage the credibility of their witness and even contradict their very nature (no. 1.2). And yet, third, the new relationships of the churches in the ecumenical movement are acknowledged with gratitude. They make it possible "to recognize a certain degree of communion already existing between them." But again, a note of realism prevents naïve optimism by stating that the churches have failed to draw consequences for their lives from the communion and agreements they have already achieved (no. 1.3). After this integration of the goal of Christian unity into the history of the Triune God with creation, humanity, Church and ecumenical movement, the report proceeds, fourth, to its central statement on the visible unity of the Church. This is done, in addition to the traditional and ambivalent term "unity," with the help of the term "koinonia" that has become more and more prominent in recent decades. The decisive section, a kind of "unity formula" of Canberra, describes the basic conditions and forms of koinonia or full communion:

> The unity of the church to which we are called is a koinonia given and expressed in the common confession of the apostolic faith; a common sacramental life entered by the one baptism and celebrated together in one eucharistic fellowship; a common life in which members and ministries are mutually recognized and reconciled; and a common mission witnessing to the gospel of God's grace to all people and serving the whole creation. The goal of the search for full communion is realized when all the churches are able to recognize in one another the one, holy, catholic and apostolic church in its fullness. This full communion will be expressed on the local and the universal levels through conciliar forms of life and action. In such communion churches are bound in all aspects of their life together at all levels in confessing the one faith and engaging in worship and witness, deliberation and action (no. 2.1).

This formula reflects a significant evolution and, I believe, a great progress in the clarification of the theological criteria and foundations of a vision of visible unity. Already recognizable in the opening paragraphs of the statement, the comprehensive horizon is now also expressed in the "unity formula" itself and its communion-ecclesiology. The influential role of this ecclesiology is partly due to the contributions of Roman Catholic and Orthodox theologians in Faith and Order. This ecclesiology serves as the framework in which the individual statements are held together and related to each other (for example those on local and universal, or unity and diversity). In describing full communion, the four classical marks of the Church are for the first time included. It is in the mutual recognition of the presence of these marks that the goal of the search for full communion will have been reached – but on the basis of and together with the earlier mentioned fundamental agreements on faith, the sacraments and ministries, witness and service. Possible institutional forms of such a communion are left open and are no longer oriented towards an organic union.

Fifth, and this is also a new element, the Canberra statement is further broadened by referring to the connection between unity and diversity: "Diversities which are rooted in theological traditions, various cultural, ethnic or historical contexts are integral to the nature of communion." However, such diversity is not legitimate "when, for instance, it makes impossible the common confession of Jesus Christ as God and Saviour" and of the salvation of humanity as proclaimed in Holy Scripture and preached by the apostolic community (no. 2.2). This is a first careful outline of the connection between unity and diversity that needs further clarification. Sixth and finally, the Assembly challenges all churches to draw consequences for their relationships from the theological convergences that have been achieved in Faith and Order studies, for example in view of mutual recognition of baptism, already possible forms of eucharistic hospitality, steps towards mutual recognition of ministries and towards a renewed commitment to justice, peace, and the integrity of creation (nos. 3.1 and 3.2).

The less than two pages of the Canberra statement represent the most concise, clear, and comprehensive statement of the visible unity of the Church coming from Faith and Order and the WCC so far. This statement was accepted by official representatives of all major Christian traditions and thus enjoys potentially a broad recognition that deserves much wider attention. It presents (1) impulses and guidelines for further theological ecumenical reflection[44] and, most importantly, (2) its main elements and thrusts are foundational (in most cases without reference) for recent decisions of churches to enter into full communion.[45]

Concerning further theological ecumenical reflection in Faith and Order, the report of the Fifth World Conference on Faith and Order at Santiago de Compostela in 1993 could be regarded as a broad, detailed interpretation and development of the basic ideas of the unity formula of Canberra.[46] Its three foundational pillars – common faith, common sacramental and spiritual life, and common witness – accordingly guide and inform the themes of the section reports of Compostela: "Confessing the One Faith to God's Glory"; "Sharing a Common Life in Christ"; and "Called to Common Witness for a Renewed World." Having as their background the report of the first section on "The Understanding of Koinonia and Its Implications," these three section reports develop their themes in the form of biblical, historical, and systematic arguments, including the description both of still existing and dividing differences and of the progress that ecumenical theological dialogue has made in recent decades. The section reports also present further explications of their themes in relation to the diverse cultural and social contexts of the present world, and they identify issues that need further study, dialogue, and agreement. The report of Santiago de Compostela thus presents a broad elucidation of the concept of visible unity prepared by Faith and Order and adopted especially by the Assemblies of the WCC in New Delhi, Nairobi, and Canberra. A wealth of material for further study and steps toward greater unity is here available.

The same conclusion also applies to a similar effort by Faith and Order to continue the reflection on and clarification of concepts of Christian unity. We find this in the new Faith and Order study on *The Nature and Mission of the Church*,[47] the long awaited ecclesiology study that is modestly subtitled "A Stage on the Way to a Common Statement." The new text of 2005, based on an earlier draft publication of 1998, seeks to bring together and integrate into a systematic ecclesiological presentation the results and insights of Faith and Order studies (in some cases by including quotations that are not identified as such).[48] These references are a kind of reception by Faith and Order of its own theological history and signify an awareness of continuity that is part of its methodology. The text does not contain a separate and systematic thesis on the unity of the church. Rather it describes in several places in more detail the basic convictions about the unity of the church as last presented at Canberra in 1991. For example, the Canberra statement is quoted in paragraph 66 on the realization of the goal of the search for full communion. Further considerations are added. For example, following paragraph 63 in the boxes with the (misleading) title "Limits of Diversity?" three different models of a structural implementation of visible unity are sketched. Though this is helpful for further discussion, nevertheless, it should be possible to move some steps beyond a simple description and to outline convergences. A systematic statement on the unity of the Church could be central to the preparation of a convergence text on the nature and mission of the Church.[49]

A further implication of Faith and Order's concepts of unity is their historical impact. The test of all ecumenical agreements is *reception*, which is their impact on theological and ecclesial history. Do they influence this history and do they even help to change this history? There is no question that the statements on concepts of Christian unity discussed and worked out by Faith and Order during the last eighty years have influenced ecumenical studies and reflection in general. A specific and historical impact of these concepts of unity can be found in recent decisions of churches to enter into relationships of full communion. These decisions are based on statements that formulate agreement in faith, agreement on sacramental theology and fellowship, agreement enabling recognition and reconciliation of ministries including the office of bishops in apostolic succession, and agreement on a common commitment to joint witness and service. These agreements and the decisions based on them that enable full communion include concrete consequences, for example, mutual participation in episcopal consecrations, exchangeability of ministries, full and reciprocal eucharistic sharing, common conciliar deliberations and exchanges, recognition of diversity of historical and confessional identities and church structures, practical cooperation and forms of theological and spiritual sharing.

On these lines the Faith and Order statements on the visible unity of the Church clearly contributed to the following declarations of full communion: (1) between most of the Lutheran, Reformed and United churches in Europe in the Leuenberg Agreement of 1973[50]; (2) between the Evangelical Lutheran Church in America and three Presbyterian and Reformed churches in the USA (1997)[51]; (3) between all Anglican churches in Great Britain and Ireland and most Lutheran churches in Northern Europe in the *Porvoo Common Statement* of 1992[52]; (4) between the ELCA and the Moravian Church in America in 1999 and 2000[53]; (5) between the Episcopal Church in the USA and the ELCA in 2001[54]; and (6) between the Anglican Church of Canada and the Evangelical Lutheran Church in Canada in 2001.[55]

4. Conclusion

In a church historical perspective, the last one hundred years stand out as a reversal of the many centuries before that were darkened and torn by Christian divisions, conflicts, and controversies. The new era of church history is deeply marked by the ecumenical movement that has received strong impulses and important orientations from the Movement and Commission on Faith and Order since 1910. Faith and Order, since 1948 part of the WCC and since 1968 with an official membership that includes Roman Catholic theologians, has significantly contributed by its theological work to changed relationships between Christians and churches. In the framework of Faith and Order's general impact on theological thinking and church relationships, the concentrated and continuous effort to envisage the conditions and contours of the "unity we seek" has been at the centre. The abundant material that is the fruit of this effort so far in the form of Faith and Order studies, consultations, Commission meetings, and World Conferences has been summarized and ordered in its outlines in this article. This has been done in the hope of filling a gap and of strengthening the "ecumenical memory." May Faith and Order's work, inspired by the Holy Spirit and solid theological minds, continue to provide direction and encouragement in the common ecumenical task of envisioning and furthering the visible unity of the churches.

---

1 Cf. Tissington Tatlow, "The World Conference on Faith and Order," ch. 9 in Ruth Rouse and Stephen Charles Neill, ed., *A History of the Ecumenical Movement 1517-1948*, 3rd. ed. (Geneva: WCC, 1986), especially pp. 420-41. For this survey up to 1937 I have also used Günther Gassmann, *Konzeptionen der Einheit in der Bewegung für Glauben und Kirchenverfassung 1910-1937* (Göttingen: Vandenhoeck & Ruprecht, 1979), pp. 291-97.

2 Leonard Hodgson, ed., *The Second World Conference on Faith and Order, held at Edinburgh, August 3-18, 1937* (London: SCM Press, 1938), pp. 220-69, in DH 1, pp. 40-74.

3 *Edinburgh 1937*, p. 251, in DH 1, p. 62.

4 *Edinburgh 1937*, pp. 251-52, in DH 1, pp. 62-63.

5 *Edinburgh 1937*, pp. 252-57, in DH 1, pp. 63-67.

6 Oliver S. Tomkins, ed., *The Third World Conference on Faith and Order, Lund, August 15th to 28th, 1952* (London: SCM, 1953), pp. 11-65, in DH 1, pp. 85-130.

7 *Lund*, p. 15, in DH 1, pp. 85-86.

8 *Lund*, p. 18, in DH 1, p. 88.

9 *Lund*, pp. 33-34, in DH 1, pp. 103-4.

10 *Lund*, pp. 60-65, in DH 1, pp. 125-30.

11 W. A. Visser't Hooft, ed., *The New Delhi Report: The Third Assembly of the World Council of Churches 1961* (London: SCM, 1962), pp. 116-22, in DH 1, pp. 144-50.

12 *Minutes of the Faith and Order Commission 1960, St. Andrews, Scotland*, Faith and Order paper 31 (Geneva: WCC, 1960), p. 113.

13 *New Delhi*, p. 116, in DH 1, pp. 144-45.

14 *New Delhi*, pp. 117-22, in DH 1,p p. 145-50.

15 *New Delhi*, pp. 120-21, in DH 1, pp. 148-49.

16 *New Delhi*, pp. 121-22, in DH 1, pp. 149-50.

17 *New Delhi*, p. 118, in DH 1, p. 147.

18 *The Fourth World Conference on Faith and Order, Montreal 1963*, Faith and Order paper 42, ed. P.C. Rodger and L. Vischer (London: SCM, 1964), pp. 50-61, in DH 2, pp. 10-18.

19 *Montreal*, pp. 50-61, in DH 2, pp. 10-18.

20 *Montreal*, p. 50, in DH 2, p. 10.

21 *Montreal*, p. 52, in DH 2, p. 11.

22 *Montreal*, p. 53, in DH 2, p. 12.

23 Norman Goodall, ed., *The Uppsala Report 1968*, Official Report of the Fourth Assembly of the World Council of Churches, Uppsala, July 4-20, 1968 (Geneva: WCC, 1968), esp. pp. 12-18. Also in *Uppsala 68 Speaks*, Section Reports (Geneva: WCC, 1968).

24 *Uppsala*, p. 17.

25 *Uppsala*, p. 17.

26 Survey and texts in DH 2, pp. 203 and 209-39, cf. also *Councils and the Ecumenical Movement*, World Council Studies 5 (Geneva: WCC, 1968); report again in DH 2, pp. 209-17. Cf. also the important contribution of the West German Ecumenical Study Committee on *Councils, Conciliarity and a Genuinely Universal Council*, Faith and Order paper 70, *Study Encounter*, 10, no. 2 (1974).

27 *Uppsala*, p. 17.

28 *Uppsala*, p. 17.

29 Commission on Faith and Order, *Church and World: The Unity of the Church and the Renewal of Human Community*. Faith and Order paper 151 (Geneva: WCC, 1990).

30 *Church and World*, p. 36.

31 Commission on Faith and Order, "The Unity of the Church: Next Steps," Report of the Salamanca Consultation on 'Concepts of Unity' and 'Models of Union,' September 1973, in *What Kind of Unity?* Faith and Order paper 69 (Geneva: WCC, 1974), pp. 119-31; *Ecumenical Review* 26, no. 2 (1974): 291-303, in DH 2, pp. 35-44.

32 Commission on Faith and Order, *Accra 1974: Uniting in Hope*, Faith and Order paper 72 (Geneva: WCC, 1975), pp. 110-23, in DH 2, pp. 50-66.

33 *Accra*, p. 115, in DH 2, p. 54.

34 David M. Paton, ed., *Breaking Barriers, Nairobi 1975*, The Official Report of the Fifth Assembly of the World Council of Churches, Nairobi, 23 November-10 December, 1975 (London: SPCK; Grand Rapids: Eerdmans, 1976), p. 60, in DH 2, p. 3.

35 *Nairobi*, p. 60, in DH 2, p. 3.

36 *Nairobi*, p. 60, in DH 2, p. 3.

37 *Accra*, p. 60.

38 *What Kind of Unity?* pp. 123-24, in DH 2, pp. 40-41.

39 Commission on Faith and Order, *Sharing in One Hope*, Reports and documents from the meeting of the Faith and Order Commission, 15-30 August 1978, Ecumenical Christian Centre, Bangalore, India, Faith and Order paper 92 (Geneva: WCC, 1978).

40 *Bangalore*, p. 240, in DH 2, p. 78.

41 Commission on Faith and Order, *Baptism, Eucharist and Ministry*, Faith and Order paper 111 (Geneva: WCC, 1982).

42 *Confessing the One Faith. An Ecumenical Explication of the Apostolic Faith as it is Confessed in the Nicene-Constantinopolitan Creed (381)*, Faith and Order paper 153 (Geneva: WCC, 1991).

43 *Signs of the Spirit: Official Report, Seventh Assembly of the WCC, Canberra, Australia, 7-20 February 1991* (Geneva: WCC; Grand Rapids: Eerdmans, 1991), pp. 172-74. Together with my colleague John Radano, I have put together a Study Document for the Joint Working Group between the Roman Catholic Church and the World Council of Churches on *The Unity of the Church as Koinonia: Ecumenical Perspectives on the 1991 Canberra Statement on Unity*, Faith and Order paper 163 (Geneva: WCC, 1993). Furthermore, John Radano and I wrote its section on "The Canberra Statement in Historical Perspective," pp. 4-9.

44 "The statement, therefore, sets a new stage for the continuing reflection on the nature of the unity we seek." Gassmann and Radano, eds., *The Unity of the Church as Koinonia*, note 15, p. 9.

45 Editor's note: Delegates at the WCC 9th Assembly in Porto Alegre, Brazil, adopted a further statement inviting the churches to continue their journey together, as a further step towards full visible unity. *Called to be One Church: An Invitation to the Churches to Renew their Commitment to the Search for Unity and to Deepen their Dialogue* [The Porto Alegre Ecclesiology Text], in *God, in Your Grace...: Official Report of the Ninth Assembly of the World Council of Churches*, ed. Luis N. Rivera-Pagán (Geneva: WCC, 2007), pp. 255-61, in GA III, pp. 606-10.

46 Thomas F. Best and Günther Gassmann, ed., *On the Way to Fuller Koinonia*. Official Report of the Fifth World Conference on Faith and Order (Geneva: WCC, 1994), p. 228.

47 *The Nature and Mission of the Church. A Stage on the Way to a Common Statement*, Faith and Order paper 198 (Geneva: WCC, 2005).

48 For example, nos. 66, 71 or 88.

49 Editor's note: The convergence statement which brought the current phase of the Faith and Order ecclesiology study to a conclusion was circulated to the WCC member churches for study and formal response in September 2012. *The Church: Towards a Common Vision*. Faith and Order paper 214 (Geneva: WCC, 2013).

50 *Konkordie reformatorischer Kirchen in Europa: Agreement between Reformation Churches in Europe* (Frankfurt am Main: Lembeck, 1993).

51 Keith F. Nickle and Timothy F. Lull, eds., *A Common Calling. The Witness of the Reformation Churches in North America Today* (Minneapolis: Augsburg, 1993); and *Formula of Agreement between the Evangelical Lutheran Church in America, the Presbyterian Church (U.S.A.), the Reformed Church in America and the United Church of Christ on entering into full communion on the basis of "A Common Calling,"* (1997); pcusa.org.

52 *The Porvoo Common Statement*, Conversations between the British and Irish Anglican Churches and the Nordic and Baltic Lutheran Churches (London: Council for Christian Unity of the General Synod of the Church of England, 1993).

53 *Following Our Shepherd to Full Communion*, Report of the Lutheran-Moravian Dialogue with Recommendations for Full Communion in Worship, Fellowship and Mission (Chicago: Evangelical Lutheran Church in America, 1998).

54 *Called to Common Mission: A Lutheran Proposal for the Revision of the Concordat of Agreement* (Chicago: Evangelical Lutheran Church in America, 1998).

55 *Called to Full Communion: The Waterloo Declaration* (Waterloo: Anglican Church of Canada, 2001).

✝ CHAPTER 16

From Mutual Recognition to Mutual Accountability: A Next Step for the Ecumenical Movement[1]

by Thomas F. Best

It is a privilege and a pleasure to write in recognition of Monsignor John Radano's contributions to the life and work of Faith and Order, to the World Council of Churches, and to the cause of the unity of the Church. This *Festschrift* offers a welcome opportunity to thank Monsignor Radano for his many years of service as liaison between the Pontifical Council for Promoting Christian Unity of the Catholic Church and the Faith and Order Commission of the World Council of Churches. It is fitting that the following lines should refer at some points to the experience and reflection of the United and Uniting churches and discussions between Christian World Communions as well as between certain churches at the national level, for John Radano has made important contributions in both contexts. For example, he served as the Catholic observer at several of the International Consultations of United and Uniting Churches – and indeed preached during one of the daily worships at Consultations in Ocho Rios, Jamaica, in 1995 and Driebergen, The Netherlands, in 2002.[2] He has been instrumental in crafting, and tireless in promoting, the "Joint Declaration on the Doctrine of Justification" agreed by the Lutheran World Federation and the Catholic Church.[3] And in recent years, he has been a valued partner in developing the idea of mutual accountability as a pathway forwards for the ecumenical movement.[4]

My aim in the following is to suggest that *mutual accountability* is a decisive dimension of the church and the churches' relationships with one another and to suggest that it should become a major theme for the churches in their life and work. As mutual accountability is fundamentally an ecclesiological issue, this discussion will begin with a review of some relevant ecclesiological issues and trends within the ecumenical movement, then show how these lead directly to the notion of mutual accountability as a next stage on the churches' ecumenical journey.

I. Theology, Ecclesiology, and the Relationship of the Churches

Early sources of the modern ecumenical movement, such as the overseas mission context and lay initiatives such as the Sunday school movement, more often appealed for Christian cooperation on practical grounds – theological and ecclesiological debates being considered sources of division rather than reconciliation. Yet ecclesiological themes have been central to ecumenism from the early 20th century on, as embodied not least in the early work of Faith and Order (Lausanne, 1927) but also through bilateral dialogues (the Bonn Agreement, 1931) and church unions (Canada, 1925; Thailand, 1934). Several enduring themes were identified from the beginning of ecumenical ecclesiological reflection; these included in particular the questions of the nature of the church, the nature of the unity of the church, and the relationship between the church and "the world," including the relation of "non-theological" (e.g. historical, cultural, and social) factors to ecclesiological reflection. All these themes had been identified as central to the search for Christian unity by the time of, for example, the second world conference on Faith and Order (Edinburgh, 1937).[5]

As the ecumenical movement took more concrete form at the global level, a further group of questions became both more evident and more pointed: questions about the relationship of the churches with one another. The 147 churches which formed the World Council of Churches (WCC) at Amsterdam in 1948 did so on the basis of a common acceptance of "our Lord Jesus Christ as God and Saviour." But as the diverse churches experienced life as members of a common, visible fellowship, they found themselves confronted by fundamental questions about the ecclesiological implications of membership in such an organization as the WCC. For example, how far are individual member churches bound by statements made by the WCC as a whole? And, perhaps most pointedly, how far does membership in the WCC imply that a particular church recognizes other WCC members as "churches" in their own full understanding of the term?

These issues were addressed in 1950, just two short years after the founding of the WCC, in the famous "Toronto Declaration." This is now remembered more for its negative than its positive statements. But it is important to note that Toronto insisted that since Christ is the "divine head of the body," membership in the one Church of Christ necessarily "is more inclusive than the membership of their own [e.g., each particular] church body." Thus, *the wholeness of Christ's body* is the fundamental ecclesiological affirmation, within which the more familiar negative statements of Toronto must be read – particularly the clarification that membership in the WCC "does not imply that each church must regard the other member churches as churches in the true and full sense of the word."[6]

From the beginning, and more so as a wider range of churches sought entrance, discussions had been held towards a more expansive theological basis for the WCC. In order more fully to express the faith of the member churches, within fifteen years explicit references to the Trinity and to the Scriptures were added to the WCC's Basis.[7] With these theological expansions, the Basis of the WCC has, by and large, stood the test of time (though in recent years there has been a renewed discussion about adding an explicit reference to baptism). In contrast, the ecclesiological issues raised by WCC membership have not finally been resolved. Indeed, they have resurfaced explicitly in the discussions about Orthodox participation in the WCC, not least in the distinction drawn between churches which understand themselves as a normative expression of the Church, and those which understand themselves as one among several, fully valid expressions of the Church.[8]

But although this matter has not been settled, it is essential to note what still remains from the Toronto discussion in 1950: the insistence that the Church, the body of Christ, is one and the churches are members together of that one body. As we shall see, this has deep implications for the notion of mutual accountability.

II. Comparison, Convergence, and Koinonia

A. *The Goal and Method of Dialogue: From Comparison to Convergence*

The above discussion needs to be complemented by a review of the methods which have been used in ecumenical theological and ecclesiological work. There is general agreement that this work has been characterized by a shift from *comparison* to *convergence*. Until about the mid-twentieth century, the challenge was in winning increased understanding among the churches, separated as they were by decades – indeed centuries – of separation and suspicion. Dialogues focused on the churches informing others about their own beliefs, practices, and ethos in order to foster mutual understanding and respect.

This "comparative" method is still necessary and helpful as new partners enter the ecumenical dialogue. For churches which are still learning about one another's fundamental beliefs and identities, it represents an essential first stage on the ecumenical journey. Yet its role as the paramount paradigm for ecumenical dialogue ended with the third world conference on Faith and Order at Lund in 1952. Even as he celebrated the achievements of the method of "comparative ecclesiology," then Faith and Order Commission Secretary Oliver Tomkins insisted on the need to move beyond it:

> As a result of forty years of patient and careful work, there now exists a considerable literature setting forth the distinctive theological convictions of the main Christian traditions... I would yet suggest that we who are called by our churches to work at the heart of this enterprise have reached a limit in what can be profitably done in mutual explanation.[9]

Lund went on to lay out the famous "Lund Principle," stated originally as a question:

> A faith in the one Church of Christ which is not implemented by *acts* of obedience is dead. There are truths about the nature of God and His Church which will remain for ever closed to us unless we act together in obedience to the unity which is already ours... Should not our churches ask themselves...

whether they should not act together in all matters except those in which deep differences of conviction compel them to act separately?[10]

With one stroke the terms of ecumenical engagement were shifted: it is the churches' "acting together" – including engaging in common theological and ecclesiological reflection – which should be the norm, with separate action and reflection by the churches a reluctant last resort. It is important to understand that this conviction was not an expression of an "ecumenical activism"; rather it resulted from an understanding of the body of Christ as one, with its members called to a common faith, life, and witness.

Such an approach meant that the focus was no longer on what Tomkins called "the distinctive theological convictions" of the particular churches, but on *what the churches could say together* about the Church. The approach focuses on aspects of confession and practice on which the churches already agree, enabling them to speak with one voice. Further, the churches' common conviction that – despite their differences in understanding and practice – fundamentally they share the same faith enables them to explore together the areas in which they continue to differ. Where they disagree, churches hold to their convictions yet continue in the search for a common understanding of the faith which transcends their differences. Thus, this approach does not result in a "lowest-common-denominator" ecclesiology; indeed, the By-Laws of the Faith and Order Commission specify that "differences are to be clarified and recorded as honestly as agreements."[11] It is precisely such clarification that enables the churches to address their remaining differences effectively together.

This dynamic of *rapprochement* has led to this being called the "convergence" method. Through this approach, the churches have gained a new awareness of the degree to which they hold together certain ecclesial convictions; and they have been encouraged to appreciate the convictions of others. In some cases, churches have developed or re-evaluated their theological and ecclesiological positions, based on their experience of dialogue with others. In some cases, churches have discovered, through re-examining apparently divisive terms and formulations that, in fact, they share a common faith. The best-known recent example of this, and a key result of recent dialogues, is seen in the Eastern Orthodox-Oriental Orthodox dialogue:

> In the light of our four unofficial consultations (1964, 1967, 1970, 1971) and our three official meetings which followed on (1985, 1989, 1990), we have understood that both families have loyally maintained the authentic Orthodox christological doctrine, and the unbroken continuity of the apostolic tradition, though they may have used christological terms in different ways.[12]

It must be stressed that this method proceeds (indeed lives) from the living, personal engagement of those who are entrusted with representing the various churches in their dialogues. At dialogue meetings, agreements and differences are stated, possible ways forwards are tried out, failures are acknowledged – all within a context of growing trust fostered by a common experience of work, meals, and sharing on both professional and personal levels. And, within this context, common worship plays a key role, insofar as the dialogue partners are able to share in it. Thus, over the course of a successful dialogue the participants develop a commitment to the common work, and to one another within the framework of the work. Of course, this personal dimension does not in itself guarantee the success of a dialogue. The dialogue results must be coherent and compelling in their own right, all the more so since the direct experience of the dialogue is not shared by those who did not take part in it. Yet the personal dimension, and especially the common commitment to the work of the dialogue, remains essential. This too has deep implications for the theme of mutual accountability.

B. *The Special Place of* Baptism, Eucharist and Ministry

The most significant result of the convergence method has been *Baptism, Eucharist and Ministry* (BEM).[13] Even more telling than the facts and figures about BEM – its many translations, reprintings, and responses both official and unofficial – is the fact that it continues to inspire formal agreements among churches, and to inform ecclesiological work done both ecumenically and within individual churches. These are the most telling signs that BEM has been "received" in a substantial way by the churches and within the ecumenical movement.[14]

Three aspects of BEM have, I believe, special significance for this discussion. The first is that BEM was the result of a process, one which had involved the churches closely over the twenty years of its production. The churches responded to drafts of the sections on eucharist, baptism, and ministry as incorporated in the text sent from the Faith and Order Accra Plenary Commission meeting in 1974; after the transmission of BEM to the churches from the Lima Commission meeting in 1982 they took part in an unprecedented way in responding to the text.[15] Faith and Order then continued the dialogue with a careful analysis of the churches' responses, identifying the issues which, according to the churches, most needed further work.[16]

A second aspect was the way in which BEM integrated theology and practice. Precisely as a theological and ecclesiological text, BEM insisted that the church's faith must be expressed in its life in the world, through engagement in efforts to make human life more just and peaceful. The signature example of this in BEM is its statement on the implications of the eucharist for the ethical engagement of the church: "The eucharist embraces all aspects of life... All kinds of injustice, racism, separation and lack of freedom are radically challenged when we share in the body and blood of Christ."[17] The text on baptism makes this point in equally strong terms. Thus BEM, for all its focus on three aspects of the church's nature and life, is fundamentally a text about the *wholeness* of the church.

A third aspect is the approach which was taken in sending BEM to the churches for response "at the highest appropriate level of authority." Strikingly, churches were not asked for a denominational "reading" of BEM – how far it corresponded to their own doctrine and practice – but were asked to indicate "the extent to which your church can recognize in this text the faith of the Church through the ages."[18] Behind this, of course, lay the distinction drawn by Faith and Order at its fourth world conference in Montreal in 1963, between the Tradition ("the Gospel itself, transmitted from generation to generation in and by the Church") and the traditions ("both the diversity of forms of expression and also what we call confessional traditions, for instance the Lutheran... or Reformed").[19] Again, at one stroke the terms of ecumenical dialogue were changed. The BEM process was about the faith of the *Church* rather than the particular beliefs of the various *churches*: each church was invited to judge its own position against a common, more fundamental standard.

C. Models of Unity

We have examined several key themes in ecclesiological reflection, and reviewed the chief methods by which ecumenical dialogue has been pursued. One further dimension of ecumenical ecclesiological reflection remains to be reviewed: the discussion of models of unity.[20] The first of these, *organic unity*, was defined at the second world conference on Faith and Order in Edinburgh in 1937 as:

> the unity of a living organism, with the diversity characteristic of the members of a healthy body... In a church so united the ultimate loyalty of every member would be given to the whole body and not to any part of it. Its members would move freely from one part to another and find every privilege of membership open to them. The sacraments would be the sacraments of the whole body. The ministry would be accepted by all as a ministry of the whole body.[21]

While it has been most fully realized in the full structural unions of the United Churches, it is important to note that it may take other forms; Edinburgh refers to "*some measure* of organisational union," and speaks of preserving "the relative autonomy of the several constituent parts" [of the body] through the "federal" principle.[22] Despite later misunderstandings, the word "organic" guards the *diversity* of the body; organic union does not signify any kind of uniformity. Beyond the fleeting reference to "the 'federal' principle," however, no advice is offered as to the structural form or shape of union.

The WCC assembly in Nairobi in 1975, drawing on Faith and Order discussions at Salamanca in 1973,[23] developed the structural implications of organic union in terms of *conciliar fellowship*:

> The one Church is to be envisioned as a conciliar fellowship of local churches which are themselves truly united... each local church possesses, in communion with the others, the fullness of catholicity, witnesses to the same apostolic faith, and therefore recognizes the others as belonging to the same Church of Christ and guided by the same Spirit.[24]

Meanwhile, a second model of unity, *reconciled diversity*, was proposed by Christian World Communions in 1974. This stresses the principle of diversity more strongly, to the point of affirming the continuation of the present confessions as legitimate expressions of the church.[25] The confessions, each of which is understood to preserve valuable elements within the body of Christ as a whole, should "lose their divisive character and [be] reconciled to each other."[26] Again, no specific ecclesial structure is identified, beyond the suggestion that such a "unity in reconciled diversity" would be "ordered in all its components in conciliar structures and actions."[27] What is the relationship of the "federal principle" in organic union, and "conciliar fellowship," to the "conciliar structures and actions" of reconciled diversity? This is a fascinating question indeed – and one which has never been answered.

A third model of unity, the *communion of communions*, did suggest some concrete structural implications. On this view, each communion should be understood as a *"typos,"* or unique configuration of ecclesial characteristics, which could be preserved within an overarching ecclesial framework.[28] As originally suggested, this framework would embrace common sacraments and dogma, a structure for ministry, and a unique role for the ministry of the bishop of Rome on behalf of the unity of the church.

Thus, the first two models of unity described above did not offer sufficient guidance on the form which unity might take. While the third model did spell out possible structural implications, it goes without saying that they did not commend themselves to every church. Meanwhile the language of "conciliarity" has proved compelling to many, and has been used repeatedly in ecumenical discussion, but it is still not clear how it would actually function in concrete terms.

D. Koinonia

The notion of *koinonia* ("fellowship" or "communion") emerged during the 1970s as a fourth model of unity and has figured prominently in discussions of the unity of the church since that time. This model does not, and indeed did not intend to, address questions of the structural form of unity; it points instead to the *nature of the relationships* among the churches. Its focus is upon "the intimate, mutually sustaining and challenging bonds – both spiritual and material – linking them within, and to, the one Body of Christ."[29]

The scriptural basis of the term is significant. In the New Testament, "koinonia" points to participation in spiritual things (the gospel, Phil. 1:15; faith, Philem. 6; Christ's body and blood, 1 Cor. 10:16; the divine nature, 2 Pet. 1:4, sufferings of one's own, 2 Cor. 1:7, Heb. 10:33, or, strikingly, of Christ, Phil. 3:10, 1 Pet. 4:13) *and* in material things (Paul's collection for the "Saints" in Jerusalem, Rom. 12:13, 15:26-27, 2 Cor. 8:4, 9:13, also 1 Tim. 6:18).[30] Thus, the concept of koinonia has proved helpful ecumenically because it offers a basis in scripture both for the churches' material support for one another and for their spiritual bonds with one another and with Christ. It has provided a biblical foundation for the churches' search for unity, but also for their common engagement in diakonia and mission; it is a term that speaks to the wholeness of the church, its nature, and its life.

By the time of the WCC's seventh assembly at Canberra in 1991, koinonia had become a principal conceptual framework for common reflection on the church and its unity. Faith and Order prepared the assembly's statement on the unity we seek; and the text, *The Unity of the Church as Koinonia: Gift and Calling*, brought together many aspects of the ecclesiological work done in the ecumenical movement up to that time. Unity is defined as

> A koinonia given and expressed in the common confession of the apostolic faith; a common sacramental life entered by the one baptism and celebrated together in one eucharistic fellowship; a common life in which members and ministries are mutually recognized and reconciled; and a common mission witnessing to all people to the gospel of God's grace and serving the whole of creation.[31]

This koinonia is also characterized as a state of "full communion," which

> is realized when all the churches are able to recognize in one another the one, holy, catholic and apostolic church in its fulness. This full communion will be expressed... through conciliar forms of life and action. In such communion churches are bound in all aspects of their life together at all levels in

confessing the one faith and engaging in worship and witness, deliberation and action.[32]

The linking of koinonia with full communion has proved inspiring and empowering for the churches' search for visible unity. It would be so, all the more, if the shape and form of that "full communion" were defined more precisely.

E. Mutual Recognition

A final topic for review is itself not a model of unity but plays an important role in the search for visible unity. *Mutual recognition* signifies that the churches concerned discern in one another the one true church of Christ. There are lively discussions as to "degrees" of recognition, or which elements of the church must be "discerned" in order to enable recognition. But the concept has provided a powerful platform for the churches to affirm their common fellowship within the one body of Christ.

Mutual recognition has been most firmly established in respect of baptism. This has been the case among many Protestants since the beginning of the 19th century and has gained momentum since the full commitment of the Roman Catholic Church (on the very basis of our common baptism into Christ) to the ecumenical movement. Indeed, for many churches and Christians it is baptism – and especially the mutual recognition of baptism – which is the basis for their ecumenical engagement.[33]

Mutual recognition, however, has been important in many other ecumenical contexts, both ecclesial and geographical. At the regional level, this is exemplified by the Leuenberg Church Fellowship in Europe, agreed in 1973 and known since 2003 as the Community of Protestant Churches in Europe. This established mutual recognition of ministries and presidency at the eucharist among Lutheran and Reformed churches, and now encompasses some 94 Lutheran, Methodist, Reformed, and United Churches from Europe and South America. At the global level the WCC assembly at Vancouver in 1983, building upon the Faith and Order Plenary Commission in Bangalore in 1978,[34] identified three "marks" proper to "a strong Church unity": a common understanding of the apostolic faith; a common confession of the apostolic faith including *full mutual recognition* of baptism, the eucharist and ministry; and common ways of decision-making and teaching authoritatively."[35] Intensive ecumenical work has been done on the first two of these areas; strikingly, the area of common decision-making and authoritative teaching has proven more difficult to tackle.

III. From Mutual Recognition to Mutual Accountability

We have explored a number of ecclesiological themes as developed within the ecumenical movement. The following have emerged as central points:

1. The Church, the body of Christ, is one and the churches are members together of that one body.

2. Therefore common reflection and action by the churches – and insofar as possible in all aspects of the life of the Church – should be the norm rather than the exception.

3. The commitment of church representatives – and, behind them, the churches themselves – to the process of dialogue among the churches is essential.

4. Such dialogues must include all aspects of the life of the church including faith, confession, worship, witness, service, and diakonia.

5. Visible church unity requires some structural embodiment, best imaged in "conciliar forms of life and action." The form of these "conciliar forms" is not yet clear.

6. In the meantime, the churches' *mutual recognition* of one another – especially as grounded in their common baptism into Christ – provides a basis for ecumenical reflection and action.

7. But to make their unity both effective and visible, the churches are called to "common ways of decision-making and teaching authoritatively." The form which this would take is also not yet clear.

Given that a considerable degree of mutual recognition – with whatever qualifications – exists among the churches, I want now to suggest that the next stage of the ecumenical movement should be characterized by a movement from *mutual recognition* to *mutual ac-*

countability. The full understanding and implications of "mutual accountability" have still to be discerned by the churches. But it signifies at least that each church takes responsibility for its own actions as a member of the one body of Christ. It signifies that each church, before acting, considers the consequences of its actions for other churches, as fellow members of the one body of Christ. It recognizes that, in today's world, there are hardly any "purely internal" documents or actions; rather, virtually all that we say and do as churches, both internally and externally, has an impact upon all the other members of the one body of Christ. And it seeks continually to make the unity which is ours as members together of the one body of Christ, both more visible and more effective in witness and service.

If the meaning and significance of mutual accountability is not yet fully clear, there have been earlier intimations of its meaning and significance for the churches and the ecumenical movement. Here four intimations may be mentioned briefly. A first intimation is the experience of the United churches, such as the Church of North India, which have been formed through the fusion of previously divided denominations.[36] In such unions, churches move from the partnership and cooperation of separate ecclesial bodies to full structural integration within a single ecclesial body. In Martin Cressey's memorable turn of thought, before the union some distance always remains between the partners, some possibility of repudiating the statements or actions of one's partner churches; whereas

> the step of union closes that gap and removes the possibility of that self-distancing. In the united church I have to take responsibility [for] the views and actions of fellow-members. Of course, there will be matters on which we can agree to differ, within the constitution of the united church, but there will also be a common commitment.[37]

In short, no expression of mutual accountability is more complete than living in full unity within one ecclesial body.[38] But sometimes full structural integration is not practicable, and in such situations some churches have found less complete, yet still significant, expressions of their special relationship within the one body of Christ. For example, the Christian Church (Disciples of Christ) and the United Church of

Christ have entered into a formal and solemn partnership in which each church invites representatives from the other to its highest governing body, with both voice and vote. Even more striking, the two churches have formed a common organization – the Common Global Ministries Board – to pursue overseas mission and development work. It is, to my knowledge, a unique example of such intimate cooperation between churches. And it is durable, having celebrated its twenty-fifth anniversary in 2015.

A second intimation of mutual accountability is found in the results of bilateral discussions between certain Christian World Communions, as well as between certain churches at the national level. A striking example in the latter category is the Anglican-Lutheran *Waterloo Declaration* issued by the Anglican Church of Canada and the Evangelical Lutheran Church in Canada. Under the rubric of "mutual accountability," the Anglican-Lutheran International Working Group reports on this dialogue as follows:

> 48. Commitment 5 of Waterloo commits the churches "to establish appropriate forms of collegial and conciliar consultation on significant matters of faith and order, mission and service." Commitment 6 is "to encourage regular consultation and collaboration among members of our churches at all levels, to promote the formulation and adoption of covenants for common work in mission and ministry, and to facilitate learning and exchange of ideas and information on theological, pastoral and mission matters". Commitment 7 is "to hold joint meetings of national, regional and local decision-making bodies whenever practicable."[39]

This proposal encourages "collegial and conciliar consultation" on a regular basis in decisive areas of the life of the church, and seeks to promote common witness and life among the churches so far as practicable. What is most significant is the assumption that serious dialogue among churches, dialogue leading to agreement on matters of faith and life, will necessarily lead to concrete expressions of mutual accountability in the lives of the churches concerned.

A third intimation comes from the broader ecumenical context, specifically from work to bring together the fields of ecclesiology and

ethics. Recent efforts in this area have sharpened the churches' awareness that they should reflect and act together rather than separately
– that the ecumenical dimension touches the life of the church as a
whole, including the churches' prophetic witness in the world:

> Is it enough to say... that ethical engagement is intrinsic to the
> church *as* church? Is it enough to say that, if a church is not
> engaging responsibly with the ethical issues of its day, it is not
> being fully church? Must we not also say: if the churches are
> not engaging these ethical issues *together*, then *none of them
> individually is being fully church*?[40]

That is, the churches are called to exercise their mutual accountability also in practising moral discernment and ethical decision-
making. To face together today's increasingly sensitive and complex
ethical issues will indeed be a challenge for the churches. But seeking
a common approach to such issues, and continuing the conversation
even when they differ on specific ethical questions – to be of one heart,
if not always of one mind – can only enhance the credibility of the
churches' witness to the world.

These impulses towards mutual accountability seem to have co-
alesced around the turn of the millennium 2000, as exemplified in
the substantial dissertation of Olav Fykse Tveit which suggests that
"Mutual accountability as ecumenical attitude is a combination of
reliability, faithfulness, trustfulness, solidarity, openness, and ability
to give and take constructive critique".[41] As we shall see, ecclesiological
and theological depth would be added to this through the work of the
WCC's Faith and Order Commission (of which Tveit was a member).

A fourth intimation of mutual accountability comes from the WCC
assembly in Porto Alegre in 2006. Based on work done by Faith and
Order[42] this text, *Called to be the One Church*, was adopted unanimously at the assembly by WCC member churches as "an invitation to
the churches to renew their commitment to the search for unity, and
to deepen their dialogue."[43] It offered the most detailed ecumenical
discussion of mutual accountability to this point:

> The relationship among churches is dynamically interactive.
> Each church is called to mutual giving and receiving gifts and
> to *mutual accountability*. Each church must become aware

of all that is provisional in its life and have the courage to acknowledge this to other churches. Even today, when eucharistic sharing is not always possible, divided churches express mutual accountability and aspects of catholicity when they pray for one another, share resources, assist one another in times of need, make decisions together, work together for justice, reconciliation, and peace, hold one another accountable to the discipleship inherent in baptism, and maintain dialogue in the face of differences, refusing to say "I have no need of you" (1 Cor.12:21). Apart from one another we are impoverished.[44]

This text offered a glimpse of the possibilities – and challenges – which the notion of mutual accountability offers to the churches on their ecumenical journey. In adopting the text unanimously as a basis for reflection and action, all WCC member churches *committed themselves* to explore the implications of their mutual accountability to one another as members together of the one body of Christ: the churches have acknowledged that they are not only related; they are intimately *inter*-related – and indeed *are* impoverished without one another. Surely this may be seen as the extension and consequence of Edinburgh 1910's primal affirmation: that Christians and the churches, in every time and place, need one another in order to manifest fully the one Body of Christ.

IV. Decisive New Developments

The notion of mutual accountability, challenging as it is, has proved to be compelling for the churches. Most importantly, it underlies the recent, watershed Faith and Order convergence text *The Church: Towards a Common Vision*.[45] This convergence text – only the second in Faith and Order's long history, the first being *Baptism, Eucharist and Ministry* – asserts that, in today's ecumenical situation, mutual accountability is intrinsic to the lives of the churches at all levels:

Every Christian receives gifts of the Holy Spirit for the up-building of the Church and for his or her part in the mission of Christ. These gifts are given for the common good (cf. 1 Cor. 12:7; Eph. 4:11-13) and place obligations of responsibility and mutual accountability on every individual and local community and on the Church as a whole at every level of its life.[46]

Perhaps controversially, the text asserts that

> A pastoral ministry for the service of unity and the upholding
> of diversity is one of the important means given to the Church
> in aiding those with different gifts and perspectives to remain
> mutually accountable to each other.[47]

Crucially, the notion of mutual accountability is also evoked in dealing
with today's controversial, potentially divisive ethical issues:

> Thus *koinonia* includes not only the confession of the one faith
> and celebration of common worship, but also shared moral
> values, based upon the inspiration and insights of the Gospel.
> Notwithstanding their current state of division, the churches
> have come so far in fellowship with one another that they
> are aware that what one does affects the life of others, and, in
> consequence, are increasingly conscious of the need *to be ac-
> countable to each other* with respect to their ethical reflections
> and decisions. As churches engage in mutual questioning and
> affirmation, they give expression to what they share in Christ.[48]

And this has found a clear echo in current ecumenical reflection,[49]
stressing as it does the churches' bonds of common concern and their
commitment to one another:

> A fellowship between churches and denominations requires
> not only mutual recognition, but also assumes that there is a
> willingness to make a *commitment* to each other. Such a com-
> mitment implies a willingness to be accountable to each other.
> Everything a church or denomination does is of concern for
> the other.[50]

Thus mutual accountability poses a challenge – and opportunity –
for the churches. Its full meaning will be revealed only as the churches,
wrestling with the full implications of their belonging to one another
within the one body of Christ, move from mutual recognition to the
next stage of their common confession, life, and witness: from mutual
recognition to mutual accountability.

---

1   As a basis for these reflections on mutual accountability, I review and develop some material
    explored initially in my article "Ecclesiology and Ecumenism" in *The Routledge Companion to
    the Christian Church*, ed. Gerard Mannion and Lewis S. Mudge (New York, London: Routledge,
    2008), pp. 402-20.

2   John Radano, "Homily on John 11:1-53: Toward Unity, Toward Life," in *Built Together: The Present Vocation of United and Uniting Churches (Ephesians 2:22)*, The Sixth International Consultation of United and Uniting Churches, Faith and Order paper 174, ed. Thomas F. Best (Geneva: WCC, 1996), pp. 158-61; "Homily on John 21:1-14," in *With a Demonstration of the Spirit and of Power*, The Seventh International Consultation of United and Uniting Churches, Faith and Order paper 195 (Geneva: WCC, 2004), pp. 168-72.

3   See recently John A. Radano, *Lutheran and Catholic Reconciliation on Justification: A Chronology of the Holy See's Contributions, 1961-1999, to a New Relationship between Lutherans and Catholics and to Steps Leading to the Joint Declaration on the Doctrine of Justification* (Grand Rapids, Eerdmans, 2009).

4   Thomas F. Best, "A Tale of Two Edinburghs: Mission, Unity, and Mutual Accountability," *Journal of Ecumenical Studies*, 46, no. 3 (Summer 2011): 311-28, esp. 326-28; and John A. Radano, "Mutual Accountability: Building Together on the Achievements of the Ecumenical Movement," *Journal of Ecumenical Studies*, 47, no. 3 (Summer 2012): 333-54.

5   See "Report of Section III, The Nature of the Church," in H. N. Bate, ed., *Faith and Order: Proceedings of the World Conference, Lausanne, August 3-21, 1927* (London: SCM, 1927), pp. 463, 464, 469; Leonard Hodgson, ed., *The Second World Conference on Faith and Order: Edinburgh 1937* (New York: MacMillan, 1938), pp. 252-53, 258-59.

6   For the citations in this paragraph see Willem A. Visser't Hooft, *The Genesis and Formation of the World Council of Churches* (Geneva: WCC, 1982), III.3, p. 114; IV.4, p. 117; IV.1, p. 116; and IV.3, p. 117 respectively.

7   See *Dictionary of the Ecumenical Movement*, 2nd ed., s.v. "WCC, Basis of" by T. K. Thomas, pp. 1238-39, esp. p. 1239.

8   See "Final Report of the Special Commission on Orthodox Participation in the WCC," B.III, no. 15 (Geneva: WCC, 2002); http://www.oikoumene.org.

9   Oliver S. Tomkins, "Implications of the Ecumenical Movement," *Ecumenical Review* 5, no. 1 (October 1952): 19-20. Tomkins was speaking to the Third World Conference on Faith and Order at Lund.

10   "A Word to the Churches," *Third World Conference on Faith and Order, Held at Lund August 15th to 28th, 1952* (London: SCM, 1953), p. 16, in DH I, p. 86.

11   This formulation of this principle is taken from the "By-Laws of the Faith and Order Commission," 3.2.ii, see *Minutes of the Standing Commission on Faith and Order: Aghios Nikaolaos, Crete, 2005*, Faith and Order paper 200 (Geneva: WCC Commission on Faith and Order, 2005), p. 98.

12   Proposals for the Lifting of Anathemas, no. 1 in "Communiqué, Joint Commission of the Theological Dialogue Between the Orthodox Church and The Oriental Orthodox Churches, Geneva, November 1-6, 1993," in GA III, pp. 4-7. For earlier stages of the dialogue see "Communiqué: Chambésy, Geneva, Switzerland, 15 December 1985," in GA II, p. 190; "Communiqué: Anba Bishoy Monastery, Egypt, 24 June 1989," in GA II, pp. 191-93; "Second Agreed Statement and Recommendations to the Churches: Chambésy, Switzerland, 28 September 1990," in GA II, pp. 194-99.

13   See the most recent, 39th printing: *Baptism, Eucharist and Ministry*, 25th anniversary printing with additional introduction, Faith and Order paper 111 (Geneva: WCC, 1982-2007).

14   See Thomas F. Best and Tamara Grdzelidze, eds., *BEM at 25: Critical Insights into a Continuing Legacy*, Faith and Order paper 205 (Geneva: WCC, 2007) and, for a recent critical review of the origin and lasting effect of BEM, see Lukas Vischer, "The Convergence Texts on Baptism, Eucharist and Ministry: How Did They Take Shape? What Have They Achieved?" in *Ecumenical Review* 54, no. 4 (October 2002): 431-54.

15 See Max Thurian, ed., *Churches Respond to BEM: Official Responses to the "Baptism, Eucharist and Ministry" Text*, vols. I-VI, Faith and Order papers 129, 132, 135, 137, 143, 144 (Geneva: WCC, 1986-1988).

16 *Baptism, Eucharist & Ministry 1982-1990: Report on the Process and Responses*, Faith and Order paper 149 (Geneva: WCC, 1990).

17 BEM, "Eucharist", no. 20.

18 BEM, "Preface", p. x.

19 "Report of Section II: Scripture, Tradition and Traditions," no. 39, in *The Fourth World Conference on Faith and Order: Montreal 1963*, Faith and Order paper 42, ed. P. C. Rodger & L. Vischer (London: SCM, 1964), p. 50.

20 A helpful survey up to the emergence of the koinonia "model" is Paul A. Crow, Jr., "Ecumenics as Reflections on Models of Christian Unity", *Ecumenical Review* 39, no. 4 (October 1987): 389-403.

21 Hodgson, ed., *Edinburgh 1937*, p. 252.

22 Hodgson, ed., *Edinburgh 1937*, p. 253 (italics mine).

23 See Commission on Faith and Order, "The Unity of the Church: Next Steps," Report of the Salamanca Consultation on 'Concepts of Unity' and 'Models of Union,' September 1973, in *What Kind of Unity?* Faith and Order paper 69 (Geneva: WCC, 1974), pp. 119-31; *Ecumenical Review* 26, no. 2 (1974): 291-303; *Documentary History of Faith and Order, 1963-1993*, Faith and Order paper 159, ed. Günther Gassmann (Geneva: WCC, 1993), pp. 35-44.

24 "Report of Section II: What Unity Requires," no. 3, in David M. Paton, ed., *Breaking Barriers, Nairobi 1975*, The Official Report of the Fifth Assembly of the World Council of Churches, Nairobi, 23 November-10 December, 1975 (London: SPCK; Grand Rapids: Eerdmans, 1976), p. 60.

25 *Dictionary of the Ecumenical Movement*, 2nd ed., s.v. "Reconciled Diversity," by Harding Meyer, pp. 960-61.

26 "Statements of the Assembly: 3. Models of Unity," no. 15, in Arne Sovik, ed., *In Christ: A New Community*, Proceedings of the Sixth Assembly of the Lutheran World Federation (Geneva: Lutheran World Federation, 1977), p. 174.

27 "Statements by the Seventh Assembly: Statement on 'The Unity We Seek,'" in Carl H. Mau, Jr., ed., *Budapest 1984: Christ, Hope for the World*, Official Proceedings of the Seventh Assembly of the Lutheran World Federation, LWF Report 19/20 (Geneva: Lutheran World Federation, 1985), p. 175.

28 See the address of Cardinal Johannes Willebrands at Great St. Mary's Church, Cambridge, England, January 18, 1972, during the Week of Prayer for Christian Unity, in Joseph W. Witmer and J. Robert Wright, ed., *Called to Full Unity: Documents on Anglican-Roman Catholic Relations, 1966-1983* (Washington: United States Catholic Conference, 1986), pp. 45-53.

29 *Dictionary of the Ecumenical Movement*, 2nd ed., s.v. "Unity, Models of," by Thomas F. Best, pp. 1173-75, quotation p. 1174.

30 Thomas F. Best, "The Issues Beyond the Issues: Possible Futures for the Faith and Order World Conference," *Ecumenical Review* 45, no. 1 (January, 1993): 59-60.

31 Michael Kinnamon, ed., *Signs of the Spirit: Official Report, Seventh Assembly, World Council of Churches* (Geneva: WCC; Grand Rapids: Eerdmans, 1991), pp. 172-74, para. 2.1.

32 Kinnamon, ed., *Signs of the Spirit*, pp. 172-74, para.2.1.

33 See Thomas F. Best, ed., *Baptism Today: Understanding, Practice, Ecumenical Implications,* Faith and Order paper 207 (Collegeville, Minn.: Liturgical Press; Geneva: WCC, 2008); and *One Baptism: Towards Mutual Recognition,* Faith and Order Paper no. 210 (Geneva: WCC, 2011).

34 *Minutes and Supplementary Documents from the Meeting of the Commission on Faith and Order,* Ecumenical Christian Centre Whitefield, Bangalore, India, 16-30 August 1978, Faith and Order paper 93 (Geneva: WCC Commission on Faith and Order, 1979), pp. 40-42.

35 David Gill, ed., *Gathered for Life: Official Report, Sixth Assembly, World Council of Churches, Vancouver, Canada, 24 July-10 August 1983* (Geneva: WCC; Grand Rapids: Eerdmans, 1983), p. 45, nos. II.6-8, italics mine.

36 The Church of North India incorporates an astonishing range of ecclesial types, having been formed from Anglican, Baptist, Congregationalist, Disciples, Methodist, Brethren, and Presbyterian churches.

37 See Martin Cressey, "Where and Whither? An Interpretive Survey of United and Uniting Churches, With a View to their Contribution to the Fifth World Conference on Faith and Order to be held in 1993," in *Minutes of the Meeting of the Standing Commission on Faith and Order held at Centro Nazareth, Rome, Italy, 19-26 June 1991,* Faith and Order paper 157 (Geneva: WCC Commission on Faith and Order, 1992), p. 61.

38 See most recently Thomas F. Best, "United and Uniting Churches as Models of Mission and Unity," in John Gibaut and Knud Jørgensen, eds., *Called to Unity: For the Sake of Mission,* Regnum Edinburgh Centenary Series, no. 25 (Oxford: Regnum Books, 2015), pp. 141-53.

39 Anglican-Lutheran International Working Group, "Growth in Communion: Porto Alegre, Brazil, 2002," in GA III, p. 385. Note that "mutual accountability" is one of the factors with respect to which the international group has evaluated all the dialogues between Anglican and Lutheran churches at the regional and national levels, see p. 377. For a detailed and incisive study of the *Waterloo Declaration* see Michael Root, "Consistency and Difference in Anglican-Lutheran Relations: *Porvoo, Waterloo,* and *Called to Common Mission,*" in Marsha L. Dutton and Patrick Terrell Gray, eds., *One Lord, One Faith, One Baptism: Studies in Christian Ecclesiality and Ecumenism in Honor of J. Robert Wright* (Grand Rapids: Eerdmans, 2006), pp. 296-315.

40 "Costly Commitment: Report of the Consultation at Tantur Ecumenical Institute, Israel, 1994," no. 17c, in Thomas F. Best and Martin Robra, ed., *Ecclesiology and Ethics: Ecumenical Moral Engagement, Moral Formation and the Nature of the Church* (Geneva, WCC, 1997), p. 29.

41 Olav Fykse Tveit, *Mutual Accountability as Ecumenical Attitude: A Study in Ecumenical Ecclesiology Based on Faith and Order Texts 1948-1998* (Oslo: Norwegian School of Theology, 2001), pp. 310. See now Olav Fyske Tveit, *The Truth We Owe Each Other: Mutual Accountability in the Ecumenical Movement* (Geneva: World Council of Churches, 2016).

42 The notion of mutual accountability already figures prominently in the penultimate Faith and Order ecclesiology text *The Nature and Mission of the Church: A Stage on the Way to a Common Statement,* Faith and Order paper 198 (Geneva: WCC, 2005); see nos. 28, 62, the box after no. 63 (d), no. 74 (with strong reference to baptism), and nos. 83, 94, 96. No. 117 refers to churches engaging in "mutual questioning and affirmation."

43 *Called to be the One Church* [The Porto Alegre Ecclesiology Text], no. 7 in *God, in Your Grace...: Official Report of the Ninth Assembly of the World Council of Churches,* ed. Luis N. Rivera-Pagán (Geneva: WCC, 2007), p. 257, in GA III, p. 608; http://www.oikoumene.org.

44 *Called to be the One Church,* no. 7.

45 *The Church: Towards a Common Vision,* Faith and Order paper 214 (Geneva: WCC, 2013). See also the related text *One Baptism: Towards Mutual Recognition,* Faith and Order paper 210 (Geneva: WCC, 2011) and see, for the close links between the two texts, Thomas F. Best, "A Faith

and Order Saga: *Towards One Baptism: Towards Mutual Recognition*," in Glaucia Vasconcelos Wilkey, ed., *Worship and Culture: Foreign Country or Homeland?* (Grand Rapids: Eerdmans, 2014), pp. 302-19.

46   *The Church: Towards a Common Vision*, no. 18. See also the reference to churches relating "in a spirit of mutual respect and attention," no. 24. Regrettably, *The Church: Towards a Common Vision* appears to have lost the strong link between mutual accountability and baptism; cf. *The Nature and Mission of the Church*, no. 74, and *The Church: Towards a Common Vision*, no. 41.

47   *The Church: Towards a Common Vision*, no. 29.

48   *The Church: Towards a Common Vision*, no. 62, emphasis mine. See also the exploratory comments in the box following no. 63.

49   See the works by Thomas F. Best and John A. Radano cited in note 4.

50   Harald Hegstad, *The Real Church: An Ecclesiology of the Visible*, Church of Sweden Research Series 7 (Cambridge, England: James Clarke; Eugene, Oregon: Wipf & Stock, 2013), p. 217. Hegstad also cites Olav Fykse Tveit, *Mutual Accountability as Ecumenical Attitude*, p. 310, and Ola Tjørholm, *Kirken – Troens mor, et økumenisk bidrag til en luthersk ekklesiologi* (Oslo: Verbum, 1999), p. 99.

✝ CHAPTER 17

A Pilgrimage Towards Christian Unity: A Baptist-Evangelical Discussion with the World Council of Churches

by Denton Lotz

t is an honour to dedicate this paper to our friend Monsignor John Radano, with whom I served for twenty years in the annual meetings of Secretaries of the Christian World Communions. In addition, we worked closely together planning the significant "theological conversations" between the Baptist World Alliance (BWA) and the Pontifical Council for Promoting Christian Unity. John Radano was a regular attendee at our BWA Congresses. He became friends with many Baptist leaders from around the world. All of us respected his keen intellect, his love for Christ and the unity of the Church. We did not always agree, especially on the Marian dogmas. Yet he represented the Catholic position well with force and gentleness. "Jack," as his friends call him, is held in great respect by Baptist and Evangelical scholars.

The program planning committee of the Secretaries of Christian World Communions met in May 2006 to prepare for its annual meeting, which that year was to be held in October in Rome. The program committee chose the theme of the present state of the modern ecumenical movement and the search for unity as expressed in the World Council of Churches (WCC). As often happens when one is not present at a meeting, I was asked as a Baptist leader and Evangelical to give an alternative and critical view of the WCC and its search for unity. This paper contains many extracts from that overview.

My personal background may offer better insight and perspective, and therefore I would like to begin with a review of my pilgrimage and understanding of Christian unity. My maternal grandparents were from Italy and settled in Pennsylvania, where my grandfather worked in the coal mines. He was suffering from leukemia and was ministered to by the Waldensians and then the Presbyterians and Methodists. Of course, coming from Italy my grandparents were Catholics, but when they moved from the city to the country to become farmers they became Methodists. My paternal grandparents were from Germany, having become Baptists under the preaching of Johannes Gerhard Oncken, the founder of the modern-day Baptist movement in Germany. In New York City, I was brought up as a minority Baptist among a majority of Jewish and Catholic friends. My father was a street evangelist in New York City and I remember as a young boy undertaking mission work among the alcoholics on the Bowery. Early in life, I had a strong sense of the change in a person's life brought about by repentance and conversion to Christ. Conversion was never seen as from one denomination to another, but always conversion to Christ (John 3:7).

The youngest of four brothers, I received an ROTC scholarship to the University of North Carolina, where I was very involved in student and ecumenical Christian ministries. I became a First Lieutenant in the Marine Corps on Okinawa. During the Vietnam War, when Kennedy was president, I was sent to Danang, Vietnam. The day I left Vietnam, our waitress turned out to be part of the Vietcong and blew up the officers' quarters where I had been staying. My close friend was killed. This incident was one of many events which precipitated my accepting God's call to Christian ministry. On the plane back to Japan, I determined to be an ambassador for Christ and not the US government. I entered Harvard Divinity School, and there my real experience of ecumenicity began. George Florovsky was my academic advisor (Orthodox), Krister Stendahl was my professor of New Testament (Lutheran), George Ernest Wright, professor of Old Testament (Presbyterian), George Hunston Williams, professor of Church History (Congregationalist), James Luther Adams, professor of Ethics (Unitarian), etc. Serving as an Associate Minister at Memorial Church under Charles Price (Episcopal liturgist, professor, and preacher at Memorial Church), I had the privilege of meeting many national and international Christian leaders. It was an honour to take part in the civil rights movement and to be a driver for Martin Luther King Jr. when he visited Harvard.

After Harvard Divinity School, I completed my doctorate at the University of Hamburg, Germany, with Bishop Stephen Neill as my "Doktorvater," Anglican bishop and former deputy general secretary of the WCC. I also studied in Hamburg with Professor Helmut Thielecke, often serving as his interpreter. Previously I had studied in Göttingen with Professor Jeremias. I will never forget the Bible studies in his home, which he made available to Student Mission Deutschland (German Intervarsity). I also heard the lectures of Otto Weber, Walter Zimmerli, Hans Conzelmann, and even Friedrich Gogarten.

Following my doctoral studies, I served as American Baptist Fraternal Representative in Eastern Europe during the Soviet period. I had my office at the Ecumenical Center in Geneva, and often enjoyed tea with Willem Visser't Hooft, Eugene Carson Blake, and Philip Potter. Konrad Raiser and I were students together at Harvard.

This introduction, I hope, will show that I am not anti-ecumenical or anti-WCC, of which I was sometimes accused at Christian World Communions meetings because I gave an alternative, Evangelical view of Christian unity. On the contrary, I have great respect for all the above-mentioned leaders, many of whom would share my concerns, I believe. I affirm and appreciate very much the historical role the WCC has played in working for Christian unity. But, a paradigm shift has occurred and the concern of this paper is whether or not we need a new paradigm for our future work and search for Christian unity.

I. Historical Perspective of Why Many Baptists and Evangelicals Are NOT Members of the WCC

My concern, and that of many Baptists and Evangelicals, is that we not forget the history of the beginnings of the modern ecumenical movement, and consequently that of the WCC. We know from the history of the modern missionary movement that the present-day movement for unity did not just happen. The origins of the quest for Christian unity are from the 19th century, the "Great Century" of missions! Evangelicals are not unaware that certain decisions in the 20th century concerning missions and unity were made that had a deleterious effect on Evangelical membership in the present-day WCC. Many streams led to the ecumenical movement as we know it today, the first being the 1910 Edinburgh World Missionary Conference and the consequent world missionary conferences. Later, in 1927, Faith and Order began and became another stream of the modern ecumenical movement, concentrating on questions of doctrine and ecclesiology. Eventually, many Baptists and Evangelicals would maintain that Faith and Order and questions of doctrine and church order had triumphed over the 1910 concern for world evangelization. Having lost its vision of "the evangelization of the world in this generation," which was the original watchword of the beginning movement for unity led by such men as John R. Mott, the ecumenical movement of the WCC drifted more into a discussion of doctrinal and social issues. Such discussions left most Baptists and Evangelicals behind. But I am getting ahead of the discussion!

Now let me give a brief review as to why many Baptists[1] and other Evangelicals are *not* members of the WCC and yet affirm the search for Christian unity.

1. Evangelical Concern about WCC Commitment to World Evangelization

In 1968 at the Uppsala Assembly of the WCC, the Anglican Evangelical pastor and theologian John R. Stott commented on the Renewal in Mission document presented to the Assembly. He said that he did not find in the report any concern for the spiritual hunger of humanity comparable to that which had been expressed regarding physical hunger and poverty. Stott maintained that the priority concern of the Church should be in relation to the millions of people, who, being without Christ, are perishing. Stott emphasized,

> The World Council confesses that Jesus is Lord. The Lord sends his Church to preach the Good News and make disciples. I do not see the Assembly very eager to obey its Lord's command. The Lord Jesus Christ wept over the city which had rejected him. I do not see this Assembly weeping similar tears.[2]

A delegate from the Congo, R. Buana Kibongi, expressed similar concerns. Sir Kenneth Grubb, another delegate from the Church of

England, said Stott had made the point he himself wished to make. Statements of Stott and others were spread widely within Baptist and Evangelical circles.

A decade earlier, in 1958, in Accra, Ghana, at the last meeting of the International Missionary Council before it was integrated into the WCC and became the Commission on World Mission and Evangelism (CWME), fears of the downplaying of mission and evangelization were expressed. Now, almost 50 years later, the CWME no longer exists and has been dispersed throughout the WCC structure in a new division or cluster called "Unity, Mission, Evangelism and Spirituality," which has yet to be defined. Those who opposed the integration of the International Missionary Council into the WCC at the 1961 Assembly in Delhi, India, were prophetic in their warnings! More recently, a message from the Bossey Seminar, *Towards a New Ecumenical Agenda on Evangelism for the 21st Century*, stated very clearly that

> without giving evangelism a proper priority and prominent place in the work of the WCC, the urgently needed broader ecumenical approach and collaboration with non-member churches in both the Pentecostal and charismatic, and the evangelical tradition (which is also a driving force behind proposals for a Global Christian Forum) would be hindered in the future.[3]

The fact is that the lack of concern for world evangelization in the WCC is one of the main reasons that many Baptists and Evangelicals have not participated more fully. The question may be asked whether or not this new emphasis on evangelism is a real concern of the WCC, or is it because of what Bossey calls a "dramatic decline in membership and stagnation in evangelization" among some WCC churches and the knowledge that if there is to be involvement of charismatics and Evangelicals then evangelism must be high on the agenda. In other words, is it a real concern or is it just window dressing?

2. Understanding Edinburgh 1910, the Initial Beginning of the Modern Ecumenical Movement

To understand where we are today, we must go back to Edinburgh 1910 and the first World Missionary Conference. Baptists and Evangeli-

348

cals were very involved in the Edinburgh 1910 conference. One could make a strong case that Edinburgh 1910 was really the forerunner of the WCC. As mentioned above, however, parallel to that movement were the later streams of Faith and Order and Life and Work. Baptists and Evangelicals would say that Faith and Order and Life and Work triumphed over Edinburgh's concern for world evangelization, which was the initial impetus for the modern-day ecumenical movement. Kenneth Ross, Secretary of the Church of Scotland World Mission Council, notes the growth of the Evangelicals since 1961 and maintains, "Though in strictly institutional terms it is the World Council of Churches that is heir of Edinburgh 1910, in terms of promoting the agenda of world evangelization, the Lausanne movement might be seen as standing in direct continuity."[4]

a.) *Lausanne 1974:* Since 1961 and the integration of the International Missionary Council into the WCC, the fears of mission agencies and Evangelicals have been realized in that they saw this integration as a failure. There was no deepening concern of the WCC for world evangelization. Partly as a reaction to this lack of concern for world evangelization, under the leadership of the evangelist Billy Graham, Evangelicals met in 1966 in Berlin and in 1974 in Lausanne and took up the call and summoned again the Christian Church worldwide to "the evangelization of the world in this generation." Any student of missiology will know the fantastic growth of the Church in the Two-Thirds World is to a certain extent more in tune with the Lausanne call to world evangelism than that of the WCC. Philip Jenkins in *The Next Christendom* outlines the growth of the Church in the Two-Thirds World.[5] One could say that the Lausanne Movement for World Evangelization, together with the ensuing church and para-church alliances growing out of it, is perhaps the largest and most powerful Protestant ecumenical movement today.

Too often the term "ecumenical" has been defined in narrow terms, only relating it to the institutional body known as the World Council of Churches. However, another form of unity, going back to Paris in 1845 and the formation of the Evangelical Alliance, has gained prominence in many churches overseas precisely because of its emphasis on mission and evangelism. The fact is that Amsterdam 2000, the follow-up missionary conference to Lausanne, with 12,000 evangelists in attendance from all over the world, was perhaps as ecumenical a gathering as the 3,500 that gathered for the WCC Assembly in Porto Alegre, Brazil, in 2006. A paradigm shift in our understanding of the ecumenical movement has occurred. In 1952, Evangelicals on a world level, continuing the movement from 1845 of the Evangelical Alliance, re-formed on a world level into the World Evangelical Alliance (WEA). If indeed the WEA represents more than 450 million Protestant Christians, as the WEA leadership states, then it numbers more Protestants than are in the WCC. Thus, we must expand the definition of "ecumenical" to include more than those churches related only to the WCC. Indeed, Evangelicalism represents a new and growing form of ecumenism beyond the institutional structures of the WCC. To fail to grasp this is to miss one of the great paradigm shifts in world Christianity during the past 100 years!

b.) *Christian Unity, Students and World Evangelism*: Baptists and Evangelicals were concerned about unity right at the beginning of the 19th-century missionary movement. In 1810, the English Baptist pioneer missionary to India William Carey proposed a "pleasing dream" that all mission agencies meet in South Africa to discuss unity. It was not old men in long black robes that originally inspired the modern-day ecumenical movement. Rather, the move for unity came from the mission field, according to Bishop Stephen Neill. In his mission lectures at Hamburg University in Germany, Neill reminded students that overseas, those of other religious traditions who were interested in becoming Christian would ask, "What kind of Christian should I become? An Anglican, a Baptist, a Methodist, a Presbyterian, etc.?" It was from this confusion among non-believers, which denominationalism brought to the mission field, that the quest for Christian unity emerged, Neill insisted. In North America, thousands of students from the whole spectrum of Protestant denominations were inspired by the watchword for world evangelization, "The evangelization of the world in this generation," and went out as missionaries for Christ. They were the best and brightest of their colleges. It became indeed a world student movement. Among these students, there was a great spiritual unity beyond denominationalism. They formed the Student Volunteer Movement for Foreign Missions which was interdenominational and a forerunner of the ecumenical movement. The volunteer movement on a world level became the Student Christian Movement, and eventually the World Student Christian Federation. Denominationalism was not highlighted, but mission and world evangelism was what held Christian students together. In the early part of the 20th century, after Edinburgh 1910, figures such as John R. Mott, John H. Oldham, Robert E. Speer, Sherwood Eddy, William Temple, Nathan Soderblom, and Karl Heim all worked together. Indeed, thousands of the best and brightest were on a mission to the world. (The secular film *Chariots of Fire* captured the emotion and passion of this student generation.) A sad commentary on the state of the student movement in mainline churches was when in 1965 the University Christian Movement in the USA voted itself out of existence.

Of course, many churches and leaders in the WCC are very concerned about the missionary movement today. However, it does appear that the heritage of the student movement has been left to Evangelical student groups such as InterVarsity Christian Fellowship, Campus Crusade for Christ, and Youth with a Mission. In contrast to the WCC's apparent waning interest in world evangelization, the Lausanne movement and other Evangelical movements continue to flourish. It is perhaps this fact – more than any other – that has caused the WCC to propose a Global Christian Forum, a new and perhaps more inclusive alignment of Christians worldwide. The first meeting of the Global Christian Forum was held in Nairobi, Kenya, in November 2007. The question remains whether or not this forum will become in the 21st century the new movement for Christian unity worldwide.

3. Dialogue with World Religions, Social and Personal Ethics

Somewhat related to the whole question of mission, relative to the WCC, is its dialogue with other religions. A weak Christological stand by some ecumenical leaders is a hindrance to further unity with many Baptists and other Evangelicals. For example, Evangelicals do not understand statements coming out of the Lariano/Velletri meetings of May 12-16, 2006, when the Vatican and WCC issued a report that states, "All should heal themselves from the obsession of converting others."[6] Of course, any type of proselytism that uses unfair means for conversion is wrong. However, to whom is this statement about the "obsession" of converting others directed? To member bodies of the WCC, or those outside? To Evangelicals? Is the "obsession" that is to be condemned the proclamation that faith in Jesus Christ is necessary to understand who God is? This apparent negative view of evangelism among some WCC divisions is not a sudden concern for Evangelicals but goes back to the 1970s, when the WCC engaged in a series of dialogues with other world religions. There was a feeling among many Evangelicals that the "dialogue with other religions" gave tacit affirmation of relativism and lacked a clear call to conversion for all peoples. This was John R. Stott's concern expressed at the Assembly in Uppsala in 1968.

Vinay Samuel and Chris Sugden, in a 1982 article affirming Evangelical dialogue with other religions, nevertheless stated the Evangelical rejection of WCC dialogue in this way: "So, the concern to convert people from other religions became secondary at best and often did not come into the picture at all, lest it undermine the fragile commonality that was being discovered after decades of distance."[7] The situation among Evangelicals has changed dramatically, particularly after the 9/11 World Trade Center attack and the so-called war on terror. Most responsible Evangelical leaders see that some type of discussion with other religions is necessary just to prevent further war and bloodshed.

Space does not permit a critique of other aspects of WCC life that make membership in the WCC very difficult for many Baptists and Evangelicals. But, another objection needs to be stated. For too long there has been within both the Evangelical and the ecumenical world a separation between personal and social ethics. To some in the WCC, Evangelicals appear weak on emphasizing social concerns but strong on concerns of personal morality.[8] On the other hand, some Evangelicals feel it is just the opposite with member bodies of the WCC. They are strong on social ethics but weak on personal ethics. For example, many of the delegates from Africa and the Two-Thirds World at the WCC Assembly at Porto Alegre in 2007 were shocked and dismayed at the discussions on human sexuality and the affirmation by some WCC leaders of the homosexual and lesbian lifestyle.

These are briefly some of the issues which separate Evangelicals from the movement for Christian unity as expressed in the WCC. Let me state for the record, however, that a more in-depth and scholarly study is needed to bring us up to date as to where Evangelicals and the present Evangelical movement stand. This article in no way claims to be an exhaustive or representative study. Rather, as stated above, these are my personal thoughts and presented with the hope and concern for more Baptist and Evangelical involvement in the movement for Christian unity. It is encouraging to know that a new movement of younger Evangelicals understands, as did their predecessors, the biblical call for unity. The question is "What type of unity?" Perhaps for that reason, there is sympathy and gratitude for the new coalition calling for a Global Christian Forum of all Christians beyond the issues that have divided us and a new commitment to Jesus and his prayer for unity in John 17.

4. Statistics: Baptists and Evangelical Representation in the WCC

In conclusion, it needs to be asked who speaks for Baptists and Evangelicals. One should not forget there are many Baptists and Evangelicals who are totally committed to the WCC's vision of full and visible unity. Glenn Garfield Williams and Keith Clements were two of the leading figures in the leadership of the Conference of European Churches. As stated in footnote 1 above, of the community of 110 million Baptists in the Baptist World Alliance (BWA), perhaps as many as 50 percent are involved in conventions that are members of the WCC. The BWA has 232 member bodies. Of these, 25 are members of the WCC. In my critical observations above, I have tried to represent the viewpoint of the remaining BWA member bodies not in the WCC... many of these, however, are members of national councils of churches, particularly in Asia and Africa![9]

One should remember that the term "evangelical" is a broad term that includes the whole spectrum of Protestantism. It is good to make the distinction between "conservative Evangelicals" and "conciliar Evangelicals." Conservative Evangelicals tend towards sectarianism and isolationism, tending in fact towards fundamentalism and a rejection of any type of theological conversations with other Christian groups. Conciliar Evangelicals, on the other hand, are open to conversations and very involved in the academic disciplines. In fact, a rediscovery of Patristics and the early Church Fathers has brought them into conversation with Catholic and Orthodox theologians from whom they had been separated and had refused any type of discussion a generation ago. Conciliar Evangelicals would be open to participation along with charismatics in the Global Christian Forum and other groups concerned about Christian unity.

Finally, any movement, if it is to succeed in the next generation, needs to be aware of history and changes that have occurred in our common understanding. Of course, the term "paradigm shift" is the catch phrase used to describe such changes. The WCC in calling for a Global Christian Forum has recognized the paradigm shift of the church from the Northern hemisphere to the Southern hemisphere. It is recognition that the charismatic and Evangelical movement has in many places of the world become the dominant expression of the Christian faith. Whether the Global Christian Forum will be the instrument for bringing in greater unity is yet to be seen.

Perhaps 100 years after Edinburgh 1910, a new form of unity, beyond the institution of the WCC, will arise. Could it be that the WCC needs to die and something new arise? I believe this question is probably relevant for all Christian World Communions. The fact is that for many Baptists and Evangelicals, the Lausanne movement for world evangelization has in recent years been a more attractive movement for unity than the WCC. Unfortunately, for most of our younger theologians and especially laity, the WCC is not even on their radar screen, except as a footnote. But, the prayer of Christ for unity in John 17 and the Apostle Paul's admonition in Ephesians 4 is a reality with which all Christians should be constantly confronted. We do not yet know the form of that new unity, but for countless lay people, Bible study groups in thousands of villages do show a unity beyond the institutional structures of the present ecumenical movement. For Evangelicals, visible unity is not in a building or institution, but it is best demonstrated in a common witness, in word and deed, to the saving power of Jesus Christ. It is for that unity that Baptists and Evangelicals will join hands and hearts with all who name the name of Christ, within or outside of the WCC.

It is important to mention here that the Roman Catholic Church is not a member of the WCC, although the Orthodox churches are. Baptists and Evangelicals enjoy regular theological conversations with both Catholics and Orthodox, often finding these conversations more in agreement with their faith than those with liberal Protestantism. Evangelicals find essential agreement with Catholics and Orthodox on crucial doctrines such as the Trinity, the divinity of Christ, the atonement, the resurrection and a biblical worldview on moral behaviour.

In 2010 in Edinburgh, the WCC gathered representatives of the member churches to celebrate the 100th anniversary of the 1910 World Missionary Conference. This celebration called the ecumenical movement's attention back to its origin in the work of world evangelism. In October the same year, the Third Lausanne Congress on World Evangelization was convened in Cape Town.[10] The Cape Town gathering consciously affirmed itself as carrying on the work of the 1910 Edinburgh conference. Could it be that both Evangelical and ecumenical theologians will rediscover the original watchword for unity, "The evangelization of the world in this generation"? Then we will have come full circle and affirm "mission and unity" as the key to future cooperation and an enlarged vision of ecumenicity. May that be our prayer!

It is fitting to close this paper with the *Lausanne Covenant*'s call for unity:

> We affirm that the church's visible unity in truth is God's purpose. Evangelism also summons us to unity, because our oneness strengthens our witness, just as our disunity undermines our gospel of reconciliation. We recognize, however, that organizational unity may take many forms and does not necessarily forward evangelism. Yet we who share the same biblical faith should be closely united in fellowship, work and witness. We confess that our testimony has sometimes been marred by sinful individuals and needless duplication. We pledge ourselves to seek a deeper unity in truth, worship, holiness and mission. We urge the development of regional and functional cooperation for the furtherance of the church's

mission, for strategic planning, for mutual encouragement, and for the sharing of resources and experience.[11]

---

1   I use the term "many Baptists" so that it will be understood that I am not speaking for all Baptists. In fact, this article is my personal opinion and does not necessarily represent that of the BWA or other Baptist groups. Of the 232 BWA member bodies, only 25 are members of the WCC. These 25 Baptist WCC members comprise more than 50% of Baptists worldwide. This is due largely to the four large African American Baptist conventions which are WCC members, i.e., National Baptist Convention, USA, Inc., National Baptist Convention of America, National Missionary Baptist Convention of America, and the Progressive National Baptist Convention, Inc.

2   Norman Goodall, ed., *The Uppsala Report 1968* (Geneva: WCC, 1968), p. 26.

3   Report of the Bossey Seminar, "Mission as Proclamation of the Gospel: Towards a New Ecumenical Agenda for Evangelism in the 21st Century" (Ecumenical Institute Bossey, June 6-12, 2006), in *Ecumenical Letter on Evangelism* 2 (August 2006); http://www.wcc-coe.org/wcc/what/mission/evlet2-2006-e.html.

4   Kenneth R. Ross, "The Centenary of Edinburgh 1910: Its Possibilities," *International Bulletin of Missionary Research* 30, no. 4 (October 2006): 178.

5   Philip Jenkins, *The Next Christendom: The Coming of Global Christianity* (Oxford: Oxford University Press, 2002).

6   "Report from the Inter-Religious Consultation on 'Conversion – Assessing the Reality,'" *Pro Dialogo Bulletin* 122, no. 2 (2006): 210-13.

7   "Dialogue with Other Religions: An Evangelical View," ch. 7 in Vinay Samuel and Chris Sugden, eds., *Sharing Jesus in the Two Thirds World: Evangelical Christology from the Contexts of Poverty, Powerlessness, and Religious Pluralism,* Papers of the First Conference of Evangelical Mission Theologians from the Two Thirds World, Bangkok, Thailand, March 22-25, 1982 (Grand Rapids: Eerdmans, 1984), p. 125.

8   Of course the Baptist tradition of social engagement is strong. Walter Rauschenbush's call for a "Social Gospel," and Martin Luther King's fight for human dignity, as well as Jimmy Carter's concern for peace and justice are all excellent models of Baptist and Evangelical concern for social involvement of the church!

9   Baptist World Alliance, "Statistics", http://bwanet.org; World Council of Churches, "Member Churches", http://oikoumene.org. Baptists do not count infants as members. Therefore, statistics for churches that practice "believer's baptism" are of course lower than paedobaptists. Statisticians for the WCC and other organizations generally triple the number of adult believers to get comparative numbers. For example, the BWA has 40 million baptized believers, which represents a community of approximately 120 million. In addition, there is probably a further 50 million in other Baptist groups that do not belong to the BWA. See *International Bulletin of Missionary Research* 30, no. 1 (January 2006): 29, where the BWA membership number of 110 million is transposed.

10   *Christ Our Reconciler: Gospel, Church, World.* The Third Lausanne Congress on World Evangelization, Cape Town, October 17-24, 2010, ed. Julia E. M. Cameron (Downers Grove, Illinois: IVP Books, 2012).

11   *The Lausanne Covenant,* "No. 7 – Cooperation in Evangelism," in *Let the Earth Hear His Voice,* International Congress on World Evangelism, Lausanne 1974, ed. J. D. Douglas (Minneapolis: World Wide Publications, 1975), p. 5.

† CHAPTER 18

Breaking New Ground: The Global Christian Forum

by Huibert van Beek

H onesty compels me to say right from the beginning of this article that in all the discussions on the Global Christian Forum of which I have been part since 1998, seldom or ever has there been an allusion to the *500th anniversary of 2017*. There are at least two reasons for this. First, the *Forum* (as it will be referred to hereafter) is not addressing directly the division that occurred in the church of the West at the time of the sixteenth-century Reformation. Second, the Evangelical and Pentecostal churches – the part of Christianity with which the Forum is particularly most concerned – do not usually cultivate a strong sense of belonging to Reformation history. Having said this, there is no doubt that the Forum seeks to promote Christian unity: if not its full restoration, at least the overcoming of separations and divisions that are characteristic of our time, and which have further divided the church after the great schisms of the past.

The Background

In 1998, the World Council of Churches celebrated the fiftieth anniversary of its foundation in 1948. This was an opportunity not only to rejoice and give thanks to God for the fruits of the ecumenical movement, but also to engage in a thorough reflection on the nature and calling of the Council. A process called *Towards a Common Understanding and Vision of the World Council of Churches* was initiated at the beginning of the 1990s,[1] and the results were presented in the form of a policy statement to the Eighth Assembly of the WCC in December 1998 in Harare, Zimbabwe. The focal point of the *Common Understanding and Vision,* or CUV as it is commonly called, was the understanding of the WCC as a *fellowship* of churches. While the main thrust of the CUV document consists of spelling out the meaning of that concept and its implications for the WCC and the churches, in its final chapter there is an observation that this fellowship will not be complete as long as the Catholic Church on the one hand, and the Evangelical and Pentecostal churches on the other hand, are not fully part of it. The observation needs some clarification. The Catholic Church has been deeply committed to the ecumenical movement since the Second Vatican Council and, although not a member, has significant relationships with the WCC, for example, through the Joint Working Group and the Faith and Order Commission. It is involved in a large number of theological dialogues with churches and communions that are in WCC membership. When it comes to the Evangelical and Pentecostal churches, the vast majority of them do not relate to the WCC and do not participate in the ecumenical movement at all. Thus, the situations are not comparable. But from the point of view of the WCC, the two groups have in common that they are not included in its membership. By noting this, the CUV acknowledged that fifty years after its foundation and at the end of the century that saw the birth of the modern ecumenical movement, the vision of the WCC as a Council embracing the whole Church of Christ had not come to be. Statistically speaking this leads to a fairly sobering assessment. Assuming that the Catholic Church counts for about half of the total Christian population of over two billion and that the estimated number of over six hundred million Evangelical and Pentecostal Christians is correct, the WCC represents roughly a quarter of Christianity in the world. This is corroborated by its own statistics, which indicate a total membership of its member churches between five and six hundred million.[2]

Although a further analysis of the CUV statement is not intended here, for the purpose of what follows it is interesting to note the implicit tensions between the concepts of *membership* and *fellowship* with which the document was struggling. Part of the intention behind the CUV was to create some space beyond the limits of membership. The document says that the Council *is* a fellowship that *has* an organizational structure.[3] Fellowship is understood as being based on *participation* motivated by communality of vision and purpose, whereas an organization is based on formal membership. The distinction made here could mean that there is, or should be, some room for participating in the fellowship without being a member formally. That is what the Catholic Church actually does. But when the CUV speaks about fellowship it is referring to the Basis of the WCC, which states: "The World Council of Churches is a *fellowship* of churches which confess ..."; and acceptance of the Basis is one of the main conditions for membership. In other words, formally speaking, membership is required in order to become fully part of the fellowship. In an attempt to solve this dilemma, the WCC created a new category of affiliation called *Churches in Association with the World Council of Churches*, which requires agreement with the Basis but not with the other criteria for membership. Until now, no church has come forward with the desire to use this new opening, which is probably not yet well known, and it is not clear whether this is a satisfactory solution. Underlying the debate is the concern that participation without the commitment that is reflected in membership may eventually weaken the fellowship rather than enrich and strengthen it.

At the drafting stage, the CUV document had one additional chapter that did not make it to the final draft. It was a proposal to transform the Assembly of the WCC into a *forum* where a much broader representation of the Christian family would become visible than only the part of it constituted by the member churches. As could be expected, the governing bodies did not want to give up the Assembly, which is indeed the only and unique moment in the life of the Council when all the member churches are assembled and the fullness of the fellowship is tasted, albeit imperfectly. But the idea of a *forum* remained, as a concept for widening the table and moving beyond some of the limitations of the configuration of the WCC and the ecumenical movement at the end of the twentieth century. The need for such a forum could also be stated in other terms, a bit more bluntly. The Catholic Church has made it clear more than once that it does not intend to become a member of the WCC as it is. Nor is WCC membership on the agenda of most of the Evangelical and Pentecostal churches, and it is unrealistic to expect that this will change in any foreseeable future. In other words, the WCC as it is has reached the point where it probably will not attract many more churches to join. There is still a reservoir of churches on the outskirts of the Evangelical movement and churches that are yet emancipating from missionary tutelage, but it is relatively small. Recognizing these realities does in no way mean to say that the WCC has run its course. On the contrary, it remains the most representative body of the churches in the world. It includes not only all the mainline Anglican and Protestant denominations but also the Orthodox churches. What it stands for – visible unity, justice, peace, common witness, renewal, mission and evangelism – is as needed today as it was when the Council was created. It stands at the heart of a movement that is much broader than the Council alone, with the Catholic Church, with groups and networks dealing with numerous issues, with individuals and groups from Evangelical and Pentecostal constituencies participating in various ways. The potential of the movement is enormous and the WCC is an indispensable instrument of it all. If it were to go out of business today, it would have to be recreated tomorrow. One could also argue that a smaller WCC is probably better equipped to play a leading role than if it was larger and more representative of the totality of Christianity in the world.

The statistical picture of 50% Catholic, 25% WCC, and 25% Evangelical and Pentecostal needs to be completed with some further observations. First, the trends that can be observed in the Christian church worldwide show that the centre of gravity of Christianity is rapidly shifting away from Europe and North America to the South: Africa, Latin America, the Caribbean, the Pacific, even Asia. These are the regions where the churches are growing, where new churches are being planted almost by the day, where new denominations come up and take the place of older ones. Second, new forms of being church are emerging, including mega-churches, non-denominational churches, independent churches, indigenous churches, charismatic groups, as well as new networks, agencies and para-church bodies. The Christian church is rapidly acquiring new and multiple faces, and these new manifestations of the church are mostly found in the South.[4] Third, most of this vitality and growth is taking place outside the ecumenical movement and among churches that are not members of the WCC, in particular within the Pentecostal churches. The Pentecostal/charismatic movement has grown in less than a century from a few dozen people "slain in the Spirit" to over 500 million followers today. This is not to say that there is no life and growth in the churches belonging to the WCC. There are life and growth, for example, in the South among churches that grew out of the nineteenth-century missionary movement and have taken root in the cultural and social context of their people. Some of the Orthodox churches have also experienced amazing renewal, such as in Albania, and others have developed new practices of mission, such as the Greek Orthodox Church of Alexandria in many African countries.

A Proposal

Although not necessarily stated so explicitly, these new realities of world Christianity were behind the proposal of a Forum of Christian Churches and Ecumenical Organizations made in 1997-98 by Konrad Raiser, at that time general secretary of the WCC. Several of the Christian World Communions, and in particular the Pontifical Council for Promoting Christian Unity, were consulted before it was launched. It was felt that without the Catholic Church, there was little reason to pursue the idea. The Catholic reaction was cautious, to say the least, and certainly not enthusiastic. There was fear, as there was in the WCC and with other partners, that such a forum could easily become an alternative option for churches that would want to reduce their ecumenical commitment. One should not forget that this discussion came at the time of growing criticism of the WCC in the Orthodox churches and the prospect that some of these churches might withdraw their membership. It was also feared that in spite of all good intentions, a proposal of this kind would sooner or later result in the creation of a new international ecumenical body that would require financial and human resources from the participating churches and organizations. In a time of diminishing support for ecumenical structures, this was not a stimulating prospect. The question that kept coming back was "why?" Why is a forum needed?

A first consultation was convened by the WCC in August 1998. It produced a document entitled *Proposals Regarding a Forum of Christian Churches and Ecumenical Organizations,* in which it offered a response to the "why" in the following terms:

The proposed Forum is *possible* because of the unity which is already given in Christ. It is *called for* because of our common faith in a reconciling God whose church knows itself summoned to become God's reconciled and reconciling people.[5]

and:

A more effective, more sustaining, more inclusive network of relationships is needed to bring differences of understanding among the partners into a mutually committed dialogue so that all may find their way to a clearer discernment and a more faithful obedience.[6]

The document then outlined the style of the proposed Forum, the basis and criteria for participation, and the range of representation including the Catholic, Orthodox, Evangelical, Pentecostal, Anglican, and Protestant families represented in the Conference of Christian World Communions, as well as regional ecumenical organizations, international ecumenical organizations and the World Council of Churches. It proposed guidelines for the size, process, and content of Forum meetings, the organization and the funding, and stated that an initial Forum meeting might take place as early as 2001, with some 150 to 250 participants. The Eighth Assembly of the WCC, meeting in December 1998 in Harare, Zimbabwe, commended the proposal for serious attention and encouraged the Central Committee of the WCC to continue the process of consultation, especially with the Catholic Church and Pentecostals. The Assembly also echoed some of the concerns, carefully worded in no less than nine points ranging from the role of the WCC in initiating the Forum, the distinction between the WCC and the Forum, and between participation in the Forum and committed membership in the WCC, to the respect for the distinctive self-understanding of each ecclesial family, the need for inclusiveness, and the modesty of the organizational structures required to make the Forum happen.[7]

The August 1998 Consultation was itself anything but representative of that grand gathering of the Christian church the Forum was supposed to realize. There was one Catholic and one Pentecostal participant. All the others were in one way or another part of the WCC constituency in its broader sense. The meeting appointed a small Continuation Committee from among the participants which of necessity reflected the same limitations. Who could have expected something new to emerge from such a small beginning?

Exploring

The obvious step that had to be taken at this stage was to find out if there was any interest in Evangelical and Pentecostal circles in exploring and pursuing the idea of a Forum in which they would sit at the table with those to whom they had not previously sought to approach; namely, the WCC, its member churches, and the Catholic Church. This happened in September 2000, when the members of the Continuation Committee sat down for a long weekend with a group of Evangelical and Pentecostal leaders from various parts of the world. The meeting took place at Fuller Theological Seminary in Pasadena, USA, a stronghold of the Evangelical movement and a place of learning for many Evangelicals and Pentecostals. The committee had on purpose chosen to hold this conversation on *Evangelical ground*, in order to demonstrate its seriousness and make it easier for its interlocutors to accept the invitation. The response to the idea of a Forum that would seek to bring together all the main Christian traditions was amazingly positive and affirmative. There was a shared feeling at this meeting that it was the right moment, that the time had come to look for ways that would make it possible to overcome the divisions of the twentieth century between those who had embraced the ecumenical movement and those who had opted for the Evangelical or Pentecostal ways of understanding and living out the faith. It may well have been that the symbolism of the year 2000, the transition from the second to the third millennium on which there had been so much emphasis, not least in the churches, had something to do with the receptive posture of the participants. But subsequent developments of the Forum process have helped to see more clearly a fundamental pattern that is underlying much of what is happening. For ecumenists, the twentieth century will go into church history as the age of the ecumenical movement. For Pentecostals, it will be the great century of Pentecostal and charismatic revival of the church. Ecumenism as we know it today had its beginning in the World Mission Conference in Edinburgh in 1910. Pentecostalism is usually dated back to the Azusa Street revival in

Los Angeles in 1906. The two movements are contemporaneous and both have their roots in the Evangelical and Holiness movements of the nineteenth century. Yet they have developed largely in isolation from one another. Each has marked the church profoundly, but each has impacted different sectors of the church. There have been some attempts at building bridges or creating intersections, such as the work of the Pentecostal pioneer David du Plessis, but the hallmarks of their relationships have been more often suspicion or hostility than respect or affection. This is all the more remarkable when one takes into account that both movements claim to be the fruit of the Spirit. The ecumenical movement would not be able to understand itself if it did not believe that the extraordinary renewal it has witnessed in so many churches and among so many Christians is the work of the Holy Spirit. The Pentecostal movement is by its very nature Spirit-driven. "All were made to drink of one Spirit," says St. Paul in his first letter to the divided Corinthians. Twentieth-century church history has shown once again that Christians who quench their spiritual thirst from the same source do not necessarily travel the same road.[8]

The ecclesial picture of the past century is more complex than what has been suggested so far. When the Ecumenical and Pentecostal movements emerged in the early 1900s, it seemed as though the Evangelical movement had come to a deadlock in the trap of fundamentalism, at least in the USA. But it found a fresh departure in the *new evangelicalism* of the 1940s that led to the creation of the National Association of Evangelicals in the USA and the revival of the World Evangelical Fellowship (now Alliance, WEA). Since then, the Evangelical movement has been going from strength to strength. The WEA claims today to represent over 600 million Christians organized in more than 120 national Evangelical alliances or equivalent bodies. This number includes many Pentecostals as well as many Christians belonging to churches that are members of the WCC. No statistics are available, but it can be said safely that in a good number of Protestant and Anglican churches, ten percent or more of the membership identifies itself as Evangelical and takes part actively in networks of the Evangelical movement. Similarly, the Pentecostal movement has been marked in the latter half of the twentieth century by a *second wave*, the charismatic revival that swept through many of the *established* churches. Thus, when the unprecedented growth of Pentecostalism is mentioned, one should not lose sight of the fact that here again there is considerable overlap in the statistics. The Catholic Church alone counts about 120 million charismatics among its flock.

What this pattern of separated yet intertwined movements of renewal says is that the church *as a whole* has been shaken to the bones in the twentieth century. It means that the ecumenical movement is challenged by Evangelical, Pentecostal, and Charismatic realities that it cannot ignore, and vice versa the Evangelical, Pentecostal, and Charismatic movements have to face the questions that ecumenism is putting before them. It calls for an awareness and recognition on *all* sides that the same Spirit is at work also in the other. When that is acknowledged, the common challenge becomes to seek to discern *together* what the Spirit is saying and where the Spirit is leading the church. It would seem that herein lies at least a partial explanation of the attraction that the Forum proposal met already at its early stages.

Shaping

Another question was how to shape the Forum? The group that met in September 2000 spoke about an independent development of the Forum idea, exploring ways beyond the existing ecumenical structures. It produced a set of possible purposes, emphasizing mission, wholeness, and relationships that could lead to common witness.[9] The Continuation Committee felt that there was wisdom in carrying on with a tentative, empirical approach rather than moving at once to convening a major global meeting as the 1998 Consultation had proposed. This led to the suggestion to test at a smaller scale what a Forum might look like. Three objectives were formulated: a) to expand and deepen the dialogue with Evangelicals and Pentecostals, b) to involve a more widely representative group of the various Christian traditions, and c) to decide on a Forum event and give guidance regarding the process.

One of the considerations was how to compose such a Forum meeting so that it would be representative of all the traditions and yet allow for a fair balance between the two components, the Ecumenical group and the Evangelical/Pentecostal group. Those on the Evangelical/Pentecostal side said that they were the ones who had been rejected and excluded by the *mainline* churches and therefore should be given ample space at the new table. If they were to find themselves in a minority position opposite the older traditions, they would feel threatened and not be able to speak their mind freely. In other words, the two sides should be on equal footing and one of the conditions for that to happen would be to ensure more or less equal numbers. The committee decided in favour of this option, which since that time has become almost a constitutive principle of the Global Christian Forum. In all its meetings thus far, care has been taken to make sure that approximately half of the participants are Evangelicals and Pentecostals, with the other half made up of Anglicans, Catholics, Orthodox, Protestants, etc. Although the model does not provide a representation in proportion to numbers, the experience is that it creates an adequate setting for a beginning dialogue between two large sectors of Christianity that hitherto have been little or not at all in conversation with one another. Another related principle is that in Forum meetings the participants sit at tables grouped in a square or rectangle so that all are equal and face one another.

A second consideration was about the methodology of a Forum meeting. Should it proceed in the way dialogue meetings usually do, with a theme chosen in advance, papers presented by experts representing different traditions, discussion in groups and plenary, drafters and a final report reflecting the consensus the group was able to reach? Instinctively, the committee felt that such a classical working method, very common in ecumenical circles, might not be the most appropriate choice for the entirely new experiment it was working on. For one thing, it would probably put at a disadvantage the Evangelical and Pentecostal participants who would be less at ease and familiar with the methodology than their ecumenical partners. The thinking of the committee went therefore in a different direction, more inductive, inviting the participants to come up with priorities as they saw them and to build their own conversation. The exercise should begin with a thorough round of personal sharing and introductions and the outcome be left open. In between, the committee as the organizer should give some guidance but leave maximum space for the process of the meeting to find its own way. The history, background, and purpose of the Forum should be presented with utmost transparency, inviting input and participation and explaining the role of the WCC in initiating the proposal. The objectives for the meeting set by the committee should be put before the group right from the start.

Experimenting

This Forum experiment took place in June 2002, again at Fuller Theological Seminary, with about sixty participants, from all parts of the world and "all parts of the Body of Christ"[10] (African Instituted, Anglican, Baptist, Catholic, Disciples, Evangelical, Friends, Holiness, Lutheran, Mennonite, Moravian, Methodist, Old Catholic, Orthodox [Eastern and Oriental], Pentecostal, Reformed, Salvation Army, and Seventh-day Adventist). It was a watershed for the Forum process. The personal presentations spontaneously developed into an extraordinary spiritual sharing of faith stories of individuals and their faith communities that took more than a full day. The participants responded creatively to the open-ended, inviting shape of the meeting and decided to rework and improve the Forum purposes suggested two years earlier into a *Provisional Purpose Statement.*[11] It led to an animated discussion on a *basis* for participation in the Forum. The document adopted in 1998 had simply taken the words of the Basis of the WCC.[12] The same was again proposed, but some objected that it might identify the Forum too closely with the World Council. To come up with a different wording was not easy, because opinions diverged on how to state in a brief sentence the basic tenets of the Christian faith. How inclusive should it be? How open, to enable the broadest possible range of traditions to feel free to join? The formulation that was eventually accepted by all was offered by the oldest traditions present in the meeting, Catholic and Orthodox, and warmly welcomed by the youngest, Evangelical and Pentecostal: "... Christian churches and interchurch organizations which confess the triune God and Jesus Christ as perfect in His divinity and humanity." It reflected a consensus that the Forum was expressing its roots in the language of the early church where all could find common ground. The meeting understood it to be *provisional* because the Forum was still taking shape. Yet it has stayed, it has functioned, none of the subsequent Forum meetings has called it into question, and at the global Forum gathering that took place in November 2007, it was unanimously affirmed and renamed as a *guiding* statement.

The meeting contributed another suggestion: that the Forum should be understood as a *process* rather than an event. The focus should be on broadening the scope, widening the circle, and drawing in more people, for example by holding similar Forum meetings in various regions of the world. In the same spirit, it was recommended that the committee should be enlarged and become more representative of the different traditions, regions, and gender. Thus, this first test of the Forum not only affirmed the concept – although many questions remained unanswered – it also provided a whole new perspective and became a model for the future. In this regard, particular mention should be made of the experience of sharing the faith stories, or *faith journeys,* as it came to be called. Its impact was in particular due to the Pentecostal and Evangelical participants for whom this was a well-known practice and who set the example. For the others, it was a revelation. Since then, the sharing of faith journeys has been a feature of all the Forum meetings. It is done on the first day and has proven to be an effective means of creating confidence and trust between Christians coming from very different traditions, some of which have been very little or not at all in conversation with one another. It is also experienced as a refreshing and innovative way of beginning a meeting. This methodology, combined with a flexible and open-ended agenda that offers as much room as possible for input from around the table, has become the typical meeting style of the Forum and one of its strengths. It is not a judgment on other, more academic styles that have their value in their own contexts. The Forum seeks to bring together two broad *streams* in Christianity that have been separated by deep-seated misgivings, ignorance, and lack of trust. For that to happen it has developed its own way of doing things in its specific context, not by design but empirically. Putting it in more spiritual terms, the Forum has experienced that when space is not filled beforehand, God's Spirit may be freer to move, and the results may be received as a gift of the Spirit. It is not by accident that the *Guiding Purpose Statement* speaks of creating a *space* as the aim of the Forum,

> an open space wherein representatives of a broad range of Christian churches and interchurch organizations, which confess the triune God and Jesus Christ as perfect in His divinity

and humanity, can gather to foster mutual respect, to explore and address together common challenges.[13]

Regional Consultations

In response to the call for a broader and more inclusive process, the Committee sat down and planned a series of four consultations in major regions of the world for the period 2004-2007. At the same time, it kept the goal of holding a global Forum as an *event* that could be scheduled as the *culmination* of the whole process. The regional meetings took place successively in Asia (2004), Africa (2005), Europe (2006), and Latin America (2007).[14] All four were more or less of the same size – about sixty people – and similar in composition, flow, and outcome. Each one also had its own aspects depending on the particularities of the region. Each time there was a strong affirmation of the Forum and of the meeting style. In Asia, Africa and Latin America, suggestions for follow-up at the level of the region were made, some of which have already resulted in new initiatives. For example, the Evangelical Fellowship of Asia has joined an already existing cooperation between the Federation of Asian Bishops' Conferences (Catholic) and the Christian Conference of Asia (the regional ecumenical body). In the Europe meeting, the emphasis was put on the relevance of the Forum proposal for national and sub-regional situations in Europe. These regional consultations have achieved a major purpose of broadening and strengthening the support base of the Forum. They have made it possible to draw in many Evangelical and Pentecostal churches and groupings that otherwise would not have been reached. The response of Evangelical and Pentecostal leaders in the South to the invitation of the Forum has been remarkably more positive than that of some of their counterparts in the North. This is also true for central and eastern Europe. In Africa and Asia, the distinctions are not as clear as in some parts of Europe and North America, especially on the ground, and there is a real desire to open up to each other and join hands. In the Africa regional meeting, several examples were given of Catholics, Protestants, and Evangelicals/Pentecostals getting on very well with each other in confronting issues like armed conflict, political upheaval, HIV/AIDS, etc. Another significant result of the regional meetings has been the involvement of the Catholic regional episcopal conferences, particularly in Asia and Latin America. The Anglican and Protestant participation in the Forum, and to some extent the Orthodox presence, have also been strengthened considerably through the regional process. Perhaps the most important lesson has been that the Forum is not simply a proposal "from the top." It meets with realities and expectations at all levels and in all regions. Developments similar to the Forum can be observed in a number of places, for example, Christian Churches Together in the USA, the new Christian Council in Norway, the Christian Association of Nigeria, the Christian Federation of Malaysia, and others, which have not resulted from the Global Christian Forum as such. The interaction between these new structures and the Forum holds the promise of encouraging and enabling *Forum-type* initiatives elsewhere, in national or regional situations. The follow-up of the Global Christian Forum is no longer a matter of a limited number of propositions by the Committee. It has to be multi-faceted and diverse, initiating, responding, informing, mobilizing, and enabling in a variety of places, locally, nationally, and regionally, while at the same time furthering and deepening the process at the global level.

A Global Gathering

Before the series of regional meetings was over, the Committee began the preparations for a global Forum *event*. It took place in November 2007 in Limuru, near Nairobi, Kenya. With some 230 representatives of all the main Christian traditions at a high level of leadership, it was a faithful accomplishment of the vision that was projected in 1998 and gradually refined as the process developed. It was probably the most diverse and representative gathering of the Christian Church worldwide since the ecumenical movement began about a century ago. The most significant result of the Limuru Global Forum has been that it has established the Forum firmly in today's ecumenical and interchurch landscape. The Forum is no longer an experiment, it is a reality. The leaders of the Evangelical and Pentecostal movements, the Catholic Church, the Orthodox churches, the Anglican and Protestant world communions, the African Instituted Churches, and the World Council of Churches all wholeheartedly said "yes" to it. The meeting did more. It approved a set of proposals for the future including a thorough evaluation of the process since 1998, the renewal of the committee, and the convening of a consultation to map out a long-term program, all of which were implemented by the end of 2008.[15] A breakthrough happened when Pentecostal leaders present at the event asked that the Pentecostal World Fellowship be listed with the other churches, church families, and organizations as signatories of the Message.[16] The sharing of faith journeys at this meeting was a learning experience. Because of the size of the gathering, it could not happen in plenary, as had been always the case. It was therefore done in groups of thirty that were composed carefully so as to reflect the diversity in terms of traditions, regions, gender, etc. There was some apprehension that people might complain not to have heard all the stories. But it turned out that in a smaller group the experience was, in fact, more intense and more effective than in a larger setting. These personal testimonies, together with the Bible studies and the moments of celebration and prayer, were the texture weaving the meeting into a community of people recognizing each other as brothers and sisters who call on Jesus Christ as their Lord and Savior.

Consolidating and Expanding

In 2008, three independent research and study centres evaluated the process from 1998 to 2007, including the global gathering. On the basis of the evaluation results and the outcome of the global gathering, a framework for a three-year plan was elaborated at a consultation that took place in November 2008 in New Delhi. Subsequently, the Committee finalized this three-year program 2009-2011, with the intention to have it culminate in a second global gathering towards the end of the year 2011. The Committee itself was gradually enlarged and made more representative of the range of church families participating in the Forum, in particular with the inclusion of the Pentecostal World Fellowship, the Ecumenical Patriarchate, and several Christian World Communions that previously had not been part of it. The name "Continuation Committee" was abandoned in favour of "Committee of the Global Christian Forum," signifying the shift from an initial, provisional stage to the reality of a new development in the pursuit of Christian unity and common witness.

The primary focus of the 2009-2011 program was to consolidate and expand the regional process. Regional follow-up meetings were held in Africa, Asia, Europe (Nordic-Baltic sub-region), and Latin America. The program also foresaw the convening of consultations in regions where the Forum had not yet been tried, e.g. the Middle East, the Caribbean, and the Pacific, but some of these had to be postponed to a later time because of insufficient financial and staffing resources. A GCF Team Visit did take place to the Middle East, which turned out to be an effective new means of introducing and communicating the Forum vision.

A New Phase

Alongside the deepening and multiplying of opportunities for the widest possible range of Christian traditions to meet and get to know each other, the Committee had to confront a fundamental question in the period following the Limuru global gathering: the role of the Global Christian Forum with regard to themes and issues of Christian unity. There was agreement that the Forum should not duplicate the work done in places like Faith and Order and the bilateral theological dialogues. Until then, no Forum consultations with a specific thematic focus had been organized. Discussions in the meetings had mostly been on general questions emerging from the life and mission of the churches, and not with the intention to reach conclusions or consensus. On a few occasions, there had been a beginning of grappling with more controversial questions, such as proselytism and interreligious dialogue. These attempts had shown that the Forum approach could provide a favourable context for such conversations. The conviction that this should be the specific role of the Forum was gaining momentum. The question was therefore whether the time had come to begin to address intentionally the tough issues that are dividing the ecumenical and Evangelical/Pentecostal movements. One of the criticisms directed at the Forum, particularly from the ecumenical side, was indeed that it was avoiding any serious discussion on such difficult questions, and that this was the price paid for preserving the meeting space it had been able to create. On the other hand, Pentecostal members of the Committee and other Pentecostal Forum participants felt strongly that it was too early to put divisive issues, such as proselytism, on the agenda of the Forum, and that much more time was needed to bring about the atmosphere of trust that would make this possible. They feared that it might jeopardize all the progress made and foreclose any future move to bridge the gap between their churches and the ecumenical movement.

The debate remained unresolved until the convening of the second global gathering, which took place in October 2011 in Manado, Indonesia. Referring to the Guiding Purpose Statement of the Forum, the participants in this meeting declared:

> We have heard the Spirit calling us, not only to foster respect for one another, but now also to move forward together in addressing common challenges. GCF participants believe that the Forum has the potential to be a space for discussing relevant topical issues, even and perhaps especially where we are not in agreement with one another.[17]

While providing this clear guidance for the Global Christian Forum to enter a new phase, the Manado gathering also emphasized that it should continue being a platform for building relationships, globally, regionally, and nationally, and seek to be ever more inclusive of the diversity of world Christianity.

From 2012 onwards, the GCF Committee initiated a consultative conversation with the Pentecostal World Fellowship, the Pontifical Council for Promoting Christian Unity, the World Council of Churches, and the World Evangelical Alliance. The intent of this consultation was to identify which *common challenges,* on the fault line between the ecumenical and Evangelical/Pentecostal streams of world Christianity, the Forum should begin to address. Two were specifically named: the persecution of Christians and proselytism. Since then, processes have been designed and implemented to deal with these themes. The first led to the global consultation on "Discrimination, Persecution and Martyrdom: Following Christ Together," which was held in Tirana, Albania, in November 2015. The second is somewhat different in nature and still on course at the time of completing this article. One of its aims is to produce a set of guidelines for "Christian witness in a world of many Christian faith traditions," on the model of the document *Christian Witness in a Multi-religious World,* published jointly by the Pontifical Council for Promoting Christian Unity (PCPCU), the WCC, and the WEA in 2011.

The findings of these thematic reflections will feed into the third global gathering of the Forum, which is scheduled to take place in April 2018 in a Latin American context, possibly in Cuba. It is hoped that this event will provide further guidance for the development of the Global Christian Forum, which by then will enter the third decade of its journey.

A Personal Word

Monsignor John Radano – Jack, as we call him affectionately – was on the Committee of the Global Christian Forum since 1999, which was practically from the beginning, until his retirement in 2008. He did not miss a single of the thirteen committee meetings in these years, and has been at all six consultations and the global gathering. That faithfulness to the commitment he had taken was a mirror reflection of the impressive faithfulness to the Catholic Church he represented, his Church, and which transcended all his interventions. As the Catholic Church was rather reserved at the beginning, so was Jack. He kept asking *why* a Forum, what is the purpose, what does it do that is not already done elsewhere? He could drive some of us to the brink of exasperation, but he was also the one who at the next session would come with some ideas scribbled on a piece of paper, to help us move ahead. As the first signals came that our Evangelical and Pentecostal partners found mission and evangelism as important as unity, he would keep on pressing for Christian unity to be *the* focus of the Forum. When the consultations began to show that the Forum had a purpose, Jack acknowledged that gladly – and proposed that we continue organizing such meetings, to bring in ever more people and make that the goal of the process. When we started discussing the global *Forum event* scheduled for 2007, he pressed again the question why. What is the decisive argument for calling such a meeting? He obliged us to formulate the answer: because there is currently no place globally where all the Christian traditions can come together. Once convinced, Jack quietly set out to bring his Church on board. We can only guess how much energy and time it has taken him. But if we are today where we are, it is in no small measure thanks to Jack. On behalf of the Committee, I would like to celebrate that and to give thanks to God for the journey Jack has travelled with us.

1   WCC, *Towards a Common Understanding and Vision of the World Council of Churches* (Geneva: WCC, 1993); available at http://oikoumene.org.

2   *A Handbook of Churches and Councils: Profiles of Ecumenical Relationships*, ed. Huibert van Beek (Geneva: WCC, 2006), p. 14.

3   *Towards a Common Understanding and Vision of the World Council of Churches*, no. 3.13.

4   See for example Philip Jenkins, *The Next Christendom: The Coming of Global Christianity* (Oxford: Oxford University Press, 2002).

5   WCC, *Proposals Regarding a Forum of Christian Churches and Ecumenical Organizations* (Chateau de Bossey, Switzerland, August 26-29, 1998), no. 4; included as Appendix II of the Report of the Policy Reference Committee I, in WCC, *Together on the Way: Official Report of the Eighth Assembly of the World Council of Churches*, ed. Diane Kessler (Geneva: WCC, 1999), pp. 173-76.

6   WCC, *Proposals Regarding a Forum of Christian Churches and Ecumenical Organizations*, no. 2.

7   WCC, *Together on the Way*, pp. 168-70.

8   I have dealt more extensively with this issue in my article "Pentecostals-Ecumenicals Dialogue" in André Droogers, Cornelis van der Laan, and Wout van Laar, eds., *Fruitful in this Land: Pluralism, Dialogue and Healing in Migrant Pentecostalism* (Zoetermeer, Netherlands: Uitgeverij Boekencentrum, 2006), pp. 81-92.

9   Global Christian Forum, *Communiqué* (Pasadena, California, September 11, 2000); http://www.ecu.net/?p=8943.

10   This expression, that reflects so nicely the intent of the Forum, was suggested for the first time in 2005. It is used here retrospectively.

11   Global Christian Forum, *Guiding Purpose Statement* (Limuru, Kenya: November 9, 2007); http://www.globalchristianforum.org

12   WCC, *Proposals Regarding a Forum of Christian Churches and Ecumenical Organizations*, no. 9.

13   Global Christian Forum, *Guiding Purpose Statement*.

14   In the USA an initiative similar to the Forum, *Christian Churches Together in the USA*, began in 2001. In Canada, the Canadian Council of Churches was developing into a forum. The Committee was therefore of the opinion that a regional consultation in North America was not a priority. The possibilities of consultations in the Caribbean, the Middle East, and the Pacific were kept open for a later period.

15   *Revisioning Christian Unity – The Global Christian Forum*, ed. Huibert van Beek (Oxford: Regnum Books International, 2009), p. 119.

16   *Revisioning Christian Unity*, p. 115.

17   Guidelines from the Second Global Gathering of the Global Christian Forum, 4-7 October 2011, Manado, Indonesia; http://www.globalchristianforum.org.

POSTSCRIPT

Monsignor John Radano: The Person

by Anthony J. Farquhar

My friendship with Monsignor Radano began as a result of a letter from the late Bishop Pierre Duprey which invited me to serve as co-chairman of the third phase of the dialogue with the World Alliance of Reformed Churches. After much ecumenical soul-searching, I accepted the invitation and found myself studying the reports of the first two phases – rather similar to someone trying to join in a serial story and reading the paragraph *New Readers Begin Here*. For a Belfastman, this was a leap into the depths of the ecumenical unknown.

Then came information as to the venue in Venice, how to master the *vaporetto* system – eventually negotiated with the assistance of a staff member from the Pontifical Council – and a letter from a Monsignor John Radano – up to that point just a frequently recurring name in the *Information Service* of the Pontifical Council for Promoting Christian Unity.

On arrival at the retreat house, I then met the Monsignor himself. He had suggested a preliminary meeting on the first evening between the joint secretaries and the co-chairman. I looked on with a certain amount of apprehension at the timetable proposed for the next six days. One of the Monsignor's first proposals was to suggest the possibility of some additional sessions on some evenings after dinner. In an instant, I recognized that here was a man of dedication and intense commitment to work. Yes, Monsignor Jack may not be a theological syncretist or a dogmatic compromiser, but he had obviously absorbed what I, as an Irish Catholic, in times when the limits of demarcation preceded the ecumenical movement, had always attributed stereotypically to be the Protestant work ethic.

In the opening 'Getting to know you' session, I also realized that here was a man of encyclopedic knowledge, not only of previous phases of the dialogue but also of other dialogues, clearly recognizing where we had come from and where our planned dialogue should lead us, not in the sense of a predetermined final report but rather in the sense of carrying out our mandate within our given parameters. This was going to be hard work, but even then I had confidence that working with this man would broaden my own ecumenical experience.

In subsequent years, our dialogue members travelled to different international venues – some of them in situations of considerable socio-political complexity, viz. South Africa, Northern Ireland, and Canada. In his preparatory work, Monsignor Radano, along with Rev. Dr. Odair Mateus, his Reformed counterpart, always managed to make available speakers who would give a sharp analysis of local situations while retaining the universal vision. There were changes in personnel, but he always managed to maintain a consistent through-flow.

There were certainly occasional times of tension in the wider ecumenical scene, but at those times above all, he showed admirable ecumenical integrity and honesty. I recall one particularly forthright session when certain historical hurts and grievances were being aired; I recalled again the letter of invitation to be a co-chair of the dialogue and in particular the comment that I had been involved in similar work at difficult times in Northern Ireland's history. We in Ireland have seen all too often the ways in which differences, long felt and deeply rooted, can drive wedges within generations. Monsignor pointed out gently that such hurts were often genuinely and deeply felt, but the main threat to ecumenical advance came when one group felt it had a monopoly on hurt. It is, he said, rather when the energy that comes from appreciation of another's hurt and pain is harnessed and properly redirected that we can make a special contribution to ecumenical advance. In his company, I learned increasingly that it is not only by sharing the richness of each other's tradition but also by appreciating its sense of hurt that we can grow – as also indeed by expressing our own hurt in such a way that it can be understood by others and assist them to grow. This ecumenical insight has proved to be of invaluable assistance to me in our Irish socio-political times of change.

In addition to his talent for facilitating people to move from where they are to a new ecumenical level – to move from the *terminus a quo* to the *terminus ad quem* – the one dimension which he always un-apologetically kept to the forefront was the spiritual one. I have spent almost all of my life in ministry in the Irish situation, where religion is increasingly portrayed as something divisive in society. Perhaps for that reason, I have always had a very sharpened sense that true ecumenism and respect for another's religious tradition is based on an unapologetic profession of faith and prayer in one's own.

> Prayer for unity is the royal door of ecumenism: it leads Christians to look at the Kingdom of God and the unity of the Church in a fresh way; it deepens their bonds of communion; and it enables them to courageously face painful memories, social burdens and human weakness.[1]

This commitment to prayer has shone through every part of the Monsignor's work in which I have had the privilege of sharing. From his earliest preparation for our first meeting he always laid great stress on the role of prayer and its importance in our program – be that prayer within one tradition or be it communal along with those of other traditions. His planning for worship is just as meticulous as his planning for the sessions of the dialogue discussion. I often thought of that lovely opening of St. John Paul II to the first World Day of Prayer for Peace at Assisi, when he reminded all assembled there that we had come, not for a conference on peace, but for prayer. Monsignor John had always brought us to our meetings prepared for both. Our dialogue sessions never sidelined the importance of prayer.

He has been constant in his conviction that our journey is towards the *Terminus ad Quem* – with capital letters – and in doing so he has given an outstanding example to his own denominational colleagues and to all his ecumenical partners.

He has helped so many people to remove the blinkers that lead to tunnel vision and to capture the universally ecumenical. Even for that alone, a Catholic from Northern Ireland would be truly grateful.

Since our final meeting, I have been privileged to witness the process by which the fruits of many weeks' ecumenical study and discussion, spread over many years, are distilled into the form of a final report. I have learned so much from Jack and his Reformed counterpart, Odair, as they worked together towards producing that report. For me, it has been remarkable to see how a systematized final version is produced. I will always read the final reports of any other dialogues in a fresh light.

I would not wish this Postscript to leave readers with an image of an American Monsignor who was totally other-worldly or rarefied. So I hope I may be excused for including just one anecdote.

It was a Sunday in Northern Ireland during our meeting of the WARC dialogue. The Reformed members had gone off to attend services in various Protestant churches in the area. The Catholic group went to concelebrate Mass in St. Colman's Cathedral, Newry, County Down, with the Bishop of the Diocese of Dromore. The Diocese of Dromore, and Newry in particular, border on the Archdiocese of Armagh.

This was no ordinary Sunday. Armagh's claim to ecclesiastical fame may well be that it contains two primatial sees – one Roman Catholic and one Anglican (Church of Ireland). However, on that particular September Sunday, its claim to fame lay elsewhere. Armagh was playing in (and with quite a good chance of winning) the All Ireland Football Final in Dublin. Now I know that the people of both Armagh and Down show great ecumenical commitment, but I suspected that a large number of the congregation – and even perhaps their bishop – would be heading off on the busy road to Dublin immediately after Mass was over. I knew that back at the Retreat House I would be chairing the afternoon session of the dialogue and my halo was shining bright with the polish of ecumenical commitment and self-righteousness!

It fell to me to select one of our members to address the congregation. Now there were members of that dialogue team who could have spoken uninterruptedly on ecumenism at such length that not only would the members of the congregation not have been released in time to travel to Dublin, but they might have been fortunate to be able to watch even the second half of the game on television. So, realizing that a non-Irish accent would emphasize the international composition of our membership, I settled on Monsignor Radano to address the congregation.

He told them of the work of the dialogue with the World Alliance of Reformed Churches. They listened well. But then I heard him move on. Memory tells me that he had begun to speak of Pentecostals and Mennonites – and then it happened – I heard him announce that he would say no more. He told them that they might gather from his accent that he knew more about American baseball scores in general and the New York Yankees in particular than he did about Irish football games, but he assured them that he realized that this was a day of a very big game, that he hoped that they would have a safe journey and that they would gain the result they hoped for. Our liturgists may not have totally approved, but Jack's sporting aspirations were greeted with a round of loud applause. For that Sunday morning congregation, the work of the Pontifical Council for Promoting Christian Unity would never ever go unheralded, and Pentecostals and Mennonites would become their friends for life. The dazzlingly bright light of Jack's pastoral relevance had shone through.

I hope this doesn't seem to trivialize the man. On the contrary, it is his facility to combine theological analysis and academic giftedness with an ability to meet and respect people where they are and then lead them a little further on that has made him such a wonderful and powerful contributor to world ecumenism. Now that Monsignor John/Jack is back in his native place, no doubt he has brought back with him those talents and that expertise which he carried from there many years ago – talents now honed and fashioned by many years of international work and dedicated commitment.

I know that this *Festschrift* will be filled with the writings of people whose contributions will capture, better than I could ever do, the Monsignor's theological acumen but I consider it a wonderful ecumenical privilege to have been invited to contribute this Postscript on Monsignor John Radano – the person.

For about twenty years, I have been privileged to see in close-up his immense contribution to ecumenism. I have tried to use this Postscript as an aid to highlighting what I see as the ideal qualities of the true ecumenist. So may I finish by saying a prayer of thanks to the *Terminus ad Quem.*

> Thank you, Lord, for what Monsignor Radano has given to
>   ecumenism;
> thank you for the inspiration he has been to so many people;
> thank you for the many ecumenical graces that you have
>   bestowed
> through his humility, his caring, his clear-mindedness,
>   his self-discipline
> and his prayer.

> *Ad multos annos.*

---

1   Walter Kasper, *A Handbook of Spiritual Ecumenism* (Hyde Park, NY: New City Press, 2007), p. 11.